The Things Which Become

SOUND DOCTRINE

The Things Which Become

SOUND
DOCTRINE

The life of Aaron M. Shank

Aaron M. Shank

Chester C. Weaver Jr.

ISBN 978-1-68001-028-2
Library of Congress Control Number: 2020932533

For additional titles, contact:

Sermon on the Mount Publishing
P.O. Box 246
Manchester, MI 48158
(734) 428-0488
the-witness@sbcglobal.net
www.kingdomreading.com

Our Mission
To obey the commands of Christ and to teach men to do so.

First Printing—March 2020—2,500 copies
Second Printing—POD edition

Behold,

Marjorie and Aaron Shank

Mennonite leaders

who

were

no

dualists,

but whose lives demonstrated

the beauty and wholeness

created by knowing Jesus Christ.

This book is dedicated to:

Milford, Richard, Ruth, Louise

who witnessed their parents' character strength firsthand,

Wesley, Duane, Violet, Fern,

Justin, Ernest, Quentin, Lily,

our children who have reaped the character benefits
of this story though unperceived,

All my students through the years.

This story is your teacher's Character Sketch.

CONTENTS

CREDITS &
ACKNOWLEDGEMENTS

FIRST OF ALL, I am indebted to God, who providentially placed me in a time and place where I could be influenced for good by worthy character models such as Aaron Shank. I am indebted to Aaron and Marjorie's children, Milford and Louise, for the pictures, information, and fact-checking which they provided. After Aaron's death in 2003, Jeff Jarmon, a first-generation Mennonite pastor who ministered with Aaron Shank, nearly completed the project which I had laid down in 1996. When he turned the project over to the Shank family, it rested for a few years until I picked it up again in 2019. The bulk of the research was done while Aaron and his working contemporaries were living and active, and to each of them I owe a deep debt. Steve Ebersole has stood by through the years to help the project along wherever he could.

The Pilgrim Mennonite Conference sponsored the project at the beginning and has provided the recordings of Aaron's preaching through the years. David C. and Lucille Shank Allen prepared the genealogy of Erasmus Coffman Shank, and their son, D. Charles Allen, Jr., gave permission to copy and use the material included on p. 35-36. Romaine Stauffer provided Aaron's genealogy.

I offer special thanks to Teacher Shirley Ebersole who cared and who regularly asked about the project status through the years. Thanks to Gardell and Karla (Boll) Strite for allowing me to include a personal letter Karla wrote as a teenager to Aaron and Marjorie, which the Shanks valued highly and kept among their papers. I am indebted to Ann Olesh Showalter for her pictures and her frank statements about the Aaron Shank she knew. I appreciate the time and effort Ruth Wadel, Joanne Weaver, Ivan Martin Jr., Lorene Mast, the Ben Eshbach family, Daniel Stover, Lily Weaver, Ethan Weaver, John G. Landis, Ervin and Darlene Martin, and Galen Martin expended in providing the pictures they did. MennoMedia graciously allowed me to use the cover of the September 1968 *Family Worship* magazine. Glenn Showalter provided the 1959 program sample and the first-hand witness of his childhood memories as he participated in the significant events surrounding the formation of the Mennonite Christian Brotherhood (now part of Nationwide Fellowship) which took place in eastern Pennsylvania. Ivan Martin Sr. provided his clear memories of the events which involved the Defenders of the Faith meetings and the later development of the Mennonite Messianic Mission. Daniel Stover provided valuable information via the Gingrichs Mennonite Church and Cemetery history book.

Thanks also to Edsel and Jennifer Burdge, Justin Ebersole, Clement Ebersole, Eastern Mennonite Publications, the Lancaster Mennonite Historical Society, and others who have given valuable aid as the book neared publication.

I am indebted to Andrew V. Ste. Marie for his friendship and for his superb help in properly preparing and publishing the book. God bless your further scholarly research and publication of other projects. An open door is before you.

A special thanks to Aaron's nephew, Don Martin and wife Mildred, who cared enough about the project to volunteer copyediting help as the project came to completion. Also, thanks to Dan Faus for his Lebanon County farm/mission board story gleaned at the last minute from conversation at his mother's funeral. Your mother wanted to read this story.

Thank you, Curtis and Janice, for extending hospitality to me while I was completing my work in Pennsylvania. Thank you, Barbara, for standing by and providing the freedom that this project required through the years.

I accept responsibility for any and all errors which may present themselves and I welcome corrections which may be forthcoming. Readers may reach me at chesterweaver@pcfnet.net.

INTRODUCTION

WHAT SETS ONE man's life apart, making it worthy of special consideration? Do not all men have a story to tell by the time they reach their fourscore years? Why are there not more biographies?

Most men's lives flow with the currents of their times. It is easier by far to go with the flow than to move upstream against the current. It takes a strong man to make progress counter to the current. It requires a vision—a vision of a greater good upstream, not downstream. The strength of that vision drives great men to exert great effort to achieve the goal at the source of the waters.

Such can be said of the man Aaron Shank. He moved upstream all his life. Early in life he received a clear vision of what God requires of man. His father first inspired it, and then by his own study of the Scriptures the vision became fully developed in his own heart. Other men, such as George R. Brunk I, became living models of the vision. This vision drove him, tempered him, humbled him, inspired him, and presented him with more work than he would ever get accomplished. In his own words he would say, "When I think of all that my Savior accomplished in three years, I am profoundly embarrassed."

Early in his ministry, Aaron made sound doctrine a defining goal of his ministry. Times have ebbed and flowed since then. Men and movements have swayed and shifted. Sound Biblical doctrine has remained fixed and immoveable. Standing by that soul-anchoring truth is the subject of this biography. It is to his credit that he did not shift.

This remarkable stability is a silent sermon in itself. This biography attempts to trace that stability through all the swirling dust and dirt that the changing times have stirred up. It attempts to chronicle the words and movements of a man who sensed and carried a burden for the Mennonite church to be true to the Scriptures. Aaron would be pleased if his story inspires a few more to hold onto the Rock in the coming generations until Christ returns.

This story of his life is meant to inspire other lives to the same noble purpose that Aaron held. All men in all ages whose work made a difference in their times carried an enormous burden for the truth. Aaron certainly has made a difference. If others can catch his vision and dedicate their lives to the same cause for which he gave his energies, then his life will not have been fruitless. Who will be the next to do it?

Empty flattery would offend Aaron. He was too aware of his own humanity to bask in praise. In fact, he wondered whether this project should be attempted. But if the truth for which he gave his life, time, and energies is reiterated one more time, he would be satisfied. In his later years Aaron said publicly, "I am just getting started and it is already time to quit." Hopefully the written record of his work will extend his efforts into the future, granting him extra opportunity to promote the truth.

This record is not intended to be earthly applause. The following pages present a flesh-and-blood human, complete with his share of shortcomings and failures. No one was more aware of them than Aaron himself. At age eighty-one, he was still aspiring to be more like his Master. Through a bedroom wall early one morning, the writer heard Bro. Aaron rehearsing a song he was memorizing.

> O to be like Thee! blessed Redeemer:
> This is my constant longing and prayer;
> Gladly I'll forfeit all of earth's treasures,
> Jesus, thy perfect likeness to wear.
>
> O to be like Thee! full of compassion,
> Loving, forgiving, tender and kind,
> Helping the helpless, cheering the fainting,
> Seeking the wand'ring sinner to find.

O to be like Thee! lowly in spirit,
Holy and harmless, patient and brave;
Meekly enduring cruel reproaches,
Willing to suffer, others to save.

O to be like Thee! Lord, I am coming,
Now to receive th'anointing divine;
All that I am and have I am bringing;
Lord, from this moment all shall be thine.

Refrain:
O to be like Thee! O to be like Thee!
Blessed Redeemer, pure as Thou art;
Come in Thy sweetness, come in Thy fulness;
Stamp Thine own image deep on my heart.

When asked later about the song, Aaron simply said, "I am trying to memorize that song because it is so meaningful." I was impressed! A man in his eighties memorizing a song! I was in my forties and was not memorizing songs.

The quality of Aaron's character became etched on my soul that day. This minor incident provides color and light for his entire life. Once I understood this fact, everything else fell into place. Even though Aaron chose the book title as *The Things Which Become Sound Doctrine*, Aaron is best understood by his simple interest in being like Christ. His decisions, his behavior, his marriage, and his ministerial work were illuminated and colored by his efforts to be like Christ in all he said and did. In the end, his simple interest in Christ-likeness has become his most enduring legacy, even overshadowing his stated interest in a legacy of sound doctrine. Aaron practiced what he preached. He was no dualist.

It is hoped that this record in no way diminishes Aaron's earthly testimony by undeserved earthly applause. And yet this story deserves to be written and read. You will understand why.

As was stated, Aaron was not so sure this book should be published. When he relented, he stipulated, "It can be published after I am gone."

He has now been gone for more than fifteen years. "If it can be of some help to those coming on, you may publish it." The time has come for publication.

His colleague, David Thomas, former Moderator of Lancaster Conference, held a different idea. "I want to read this story. The events are like yesterday. My children will not want to read this story!" David went on to his reward back in 2000, nearly twenty years ago, having never read this story. Maybe, just maybe, his children will read it.

At Aaron's funeral, daughter Ruth stated, "I did not know Dad was such an important man." Maybe she did not, but others did. That is why this book is now being presented to interested readers. Did even Aaron know the significance of his own life? Marjorie knew something about the significance, because she made sure that all her personal journals were consumed by fire during her lifetime lest anyone discover her responses and feelings related to the significant events of their life together.

Son Richard must have missed the significance altogether, because he missed the funeral in 2003. Many others did not. Today, more people than just those who attended Aaron's funeral remain interested in Aaron's significant contribution to conservative Mennonite history. To be sure, Aaron did not set out to alter the course of conservative Mennonite history, but alter it he did. Some readers would like to retrace those altering steps today. Others deserve the history they never experienced but whose lives, nevertheless, have been impacted by that which had happened before their time.

The idea for the book happened one day when Bishop Harold Good said to a friend, "You know, Aaron's story ought to be written." I overheard that statement that day and the idea remained with me. I was not closely associated with Aaron's story because I lived in Cumberland County, Pennsylvania, over an hour west of Aaron's Lebanon County. But when in 1986 the Lebanon District asked our family to consider moving to Texas to be a part of the new Grays Prairie settlement southeast of Dallas, Texas, the entire picture changed. Then Aaron and Marjorie did become a real part of our lives.

When the Pilgrim Mennonite Conference commissioned me to write the story, I travelled back to Pennsylvania in the 1990s to interview the key figures in Aaron's story. I remain grateful that I had the opportunity to do live interviews with these people, most of whom have now passed to their rewards. Aaron himself reviewed the basic manuscript to ensure accuracy.

While effort has been made to ensure the accuracy of the story presented here, later in the story the documents both Aaron and others have written tell the raw facts of the story. The unaltered documents stand for themselves and offer interpretations dependent upon the perspective of the reader. What cannot be disputed is Aaron's integrity. He worked, spoke, and wrote out of a heart loyally dedicated to Jesus Christ, his Master and Lord.

Chester Weaver

CHAPTER 1

The Generations Before

THE DAY WAS Friday, February 5, 1915. That day God placed a baby boy into the arms of Mary May (Miller) Shank; John M. Shank and his wife named him Aaron Martin. Four siblings welcomed him into their family: Paul, Naomi, Mark, and Ralph. Walter, Gladys, and Mary Louise would follow to complete the family.

God used the Shank home to prepare a man of Christian integrity and doctrinal stability. The Mennonite Church would need such men in the last half of the twentieth century. From the solid Biblical foundations of the Anabaptist movement four centuries earlier, the Mennonite Church struggled to retain its identity. Protestant theology and practice had been impacting the Swiss Brethren American immigrants ever since their arrival on North American shores. Cut off from their German writings by the new Protestant English environment, their past had begun to fade. The days were spiritually perilous. Many were choosing to regard Mennonite practices as cultural relics to be abandoned—rightly discarded—in favor of "enlightened Christianity." Others clung to cultural options which could not be defended with Biblical authority. Still others eagerly took advantage of the economic opportunities America offered and squandered their energies on obtaining wealth. Countless numbers of Mennonite offspring had been lost to the Protestants. This state of affairs in America had continued for more than one hundred fifty years. The Swiss Brethren Mennonites desperately needed men who possessed extensive Scriptural knowledge and the ability to motivate people with the truth of God's Word. Where were they? Only a few Mennonite men during those one hundred fifty years had possessed such qualifications.

Beginning with John M. Brenneman and John F. Funk in the American Civil War era, the Mennonite landscape began to change. The Spirit of God began to blow the American Mennonite embers back into flame. A number of outstanding Bible teachers such as John S. Coffman and George R. Brunk I called the Mennonites of their day back to Christ and the Scriptures, the ultimate sources of spiritual authority. These men and others sounded the clear message of Bible truth against a backdrop of deepening Mennonite apostasy. In his own time, Aaron Shank would join that number.

Where did Aaron come from? What influences blended to prepare him as a Mennonite leader? What was Aaron's unique contribution to his time?

Roots

John M. Shank (1880) and his wife Mary (1881) were both born in Ohio. John was born in Allen County, near Elida, and his wife Mary in Wayne County, but neither family remained in Ohio. The Shanks moved to Concord, Tennessee and the Millers to Cass County, Missouri.

After a Mennonite colony was formed at Denbigh, Virginia (now a part of Newport News), both the Millers and the Shanks relocated to Denbigh. Most

Christian and Abi (Yoder) Miller.

of the families moving there came in hopes of obtaining cheap land. Instead of moving west, these two families moved east. The Shank and the Miller families experienced the normal rigors of pioneering in a new settlement anywhere, creating a home, working a farm, and for Mennonites, building a congregation. Money was scarce.

When Mary was eighteen years old, her father Christian Miller with his family left western Missouri with a pair of mules, Jack and Pete, to pull their covered wagon 1,200 miles to their destination in eastern Virginia. The trip took nine weeks and two days. They arrived at Denbigh on November 16, 1899.

In addition to the demands of travel, the Miller family needed to tend to "domestic" duties such as meal preparation. The Miller women made biscuits in a Dutch oven (a heavy iron pan hung from a tripod over the fire).

Mary Miller (standing, right) with her sisters, before her marriage to John Shank.

They kneaded bread dough in the morning so that it could rise during the day's journey. In the evening they baked the shaped dough for supper. The trip was wearisome and uneventful except on two occasions.

One night at midnight, while camping near a large city, a man appeared out of the darkness with a gun and demanded money he thought was collected by selling a load of grain. He had mistaken Christian Miller for a grain salesman. It took effort, but Christian convinced the man that the wagon was crowded with sleeping children, not money.

On another occasion the mules, Jack and Pete, balked as they went up a rough and stony mountain trail. They stopped on the hill! If the mules' lack of progress presented a frustration, the possibility of them allowing the wagon to roll backwards presented a real hazard. The Miller children stood ready with stones to block the wagon wheels from rolling downhill. When the mules made any forward movement, the wheels were chocked to allow the mules additional rest and to prevent the wagon from rolling backwards. Eventually, the Millers reached a small clearing by the side of the road to which the mules pulled the wagon. The family parked right there for the night.

The next day a man with a team of horses "towed" the wagon the rest of the way up the hill. He would accept no payment except that the family would help the next people in a predicament.

Grandfather John's Marriage

John Shank learned to know Mary Miller at Denbigh. They courted and were approaching marriage when a particular incident revealed John's conscientious character. As a young man John had desired to wear a necktie, but his father would not allow him to. At his wedding, John's mother wanted him to wear one, saying, "You ought to put on a necktie just to get married. The other young fellows are doing it." But by this time John had developed personal convictions against it.

He replied, "Well, this is one young fellow who is not going to do it."

John and Mary were married on October 15, 1903, without John's tie.

Pioneering is always difficult, and pioneering at Denbigh was no exception for the young couple. To add to the difficulty, John and Mary's house with all its furnishings

John and Mary Shank's wedding picture. John refused to wear the necktie which many young men wore at their weddings.

burned to the ground a few years after they were married. In April 1911, John heated tar on the kitchen stove to prepare it for application on a newly-built shed roof. The overheated tar caught fire, which spread out of control, destroying the house and most of its contents. John and Mary, with their five children, lived in two outbuildings while the new house was constructed. To complicate matters, Mark, the second oldest, lingered between life and death with serious illness. By Christmas that year, the combined efforts of the Shanks, Millers, friends, and neighbors had the new house completed. By that time Mark was recovering from his illness.

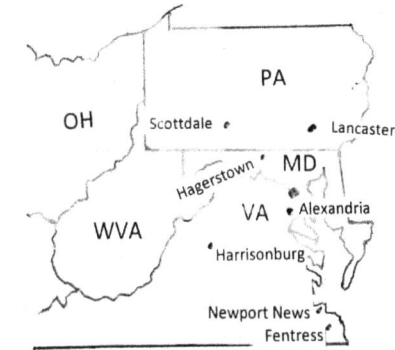

Various locations in Virginia considered for the location of Eastern Mennonite School.

Bishop George R. Brunk moved from Kansas to Denbigh in 1910, seven years after John and Mary were married, one year before their fire. The influence of Bishop Brunk upon the Shanks was profound. From their very first acquaintance, John admired Bishop Brunk's deep spiritual insights and his strong appeal for a conservative approach to the Christian life. A lifelong bond formed between these two men.

Bishop Brunk wrote, "One main reason for our coming east [from Kansas] was to press my campaign against the corrupting influences of Goshen College—the West at that time being well established in conservatism and fully warned against the influence of Goshen men—who were up to that time having free range in Virginia...."

Dedicated to battling liberal influences, Bishop Brunk and others became interested in establishing a conservative school in the East. John Shank shared the vision. John rode his bicycle all the way from Denbigh to the Fentress Congregation (forty miles) carrying a petition to arouse interest in the new school.

The Denbigh congregation, including John, wanted a "school with a prevailing religious influence in defense of the simple gospel." They wanted a school

to provide intellectual, moral, and religious development for the student; to arouse missionary interest and to train for missionary service; to give "due attention....

to the peculiar doctrines of the Church, together with special training in vocal music—looking to the strengthening of that feature of divine worship in our congregations."

To preserve a conservative school, the writers of the school constitution stated that sections related to "underlying principles and safeguard features for the church and school, shall be unchangeable."[1]

In 1926, A. D. Wenger, later principal of the new Eastern Mennonite School, published a widely distributed pamphlet of eleven pages. At the beginning of the pamphlet he raised the question, "Who should educate our children?"

He answered his question thus, "The question is no longer, shall we educate or not? That was the question some years ago. Parents could then do as they pleased. They are now compelled by law to send their children to school until a certain age limit. Books, buildings, and teachers are provided. The object is to make good citizens and brave soldiers...."

EMS Faculty in 1923. Left to right, back: Henry Weaver, A. G. Heishman, A. D. Wenger, J. L. STauffer, Henry Keener; front: Ira Franck, C. K. Lehman, Elizabeth G. Gish, Dorothy Kemrer, Daniel W. Lehman, Paul Sauder.

1 Herbert Pellman, *Eastern Mennonite College 1917-1967*, 1967, Eastern Mennonite College, pp. 16, 17.

He concluded the pamphlet by saying,

Shall we sit still until our church houses stand empty because worldly schools through their pride, pleasure, immorality, and evolution have robbed us of our children? If we do not provide *for our own*, others *will*, and they will take them from us. Thus we have been giving our sons and daughters to other denominations and to the world for over two hundred years. If we ever intend to stop, let us do it now. *It can be done.* If we in this generation cannot solve the school problem as it confronts the Church, how can it be done in the next? We can now *if we will.* Let us solve the problem before it *dissolves us.*

The intended location for the new school underwent a number of changes. Originally, the "Warwick Mennonite Academy" was to be built in the Denbigh community. Plans shifted when Bishop Brunk directed attention to another opportunity at Alexandria, Virginia. There the Hayfield Farm had a nineteen-room mansion built by George Washington in 1769. The size of the facility would serve well to establish the new school.

Then plans for the Hayfield venture stalled and a building at Assembly Park, near Harrisonburg, Virginia, hosted a special Bible term in 1916. The facility along with the surrounding twenty-three acres was purchased the following year and named Eastern Mennonite School.

John Shank had been the recording secretary of the Denbigh meetings. Now he moved to Harrisonburg to be a full-time solicitor of students and money for the new school. That same year (1917) Bishop Brunk became so ill that David Garber temporarily handled his bishop responsibilities.

Aaron was two years old when his parents made the move to Harrisonburg.

Soliciting for the school created a heavy burden for John. It took him away from home too much and his health began to break. When the doctor suggested different work, John and Mary thought that farm life would be the best option for their growing family. But farm prices were high around Harrisonburg.

John's sister, married to Irvin King, lived at Royersford, Pennsylvania. Thither they went to look for a farm, in the company of Walter Grove and his wife, another of John's sisters. But farms near Philadelphia were also expensive. They started home without making a purchase.

But Walter Grove had a brother living at Hershey, Pennsylvania, so they stopped to visit with him. They shared with Walter's brother the purpose of their trip and that they had been unsuccessful in their search for a reason-ably-priced farm.

As the group departed from Hershey and headed for Harrisburg on their homeward journey, a large shiny car drove up beside them, blew the horn, and motioned them to the side of the road. The car contained two realtors. Walter Grove's brother had contacted the realtors and told them about the Virginians' fruitless search for a farm.

The realtors offered to put the group up for the night. The next morning everyone went to see a farm three and one-half miles north of Annville (about one-half mile west of the original Dohner Mennonite Meetinghouse and the former one-room Myersdale Elementary School across the road). John and Mary liked it and purchased it for $8,500. The price was half of what they could have expected to pay in Virginia. Nevertheless, even that wartime-inflated price was too high. Before long, comparable farms in the area were selling for half of what they had paid.

The Shank family moved to Pennsylvania in the fall of 1919, but because of a misunderstanding with the seller, could not take possession of their new farm until the spring of 1920. Six children, Paul, Naomi, Mark, Ralph, Aaron, Gladys, and two parents made the trip in a Model T Ford. By the time they moved on to the farm, Aaron was five years old.

Farming was not very profitable and John was not very well physically. Mary was well and strong though and managed to keep the family warm and fed. For ten years the Shanks only paid interest on the property, no principal. Then in 1929 the Great Depression hit. The week the stock prices crashed, Mary had almost no customers at market. She brought home almost everything she had taken. John paced the floor saying, "We'll never make it. We'll never make it."

Several times the family thought they would lose the farm to bankruptcy. Somehow the Lord preserved them as they trusted Him and scraped and scraped to get by.

One day Mary sent Ralph to her husband in the field to ask for a dime with which to purchase kerosene. John looked into his purse for a while and told Ralph, "Ask Mother if we can possibly make do until the first of April when interest on the mortgage comes due."

George R. Brunk I (seated, second from left) and family. Bishop Brunk was very influential with the Shank family.

Mary did her share of scraping. She unraveled the binding strings from cloth feed bags to repair bed sheets and mend the boys' shirts.

By the late 1930's, the economy had picked up enough to allow John and Mary to pay off their farm mortgage.

John's Burden

John carried a real burden for the church. He had demonstrated that care by his interest and involvement in the development of the Eastern Mennonite School. Arriving in Lebanon County, John's burden shifted to an altogether different concern, a concern he had not faced in Virginia.

He had appreciated and had been accustomed to Bishop George Brunk's organized and vigorous leadership in the Virginia church. In contrast, the Lebanon County preachers did not come to church on a Sunday morning prepared to preach. They would gather in a meetinghouse anteroom and converse among themselves as to who would preach that morning. A standard part of the procedure was for each minister to pass the responsibility on to another in the group until someone finally consented to preach.

As a boy, Aaron also saw the ministers debating among themselves who was to preach while they were sitting on the front bench in the meetinghouse.

Eventually, one brother would arise and say, "It falls to my lot to preach ..." Then he would likely say, "While sitting here wondering what I was to preach on, this text came to my mind." One preacher used a chain reference Bible which provided some structure to his preaching. Obviously, in the absence of preparation, the preaching burden was also often absent.

Compounding this weakness, church services were held only every other week as two congregations would alternate between four buildings, Kralls, Gingrichs, Dohner, and Shirksville. Every service, whether morning or evening, had Sunday School associated with it. There were no Bible Conferences or Christian Workers Meetings and all the preaching was in German. David Westenberger served as Bishop in the district.

Church members raised and used tobacco, including the church leadership. It was common to share the Christian greeting with someone who had a "tobacco mouth." There had been spittoons in the meetinghouses, but by the time the Shanks had arrived, they were gone.

The Virginia Conference had been much more stringent in their prohibition of tobacco than Lancaster Conference had been. In Lancaster County tobacco was a valuable cash crop which provided work for the family unit. Everyone understood Lancaster as a tobacco center.

One day Mary Shank received a letter from her sister living in Virginia. The letter reported that a nephew was refused Communion privileges because of his continued use of tobacco. Mary identified with such church discipline. She yearned for the blessings of healthy church life. At times, John needed to help Mary remain satisfied with the Mennonite leadership of Lebanon County.

John Shank also missed the vigorous, healthy church life he had enjoyed in Virginia. He tried to convince the leadership to switch to English preaching.[2] He worked a long time before the leaders accepted his proposal to hold a Christian Workers Meeting. When the meetings were finally held, the event marked the beginning of Bible Conferences in the Lebanon District.

Bishop David Westenberger was a well-meaning German man, but he was not in favor of Sunday evening programs like the ones held in Lancaster County. When John pled with him to institute these programs in Lebanon

---

2 The Shank children never learned German.

County, David related the story of a bad accident involving young people returning home from one of them.[3] To him, the Sunday evening program was the reason for the accident.

Communion services were lengthy. First Sunday School would be held. Next there was a sermon on types and shadows from the Old Testament— really a retelling of the Old Testament story. Bible exposition was absent; no types were explained. The speaker would say, "You Bible readers all know this." Then followed the Communion sermon, covering the same basic theme. David Westenberger often said during the sermon, "Much could be said if memory would serve and time would allow."

The lifeless formality of the Lebanon County churches bothered John and his wife continually. They missed the church at Denbigh intensely. They had esteemed George R. Brunk highly, and now in Lebanon County no one replaced him. They also intensely missed the church discipline actively practiced in Virginia, demonstrated by the nephew being refused communion for using tobacco.

Because of these concerns, John tried to sell the farm, but farm prices had fallen, leaving him with no prospect of finding a buyer. Since relocating was not an option, John tried to work for wholesome changes within the church.

The Lebanon District only possessed a few young people. After the young men's Sunday School class was concluded in the rear of the auditorium, Aaron and his brothers would walk up front. John and Mary insisted that their sons wear plain suits, even though the other young men did not. Plain suits were not required by the church at that time, even though there was strong encouragement for the practice. Most young people did not adopt the practice until they grew up, if they wore them at all. Some members in the district never did wear them.

While none of the men wore long neckties, some wore bow ties. Some bow ties were worn under the plain suit with the top button left open and others were worn with a lapel coat. John Shank was against wearing any neckties. Virginia did not make a distinction in ties like Lancaster did. There, no one wore a tie, regardless of design. Accordingly, Aaron never wore one either.

---

3 He may have been referring to Enos Barge and Barbara Hershey being killed by a train near Bird-in-Hand in 1896 as they were travelling home from an evening young people's gathering. The complete story is recorded in *I Hear the Reaper's Song*.

Almost every time there was a call for leadership in the Lebanon District, John was named as a candidate, but the lot never fell to him. However, John's mild-mannered personality was influential and he became a leader nonetheless. Because he did not just sit back and accept the status quo, he made some enemies in the District. At Christmas time, for example, it had been the practice of the churches to give children a box of candy and an orange. John could not sit still. "Take these things hence. Candy does not belong in church." (He had seen some boys eat almost their whole box of candy prior to church dismissal.)

John and Mary Shank.

John got his point across, but some fellow church members were very upset with him for challenging the status quo. Some also strongly opposed his push for other activities beside Sunday School and preaching. Their attitude was, "This is the way it is done, this is the way it was always done, and this is the way it shall be done in the future."

While John's efforts to make positive changes in church life created opposition, no one could attack his upright life and his devotion to Christ. He was careful and godly in his behavior. His children respected him highly. When he could not work because of his poor health (he had three nervous breakdowns), his children pitied him rather than disrespecting him for his weakness. Mary was extremely loyal to him. She built him up in the children's minds. She never would say *anything* derogatory about her husband. Once while sitting in the car along the street in town, she said to the children while her husband was approaching, "There comes the most dignified man around."

John was a very sober-minded person. He did not joke and shady stories were never mentioned. He was so serious that it affected his health; his three nervous breakdowns illustrate this condition. John's basic problem was with Christian assurance. His perfectionism issued into conscientiousness of character which the children very much respected. Furthermore, his perfectionism issued into very serious Bible study. He needed to be accurate when he quoted Bible verses.

John was a disciplinarian in the home, but never disciplined in anger. He was kind to his wife and children. Sometimes Mary disagreed with him in his exercises of discipline. Since the children did not know Pennsylvania Dutch, she spoke to John in Dutch about the discipline in the children's presence.

The children never knew their father to speak unkindly about anyone. He was very sensitive to being truthful and he was sensitive about offending people. This quality was tested during the times he needed to help Mary remain satisfied with the lesser-quality leadership present in Lebanon County than she had been used to in Virginia.

The children could sense church problems or when church people were making it hard for their parents. But the parents never spoke ill of the people making it hard for them or exploited the church problems. While they spoke with concern about people, they never bad-mouthed church leaders or others.

The Shank family life was built around the church. When anything was going on, the family was there. Gladys remembers her father getting the children ready for church, combing her hair, and carrying her to the car so that she would not get her shoes muddy on the way to the car.

John was an avid reader, even though he did not have many books. He read the Bible and his commentaries. He purchased a copy of Josephus in 1902. The Shanks also owned a *Foxe's Book of Martyrs*, *Martyrs Mirror*, and *First Steps for Little Feet*. The family received periodicals such as *Farm Journal*, *Gospel Herald*, and *Sword and Trumpet*, along with the Lebanon *Daily News*.

John's reading and study prepared him to enter into discussions on a wide range of topics. He discussed political issues with knowledge and ease because of his extensive reading, his keen interest, and his long consideration of those issues. However, John would never vote because of his Two-Kingdom Concept. He talked to his family at the supper table about his views and concerns, including his concern about Mennonite drift. Sometimes he would sit in a session at the local courthouse.

Mary was not a big reader. She had only finished the fourth grade in school. She did read the church papers, especially the editorials, considering them the best part.

There were few books for young people in the Shank home. The library was meager because money was scarce. Thus, the boys read their father's books. In his father's books, Aaron discovered notes in the margins, such as "This is poison." Few books but much family reading naturally inspired John's boys to read.

John possessed an extraordinary Bible knowledge because he was a student of the Word. Aaron thought that his father probably would have ranked among the top ten men of his day with his understanding and interpretation of the Bible, but sometimes when he would stand in front of a group of people, he would need to grope for words because he was sensitive to how words were used.

Coupled with knowledge, his strong convictions motivated him to write. His most enduring piece of writing is entitled "A Time to Kill and a Time to Heal,"[4] proving that nonresistance was not God's plan for Old Testament saints.

He also wrote letters to the editors of periodicals, such as the *Readers Digest* and the local daily newspaper. On April 7, 1944, the following appeared in the local Lebanon *Daily News* as a letter to the editor.

Dear Editor:

Now and then you suddenly come to the rostrum with an illuminating and extremely refreshing editorial, contemptuously outlining the unbridgeable chasm between the American and Russian ideals and concepts of life socially, politically, religiously. Then again you abruptly descend to the nation-wide level of jubilation over "continued and increasing successes by the Russians against Nazi invaders," and appraise these military successes as seeming "too good to be true." In the light of facts such a conflicting stand, instead of making good sense only makes nonsense. In view of the obvious basic similarity of the concepts and aspirations of the world's two most powerful anti-God dictators, what can it matter to liberty-loving

4 Still in print today.

nations which of the two wins this war? The inescapable conclusion must be, in either case, a potential threat upon our social and economic freedom will remain.

At this moment not only millions of sober-minded, ordinary American citizens, but many in high officialdom are in a quandary of skepticism and confusion over the probable consequences, if and when Joe Stalin emerges from this war the dominant ruler of the Eastern Hemisphere. From the day that Hitler and Stalin became belligerents it has seemed to the writer like a gracious providence of God that these two most atheistic regimes in the world should be pitted in deadly conflict against each other. It is one of "His ways past finding out" to maintain the balance of power between the forces of good and evil. Whether it is through the providence of God that our own land of Bibles and churches has become the ally of the Godless Soviet Union, others may judge. Whether we shall reap a golden security for the billions we are pouring into Russia, or whether the reaping will be a harvest of withering disappointment, remains to be seen. The latter is by no means a remote possibility. Left alone, the aggressor totalitarian regimes might have worn themselves to a frazzle. It appears that our government is unalterably committed to the aid of the Soviets in this global war, and it is not the purpose of this letter to criticize any such government commitment. But it is an appeal to you, Mr. Editor, and to all who would mold public opinion through the printed page to keep clear the broad distinction between Russian and American ways of life. Let us have more and more editorials pointing out this incompatible difference.

In view of the ominous threat of Kremlin totalitarianism, is it not the height of folly to go on blindly eulogizing the sweeping triumphs of Russian militarism? Were it not infinitely better for us to face the facts with an undimmed eye? And to humble ourselves before the God who is able to defy men and isms and determine the boundaries of nations? And to make our prayer unto Him that He would throw His gracious arms around us for the protection of our cherished freedom?

Respectfully,

J. M. Shank

The above letter illustrates the command of words, the broad horizons, and realistic discernment of its author. What a worthy legacy to leave to one's posterity!

John did not do much preaching and moralizing to his children; he simply demonstrated practical godly living. Even when the family subsisted in the depths of poverty, John refused to report the theft of his chickens to the police. Someone told him to report it to the law, but he said, "No, the Scriptures say, 'Vengeance is mine, I will repay saith the Lord.'"

John liked music. Not only did he like music, he made his contribution to church music by composing the tune to the song "Land of Love." He used a German rendering of John, "Johanan," for his pen name.

He led music in church with a tuning fork. Sometimes he was so immersed in his music that he led the timing by swinging his hand that held the book. He liked to sing and poured his whole spirit into it. At home the family sang together also. Mark had an early tape recorder which he used to record the family singing.

John never missed family worship except when he was sick. He would read a Bible passage to the family and then lead in a kneeling prayer.

John was a steady worker rather than a pusher. He wanted his boys to be in the field by 7:00 A.M. By the time he sold the farm in 1942, his herd of cows had reached thirteen, always milked by hand. After a meal he would relax under a shade tree for a while before returning to the field. He was not lazy. He never owned a tractor for his farming; all his farming was done with horses up until he sold the farm. His biggest farming interference was his poor physical and emotional health. Aaron never felt like his father worked him too hard, nor did he feel like he let him play too much.

Years ago, children and young people sat and listened to the older people talk. Aaron remembers his father talking to J. L. Stauffer, A. D. Wenger, George R. Brunk, and David Garber. As Aaron listened, he gained lasting impressions.

John liked good men and made them his friends. Talking about qualifications for a leader as a "lover of good men," he was heard to say, "Well, the better the men, the more I love them."

One day, possibly at EMS, John was in the company of J. L. Stauffer and George Brunk. At that point J. L. Stauffer held Calvinist views and had entered a discussion with George Brunk who was staunchly opposed to Calvinism. As the discussion progressed, it became heated to the point of the men losing patience with each other. John Shank noticed that Stauffer was losing the debate. One of the men rose to leave the room but John beat him to the door and said, "You men aren't ready to separate." To Stauffer he said, "Haven't you changed your mind on the Calvinistic doctrine?"

Stauffer weakly said, "Well, yes, I think I have." He had lost the debate but apparently was not ready or humble enough to admit it. John saved the day. J. L. Stauffer became one of the church's strong, competent defenders of Arminianism and an exposer of Calvinistic errors.

John Shank was the predominant influence upon his son, Aaron. John's life was characterized as being above reproach, knowledgeable, discerning, positive, disciplined, musical, and devoted to good people. When asked if there was anything for which he ever resented his father, Aaron replied, "I wouldn't know of a thing."

CHAPTER 2

Charming Childhood

MARY SHANK WAS a very hard worker. She worked hard to erase the farm debt by going to market. By working from morning till night, she taught her children how to work. Preparing for market was a family effort; everyone had to pitch in. At the time, Mary Louise, the only child born in Pennsylvania, pitied herself for having to work so hard. In later life she enjoyed hard work and credited her early training for that blessing. Mary had succeeded with her work-ethic training for all her children.

Aaron obtained all his formal education at the Myersdale School (now the Cedar Run Mennonite Christian Day School) located across the road from the Dohner Meetinghouse. He entered first grade after the Shanks moved to Lebanon County.

On Friday evenings each week the students presented a literary program. At first the students could choose what they wanted to present publicly. Mary Shank taught her little first-grader, Aaron, the following little speech (his first public one):

Ladies and Gentlemen,

I rise before you to tell you that Christopher Columbus discovered America, and that George Washington was the first president of the United States.

Now if there is any other boy or girl here under three feet high

That can speak in public as well as I

I'd like to hear him try.

At age 9 or 10, Aaron was stricken with double pneumonia, and for several weeks his life hung in the balance. A dangerously high fever brought on delirium. Later he also suffered a severe case of diphtheria, which made breathing and swallowing very difficult for several weeks.

Aaron spent seven years in his formal schooling. His teacher at the Meyersdale School was a nephew of one of the school board members. This relationship probably accounted for his position as a teacher more than his suitability for the work. Nevertheless, after seven years of study, Aaron passed the high school entrance test, which at that time freed him from further schooling obligation.

John and Mary desired their children to obtain at least a high school education. But when they moved away from Eastern Mennonite School, they did not want their children to attend the local public high school. This was a grief to them. They had helped start a school

Aaron Shank, schoolboy.

that their children could not attend. At age 20, Aaron did return to Virginia to attend the Eastern Mennonite School's short Bible term.

By the time Aaron was about eight years old he had saved enough pennies, nickels, and dimes to equal one dollar. He took the dollar to the Annville Farmers Trust Bank and opened a savings account. Whenever he accumulated twenty-five cents, he took it to the bank and made a deposit. The account yielded 2% interest.

When the account had accumulated to about $12.00, the bank failed during the Great Depression, joining hundreds of other banks all over the country struggling under the effects of the Depression. In the process of time, the failed bank did return almost all his money in small payments. Aaron thus gained economic education outside the threshold of the schoolroom door, providing him with insight into the society around him.

Mary also supplemented her children's schoolroom education by teaching the children poetry. Gladys remembered the following lines all her life:

Little Johnny had for breakfast
Such nice milk and bread.
"Oh, it's very nasty," little Johnny said.
"Horrid stuff, I'll leave it."
Mother said you may.
You shall have for it
Though, nothing else today.

There was beef for dinner,
Beef and rhubarb tart.
When Johnny drew his chair up—
Didn't Johnny start!
For there was his basin
Filled with milk and bread.
"Eat it," said his mother,
"Or else you go to bed."

Up to bed went Johnny
Grumbling all the way, saying,
"You'll be sorry if I die today."
Oh, how bad felt Johnny,
He really thought he'd die.
No one came to see him,
No one heard him cry.
When the tea bell rang,
Johnny cried the more.

Then he saw his mother
Standing at the door.
"Are you good now, Johnny?
If you are, here's your milk and bread."
"I could eat dog biscuits!" hungry Johnny said.

Up he sat and took it.
Soon it was all gone.
Thought it quite delicious.
Better then felt John.
Now he never grumbles,
Says his food's so nice.

Children, when you're grouchy
Just think of Johnny's price.

She also tutored her children in their Sunday School memory verses,
with John making certain the lines were mastered by Sunday morning.
The children knew their verses when they got to church.

She also taught them to be
well-behaved and to be decent.
Courtesy, consideration, and po-
liteness were important virtues.
When the children used by-
words, she reminded them that
they would need to give account
of every idle word. Once when
Aaron called one of his siblings a
"nut," he had his mouth washed
out with soap.

Meyersdale school students with teacher's car.

Mary was glad for visitors even though she did not often have them.
She was especially glad for visitors from Virginia. Gospel teams from
Eastern Mennonite School found lodging there.

At age twelve Aaron sat through revival meetings while under heavy
conviction. The revivals closed and Aaron had not responded. Like many
other boys that age, he was timid. But John, his father, noticed that his
son was restless with conviction. He talked with Aaron and helped him
gain a New Birth experience. Unlike many others, Aaron made a steady
spiritual climb without relapse. Within a year of his conversion, he had
read the entire Bible from cover to cover for the first time. He would repeat that accomplishment many times throughout his eighty-eight years.

Meyersdale School photo—Aaron is second from right in the back row (under the shutter).

One morning in later years during a revival meeting time, Mary made it a point to make the beds with Gladys and asked her, "Is it not about time for you to give your heart to the Lord?" Gladys was a bit embarrassed but did not resent her mother's inquiry. The next evening, she stood in the meeting to make her need known. She was ready and just needed the extra push.

Mary was very loyal to the church and thus was careful to dress her daughters modestly and to teach them truthfulness.

When Mary and her husband needed to discuss church matters, they did not discuss the matters in the presence of the children. They retired to a bedroom to do that. At times Mary needed some help from her husband to deal with church frustrations.

Like normal children, the Shank children scrapped at times and had fun at others. On the whole, the siblings got along well and appreciated each other. One sister said, "Aaron was a little bit different. He was more serious-minded and easier to get along with."

A family tragedy occurred when Paul, the oldest son, proved to be a source of sorrow for his parents. John and Mary had moved to Harrisonburg to help start EMS so children, including their own, could attend a Christian high school. But they moved away from Harrisonburg about the time their children, beginning with the oldest, would have been eligible to attend.

Paul never put his heart into the Lebanon County farm, even though as a young teenager he could have been a great asset to his parents. One year, John and Mary sent him south to the beloved school. During this time away from the family, Paul got into the company of rowdy friends. Because of both Paul's choices and their poverty, John and Mary needed to bring Paul home. Paul resented that decision and the situation declined ever after that. Gladys remembers going to visit Paul in prison. He died as a wealthy, ungodly man at the age of 76. Some young men eventually mend their ways as they mature; Paul did not.

Another spiritual tragedy developed in the oldest daughter, Naomi. Naomi had not made a wholehearted commitment to Christ. Once when she returned by train from Virginia to Pennsylvania, she failed to wear her bonnet. (She had a sideline business making and selling bonnets and had sold even her own.) For her failure, she needed to make a public acknowledgment. John encouraged her to make the acknowledgment but she hated it, feeling like people were picking at her.

Once when Mary Louise was visiting Naomi at work in the Hershey children's home, she was shocked to find her sister going to bed without kneeling down to pray. When Mary Louise questioned her about it, she said, "I pray in bed." To Mary Louise, Naomi was not taking her Christian life very seriously.

At Hershey, Naomi became involved with one of the older boys and thought she wanted to marry him. She was not well for a while and rumors circulated about her. John and Mary staunchly defended her against the rumors they understood to be false. Nevertheless, Naomi became embittered toward the church because of what people were saying about her.

Naomi gave up her faith at age 21 while living in Virginia. Afterward she married a divorced man. Eventually she had three husbands, two of them divorcees.

These two tragedies within their own family upset John and Mary, contributed toward John's poor health, and probably hastened his death. In contrast, Aaron made choices which honored the God of his father and mother. "The steps of a good man are ordered by the Lord."

CHAPTER 3

Tender Teens

JUST BEFORE HE was a teenager, at age twelve, Aaron worked for a lawyer neighbor who had a summer cottage near the Shank farm. After working for five days, the lawyer would give him a five-dollar gold piece which he turned over to his parents.

One day the lawyer sent him to the house for a pack of tobacco. Aaron reluctantly went to the house, got the tobacco, and presented it to the man, saying, "I don't think you ought to be using tobacco. Please don't ask me to go for your pack of tobacco again."

"Ahhh," he stiffened. "You know those fellows over in Lancaster County grow the stuff." This made a deep impression on Aaron and later spurred him on to use his influence to help his brethren in Lancaster County to develop similar convictions against the production and use of tobacco.

Character and Missions

John Shenk, Aaron's older cousin, also made a deep impression upon Aaron one day when a group of young people were together. The group was discussing personalities critically when John said, "Boys, I always feel bad when we get through talking about people like this. I think we ought to stop talking about them and have prayer for them."

This impression issued into a life principle for Aaron. When he was present during negative people discussions, he would say, "Well, we have talked about these people to each other. Now we had better talk to the Lord about them."

Another boost came at about age 15. Aaron had heard his father tell his mother that he believed Ralph and Aaron could stand on their own two feet on a particular issue. With this, the boys knew their father believed in them. The belief and trust in them created a desire in them to live up to that expectation.

Early in his life Aaron immersed himself in the Scriptures. He studied it outdoors and indoors. When the horses rested at the end of the field, Aaron read his Testament. In the evenings after chores were completed, Aaron was reading his Bible again. His brothers and sisters noticed it and how it influenced his outlook on life.

Aaron's older brother Mark became a role model for Aaron. In contrast to Paul, Mark became a young man of conviction. Like his father, Mark had health problems, his affliction being a severe bronchial ailment beginning early in life at age five. Having made some mistakes in early courtship, and in response to Naomi's looseness, Mark modeled strong convictions in his later courtship with Reba Heatwole. He lectured his younger siblings on what is proper and what is improper behavior, impressing his younger brother.

Mark wanted to involve himself in church work, especially evangelistic efforts. For many years he was superintendent of the Meckville Mission. Furthermore, he used his mind and did some writing. At the age of forty, Mark sold his farm to Aaron so that he could move to Florida for health reasons and to involve himself in mission work. On the way, he and his wife, with their possessions, stopped in Tennessee to visit friends. Tennessee beckoned them and they stayed. Mark served as a licensed minister at the Concord Mennonite Church under the Virginia Conference. Later Mark did move to Florida, finally dying there at the early age of 56 with a combination of bronchial problems and spinal cancer.

In 1931, when Aaron was sixteen, the Eastern Mennonite Board of Missions and Charities opened a mission at Meckville, a very small village at the foot of the Blue Mountain, four miles north of Fredericksburg, Pennsylvania. Services were scheduled for every Sunday afternoon at 2:00 P.M. to make it possible for the Lebanon District churches to help operate the work. John and Mary took an active role in the work from its inception, even though they did not think they could afford the weekly round trip of about thirty miles. Aaron himself enjoyed participating in the work when he was at home. Although the mission board was in charge of the work, John served as one of the superintendents for many years.

The work at Meckville was started in response to several Mennonite families who had moved into the area from Virginia and West Virginia in the early 1920's. One of these families attended the District churches fairly regularly. The others did not pursue a local church affiliation, but simply attended the services held by the Brethren church in a nearby schoolhouse.

In 1924 the most interested family had attended a service at Gingrichs and asked the speaker, John S. Hess, if similar services could be held for them in a schoolhouse in the Meckville community. Hess, a mission field worker from Lancaster County, responded to this request by coming over to hold a series of revival meetings. Hess continued his interest in the area, and for six years, small groups met occasionally in the homes for worship. On August 23, 1931, when the first service was held, seventy-three persons were present.

The Mission Board decided to purchase the schoolhouse and made necessary improvements. Sunday School was held at 2:00 P.M. and preaching at 3:00. That way mission helpers from other congregations could assist without missing their own services.

One night five months later, someone burned the schoolhouse down. Within a month work began on a new building located on property owned by one of the original Mennonite families (Ritchie). In a little over two months a new brick structure was completed, with much of the labor donated by local supporters. With the commotion caused by the fire and the new facility, interest soared, and almost one hundred persons attended the first Sunday School in the new building. Soon after they were using the new building, someone stepped back into the building after an evening service and reported fire down across the hill. The Brethren schoolhouse was burning.

Even though there was nothing to the report, the report got out that the Mennonites blamed the Brethren for burning their schoolhouse and the Brethren blamed the Mennonites for burning theirs. Nevertheless, the Meckville work continued to grow. By 1937 a bus was collecting sixty or more children, bringing them to Sunday School.

The Olesh Family

This story is not complete without a special note here. John Olesh, originally from Yugoslavia, was plowing his field one day when he saw a group of conservatively-dressed men gathered across the road. He stopped his field work and approached the group to see what was going on. They told him they were planning to build a church-house there. He said he would be glad for that.

John and his family visited the new Meckville church and appreciated the teaching and the separation practiced by the church, even though they were members

The John Olesh family, Yugoslavian immigrants, joined Meckville Mennonite Church.

of the Baptist church at the time. Early in the history of the congregation, they placed their membership at Meckville.

Since Aaron worked closely with the family and knew their story, he was anxious that it be put into print. Accordingly, after Anna Olesh died, Aaron contacted Christmas Carol Kauffman, requesting that she research and write the Olesh story. Christmas Carol responded by coming to live with the family for a time in order to gather information for the story entitled *Hidden Rainbow*.[1]

Back to Virginia

Aaron was not able to return to his birthplace until he was sixteen years of age. At that time, 1931, Naomi, Ralph, Mark, and he went to Denbigh, Virginia, for an extended visit with cousins. (By that time the Shank finances had improved somewhat.) While there, a dairyman by the name of Amos Brenneman hired Ralph and Aaron for $20.00 per month plus room and board. Amos Brenneman was about forty years old and was ending his

---

1 The story behind the story is presented on pp. 217-226 of Christmas Carol Kauffman's own biography. Marcia Kauffman Clark, *The Carol of Christmas: Life Story of Christmas Carol Kauffman*, Digital Legend, 2008.

bachelorhood. He had found a wife over at Harrisonburg and needed help for several months until he could get back to Denbigh with his wife.

Amos did not pay until the boys were owed about $90.00. Ralph and Aaron were so pleased to be able to send all $90.00 home. They never even thought of keeping part of the earnings for themselves. Near the end of the three-month stay, Aaron received a personal tip from Amos of $2.50. He could hardly believe it.

Amos was very particular with his dairy and had one of the lowest bacteria counts in the county. Before the boys could milk the cows by hand, they needed to wash their hands, disinfect their hands, and clean their fingernails. Furthermore, the cows' udders needed to be washed and a few squirts of milk shot onto the floor before being caught in the bucket. By being careful like that, the dairy was able to keep the bacteria count down to almost nothing.

The milk was bottled and sold wholesale to stores. Amos would often stop at Bishop Brunk's orchard and get apples for delivery to stores in town.

Two years later, at age eighteen, Aaron went back to Denbigh, Virginia, again to work, this time on Lewis Burkholder's dairy farm. The Burkholders' daily hundred gallons or so of milk was bottled in half-pints, pints, and quarts (and cream as well) and was delivered from house to house in Newport News. The delivery would start at two in the morning, heading for the city twelve miles away. The chipped ice placed over the milk in the summer time would be all melted by the time they returned in the late morning. Lewis Burkholder paid Aaron $6.00 per week and provided room and board. Two years later his wage had risen to $12.00 per week, considered an exceptionally good wage. Again, all his wages went home.

When Aaron finished at Lewis Burkholder's, he went to the six-week Bible term at Eastern Mennonite School. His teachers there were J. Irvin Lehman and A. J. Metzler. This high point in his experience furnished much help for him later in his teaching and preaching ministry.

Return to Pennsylvania

Just before his twenty-first birthday, Aaron took a job husking the corn produced on a neighbor's twenty-acre field. The task took three weeks. While Aaron labored husking the dry ears, some boys from town had approached the same farmer about work opportunities. They were sent to the field to labor with Aaron. They erratically jerked the husks from several ears of corn and came over to watch Aaron work vigorously. After they had watched awhile, one boy said, "That is the closest thing to sin that I ever saw." The boys walked off.

Aaron turned twenty-one while working on the home farm for his father. John had made an agreement with his sons. If the boys continued working for him until they were twenty-one, John would give each of them one hundred dollars. At that point he would pay twenty-five dollars per month in addition to room and board.

A short time after Aaron became of age, George R. Brunk asked him to come to Virginia to work in his orchard. There he started out at $20.00 a month with room and board. The next month was $25.00, the difference being that Aaron had caught some muskrats the second month.

Aaron Shank as a youth.

During this time George R. was having one of his bouts with heart problems. Reclined on the sofa with a pencil, tablet, and a board, George would write as fast as he could. Commenting on his own writing habits, he said, "I go down like a submarine when I start on a subject." Brunk's writing method reflected the intensity of his personality. In contrast to many others, he did not sit and think, write and think, and wait and think. He just wrote, and what he wrote did not generally need much revision.

After working for George Brunk for several months, Aaron received word from his father that he was needed at home. Walter wanted to leave the farm and get a job elsewhere. So Aaron returned home. Not long after he left, a hailstorm struck the Brunk orchard, ruining the peach crop. With no crop to harvest, Aaron's services would not have been needed in Brunk's orchard even if he had stayed.

Aaron knew his father could not afford to pay high wages. In conjunction with the arrangement of $25.00 per month Aaron had with his father, he asked if he could raise shoats, butcher them, and sell the meat at market. John consented. This allowed Aaron to supplement his wages by several hundred dollars the following winter. Later his father raised his wages to $50.00 per month.

Those few youthful years at Denbigh under the church leadership and preaching of Bishop Brunk played an important role in helping Aaron chart his course in life. In Bishop Brunk, Aaron had found a man he deeply admired. He sought George's company and spent time discussing theological questions with him. In Aaron, Brunk found a young man who was not interested in the frivolity, fun, and foolishness typical of youth, but one who possessed an interest in the deeper things of God. Aaron was preparing himself for service in the church of Jesus Christ.

Eastern Mennonite School Mixed Chorus, 1937. Marjorie Showalter is in the second row from the front, eighth from the left (circled).

CHAPTER 4

Teachable Twenties

THE SHYNESS SO prevalent in Aaron's youth continued into his twenties. He never courted until he was twenty. In a time when couples "courted around," Aaron only had three dates. One date was with a girl from York County and the other two were with a daughter of George Brunk. Even then, he might not have courted her without her encouragement to do so. Feeling intimidated by the intellect of George's daughter, Aaron found the relationship uneasy. He did not date again until he met Marjorie Showalter at age 23.

Marjorie was in the same graduating class at Eastern Mennonite College as Aaron's older brother, Ralph. Marjorie impressed Ralph with her brilliance, good grades, likeable personality, and good sense of humor. He was already engaged to be married to Bessie McCaskey.

When Aaron went to visit Ralph at EMC to hear the rendition of "The Holy City," his eyes rested on a particular girl during the rendition. Afterward, Ralph wanted to introduce Aaron to Marjorie Showalter. Behold, it was the same girl he had particularly noticed during the rendition! Aaron and Marjorie were not acquainted at all, even though the Shanks and the Showalters had both lived in Virginia, the Shanks near Harrisonburg and the Showalters further south near Waynesboro. He was twenty-three and she was twenty-two.

During their first date, nothing was said about continuing the friendship. Aaron went home and wrote Marjorie a letter indicating his interest in a continuing friendship provided she would have a corresponding interest. She wrote back and said that she had an interest in continuing. Through

35

correspondence and occasional visits, Aaron told Marjorie that if at any time she was not interested in continuing the friendship, he was not interested either. The relationship needed mutual interest.

Aaron and Marjorie had two dates before commencement. During that time, he got acquainted with her parents in Augusta County.

The Showalter Family

Marjorie Showalter was the oldest of the eight children born to Ira S. Showalter (October 3, 1893-April 24, 1953) and Edna Mae Shank Showalter (November 20, 1893-January 9, 1975). The children's birth years are as follows: Marjorie (1916), Winfred (1919), Milton (1923), Lois (1926), Dorothy (1927), Leonard (1929), Shirley (1933), Ralph (1934).

The Ira Showalter family. L to R, back row: Leonard, Milton, Winfred. Front: Shirley, Dorothy, Lois, Marjorie. Seated: Ira and Edna; Ralph standing.

Marjorie's father was a capable man, possessing an excellent store of Bible knowledge. He shared in the lot for minister twice at Springdale but was never ordained. He was a song leader and conducted singing classes at Springdale. Even with a weak heart, he sang with a glad, full voice. Ira reminded Aaron of his own father, and he always liked to listen to Ira sing. His weak heart gave out early, at age fifty-nine.

Ira held a strong premillennial view of eschatology while his father-in-law Erasmus Coffman Shank held a strong amillennial view and actively opposed premillennialism. The two would get into warm discussions about the issue and finally needed to stop because the matter got too tense between them.

Marjorie's sister, Shirley, wrote of their father:

Dad made the Sunday mornings, before going to church, a very special time. He always woke me up by singing "I Owe the Lord a Morning Song." Even with a weak heart, he sang with a full voice and much gratitude. I was always blessed to hear him sing. It was good preparation for the worship that followed....

Erasmus Coffman Shank (Marjorie's grandfather)

Erasmus Coffman Shank, or E. C. Shank, as he was known, moved from Rockingham County, Virginia to Augusta County, Virginia sometime between 1887 and 1888. He was ordained to the ministry in the Mennonite Church near Waynesboro, Virginia in 1890. This church became known as the Springdale Church.

By 1898 he was helping to preach to the mountain families above Stuarts Draft, and helping to start the Mountain View Church. One winter the road to the Mountain View Church became impassable because the snow was so deep, so he got up very early and walked the ten miles to the church in order to hold the services on time.

Erasmus and Ida Shank, Marjorie's grandparents.

He was also spending time in the mountains of West Virginia helping in church mission work at Elkins, Franklin, Mouth of Seneca, Job, and other churches. In 1901, Erasmus and L. J. Heatwole preached seventeen sermons in a twelve-day trip. At the furthest point, they were more than one hundred miles from home. This would have all been by horse and buggy. In one of his sermons he told about one of his cows that gave twenty-eight quarts of milk a day. For West Virginia at that time, such a record was unbelievable. A woman in the back of the room was heard to remark, "Isn't that a pretty tale for a preacher to tell."

He was also preaching in other parts of the Virginia Conference, which included South Boston, Warwick River (Newport News), and Fentress (Norfolk). He was able to spend all this time for the church because of the prosperity of his dairy farm and orchard.

Erasmus held revival meetings in Knoxville, Tennessee in 1919 and later became involved in building a church there, becoming a member of the building committee and then supervising the work.

About this time, he became involved in the effort to establish a Mennonite school (Eastern Mennonite) in the Harrisonburg area and was on the original board of trustees from 1920 to 1936. In 1933-34 in a venture to give employment to students, Erasmus Shank, along with Ernest Gehman and A. D. Wenger, formed The Sharon Manufacturing Company. This company was the only company to make cast iron toys in the United States. It was located in one of the original farm buildings near the old Industrial Arts Building and what is now the Seminary Building. The toy factory employed thirteen full-time workers and more than forty students. In 1934 the NRA (National Recovery Administration) minimum wage requirements could not be met and they had to cease manufacturing. Some of the toys can be seen in the Eastern Mennonite University library museum.

Much of the success of the churches in the hills of Virginia and West Virginia could be attributed to the untiring work and the strong belief that we are living in the end times, which drove Erasmus on to preach the gospel. His successes as a farmer made it possible to provide finances to the church and school during the Depression years. He was active until near the end, when he said that his eyesight and mind were not quick enough to prepare sermons and he asked to be relieved of his duties. Erasmus Shank died in 1942 at the age of eighty-two and is buried in the Springville Mennonite Church Cemetery.

Quoted from David C. and Lucille Shank Allen, *The Genealogy of Erasmus Coffman Shank*, 2002, self-published, p. iv.

Erasmus Coffman Shank and family, c. 1912. Left to right, back row: Edna, Pearl, Ollie, Jacob; front row: Russell, Erasmus, Ida, Clayton.

Marjorie's mother, Edna Mae, had spent time at a tuberculosis sanitarium, but had recovered by the time Marjorie began courting. She was a saintly, hard-working woman. She possessed a keen mission interest and supported non-Mennonite efforts in missions. Aaron's son Milford stated years later, "We were so Mennonite that it surprised me that Grandma Showalter supported non-Mennonite mission efforts."

Both the Shanks and the Showalters were very loyal to the Mennonite Church. They both shared concerns about the liberal influences coming into the Church in their day.

Soon after Aaron and Marjorie started courting, Marjorie moved from Virginia to Reading to work because wages from the aristocratic people living there were higher than anywhere else. Her first job offered $12 per week, a high wage. For that wage she cleaned, did dishes, dusted (around many gadgets), and did other housework for an old woman and her niece who lived together. Marjorie lived in the house with them.

Aaron and Marjorie, courtship.

When the two women went to their Maine home for the summer, Marjorie went along to work for them there. While Marjorie did not particularly like her work, she especially liked her trip to Maine and wanted to revisit the New England states later after she and Aaron were married. They never got around to it.

Marjorie Showalter's graduation picture.

In Reading, Marjorie worked in two different homes. In the process of time the mission board asked her to serve at the Twelfth Street Mission, not realizing that by that time she was already engaged to be married. Marjorie consented and served there for the last six months before she was married.

Reading was about thirty miles away to the east, so the Shanks could frequently enjoy her. "Margie" inspired Gladys to memorize chapters of the Bible. She was energetic, likeable, and sociable. When Gladys served as Marjorie's maid over Milford's birth, Gladys was impressed with the amount of food that Margie canned, even in large jars.

During their courtship, Aaron and Margie visited older folks and relatives; enjoyed scenery, such as the view from the Reading Pagoda, Skyline Drive in Virginia, the Endless Caverns (Virginia); attended Bible Conferences and other church services; played board games such as checkers; and participated in other youth activities.

Teaching on courtship practices in those days was less than ideal. "Hands off," "lips off," "laps off," was preached as necessary before engagement, but after engagement, some physical liberties could be taken. An engagement kiss was considered proper and to be expected as a seal of that promise.

Aaron and Marjorie on their fourth date.

Aaron's strong emphasis on purity in courtship was influenced by his own observations of the courtship practices of his youthful days. He much preferred the higher standard of later years.

Marjorie seemed like the perfect match for young Aaron. The Eastern Mennonite School yearbook described her personality as dependable, energetic, cheerful, prompt, possessing a spirit of altruism. Though she was small, she was not easily discouraged by large tasks. Aaron found her to be conscientious and attentive to details. She was neat and thoughtful. In Marjorie, Aaron discovered a natural teacher, one who could handle children as well as read quickly with comprehension and understanding. Marjorie possessed managerial abilities, including the ability to organize.

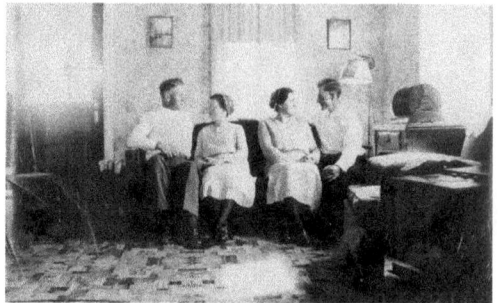

Aaron and Marjorie (left) with Mark and Reba Shank.

Courtship continued for over two years. Aaron could not see his way clear to get married because his parents needed him at home. The courtship stretched out, with engagement lasting for an entire year. Marjorie was becoming a bit impatient!

Finally, Aaron told his parents that something would need to be done. He was engaged and some change needed to take place.

The Shank family agreed to raise the roof of the summer kitchen on the home place to provide a room upstairs there. They fixed the whole building up to make a nice cozy little place for the couple to live.

The couple was married on May 29, 1940 at Springdale Mennonite Church in one of the last services in the old building. Furthermore, it was one of the first church weddings at Waynesboro, Virginia, the Southern District of Virginia Conference. Springdale, Marjorie's home congregation, was considered one of the finer (less plain) congregations of the Virginia Conference.

Simon Bucher preached the wedding sermon based on Aaron and Marjorie's chosen text of "That in all things He might have the preeminence." This wedding sermon was the first

Aaron and Marjorie's wedding picture.

wedding sermon he preached after having been commissioned as Bishop in the Mennonite Church. Bishop Joe R. Driver married them.

The wedding was held at 6:00 on Wednesday evening, May 29, 1940. The following day, May 30, had been their preference, but they moved the date ahead one day in order to accommodate John Shanks' so that no market day would be missed. Aaron's brother Walter served as best man, and a friend from the Reading Mission, Esther Swartzentruber (later Mrs. Arthur Good), served as Marjorie's bridesmaid. After the wedding, sandwiches and salad, as well as cake and ice cream, were served at Marjorie's home.

In an interesting twist of history, Marjorie Showalter had married a Shank. Her mother Edna Mae had been a Shank who married a Showalter. Aaron and Marjorie knew that they were third cousins.

Jacob Shank 1793-1871

Frances Miller Shank 1793-1836

Henry M Shenk 1817-1876	(Brothers)	Jacob Shank 1819-1889
m. Susanna Brenneman Shenk[1] 1818-1908		m. Barbara Beery Shank 1824-1868
Catherine Shenk Shank 1852-1921	(1st cousins)	Erasmus C. Shank 1861-1943
m. Martin Burkholder Shank 1854-1930		m. Ida Catherine Rhodes Shank 1862-1931
John Martin Shank 1880-1945	(2nd cousins)	Edna May Shank 1893-1975
m. Mary May Miller 1881-1975		m. Ira Samuel Showalter 1893-1953
Aaron M. Shank 1915-2003	(3rd cousins)	Marjorie Showalter 1916-1995

For their wedding trip, the new couple went to Washington D.C. for two days. John and Mary Shank were attending market and could hardly spare Aaron's absence.

Newly married—Aaron and Marjorie ready to depart on a trip.

The newly-married couple set themselves to the task of establishing a household. But the couple found living on $50.00 per month to be difficult, even with the use of the "summer kitchen" house, and Aaron told his father so. Something needed to be done. Mary could not understand why he could not make it with that kind of income. She decided that she would keep record of her and John's expenses to see what it cost them to live. That was the last Aaron's heard anything of that.

---

1 Susanna (Brenneman) Shenk was the younger sister of well-known Mennonite bishop John M. Brenneman (1816-1895) from Elida, Ohio (author of *Pride and Humility* and *Christianity and War*, as well as numerous articles in the *Herald of Truth*).

About the same time John and Mary thought it was about time for them to quit farming. They offered the farm to Aaron's for $2,500 per year rent. Aaron said that they would need the market business in order to pay that. But John and Mary were not ready to part with market, so they decided to sell the farm. They started with a price of $10,000 in the early 1940's. (They had paid $8,500 for it in 1919.) There were no nibbles. They kept reducing the price until they had a buyer at $7,500, but then that man could not produce the money.

John decided to sell the farming operation plus real estate at public auction. At the auction, the farm brought $8,000. They felt fortunate that they had not sold earlier at the lower price and still have to pay the real estate commission. The rest of the sale, including the sale of their thirteen cows, produced revenue beyond their expectations—about $6,000.00.

With the money, John and Mary bought a new house in Myerstown for $6,000.00 and moved there. Two years later, on November 16, 1945, John died in that house, aged sixty-five years.

Some of John's last words were, "In a dream last night God made it so *very* plain to me that the gateway to heaven was open, and whether I live or die, I am at peace."

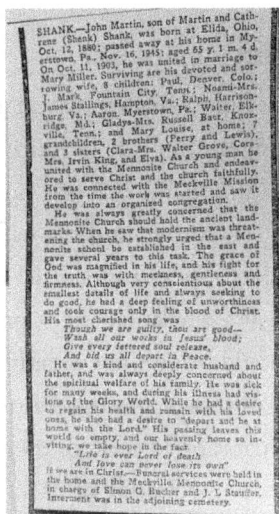

John Shank's obituary.

His obituary stated:

He was always greatly concerned that the Mennonite Church should hold the ancient landmarks. When he saw that modernism was threatening the church, he strongly urged that a Mennonite school be established in the East and gave several years to this task. The grace of God was magnified in his life, and his fight for the truth was with meekness, gentleness, and firmness. Although very conscientious about the smallest details of life and always seeking to do good, he had a deep feeling of unworthiness and took courage only in the blood of Christ. His most cherished song was

Though we are guilty, thou art good—
Wash all our works in Jesus' blood;

Give every fettered soul release,
And bid us all depart in peace.

He was a kind and considerate husband and father, and was always deeply concerned about the spiritual welfare of his family. He was sick for many weeks, and during his illness had visions of the Glory World. While he had a desire to regain his health and remain with his loved ones, he also had a desire to "depart and be at home with the Lord." His passing leaves this world so empty, and our heavenly home so inviting...

Funeral services were held in the home and in the Meckville Mennonite Church, in charge of Simon G. Bucher and J. L. Stauffer. Interment was in the adjoining cemetery.

Simon Bucher

Simon Bucher, the man who preached his wedding sermon, would play a significant role in Aaron's life. Who was this man?

Simon Bucher was ordained as a presiding elder in the Church of the Brethren. He and his wife hosted two of his wife's unmarried Mennonite aunts. These aunts often came to Gingrichs Church by trolley because the trolley tracks ran right past the meetinghouse, but sometimes the Buchers would bring these elderly sisters to Sunday evening services.

By this time the Church of the Brethren no longer officially required separation in dress or even emphasized the practice. Bucher was discouraged with his church because of this failure. For a while he would attend the Brethren services in the morning and the Mennonite services in the evening.

After he attended the Mennonite services a few times, the Mennonite ministry asked him to give testimony. He impressed everyone with his testimony, including Aaron, then in his late teens. Bucher's testimony was so different from the usual testimony in that it was fresh, enthusiastic, and employed good logic. Once started, the practice of giving this type of testimony continued.

The Shanks loved this breath of fresh air. They had the Buchers and the maiden ladies for Sunday dinner and immensely enjoyed the visits. Meanwhile the Buchers kept coming to the Mennonite services and mingled more and more with the Mennonite people.

Simon and Sally Bucher. Simon was a presiding elder in the Church of the Brethren, but laid down his ministry, joined the Lebanon District of Lancaster Conference, and was called as bishop of that district.

Finally, Simon laid down his ministry in the Church of the Brethren and became a member of the District as a lay brother. Shortly afterwards, there was a call for a ministerial ordination at Dohner. Jacob Ebersole was failing in health and thus the call for a preacher at Dohner. Counsel was taken from the District and the counsel was unanimously in favor of restoring Simon Bucher's ministry at Dohner.

Soon afterward, he held revival meetings at Dohner and crowds of people came to listen to him. Simon was an educated man and had a systematic method of preaching that was new to the district. Once again, the Shanks were able to enjoy what they had previously experienced in Virginia.

By this time the older Bishop David Westenberger had died and Bishop Noah Risser from the Elizabethtown District had been serving at the appointment of the Bishop Board. Soon after Simon was charged as a Mennonite minister, there was talk about a bishop ordination for the Lebanon District. Less than two years after receiving his charge at Dohner, the bishop ordination was held for the Lebanon District and Martin Weaver, Daniel Wert, and Simon Bucher were named.

This ordination caused no small stir in the district. Two of the nominees possessed questionable qualifications, so John Shank raised concern. Between the naming and the ordination, the John Shank household became tense, as the class of candidates for bishop contained two men the Shanks considered unqualified.

On the morning of the ordination, the presiding bishop got up and stated that they had received many letters of concern about this ordination. They studied each letter and considered the concerns. They concluded that the only thing they knew to do was to "commit the whole issue into the lap of the Lord."

The lot revealed that Simon Bucher was to be Lebanon County's new bishop. Since Simon had been ordained previously, he was re-commissioned, not re-ordained.

Simon's ordination was the beginning of a new era for the Lebanon District. The Church breathed fresh air.

Shortly after Simon was re-commissioned, he called for an ordination at Dohner. Four men were named (one vote placing a man in the lot): John Shank, Oscar Delp (not a member of the district but living there), Robert Miller, and Aaron Shank. The Shanks' membership was at Dohner but they worked at Meckville. The lot fell to Robert Miller. Aaron felt no personal call.

One family at Meckville complained before the ordination about the newly-married Aaron Shanks, "You can't have them for Dohner; we want them for Meckville."

Typical of his energetic ministerial style, ten months later Simon called for an ordination at Meckville. The Mission Board had wanted to ordain at Meckville several times, but due to some existing stressful situations, ordination proceedings were denied the congregation. Daniel Wert, from Gingrichs, had been appointed pastor there from 1935 (when John S. Hess resigned) until Aaron was ordained in 1941. The Mission Board had also appointed Mark Shank as superintendent of the mission, in which office he served until sometime after Aaron's ordination.

When Simon Bucher finally received clearance for ordaining at Meckville, Gleason Ritchie and Aaron Shank were named. (John Shank, Aaron's father, refused to carry a proxy vote for Aaron from a sister whose husband was not a member and who was unable to attend the nomination service.) This time the personal call was clear. Aaron felt a mixture of burden, strain, solemnity, and humility. The lot fell to Aaron and he was ordained as Meckville's first local minister on his father's sixty-first birthday, October 12, 1941. Aaron was twenty-six and had been married almost a year and a half.

Historically, the Mennonite Church has used the lot as an expression of gelassenheit when more than one nominee is named.[2] Proverbs 18:18 states that the lot will cause contentions to cease by removing the matter from the hands of men and placing the matter in the hands of a Sovereign God.

This did not happen in this ordination. On the day of the ordination, as the congregation met the Ritchies and the Shanks, Marjorie heard a sister say to Mrs. Ritchie, "We're sorry you weren't ordained." Then she looked at Marjorie and said, "You'll be alright too, I

The young couple at home.

think." This same family had earlier wanted Aaron as a minister for Meckville, but just before this ordination, the family had solicited votes for Gleason Ritchie.

Tension existed at Meckville for several years after the ordination and Aaron felt like he was preaching to a stone wall. These stresses were carried over from former years of worker rivalry. It required years of Scriptural ministry to reduce tension and build church support.

After he was ordained, Aaron was never told when to start preaching nor was he introduced to the congregation. The first Sunday morning after the ordination, he prepared to preach, went to the pulpit by himself, and started preaching.

2 Sandra Cronk, "Gelassenheit: The Rites of the Redemptive Process in Old Order Amish and Old Order Mennonite Communities," *Mennonite Quarterly Review* (January 1981), p. 10. The entire thirty-nine page essay provides useful historical context for the concept of gelassenheit, which was already largely lost among the Old Mennonite Church by this time. Gelassenheit, a German word with no simple English equivalent, means yieldedness, letting-go, humility, imperturbability, relaxation, etc. The term describes a life attitude toward the providence of God.

Upon his ordination, Aaron suddenly found himself to be no longer a part of the Lebanon District. Due to some opposition from the Lebanon District Ministry to the Meckville ordination, Aaron was not invited to the Lebanon District ministerial meetings. Therefore, he was not considered a part of the Lebanon District even though his membership was at Dohner at the time of his ordination. This situation lasted for about ten years.

Simon Bucher felt strongly that the situation needed to change. Meckville was somewhat a part of the District even though it operated under the Mission Board. The District had regularly sent preachers to share in the preaching there. When Simon began to make efforts to include Meckville in the District, not everyone on the Ministerial Board felt comfortable with that arrangement. Some ministers felt threatened by Aaron while Simon consistently expressed appreciation for Aaron and his ministry. This seemed to make others jealous, and thus they continued their opposition.

Ultimately, Aaron came into the District just like he went out. There was no formal exit and no formal entrance. He simply was invited to Ministerial Meetings and Meckville was considered to be a part of the District. Interestingly, Mission Board support for Meckville stopped soon after Aaron was ordained, with the understanding that it would be a part of the Lebanon District. As a self-sustaining work, Meckville had not been a part of any district for almost ten years.

The Shanks at their three-story home.

Simon invited Aaron to go along to the first Christian school promotional meeting of the District. The discussion was supposed to center on the possibility of starting a local Christian School. At the meeting, one man stood up and said, "I'd like to know why Aaron Shank is at this meeting."

Simon replied, "We invited him here."

M_____ stormed, "Why was he invited?"

Simon hedged, not knowing what to say. He turned to M_____'s father, "You are the oldest man of the district, maybe you can answer the question."

M_____'s father responded, "Why are you picking on me?"

M_____ again burst out, "Simon, I'm asking you the question!"

By this time the other people present were becoming jittery and some were crying. Aaron stood up with a smile on his face and quietly said, "I feel like I belong to the Lebanon District. I was a member of the Dohner congregation when I was ordained for Meckville. I was automatically disconnected from the District for no known reason. There was never a reason given why this happened."

These words quieted the meeting and it proceeded with business.

Real Estate

When the farm was sold, Aaron and Marjorie, along with baby Milford, needed to find another place to live. Out scouting around one day near Greble, twelve miles east of the Annville place, Aaron spotted a vacant house.

He stopped at the house on the opposite side of the road to inquire about the vacant property. He asked the lady who came to the door, "Is the vacant property for sale?"

She replied, "No. Buy this place."

Aaron was surprised. "Is this place for sale?"

She said, "Well, we talk about it sometimes."

Home for us 1945-1974
Home for Ira's 1971-?

The Shank farm, 1947.

Aaron asked, "Do you have a price?"

She said, "Come back later."

When Aaron returned, the owner said that they would sell the house and twelve acres for $4,000.00.

The large old house had been used as a store at one time. The layout of the house was undesirable, but it was a place to live and it was inexpensive. The Shanks lived there two years.

About a mile further east, Mark Shank lived on a twenty-two acre farm. When Mark decided to move to Florida, his move would vacate that farm and thus Aaron became interested in it. Aaron and Marjorie purchased it in 1944 for $7,500 and turned it into a broiler-raising operation.

Just a bit further east, an eighty-acre farm in two tracts came up for public auction in 1956. At the auction, Aaron's high bid of $12,300 was rejected. After the sale he went into the house and offered the woman $14,000, and then $15,000, but both of these bids were rejected.

The next year another auctioneer told the woman that she could not sell it at auction unless she made it absolute. Again, Aaron offered the high bid of $12,300 and this time got it. Numerous dilapidated buildings

Aaron (top of wall) working on an addition to the Shank farmhouse for his mother, Mary, to live in.

occupied one of the tracts. Thirteen were eventually demolished and some new ones erected in their place.

Aaron and Marjorie built their new ranch-style house in 1975 on the other forty-acre tract. Stephen Ebersole built his new house in 1987 on the same tract. Later, the Swatara Mennonite Church was built in 1993, again on the same forty-acre tract of land.

Many years ago when I was a young farmer, I did custom farming for Aaron Shank. I went to him for advice about milking cows and other farming related questions in Lebanon County. I was endeavoring to make a living for my family.

He told me the story of when he was a young farmer and newly ordained in the Lancaster Conference. In those days a person could loan money to or borrow from the mission board to start farming. Also in those days farming in Lebanon County was looked down on. (The idea was conveyed or at least imagined, "If you try to make a living there you will starve. Even the crows pack their lunch if they plan to go over Brickerville and into Lebanon County!!").

So Aaron applied for a loan to build a chicken house for his livelihood. The mission board sent a three-man deposition to see Aaron, to look at his plans, review his balance sheet and so forth to see if it was a good idea for the mission board to loan monies to him.

One brother asked Aaron, "How are farmers doing in Lebanon County?"

"Well," Aaron replied, "I will drive you around. You can decide for yourselves."

So they did. They drove past a number of well-kept farms of families in the Lebanon District. One of the brothers stated, "It looks like these farmers are doing very well in Lebanon County. What do they do with their money?

With a twinkle in his eye Aaron replied "When these farmers have extra money, they loan it to the mission board."

Needless to say, the committee approved Aaron's loan and extended their wish for God's blessing on his plans to build a chicken house. Aaron was a good chicken farmer for many years.

Also, as a young farmer, I took Aaron's advice, and milked cows for many years. In this way I raised my family for the Lord and endeavored to serve the church.

—*Daniel Faus*

CHAPTER 5

Tireless Thirties

MILFORD DOES NOT remember his mother resting. She did not take naps. When telling Milford to take a nap, she would say, "If only I *could* take a nap."

"It seemed that Mother had more energy than she had strength for. She seemed tired but would always keep working. It makes me weak to think of the incredible amount of effort my parents put into church, school, and home."

Marjorie was a prolific reader, but she did not read during the day. She read at night. When she attended Millersville State College much later in the summer of 1965, an uncle told her not to expect high grades in the subject she was taking. But she tried it anyway and ended up with straight A's.

By age thirty Marjorie, as a minister's wife, had lots of company. The church families would be invited by turn as she rotated round and round the church.

Aaron himself was becoming quite busy. His previous youthful Bible study served as an excellent preparation for his increasing public preaching ministry. Within five years of his ordination, he was in demand as a speaker in revival meetings across the church and had embarked on a long career as a teacher in various Bible Schools.

He conducted his first series of revival meetings in 1944 at Gingrichs in his home district. This inaugurating series lasted two weeks, as did the two held the following year at Rawlinsville and Rissers.

During his revival meetings in Lancaster County Aaron regularly included a pre-sermon talk entitled "A Love Note on Tobacco." Lancaster Conference included many tobacco growers. The justification was, "Our fathers hand-ed us a spiritual church and they grew tobacco. If they could grow it and hand to us a spiritual church, it must be all right. People who stop raising tobacco often go liberal. God wouldn't make it grow if it wouldn't be good for something. Besides, it gives us year-round work and keeps our children at home on the farm."

Aaron responded, "Noah was a righteous man too, but I guess we won't get drunk simply because Noah got drunk."

At Lancaster Mennonite School Aaron asked the students, "If it is good for human consumption, why don't we load a shipload to send out for relief? If it is worth nothing for human life and health, how can a producer accept

Aaron and Marjorie with their first son, Milford, at Aaron's first set of meetings.

$500 per acre for a commod-ity worth nothing? Tobacco growing just does not fit the 'good works for necessary uses' spoken of in Titus 3:14."

As an evangelist, Aaron determined to give tobacco a blow. During a two-week series of revival meetings at East Petersburg (1951), Aaron announced that the second Thursday night he would deliver a pre-sermon talk entitled "A Love Note on Tobacco." "I am announcing it tonight because some of you might especially want to be here that night and some of you might want to stay away."

Consequently, one man approached Aaron saying, "You better be careful what you say here. One other person who preached against tobacco here went away with a mighty small offering." Another man reminded him that he was in the heart of tobacco-growing country.

On that Thursday night Aaron related the story of the Lebanon County lawyer and what he had said about Lancaster County's tobacco production. He also publicly related the warnings that he received. Then he said, "If I was preaching for money, I would change both my message and my church."

That night Aaron extended an invitation to anyone who would commit himself to ceasing tobacco production (the only time he ever extended that invitation). One man responded, a Brethren man, who later came into the Mennonite Church. After hearing the "Love Note on Tobacco" a number of farmers became ready to discontinue production of "the weed" as it was often labeled in those days.

Aaron's anti-tobacco voice was lonely. Aaron loathed needing to be led from farm to farm during revival visitations, visiting tobacco cellars. While the home preacher was enjoying "tobacco talk" with the church tobacco strippers, Aaron was hating it. The experience added fire to his usual "Love Note on Tobacco" during the week.

At Mountville Mennonite Church after the tobacco talk, one tobacco-growing man approached him, saying, "That message can't be refuted."

Aaron replied, "You'll stop raising it won't you?"

"Oh, I don't know. I won't promise."

Later, when Aaron met him in a different setting, he reported, "We're out of the tobacco business." His was not the only response. Another man stated, "Don't think your tobacco message was unfruitful, because there is no more tobacco raising in our family."

In 1951, Aaron's own son Milford was introduced to tobacco use at age ten. At the local Mennonite School (before Myerstown) Milford's friends enticed him. These boys' fathers raised and/or smoked tobacco, but they were not a part of the Lebanon District. Since the school smoking needed to be done on the sly, they "forced" Milford to smoke so that he would not report their activity.

From the very first, Milford found tobacco pleasing to his flesh. One friend taught him how to inhale the smoke, rather than just hold it in his mouth. Milford liked the experience and smoked occasionally for a three-year period. During that time, he would occasionally get caught and the consequences were serious.

At age thirteen, as a member of the church, God faced Milford with the choice of giving up tobacco or going to hell. He had often heard his father preach against tobacco use and production. The issue pressed itself against his own soul. Against all his desires, he gave it up and has not used tobacco since.

Milford gives tribute to his father for the strong influence against tobacco. With hereditary respiratory problems combined with a love for its taste, Milford later wondered how long he would have enjoyed good health or lived had he not received such strong parental help.

Aaron not only warned his children and his churches about tobacco, but he warned others as well. Milford could usually depend upon his father to warn farm visitors or workers if they smoked, appeared shirtless, or used profanity.

Itinerate Ministry

From 1946 through 1956 Aaron averaged more than four revival series each year, plus teaching at Millwood Bible School. Millwood Bible School was a heavy load of five subjects per teacher with four classes daily during a two-week term.

Aaron was especially appreciated as a teacher at Millwood. His youthful enthusiasm and his Bible knowledge inspired many young people to vibrant Christian living. He did not hesitate to speak on issues where he had strong convictions. He just waded into problem areas and forcefully showed how the Scriptures spoke to those areas.

In 1954 and for the next several years, Aaron consented to a six-week special Bible term of three classes held at Lancaster Mennonite School. No

Left: Male teachers, Millwood Bible School; L to R: Clarence Fretz, Aaron Shank, Elias Culp, and Jacob Rittenhouse. Right: Millwood Bible School.

Lancaster Mennonite School Special Bible Term, 1954. Students in rear; teachers in front row. Aaron is in the front row, second from right.

wonder Milford later said, "It makes me weak to think about all the effort that was expended."

The various revival meetings took Aaron through Lancaster County, York County, Montgomery County, Franklin County, Dauphin County, and Juniata County, as well as his home Lebanon County, Pennsylvania. Outside Pennsylvania, he served in Tennessee, Virginia, West Virginia, Nebraska, Oregon, Alabama, and Florida. He served in Lancaster, Franconia, Virginia, and Washington-Franklin County Conferences.

Millwood Bible School students. Ruth Blank (now Mrs. David Wadel) and her sister Mary (now Mrs. Elvin P. Graybill) are in the group.

In 1949 Aaron conducted a series of meetings from July 14-24 at

Perkasie in Franconia Conference.[1] Richard Detweiler had contacted Aaron requesting the meetings, reporting that they were having problems with their sisters consistently wearing their head coverings.

During the meetings, one evening was spent on nonconformity and another on the head covering. On Sunday morning, July 24, a completely fashionable young man taught the Sunday School class. He looked miserable as he taught. The same young man responded to the invitation at the close of the morning message.

In the prayer room he poured out his heart. He said, "I've had a rebellious heart. I've influenced a lot of young people the wrong way." He begged God to forgive him for his wrong influence and to help him to be a good influence. He began to wear a plain suit. Sometime after these meetings, Richard wrote to Aaron and shared that a number of their young sisters were now wearing their coverings regularly to (public) school and elsewhere.

Three years later Aaron held a week-long Bible Conference at Rock Hill, also in Franconia Conference. Earlier in the week he had announced that he would preach on nonconformity on the last evening.

That evening, bumper-to-bumper traffic converged on the church house and a dozen tape recorders were prepared. Aaron preached the longest sermon he ever

CHRISTIAN LIFE CONFERENCE
MECKVILLE MENNONITE CHURCH

March 23-26, 1950

Speaker—KENNETH GOOD, Elida, Ohio.
Theme—The Spirit of God.

Thursday
  7:30 P.M.—His Ministry of Conviction.

Friday
  7:30 P.M.—God's Atomic Energy (The Spirit-Filled Life).

Saturday
  7:30 P.M.—The Spirit's Work in Sanctification.

Sunday
  9:30 A.M.—Sunday School Hour.
  10:30 A.M.—Sermon.
  2:00 P.M.—Grieving, Resisting and Quenching the Spirit.
  7:15 P.M.—Children's Period. Evangelistic Message.

— WELCOME —

Program for a Christian Life Conference at Meckville in 1950.

---

1 For a record of Aaron's itinerate meetings, see Appendix E.

The Summer Bible School at Meckville was so well-attended that a bus was required to transport the children.

preached—two hours. After the service the ushers went around and picked up ornamental items, including cuff links, ties, and rings, that were left lying on the benches.

Even though he often traveled, Aaron was concerned that the families at Meckville live upright lives. He was also concerned about the local unsaved people.

One night after revival meetings at Meckville, Aaron noticed that John Olesh's son Steve left immediately after the service instead of responding during the service like Aaron thought he should. Instead of visiting awhile after the service, the young man had started walking home. Evidently Steve was under conviction.

Aaron got in his car and soon caught up with Steve and asked if he would get into the car because he wanted to talk with him. He said, "I thought surely you would give your heart to the Lord tonight, but you didn't."

Steve replied, "I'm not interested."

A number of years passed and Steve (age 24) was dating the girl who would become his wife. He began to admit to himself that he was not living in Christian victory. He had been taught the truth but he was not living it. The burden of conviction continued to grow as he thought and thought about this. One night at revivals, both he and she responded. Steve would one day be deacon at Meckville.

Meckville was flourishing. A long line of incoming, respected speakers had taught and had influenced the Meckville church ever since the Mission was formed. The various special meeting programs testify to the energy and effort Meckville expended on its teaching program in the effort to build a solid congregation.

Aaron (standing in doorway) leads singing at Meckville's Summer Bible School.

When the Meckville meetinghouse was built by the Mission Board, the structure had no basement under it. During the winter of 1946-47, the congregation dug a basement under the existing structure. Furthermore, they added restrooms, drilled a well, installed plumbing, built new front steps, and graded and enlarged the church grounds.

Mark Shank got the summer Bible School work started at Meckville in 1938. Visits were made with the folks in the area as well as in Monroe Valley to solicit children for Bible School. Aaron himself would spend days at a time visiting in the community in the following years. The Bible School sessions were held from 9:00-11:30 A.M. the week after school closed for the summer and ran for two weeks.

The interest became so great (attendance as high as 160) that the church used a bus to transport children to Bible School. Additional teaching help came in from Washington County, Maryland; Virginia, and Lancaster County.

One imported teacher, Esther Rudolph, asked Aaron to come to her preschool class to talk with the children about the church. In class Aaron picked a child up, set him on his knee, and spoke in simple language to the class about what the church is.

Eventually, Aaron's sister Mary Louise Shank married Earl Martin as a result of the help from Maryland. One of the other families from that area introduced the Shank family to asparagus growing.

As the years passed, more Mennonite families moved into the area for the cheaper farmland. Cletus Doutrichs, Walter Newswangers, Daniel Reeds, Sanford Goods, Mervin Wengers, Clarence Stoners, Chester Martins, Abe Lefevers, and others were included in the number.

Gladys

Aaron's sister Gladys had always respected her older brother. When Aaron was old enough to participate in the public worship services, she could not imagine how he could pray such long prayers. His prayer list seemed so inclusive.

On August 30, 1945, Aaron was privileged to serve his sister by preaching her wedding sermon at the time she was united to Russell Baer. The text was, "To the praise of His glory." Characteristically, Aaron played on the word "bear;" "bear" and "forebear" are needed in a marriage just like Gladys was "for Baer."

After Gladys and Russell were married, they moved to Knoxville, Tennessee, to serve in the Knoxville Mission. Four years later, Russell was ready for a change.

The Lancaster Mennonite School Board was responsible for ninth and tenth grades at Kraybills Mennonite School near Mt. Joy, Pennsylvania. As a Board member, Aaron remembered Russell Baer in Tennessee and approached him about the possibility of moving to Pennsylvania to teach at Kraybills. The Baers moved to Mt. Joy in time for school in the fall of 1949.

Aaron and siblings. Left to right, back: Mark, Walter, Ralph, Aaron. Front: Gladys, Mary, Mary Louise. Paul and Naomi are absent.

Book Humor

As a young preacher, Aaron went to the Weaver Book Store in Lancaster one day. Christie Charles, manager of the store, was a persuasive salesman.

When Aaron walked into the store, Christie pulled down three or four books and laid them out. After Aaron had made his selections, he approached the checkout counter to pay. Christie started in. _____ bought this book, _____ bought that book, _____ recommended this title, etc. Don't you want them?

Aaron replied, "Yes, I want them, but I don't have what it takes to get them."

Christie would not be put off. "Your father is rich, isn't he?"

Now Aaron was ready. "Yep, I got a rich Father. Give me the books and charge them to my Father."

Christie was not ready for that.

Word Humor

One evening, Walter Newswanger, who was in charge of Meckville's midweek meetings, called Aaron and said, "We need a minute man. Would you speak on short notice tonight?"

At church Aaron got up and said, "Walter called me shortly before church time and assigned me a subject. Walter, did you know you assigned me a subject?"

"No."

"Yes, you did. You asked me to speak on 'Short Notice.'"

He then discussed the "short notices" of Scripture, such as "Be ready always to give an answer," "Be ready to suffer injustice," "Be ready for the Lord's return."

Thirty years later, Aaron was still ready at a moment's notice. At a Bible Conference at Numidia Bible School, Aaron rose and said, "I left my Bible and notes at home on a shelf in the garage. I'll give what I have."

The listeners would not have known that his notes were missing. He had the message engraved upon his heart and mind and shared it from that source.

Hay Help

It is likely that it was in this period of Aaron's life that a simple incident transpired that he would later use as an illustration of how a person's mistakes can be used to develop convictions. Aaron had cut hay for his farming operation earlier in the week, and Sunday came before it was ready to bale. On the way home from church, Aaron thought of his hay and that it likely would soon be ready to bale. On impulse he pulled to the side of the road and strolled over to a swath of hay. Kicking his foot, he turned the hay to see how it was drying underneath.

He heard a car slow down back at the road. Turning to look, he saw one of his church members stop his vehicle and lean out the window.

"Woe unto him who cannot wait until the Sabbath is over!" the brother called, half in jest, half in reproof.

To Aaron it was all reproof. He felt severely convicted and then and there resolved never to act as if he was anxious to be about work activities while it was still the Lord's Day.

But Aaron was also humble enough to use this illustration to help others grow. He was very careful not to use illustrations over the pulpit that put himself in a good light, or placed others in a negative light, but he would use illustrations that showed he could learn from his mistakes.

Doctrinal Dealing

Gleason Ritchie had been ordained as deacon for Meckville at the close of 1942. Gleason was married to Bishop Christ Lehman's daughter. Several years later when teaching the book of Romans at Meckville, Christ was confronted about the Calvinism he was teaching. But his son-in-law Gleason began to adopt Calvinistic views, influenced of course by his wife's father. He was also influenced by Abe Gish's teaching and the Scofield Bible course which he attended. The more Calvinistic he became, the less Mennonite sympathies he had. Church standards were ignored.

Simon Bucher liked Gleason as a person and was hesitant to believe that Gleason was not sincerely loyal. But at a communion service one morning, Simon's wife sat beside Mrs. Ritchie and noticed that she was wearing shoes that were in rather serious violation of the church standard. She mentioned the fact to Mrs. Ritchie. Mrs. Ritchie reacted to the admonition by later saying to someone else, "I think that is pitiful."

When Aaron needed to be away on preaching assignments, he had asked Gleason to preach, which Gleason enjoyed doing. But the peace at Meckville became disturbed. The Ritchies went to the families at Meckville to seek support for their plans for a Scofield Bible class to be held in a rented building a few miles from the Meckville church. The Bible Class started, but soon died for lack of support.

The sad state of affairs necessitated a bishop committee investigation. As a result of their first meeting with the Ritchies, the bishops terminated his ministry in June, 1950.

John Olesh (of *Hidden Rainbow* fame) warned Aaron that Meckville might lose some families.

Aaron asked John, "Are you one of them?"

"No," he replied.

"I don't think many others will leave either," Aaron said.

Two families left, Gleason Ritchies' and his father. Gleason went to the Jonestown Bible Church.

At the time this happened, Meckville had about thirty members. A year later, one baptismal class containing fifteen people boosted the membership to about forty-five.

The Ellison Family

The conversion of the Ellison family took place over this time. Austin and Elisabeth Witmer lived in the same apartment building as Arthur and Kathryn Ellison, and the Witmers invited the Ellisons to church at Meckville. The Shanks took special interest in the young Ellisons. Even before Kathryn's conversion, Marjorie brought her gifts of food, prepared and unprepared, as acts of kindness. Marjorie taught Kathryn how to cook and how to can food. When she got hepatitis, the Shanks took her into their home for a month. This act deeply impressed her. It was over this time that Kathryn had received her first Bible. But she struggled; she loved her sins and yet she hated them. She told Aaron, "If I confessed Christ and live like you claim the Bible teaches, I'd go crazy. There would not be a thing to live for."

Over the Ritchie disturbance, Kathryn decided that it would be better for her spiritually if she remain associated with the Meckville Church. A Baptist woman who had left another Mennonite church and was obviously living in sin tried to discourage her from joining the Mennonites. This ex-Mennonite had a faithful blood sister in the church at Meckville.

Aaron asked Kathryn, "Which of these two sisters is the happier?"

Kathryn replied, "The Mennonite, by far."

Aaron said, "You know, Kathryn, I think if you keep going on in your sins you will come a whole lot nearer going crazy than if you got rid of your sins." Then he said, "Frankly, I think you are pretty near getting rid of your sins."

"You think so?" she queried.

"Whenever anyone is as uncomfortable in their sins as you are," Aaron said, "they either decide to throw the whole thing away or they decide to do something about it. I think you are going to do something about it."

At the very next visit, with Evangelist James Bucher present, James asked Kathryn, "Suppose Jesus Christ came walking through that door right now. What would you tell him?"

She hung her head and said, "I'd tell Him how sinful I have been. I'd tell Him I would like Him to forgive me."

James said, "Let's get on our knees and you tell Him that."

They did so and she was converted.

Later, as a church member, she went to see the doctor in anticipation of an addition to their family. He saw immediately that a change had taken place in her life and asked Kathryn about it.

She said, "I've been converted since I was in here the last time."

The doctor questioned, "Can you be happy living a life like that?"

She answered, "Doctor, I never knew there was a peace to be had like I'm enjoying now."

Neck Ties

In 1954, the Lancaster Conference Discipline was revised. The old Discipline stated, "Long [neck] ties shall not be worn," making room for bow ties. During the Conference discussion on ties Aaron took the floor, saying, "In certain situations in the world, the bow tie is more acceptable than a long tie. In principle it doesn't matter if the tie hangs down lengthwise or sticks out the sides."

One ordained man who wore a bow tie stood and remarked, "I wear my bow tie as a mark of separation from the world and in respect to my father."

Venerable Bishop Noah Mack added, "When I was ordained, I wore a bow tie. Since some people considered it worldly, I got to thinking about it and had to agree. I just removed it and that was all there was to it."

At this time in Conference history, the bishops listened to all the discussion, but formulated the wording in the Discipline themselves. They did not take a vote in Conference on such an issue, nor did they poll the membership for direction on an issue.

The final revised wording reflected the conservative trend of the Conference: "Brethren shall not wear long neck ties nor flashy colored bow ties. Conference suggests omitting the tie." This wording stood until the revised 1968 Discipline stated, "Conference believes that wearing the necktie is a worldly practice. We maintain a testimony against its use."

Criminal Court

In early 1951, due to some involvements prior to his conversion, Arthur Ellison was called to be a witness in criminal court. Aaron sat in court with Arthur, and Arthur appeared on the witness stand wearing his plain suit. During the trial, Arthur was accused by the opposing attorney as being a "wolf in sheep's clothing."

Because Aaron did not receive an opportunity to speak with the attorney, Mr. Gingrich, that day, he wrote him a letter.

Dear Mr. Gingrich,

By way of introduction I am the man who sat by Mr. Arthur Ellison in the court room, March 5 and 6. Perhaps you can call me to mind a little better if I tell you that I was the other man in the court room who was dressed in "sheep's clothing...."

First, I was impressed with the carefulness with which you proceeded to handle the case in favor of A----------.

Secondly, I was very much impressed with the intelligence and wit you demonstrated while making your speech before the jury of the court. Your wonderful ability sold itself to me....

Thirdly, I was very much depressed with the way you could rail on the Commonwealth ... but almost in the same breath you filled the atmosphere with lying words in defense of a criminal the Commonwealth was trying to deal with. Of course you had to be "true to your profession," and it would indeed have been amusing if it were not for the fact that "all liars" shall have their eternity in the "lake of fire" and the Bible (the one you have in the court room) does not say that lying lawyers are an exception to the rule. [Quote from Rev. 21:8.] A couple thousand dollars to tell a couple lies in defense of a lying man will look fearfully foolish in the torments of hell....

Next, I was quite thrilled to note that a man of your mark and intelligence should give such a forceful argument in favor of sheep wearing sheep's clothing. Your incriminating remark suggesting that Ellison was simply a wolf in sheep's clothing was quite complimentary for our distinctive Mennonite Christian manner of dress. I felt sorry for all the other professing Christians in the court room, for your insinuation meant that their appearance was the appearance of wolves. And as for yourself, one had to conclude that you were not only wearing wolves' clothing but that you were properly dressed....

It would be wonderful indeed if your talents, abilities, and interests could be changed to focus in the direction of things that will count for God and eternity. This would also bring peace and joy to you that would far surpass your present happiness in life. Think it over, my friend....

If I can be of any help to you spiritually, do not hesitate to call on me. My services are without charge and cheerfully rendered. I will be most happy to hear from you at your convenience on this most important matter in life....

Aaron Shank

Arthur Ellison remained in the church for nearly ten years. While he withdrew his membership, Kathryn did not and remained a part of the church until she died in 2009, with her membership at Meckville, Rehrersburg, and finally at Swatara Mennonite Church.

Recounting her experience with the church at Meckville, Kathryn declared, "The people at Meckville both preached and lived what the Bible taught. They had love and compassion for people who needed Christ and they always took time to listen to people's problems and concerns."

Even though he was no longer a church member, Arthur testified in later years, while Aaron was still living, "Aaron is the same person today as he was then. He is a wonderful person for the Mennonite people."

Failure

Not all efforts at community evangelism met with the same success. Another young mother who responded to the Gospel was rejected by her husband. He locked her out of their bedroom one night. The next morning, he told her to get ready because he is going to take her away. "I can't have you around," he said.

She said, "F-----, I've got to have a little time. If I've got to leave, I must have some time to get ready. Give me till tonight."

"Okay, I'll give you till tonight."

That night she said, "F-----, where are you taking me?"

He said, "I'm taking you back to my mom."

"Your mom doesn't want me. I think you better take me to Aaron Shanks."

"No, I'm not taking you to Aaron Shanks; I'm taking you to my mom's place."

That night the Meckville church was holding a cottage meeting at his parents' house. F----- got there just before the Shanks arrived. He was leaving the house just as the Shanks were entering. To Aaron's greeting he just nodded his head and hurried away.

That evening something seemed wrong. The family seemed so depressed.

After the meeting the young mother pled to go along home with the Shanks. The Shanks took her home and she lived with them for a considerable length of time.

Eventually, her faith failed and she yielded to her husband's wishes.

Cletus Doutrich

The Cletus Doutrich family had moved to a farm in Lebanon County a few miles from the Meckville Church without even realizing the church was located there.

One evening, a neighbor who attended Meckville's Sunday evening services invited the Doutrichs to accompany them to Meckville's evening service. The narrow, bumpy, path-like road led the Doutrichs to a respectable-looking lit-up brick building back near the mountains.

Walking into the building, they were warmly welcomed by those who had gathered early. This made a deep impression, because back in Lancaster County from where they had come, they were accustomed to a segregated church experience. Older and younger people did not actively fellowship with each other at the Paradise Mennonite congregation. After a service, the fathers went out the back door, the younger men went out the side door, and the preachers went out the front door.

The impression gained at that first Meckville experience initiated a kinship feeling for the people at Meckville. The Mennonites at Meckville were invitingly different from the ones at Paradise. The Doutrichs could attest to the reputation Meckville had of being a friendly, loving church.

Sometime later, the Doutrichs ventured back themselves. But Cletus soon developed a hesitation about going because Aaron had the practice of calling on anyone present to offer the closing prayer. Cletus dreaded being called upon. He was not accustomed to being involved in church activities, such as teaching Sunday School, leading young people's meetings, and attending summer Bible School.

Another hesitation centered around Cletus's attire. He did not dress according to church regulations. It had never seemed to be an issue with the bishops in Lancaster County, at least in Cletus's mind. Even though Cletus had no conviction for plain clothing, he was much impressed by all the

LMS Special Bible Term teachers and students. Aaron is in the front row, second from right; J. Irvin Lehman is to his left. Cletus Doutrich is in the back row on the right, in front of the door frame.

plain suits he saw at Meckville. Furthermore, the people loved, respected, and appreciated their minister, who encouraged them to wear the plain suit. After attending for a period of time, he felt out of place with his fashionable attire and developed conviction for the plain suit. Accordingly, he laid aside his long tie and lapel coat and donned the plain suit.

Before long, he had assignments at Meckville, such as teaching Sunday School and superintendent work. He had never served that way before. After Gleason Ritchie left Meckville, Cletus Doutrich, as a layman, assumed responsibility for the church finances.

In 1950 or 1951 a converted Jew named Joseph Hershkovitz, serving as a Mennonite minister, preached at Meckville. In his sermon he pointed out the value of driving a stake of commitment where the believer offers himself wholly to God for His service. This was a new thought to Cletus. He had never really committed himself to the work of the Lord in a definite way.

At the close of the sermon Joseph offered the opportunity for anyone in the audience to drive a stake by publicly offering themselves to the Lord's work in a new way. Five men responded, including Cletus. Each of those five were called to leadership positions in the church later.

The Shank family in 1947. Aaron is holding adopted son Richard; Marjorie is holding Milford.

The next year, August 1951, when an ordination for a new deacon was held, Cletus Doutrich, Mervin Shirk, Austin Witmer, and Steve Olesh were named. The lot fell to twenty-six-year-old Steve Olesh. Steve had attended Meckville from boyhood and considered Aaron to be his spiritual father. He knew Aaron would look out for his best interest and felt relieved in his presence. Steve threw his energies into his church calling.

Because Aaron was receiving repeated calls to serve in evangelistic work, he sought and received permission to ordain additional ministerial help. Accordingly, Cletus Doutrich was ordained as minister on June 1, 1952, chosen by lot from a class of four men, which included Mervin Shirk, Steve Olesh, and Walter Newswanger. Aaron said that day, "The Lord was with us today."

Aaron and Louise take a bike ride.

Cletus and Esther felt accepted as part of the ministerial team.

Cletus began his ministry feeling like he was in the shadow of Aaron Shank. Aaron was knowledgeable in the Word and gifted in his preaching. Cletus had almost no experience with teaching prior to coming to Meckville in the late 1940s. What he did have, he had gained under Aaron's tutelage. Thus, he felt quite inferior to Aaron, both in Bible knowledge and in public speaking. Being charged to serve as Aaron's assistant placed a heavy burden upon Cletus, a burden he carried for years.

Growing family

The Shank household also grew during this time. After four childless years following Milford's birth (punctuated by two miscarriages), Aaron and Marjorie adopted two-year old Richard. The following year they adopted again, this time a girl, two-year old Ruth. The very next year, 1949, the Lord blessed them with a biological daughter, Louise. Milford was eight years old, Richard was four, and Ruth was three.

The demands of family life, ministry, and work placed heavy demands upon Aaron and the rest of the family. Milford remembers going to many, many church services as a child. On the way home Aaron and Marjorie would sing together, inviting the children to sing with them.

Mother Marjorie was busy in her house, busy in the church, and bustling behind the scenes so that her husband could serve the church unhindered. Many times, she needed to manage the family affairs alone.

School

Little six-year-old Milford needed to begin formal schooling, but Aaron and Marjorie were not inclined to send him to the public school, so they enrolled him in the Calvert School program and educated him at home as a temporary measure. Pennsylvania law dictated that an eight-year-old child needed to be placed in school unless the parent had college training.

At the same time the Lebanon District felt some stirrings that they should be providing a Christian Day School of their own. On October 1-2, 1949, the first Annual Christian Day School Promotional Meeting was held at Meckville with Sanford Shetler as speaker.

Meckville provided a school in the newly-excavated basement for two years. In 1951 the Smaltz Christian Day School, south of Myerstown, and Meckville Christian Day School, north of Myerstown, combined to form the Myerstown Christian Day School. A two-room school building was erected on land donated by Sidney Gingrich.

The Myerstown school did not enjoy an enthusiastic patronage. It experienced financial difficulty. Then some parents began pulling their children out to return to the public schools. Years later, in 1963, when the school could not find an upper-grade school teacher, the Board had approached Marjorie Shank as a potential school teacher, but she declined. Her youngest child, Louise, was thirteen years old.

On the final week of summer vacation, the School Board Chairman called the Shanks to report that no teacher had been found. "Could Marjorie possibly be in the classroom the following Monday morning?" Aaron was in a quandary. He wanted the school to be properly staffed, but he was not anxious for his wife to take up teaching.

The evening before school started, Aaron decided that they needed a word from the Lord. He got a slip of paper; on one side he wrote "teach" and the other side was blank, indicating no teaching. He would drop the slip of paper and whichever side was up would reveal the word. Furthermore, it needed to be confirmed with the same message on a second drop. He and Marjorie prayed about the matter.

The first drop indicated "teach." The second drop also indicated "teach." So, Marjorie scurried to make arrangements to be in the classroom the very next morning. Marjorie had no experience with teaching school. They told the Board Chairman that he should continue to look for a teacher.

Two weeks later Marjorie informed the Board that they need no longer look for a teacher; she would teach. Thus began a long tenure of teaching at the Myerstown school—nineteen successive terms. Both Marjorie and the school thrived.

In the following years, both Lebanon District parents as well as the Richland District parents shared the school. They also worked together on the School Board. The school expanded into four rooms, and by 1972, it was ready to expand again.

In that year, the vacated seven-room public school building at Millbach was purchased at public auction. The Richland patrons and board shifted to Millbach amid a few ripples. The Millbach school began with about 60 students.

The Myerstown School continued to grow, filling up the vacancy left by the departure of the Millbach students. Sidney Gingrich commented to a brother, "What would we have done with 60 more students?" The separate schools proved to be a blessing for each group.

Marjorie taught her last term at the Myerstown School in 1981-1982.

CHAPTER 6

Fiery Forties

IN 1957, AT age seventy, Simon Bucher requested permission from Lancaster Conference to ordain a bishop helper for the Lebanon District. Conference granted the permission and Simon began to make plans for an ordination. Three men were named: Aaron Shank, Sidney Gingrich, and Paul Ebersole.

A week before the nominations were taken, Aaron was painting an asphalt coating on his two-story chicken house. Not long after the job was completed, a thunderstorm washed some of the paint away. Aaron climbed onto the roof again to re-coat the washed spots. He was finishing the repair job, the last sheet, when he stepped onto some paint that had been dropped from his work on the next-to-last sheet. The paint was as slick as grease and Aaron immediately slid down the roof, shooting out from the building about six feet. The side of his chest struck a wooden post set there to anchor a wire to support raspberry vines. The post broke his fall and sent him into a roll. Everything went black for a while.

On his way down, Aaron had committed himself to God. The Lord did raise him up, but as a very sore man for a while.

The Shanks invited the family chiropractor to the ordination. He had been out to their place for meals and had taken a special interest in the family and their beliefs. The Shanks explained to him how the choice was made with the use of the lot. He refused to come, saying, "Nothing would make sense if Aaron is not ordained. I would feel too badly. He is the most dedicated man I ever met."

Before the ordination, his personal call became clear; Aaron knew he would be chosen. He prayed and fasted and tossed and turned with the burden of that responsibility. One of Milford's friends from Meckville told Milford (age sixteen) when the votes were announced, "They might as well ordain Aaron outright." The night before the ordination, Marjorie asked Aaron how he felt about the situation. Aaron informed her that the call was clear. She said, "I feel the same way."

The next day, July 4, 1957, the lot made public what Aaron and Marjorie keenly sensed in private. Aaron was forty-two.

Simon announced to the congregation that they should not shake hands very vigorously with Aaron because he was still sore from his fall. His sister, Mary Louise, pitied him for needing to shake hands at all.

Aaron promptly wrote a letter to the District ministry, expressing appreciation for Simon Bucher and his administration. Then he appealed for their support as he joined Simon. He quoted Rudyard Kipling, saying,

> When crew and captain pull together
> It takes a gale and more than a gale
> To put their ship ashore.
> For the one will do what the other commands
> Although they are chilled to the bone,
> And both together
> Can live through weather
> That neither could face alone.

Immediately, one of the District ministry who earlier had strongly opposed Aaron being a part of the District ministry reversed his opposition and lent unreserved support to Aaron. That support lasted until he died; he even requested that Aaron preach his funeral sermon.

Simon told Aaron, "You'll be my helper for a while, then we will work

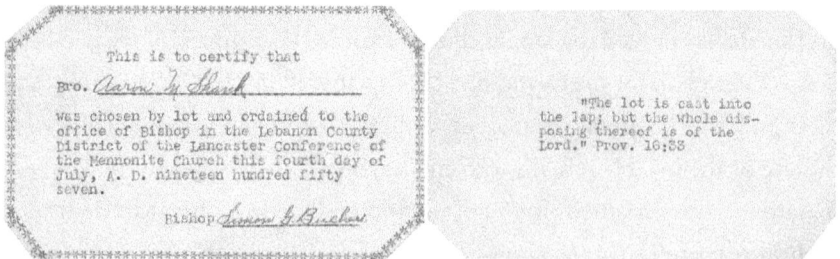

Aaron's bishop ordination certificate.

together for a while, then I'll be your helper for a while, and then I'll slip away." It happened just that way over a period of ten years.

Aaron and Simon worked together as a harmonious team, with basically no administrative differences. However, the two had some doctrinal differences. To the end, Simon held on tenaciously to his belief that nonresistance was taught in the Old Testament. In this respect, Simon agreed with the general sentiment of Lancaster Conference on the subject.

Aaron Shank and Simon Bucher.

One day at a Bible Conference, Aaron presented his viewpoint that nonresistance was solely a New Testament doctrine. Afterward, a preacher reprimanded him, saying, "You'll find that you will get along better if you accept the general concepts of the church." But Aaron was more concerned with right doctrine than he was with uncritically accepting group think.

Simon's health began to fail in the late 1960's. Aaron was so accustomed to working in tandem with another bishop, and valued the practice so much, that he requested permission from the newly-formed Eastern Pennsylvania Mennonite Church to ordain a bishop helper. On August 30, 1970, Sidney Gingrich was ordained, with Paul Ebersole sharing the lot. By that time Simon had suffered an incapacitating stroke. He finished his earthly race on July 5, 1972, aged 85 years.

Aaron always felt that Simon "was a man sent by God" who brought a new vitality and spiritual dynamic to the Lebanon District of Lancaster Conference.

The Load

Aaron was already busy in 1957 when he was ordained bishop. Now something had to be adjusted in his schedule. Both his teaching at Millwood

Bible School and the special Bible term at Lancaster Mennonite School needed to be dropped.

Revival meetings continued, with an average of four series of revivals per year from 1956 to 1965. These meetings still took him to distant places, to

Shank family asparagus harvest.

West Virginia, Virginia, Maryland, Alabama, Florida, Ohio, Nebraska, New York, as well as several counties in Pennsylvania. He only served one congregation in Franconia Conference during this time period.

The only time Aaron would not accept revival invitations was over the asparagus season. During that season, he would rise at 4 A.M. to get the knives sharpened and everything ready for the day's work. The rest of the family would rise at 5 A.M. The asparagus harvest would end between 9 and 11 A.M. By that time, there were hundreds of pounds to sort and bunch. Furthermore, the chickens needed to be tended.

Following his bishop ordination, Aaron was appointed co-bishop with Simon Bucher over thirteen congregations in western Florida and Alabama.

Steve Kolar was a hired hand who lived with the Shanks.

Previously, the churches in the South had all been served by one bishop,

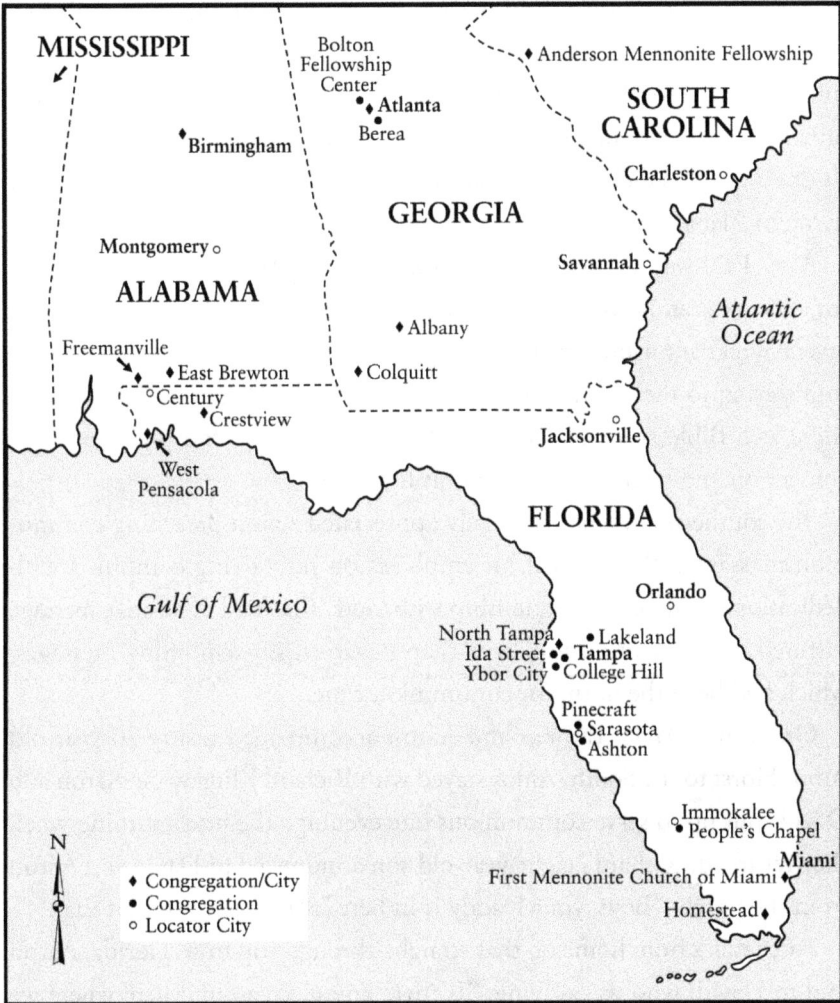

Lancaster Conference congregations in South Carolina, Georgia, Alabama, and peninsular Florida. There were additional congregations near Pensacola not shown on this map.

Leroy Stoltzfus, but the load was too much for one man. Accordingly, the southern churches were divided, with Leroy keeping the eastern part of the South along with a bishop helper, Mahlon Witmer, while Aaron and Simon took responsibility for the western part of the South.

Aaron and Simon carried this responsibility for about four years until Paul Dagen was ordained as bishop in 1961. At this bishop ordination, only the ministry of the southern churches cast votes. With only the ministry voting, only two or three nominations were required for a minister to be eligible for the lot. Mahlon Glick and Paul Dagen qualified. Paul was a licensed minister living in Alabama.

After Paul was ordained, Simon stopped going South. Aaron continued for another year. During the entire period from 1957 to 1962, Aaron spent several weeks annually, totally approximately six months of time in the South, ministering to these thirteen churches. As elsewhere, Aaron was respected there as a Bible student and a good Bible expositor who preached with conviction and held the interest of his listeners.

The southern churches especially appreciated Aaron preaching communion messages. They valued his emphasis on holy living combined with dedication to a dynamic relationship with God. This kind of positive message inspired more devotion to Christ than negative, sin-reminding messages, which had been the norm for communion time.

One time, David Thomas and Aaron accompanied nearly 70-year old Amos Horst to the South. Amos stayed with Richard Kling while Aaron and David split up to serve communions one evening. The next morning when they returned, Richard's eight-year-old son announced to David and Aaron from the porch, "Boys, your Daddy is in here." Amos never forgot that.

Forty miles from home on that straight-through trip from Florida, Aaron said to David, who was driving, "Is there any place around here where we can clean up for our wives?"

David replied, "Well, Aaron, if you are going to do that you will do it between New Danville and Lebanon." The one man was more interested in getting home, the other with being presentable when he reached home.

One day in the South, Aaron went into the Atmore, Alabama, post office to do some mailing. While he was preparing the mail, a black woman came to the same table where he was working and they exchanged greetings. When he did so, he noticed that this black woman was quite different from other women in that her modest, solid-color dress reached halfway between her knees and ankles. (These were the days when miniskirts were fashionable.) Furthermore, her long, uncut hair was covered with a modest covering.

Aaron was pleasantly surprised. He said, "Madam, you look so different from the average woman on the street in your manner of dress. Is this a personal taste that you have or might you represent some religious group? Is there religious significance in the way you appear?"

She replied, "Ah, there is religious significance to this."

Photo of the first African deputation from the Mennonite Church planted by Lancaster Conference missionaries in Tanzania. L to R, front row: Simeon Hurst, Zedekea Kisare, Ezekieli Muganda; second row: Ira Buckwalter, Orie O. Miller, Henry F. Garber, Howard Witmer; third row: Amos Hurst, Aaron Shank, Donald Lauver; fourth row: Paul N. Kraybill, H. Raymond Charles.

Aaron asked, "Who are you? What do you represent?"

She said, "We's just a small group studying the Bible and we discovered that the Bible teaches it, and we practices it," her face lit up, "and we loves it!"

To himself, Aaron thought, "What a testimony! The Mennonites have studied the Bible for centuries, know the Bible teaches it, still practice it, but a lot of us hate it. You cannot keep a doctrine alive if you hate it."

Committee Work

After he was ordained bishop, Aaron was placed on the Foreign Missions Council with responsibility to visit the foreign fields. After his first trip to Honduras, he reported to his fellow bishops how he straightforwardly dealt with the missionaries who were beginning to lay aside their plain clothing in favor of conventional Western dress. He spoke with the missionaries very directly about their failures and that they were failing the bishops' trust in them.

One of the bishops on the council, Amos Horst, asked, "How did they take that?"

"They took it well. They said that they did not appreciate hedging, being apologetic, and beating around the bush."

Two of the council members were highly offended. They were the ones the missionaries had implicated with their statement. One of them commented that Aaron's words "hit him between the eyes." This young upstart bishop knew better how to administrate than they did. Aaron had never thought about how they would feel about his statement.

By 1958, Aaron was already serving as one of three Lancaster Conference members on the Mennonite Publication Board, overseeing the Publishing House at Scottdale, Pennsylvania. He did not feel qualified to be there or have as much time as the job demanded, and consequently did not feel like he had much impact. Others felt differently, so Aaron served a total of nine years on the Publication Board.

One day at Scottdale, the Board was discussing joint publication of Sunday School quarterlies with the General Conference Mennonites. The discussion was heavily in opposition to the joint project. One Board member pointed out that General Conference women already had their hair cut, a clear violation of New Testament teaching. Another member from the West arose and said, "We might as well admit that we have women with cut hair too." Aaron sat there thinking. He could not imagine women having cut hair in the Lancaster Mennonite Conference.

A Resolutions Committee was responsible to formulate a resolution to finalize the discussion. Paul Erb, as Committee Chairman, prefaced the resolution by saying, "Brother A. J. Metzler says this resolution represents the typical editor straddling the fence. Furthermore, he says that if I don't quit straddling the fence, I'll get so bowlegged I can't walk."

The resolution recommended the joint effort but "to proceed cautiously in a joint venture with the General Conference. If at any time we sense that our principles are in jeopardy, we will at once withdraw our joint effort."

In spite of the strong opposition on the floor during discussion, only Aaron and Ernest G. Gehman voted against it. Clarence Lutz, one of the three Lancaster Conference representatives (understood as conservative), took the liberal viewpoint during discussion which, of course, influenced the vote.

Home at Meckville

With Aaron gone so much of the time, it was deemed advisable to ordain additional ministerial help at Meckville. Accordingly, Meckville experienced an impressive double ordination service in June 1958, when Stephen Stoltzfus was ordained as minister and Walter Newswanger was ordained as deacon.

Stephen had moved into the area from Florida less than two years prior. He was now to assist Cletus Doutrich in preaching. Walter Newswanger was to assist Steve Olesh as deacon.

This arrangement lasted only two years. In July 1960, Stephen Stoltzfus—alarmed by the drift in Lancaster Conference—abruptly departed to join the

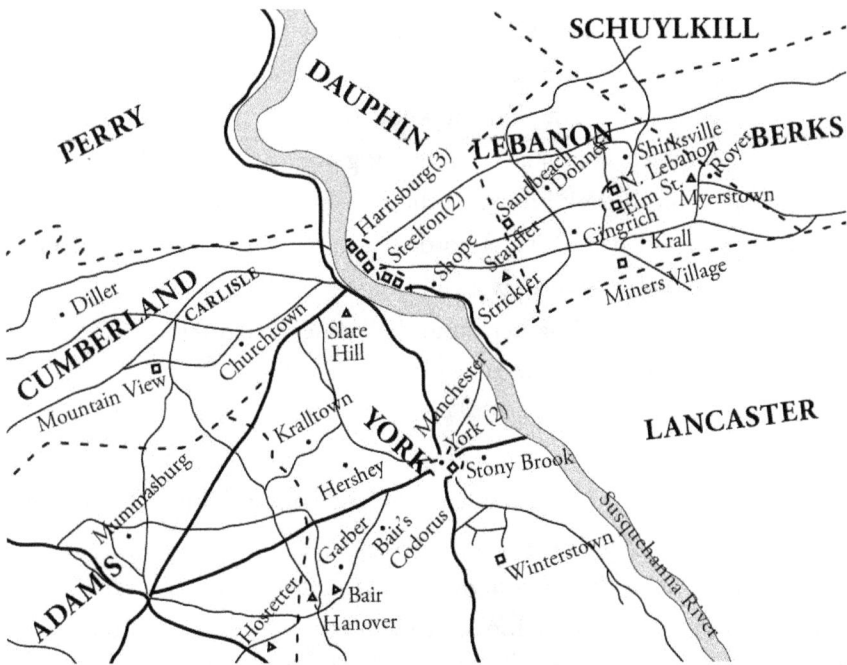

Lancaster Conference congregations in Lebanon and adjacent counties.

group of ministers forming what is now known as the Nationwide Fellowship Churches. Aaron reduced his schedule to be closer to the Meckville congregation. That year Aaron held only one series of revivals, that being at Dillers, in Cumberland County, Pennsylvania.

The Eastern Mennonite Board of Missions and Charities had requested that the strong Meckville congregation assume responsibility for the Wayside mission station near Tower City, twenty miles over the mountain to the northwest. In 1959, Meckville consented. Two years later, better meeting place accommodations were purchased at public auction on Grand Avenue in Tower City.

Alvin Snyders' and Elvin Stauffers' were asked to move to Tower City to assist with the work there. Meckville families traveled the distance regularly to support the effort. Walter Newswanger, deacon at Meckville, was licensed by Conference to temporarily take care of the pastoral needs of the congregation.

Community Salt

Milford could count on his father speaking to people who did wrong while on his property. When workers would come and work without shirts, he would remind them to be covered. When someone used profanity in his presence, Aaron would say, "Do you know whose Name you just used?" It was common to hear Aaron ask, "How is it going with you and the Lord?"

One day Milford took his car to the garage for work. Mr. S_____ said, "Your dad was just here. I had a bottle of whisky sitting here on the desk and I felt so small. He didn't say a word."

When Milford told his father about the incident, Aaron said, "That's the best compliment I ever got from an ungodly man."

Criticism

As a church leader, Aaron was a special target of criticism. The children observed this more than once.

On one occasion during a disagreement in a theological discussion at Lancaster Mennonite School, one of the students quoted Aaron Shank's position. One of Aaron's children was part of the class and heard his teacher say, "That Aaron Shank is one of the most egotistical men I have ever met."

Aaron never vented his anger about someone in the presence of his children. The children could tell when something was bothering him by the stoic demeanor that would come over his face. Aaron refused to cast the burden of church problems on his children. The most they would hear was, "Oh, church, church, church!"

One man observed that Milford failed to return to the auditorium for twenty minutes one Sunday during an All-Day Meeting. Milford, feeling sick in his stomach, told his accuser that he was not feeling well. Not satisfied, the man confronted Aaron about the matter. Aaron asked the man, "Would you feel better if I brought him down to your house and gave him a whipping?" When Aaron and Marjorie discussed the incident with Milford, Marjorie concluded with, "Maybe you should have thrown up on his shoes!"

In spite of it all, Milford always admired his father. He was pleased that his father was a church leader. Like everyone else, he would sit in a meeting engrossed and impressed with what his father was saying. He believed his father ranked among the top ten Mennonite men with his Bible knowledge.

The Shanks had a verse for everything at home. There were verses for comfort, for encouragement, for correction, and for direction. There was no

The Shank family. Standing: Milford, Aaron, Richard. Seated: Louise, Marjorie, Ruth.

mincing of words; the Bible meant what it said. Milford never questioned whether his mother was right in what she said. "The Bible was it at our house. It had the last word on everything."

Education

Marjorie loved learning, but her son Milford did not find learning easy. She would take him aside and try to explain the coming week's geometry lessons (he found mathematics difficult). She wanted to make sure Milford understood it. She was so interested in what he was learning that she would do some of his science project work herself.

Both parents saw to it that Sunday School lessons got prepared. Marjorie concentrated on the learning part and Aaron on what the Scriptures said.

The children almost never saw their parents disagree with each other. If there was a difference on a particular issue, Milford heard, "Dad feels this is the way it should be." He did not hear his mother's side of the issue.

One difference of opinion in the Shank household was over the issue of education. The Myerstown Christian Day School began in 1951. Once it was established, birth and growing pains threatened the quality of, and dampened the interest in, the church school.

Marjorie knew this and was deeply concerned. Other church families were pulling their children out of the Christian school and placing them back into public school. Marjorie and the school children wanted to follow suit. Aaron put his foot down. He had thrown his energies into the church school revival and believed it to be a worthy project that should be supported. He felt that for them to discontinue supporting the school might send a signal to the church that could seriously endanger the church school program.

So, when school began that fall, Marjorie and the children watched the school bus pass by their house without stopping to pick up the Shank children.

Within a few years, the quality of the school had improved, and interest was renewed and increased.

Shank Sons

Aaron and Marjorie tried to monitor the influences that came into their children's lives. They encouraged friendships with certain people and discouraged friendship with others, but they never created a sharp line demanding that they not associate with certain church families.

Milford basically followed the people his parents desired him to follow, but soon a serious problem developed. As Milford grew older, as many children of ordained men find it, he faced a struggle between what he knew he should do and what his human nature wanted to do. He totally believed in his head everything his father and mother taught. It all made sense. But his heart could not keep pace. He could feel the spiritual side of him pull one way and the carnal part of him pull the other way. He knew his parents desired him to be an example for oth-

Milford (seated on floor at left) participating in a Men's Prayer Circle at Lancaster Mennonite School, led by Paul Reed (upper right, seated).

ers, but he felt guilty that he was not a better example. He knew his sensual weaknesses and felt ashamed of himself.

This dichotomy produced a great conflict in his life that had a profound negative effect. He was not able to convert all that he appreciated in his father to his own life. Furthermore, Lancaster Mennonite School had teachers such as Paul Reed and John Eby who could make the Christian ideal vivid, but Milford felt he could never measure up. He knew what was right but was unable to translate that knowledge into glad obedience. This left him feeling defeated.

At this time, the Lancaster Conference was pulling loose from its own Biblical moorings. Many people began drifting from the secure positions of a separated church into the quagmire of worldliness. This acculturation was taking place among Milford's peers. Aaron saw the changes as fulfilment of the great apostasy prophesied for the last days, but many of Milford's "spiritual" leaders and his peer group saw the relaxing of traditional practices as gospel freedom. By the time he graduated from LMS in 1959, the liberal/conservative issue was swirling rapidly. Being the son of a conservative bishop in a liberalizing setting placed him in the vortex of the conflict.

Throughout all his struggles, Milford felt no lack of love and interest in him from his parents. In fact, he felt the opposite. His mother demonstrated an incredible interest in his social life and his girlfriend. His girlfriend felt close to Marjorie in the same way she did to her own mother. Milford enjoyed sharing his letters from his girlfriend with his mother. He even wanted her to read the personal parts. Milford was heartened that his mother took such an interest in his girlfriend.

Fifteen years into marriage, Milford's wife Mim wrote to Marjorie, "I'm sorry for any pain our difference in standards has caused you. But I'll always be glad I could come to you for spiritual advice and you would try your best to help me. I thank you for your Christian example....I enjoy talking with you and being with you....I'm grateful for having you as a friend....I thank you for all the counsel, love, and for bearing and forbearing with me..."

Milford liked his mother and enjoyed being identified with her. She understood him, she loved him, and she cared about him. At home she was precise about a lot of things and very punctual. She got excited if the family was late when going for any kind of appointment. Her motto was, "Take care of matters *now*, don't procrastinate."

Marjorie did struggle with taking criticism personally. Milford remembers her being offended

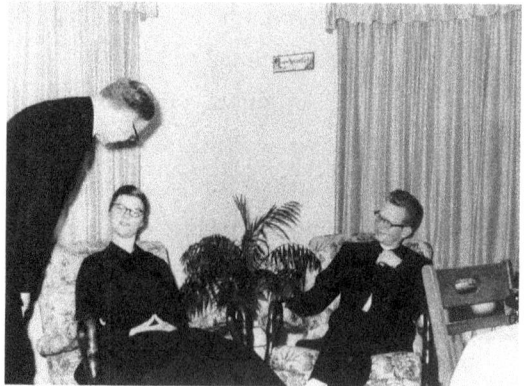

Aaron with Ruth and Milford.

from time to time. Her usual response was tears whereas her husband's response was stoic reserve.

Richard, the Shanks' adopted son, became a grief to his parents early in life. He was accepted as part of the family just like the rest, but he tended to be a loner. He never bonded with the Shank family. He preferred to be alone to play all by himself. He found school work difficult and did not appreciate Marjorie's efforts to help him. He was openly critical of his father, which caused Marjorie much anguish. Richard's behavior disturbed Milford profoundly. In retrospect, Aaron wished he had done more to deal with the loner tendencies in Richard at an early age. He attributed the family's heartache to his own failures to bond with his son.

Richard refused to attend Lancaster Mennonite School. Once when dealing with Richard, Aaron threatened to take his allowance as a disciplinary measure. However, instead he doubled the allowance in hopes of motivating interest at home. Richard remained unmoved.

A Mennonite brother who had a grievance against Aaron knew Richard was dissatisfied at home and hired Richard to work for him. He did this in spite of the fact that Richard was only sixteen and needed a work permit to quit school. Aaron knew nothing about the work agreement.

When Aaron called the man to discuss the issue with him, he was told, "The employer pays the employee. I intend to deal directly with the boy and not with his father." Nothing else could be discussed.

Soon after Richard started working away from home, he got money for a car. He went to the Justice of the Peace, and asked the Justice to help him purchase one. That happened. Aaron called the Justice to talk with him about what he had done. The Justice replied, "Maybe I goofed. But you know the courts are defending juveniles today." The whole episode took place without Aaron's signature anywhere.

As the years passed, Richard increasingly isolated himself from the Shank family. He declined to visit with any of the Shanks. Eventually, he severed himself from his parental home, even refusing to attend Marjorie's funeral in 1995. This was a difficult burden for Aaron to bear. At times, he would excuse himself from preaching messages related to the home because of the grief it gave him. He wished he would have worked harder at building a bridge of love with Richard when he was younger and would have talked more with him about his personal development as he moved into his teenage years. He did not excuse Richard for his choices, but he felt he should have somehow been a better parent.

Shank Daughters

Ruth was different. She was a delightfully social girl who fit into the Shank family life well. She was intelligent and performed well in school. She was full of promise as a young Christian. After she finished her schooling

at Myerstown and graduated from LMS, she taught at Myerstown successfully for three years along with her mother, Marjorie.

However, Ruth was having some inner struggles she was keeping to herself. Suddenly one day she said, "I'm moving out of the house, and I am leaving the church." She decided to enter nurse's training to become a registered nurse. During

Numidia Mennonite Bible School, begun by the Mennonite Messianic Mission.

her training, she met Elam Burkholder, a young man with a traditional Mennonite background who had also left the tradition of his upbringing. Elam was not educated in a scholastic sense, but was brilliant with mechanics and other business interests.

While they were dating, Ruth and Elam decided to unite with the Blainsport congregation of the Lancaster Conference. When Ruth told Aaron their plans, Aaron counseled her to come back where she went out. Ruth was not ready to do this.

Ruth and Elam were married at Blainsport on August 8, 1970, in a candle-lighting ceremony. The Blainsport experience was short-lived. From Blainsport, Elam and Ruth strayed into the charismatic movement. Ruth's choice to disregard the closely-held values of her parents

Aaron teaching at Numidia Bible School in its early days.

added to Aaron's burden. He often spoke longingly of Ruth and continued

to hope the seeds of faith sown in her life in her youth would perhaps yet bring spiritual fruit.

Aaron said of Richard and Ruth, "This has been a real blot on my life. There must have been something we could have done better to prevent all this."

Louise had an advantage over her siblings. In 1967, Aaron insisted that Louise attend the new Numidia Mennonite Bible School in December. Louise had graduated from LMS in 1967 and had her own set of struggles related to liberal influences there. While Ernest Bontrager was conducting revival meetings at Meckville, he asked Louise to be secretary at the Numidia Bible School. At Numidia, Louise rededicated her life to God.

Ira Mast attended Numidia at the same time Louise did and developed an interest in her. After an extended courtship, the two were married at Rehrersburg on September 26, 1970. In 1973, Ira was chosen from a class of four brethren and ordained deacon for the Rehrersburg congregation where Aaron served as bishop. Ira and Louise live on the Shank home place and operate the Shank Door business. They have six children.

Aaron studying, 1967.

Well-meaning counselors assured Aaron (and other leaders of that generation) that if he gave his time and energies to church work, God would take care of his family. Like other families of leaders of that period, Aaron's family was caught in the swirling battle of faithfulness to Christ versus gradual accommodation to the flesh and to the world. Liberal leaders held a strong appeal to the youth of that day. Aaron continued to bear the grief of his losses until his death.

Brakes Applied

As soon as he was ordained bishop in 1957, Aaron felt that he needed to put reins on the church to stop the worldward drift. His revival meetings took him far and wide and he could observe the churchwide general drift toward worldliness and carnality. Aaron characterized himself as the caboose on the runaway train, trying to slow the rest of the train hurtling down the track at a dangerous pace.

New on the Bishop Board, he was not the only conservative voice. In his younger days Aaron had seen the heavy balance of leadership in the Lancaster Conference as conservative. The splinters away from Conference had been liberal splinters. Conservative influences carried the day. Christian Charles, working in the plain clothing department at Hagar's department store in Lancaster city, kept finding new people coming in all the time to "go plain." These people heard teaching from Bible Conference programs that influenced the way they thought. This state of affairs existed when Aaron was ordained minister in 1941 and continued up until the early 1950's.

Nonconformity Conferences and Nonconformity Institutes were regular features in Lancaster Conference. These were directed by a Nonconformity Committee, whose responsibility was to keep the principle of nonconformity alive among the Conference membership.

At these conferences, one-half the service would be given to reviewing the Discipline and the other half would be a study of the history of the doctrine of nonconformity. One such evening meeting would be held in each district every year. Aaron was in demand as a speaker at these meetings, usually on the history side. These Nonconformity Conferences became a forerunner of the Mennonite Messianic Mission, which came into existence in 1966.

One individual recalled one of these nonconformity meetings being held in his home area west of Harrisburg, Pennsylvania, in 1964. His testimony was that Aaron gave the subject his passionate best, and stayed to shake the hands of those who came for the service. But already it was apparent there was little interest in subjects such as nonconformity. A meeting house that should have been overflowing with the size of the district it was to represent had only a sparse attendance.

A picture is worth a thousand words. This picture, printed on the cover of a Mennonite publication printed at Scottdale, Pennsylvania, in 1967, illustrates the world-assimilating mentality against which Aaron battled. He felt like a braking caboose trying to slow down a run-away train.

But Aaron's motivations were not always understood. Some well-meaning conservative brethren came to him at one point in his preaching career and wanted him to serve on a circuit, preaching against the use of musical instruments in the home. They felt that since he was outspoken and forceful for the conservative cause, he could be counted on with this concern.

"But the Scriptures do not present the right use of musical instruments in a negative light," was Aaron's reply. "The harmonious blending of tones is of heavenly origin. Dis-chords have their origins in hell. I'm afraid I won't be able to help you with your concerns."

The Lancaster Conference was the conservative conference of the Mennonite Church. Lancaster Conference preachers Martin Lehman and Richard Kling returned from a trip through the West visiting various Mennonite churches in the late 1950's. Martin said in a public meeting in the Lebanon District, "If there is anything this little preacher would like to say to the Lancaster Bishop Board, it is that they ought to assume a conservative leadership that will influence the church across the nation. The church across the nation is ready for it. There is a drifting trend and yet there is a large number of people that would love a conservative influence. If the Lancaster Conference does not offer this leadership, they will likely get help nowhere else. I would like the Lancaster bishops to sense a responsibility to get out and encourage the conservative viewpoint across the nation."

Conference sat still.

In the Lancaster Conference, the conservative shift ceased. Nothing changed for a while. Then the liberal drift started. Soon a movement of thirteen ordained men, including Mervin Baer, Roy Geigley, Harold Brenneman, and Stephen Stoltzfus splintered away from Conference to help form what would become the Mennonite Christian Brotherhood (later known as the Nationwide Fellowship movement). The group visited Aaron, desiring his bishop leadership.

Aaron sympathized with their concerns, but in his opinion, the church as a whole was not ready for a full-blown conservative movement. At the very same time, his own family needed the influence. Reflecting back, he realized that his family would probably have benefitted from involvement in that movement.

Lancaster Mennonite School

This selection of photos from the 1968 LMS yearbook give a glimpse of the variety of attire and hairstyles worn by the students.

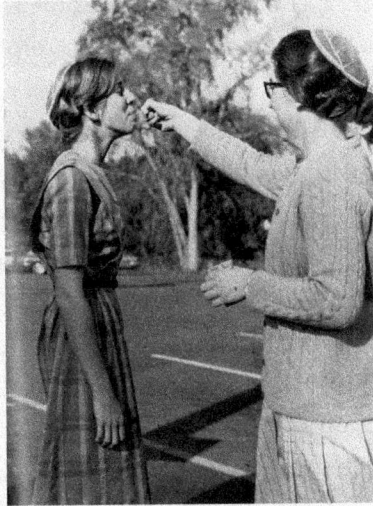

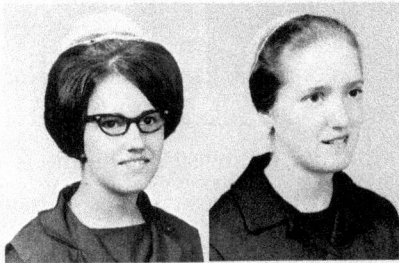

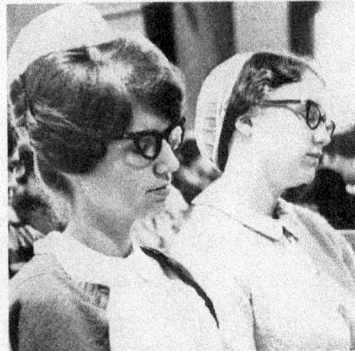

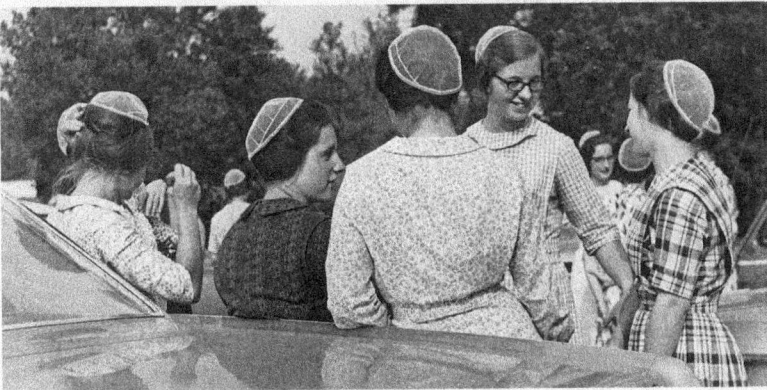

Aaron said, "I saw the balance swing to the other side and I determined to do all I could to stop the drift and help the church go the other way. At issue was who spoke on church programs." Lancaster Conference men who traveled to distant places to speak thereby picked up liberal influences. The speakers from distant places brought the same influences with them when they came to speak in the East. Even though the imported speakers spoke "correctly" to Lancaster Conference audiences, the listeners discovered the real situations behind the speakers in their home areas.

The drift was said to have been "blue-printed" by Mennonite church leaders in the West. The western Mennonite colleges were heavy liberal influences. Furthermore, there was a push for a merging of Mennonite groups. The "blue-print" called for pushing this liberal agenda through the Mennonite Publishing House at Scottdale. In this way, the conservative Mennonites in the East would be bombarded by liberal influences weekly in the form of the "church papers." The *Gospel Herald* in particular, as the official church organ, lent an official voice to the efforts to bring liberalism into both the church and the home.

While many felt that the Conference was under attack from outside influences, some serious issues lodged within the Conference itself. Conference was becoming careless with its own ordinations. Biblical qualifications for church leadership were being set aside in favor of choosing leadership with administrative ability. Leadership was viewed as having the skills necessary to run a local church in an efficient manner.

Then there was the foreign missions problem. For ten years Aaron served on the Bishop Board's foreign missions council. In an effort to cooperate with other Protestant missionaries, the Mennonite missionaries were laying aside their plain clothing. Lancaster Conference Mennonites were shocked when a deputation representing the Mission Board and the Foreign Missions Council returned from Africa and informed the church that they were met by missionaries on the field in fashionable attire. Later, Conference asked Aaron as secretary of the Foreign Missions Council to write a tract on "Marriage and the Wedding Ring." This tract (1964) was adopted as the official voice of the Lancaster Conference for foreign missionaries.[1]

---

1 This tract is no longer in print.

When the missionaries received this work, their response was, "We find that we are more effective in our evangelistic efforts using rings than without. We plan to continue using them." Some of them did, in defiance of Conference direction.

To combat these influences, Aaron often preached on nonconformity in the revival meetings he conducted. One day at Eastern Mennonite College, his brother Ralph heard someone in the hallway say, "That Aaron Shank is not fit to be an evangelist anywhere. He had revival meetings at _____ Church and preached on dress one night. At revival meetings!"

For years Aaron had been a strong promoter of the doctrines and practices held by Conference. His children knew him this way. As the Conference drifted from its former position, Aaron began to take issue with the Conference and criticize it for doing so. This shift confused them. Their father who had been "for" Conference was now "against" it.

Lancaster Mennonite High School Board of Trustees and Religious Welfare Committee, 1960. Left to right, back row: Roy Brubaker, Jacob Nauman, Victor Groff, Clarence Rutt; middle row: Amos Myer, Ray Yost, Paul Weaver, Elmer Leaman, Elam Stoner, William Horst; front row: Clair Eby, Landis Brubaker, Aaron Shank, James H. Hess, John R. Kraybill, David Thomas.

Lancaster Mennonite School was becoming a spiritual hindrance to the church by becoming an effective liberalizing influence in the Lancaster Conference. Aaron served on the Lancaster Mennonite School Board from 1949 through 1963, serving as vice-chairman from 1956 to 1963. During Aaron's entire tenure as vice-chairman, James H. Hess served as chairman. On July 7, 1962, Aaron wrote to Amos W. Weaver, principal of the school.

Dear Bro. Amos,

Greetings.

Thank you for the proposed statement of standards for the coming term at L.M.S. which you mailed to us some time ago. My response is a bit late in coming, but I do want to express my sincere appreciation for this fine outline of standards you have set up. I hope that no one felt that the standards should be watered down to fit into the trends of this "untoward generation." I also appreciate the strong logical appeal you make for adherence to the regulations you outline. Too often we lay down the law without giving any basic reason for those things required. This can lead us away from the underlying principles embodied in the regulations, which also leads into dead formalism and away from the truth....

One observes at the close of the school week when students are ready to leave the campus far too much of this "school-out of school" double standard. Students change their coverings, hosiery, and dresses to leave for the weekend. And girls who do not have these "changeable suits of apparel" are sometimes ridiculed. Again, it would be a help to both parents and students who do not have the double standards if students would all be required to arrive at school and leave the campus under school regulations.

The use of the "bobby sox" for girls bothers me some too. Our church discipline forbids the wearing of anklets. When our daughters were very small, we took the anklets off of them out of conviction. Locally, anklets are not allowed in our Christian Day Schools. And now our grown up daughters under the pressure of student influence at L.M.S. have taken to wearing these "grown up anklets." If these "over grown" anklets are a necessity to keep the feet warm, would it not be well to have the same requirement for them as hosiery, "black, or a dark shade?"

The pressure of the student environment has become terrific the past few years so that it almost seems that we are now at the stage or nearing the place in our educational advancement that many of our youth are being seriously hindered in some of the applications we believe to be necessary to maintain the principle of separation. In this past school term the father of a senior told me what has happened to his son. When I tried to give some encouragement and help to this young man, among other things he told me that student pressure in favor of disrespect for church and school standards has become so strong that it is well nigh impossible to go through school untainted and that he can hardly wait until he gets away from it all.

This young man's experience is being duplicated by numbers of other young people. This is certainly not an indictment against the school but simply recognizing a condition that now exists in our school program. In my visit to L.M.S. this past year I sensed an alarming increase in rudeness and disrespect on the part of the student body. In spite of all the benefits that have come to our youth through the church school one is faced with the question as to whether the hazards encountered through this student environment – and some faculty influence – are not becoming greater than the benefits received.

LMS principal Amos Weaver.

One more word about the standards. They are worth paying the price it costs to keep them in practice. One cannot visit the school without seeing coverings that are smaller than the required pattern, hair buns below the covering, fancy trim on some of the dresses, dresses immodestly sheer, especially at commencement time, and dress lengths that little more than cover the knee. I will always want to give my vote of appreciation for any action or measures that are taken to keep high the standards of right at L.M.S.

In closing I would like to pay a tribute of respect to you for your untiring consecrated efforts to guide the ship of school aright these many years you have served in the tremendously responsible office of Principal. We pray God to bless and reward you and grant you enabling grace as you continue to help our youth into fuller dedication and greater loyalty to Christ and the church.

Yours Sincerely,

Aaron Shank

Principal Amos Weaver responded with the following letter.

Dear Brother Shank,

Greetings:

Thank you for your very kind letter and concerns expressed. It is gratifying to know one's efforts and labors have been appreciated. This knowledge at least dulls somewhat the keen sense of disappointment in realizing one has accomplished so little. I feel like Job 3:21, "That which we hoped to avoid is upon us."

In your letter you speak of "the tremendously important, responsible office of Principal." I have always felt that way about it too, and that it was too big for me. I would have liked to have kept the standards up there where you place them. It seems this tide of "drift" has a way of enveloping and overflowing that defies all measures against it. As individuals we can refuse to go along with it but apparently cannot stop it. I not only feel unable to stop it in our school; I am pretty well convinced no one else can.

Lancaster Mennonite School officials; left to right: Clyde B. Stoner, Noah G. Good, and Amos W. Weaver.

You may, or may not, know I informed the Religious Welfare Committee several months before the close of school that I wish to resign by the end of another term. But as I think of a possible successor, whoever he may be, I am, quite frankly, fearful of the future of the school. There are so many factors and tremendous pressures from so many angles contributing to the changing scene among us the result seems inevitable. And strong, stringent measures would wreck the whole, defeating the main purpose of our school.

If someone could be found to step into my place immediately who would be able to stem the tide, effectively and constructively, I would be most happy to step aside and let him in. I know I sound like an awful egotist but I doubt if he can be found. If it is the will of the Lord and the church I shall continue for another year. I will try to do what I can with the Lord's guidance and help.

I received a few responses from Board Members, one in favor of more lenience in some areas, one or two gave a few concerns, and yours for more strictness. The rest were in general agreement without any particular suggestions or requests. The majority made no response to my letter. It's my notion no one wants my job. It's at least a consoling thought that no one is envious of you or is eager for your position.

Sincerely and Gratefully Yours,

Amos W. Weaver

One year later, on July 2, 1963, Aaron wrote to the new principal, Clayton Keener. In response to Lancaster Mennonite School rapidly accommodating liberal influences, the Lebanon District refused to provide a Board Member for the School after 1963.

Dear Bro. Keener:

Warmest morning greetings!

We missed you at the L.M.S. Board Meeting yesterday. I wanted to have a few words with you there, but since I missed that I will take a few minutes out of a very busy morning to say what is on my heart. One of the bishops on the R.W.C. [Religious Welfare Committee] urged me to contact you.

Last year I had written to Bro. Weaver in response to his invitation to do so after the proposed school standards for the coming school year were mailed out to the Board members. A copy of this letter is being enclosed for you to read....This letter may help you to understand a problem that a goodly number of us have with the change in a few of the dress standards the past few years.

There is a second problem that I have with this sanction of the skirt and blouse dress for girls, for certain activities, and that is this. Is it proper procedure for one person or a study committee to assume the authority to permit a lower standard of dress than the Conference statement of discipline allows, in a Conference controlled institution, without it at least coming before the highest governing body of the Conference?

After Bro. Clair Eby gave his report of the study committee on school standards yesterday, one of the Board members made this rather profound observation to me personally. In substance, this is what he said. "When a Church School is organized, it leads out in defending Church standards; later, it goes along with the standards, and ultimately leads away from the standards." I am not suggesting that L.M.S. is there now, but it does seem to me that if we have gotten to the place that a school committee can set up standards, we have at least taken the first step toward a school-controlled Conference, rather than a Conference-controlled School.

The Lord willing, I will have two daughters attending L.M.S. next term. As members of the Church, these two girls have never had any other dresses than the Church prescribed dress. If I may judge by past experience that some of our girls have had at L.M.S., sometime during the coming year, there will be strong student pressure brought upon them to ignore and disrespect parent and Church standards.

They will be encouraged to "borrow" other girls' outfits, and our problems at home will be increased. Frankly, I wish my daughters would not need to receive a letter from the School, suggesting that a skirt and blouse may be used at certain times at school.

Would it be too late after July Bishop Board Meeting to send out these School Standards? In view of the nature of the changes referred to above, I would like to appeal that the proposed standards be presented to our Board for approval before mailing to prospective students. Please!

Thank you in advance for your consideration to this appeal. The Lord bless you abundantly and grant you enabling grace for the tremendously important place the Church has asked you to fill. Sufficiency is of God.

Respectfully,

Aaron Shank

Clayton Keener never responded.

This correspondence offers a window into the changing climate of Lancaster Conference. It also offers a window into the Shank home, offering a glimpse of the pressures coming upon the younger family members.

Like the American society around it, the early 1960s found the Mennonite Church in a culture that exalted the individual and gave free license to challenge existing authorities.

The events of the next few years would dramatically alter the course of the Mennonite Church. Aaron was forty-eight years old.

Overleaf: LMS students pictured in the 1965 yearbook.

Betty J. Risser
Route 3, Elizabethtown, Pa.
Amos and Elizabeth Risser
General
    Shows her dimples often . . . enthusiastic
Christian . . . deserves the badge of self
lessness . . . Spanish senorita.

Marilyn J. Rohrer
Lancaster, Pa.
Harry and Evelyn Rohrer
Commercial
    Centers her interest in commercial sub-
jects . . . close friend of Nancy . . . little
live wire . . . looks forward to Saturday
nights.

Susan Rohrer
Route 2, Lancaster, Pa.
Elmer and Ruth Rohrer
General
    Tries everything at least once . . . ato
energy . . . well-liked . . . future phys
ed. teacher.

Gerald A. Ruhl
Route 1, Mount Joy, Pa.
Arthur and Esther Ruhl
Agriculture
    Good baseball player . . . no time for
study . . . worth knowing . . . spare mo-
ments find him in his shop.

Dennis Ruth
Route 3, Newville, Pa.
Marvin and Lizzie Ruth
Agriculture
    Livens dorm with popcorn and noise . . .
known by the color of his hair . . . bottom
of every riot . . . enjoys all sports.

Lauretta Mae Rutt
Lancaster, Pa.
Frank and Mary Alta Rutt
Academic
    Interested in anything that's going on
. . . not lacking in sociability . . . at ease
in front of an audience . . . optimistic.

mar L. Sauder
Holland, Pa.
and Clara Sauder
eral
terested in radios and electronics . . .
s up to few people . . . dependable . . .
life to any party.

Esther Mae Sauder
Route 2, Ephrata, Pa.
Daniel and Edna Sauder
General
Beautiful soprano voice . . . friend who
understands . . . reserved young lady . . .
faithfully attends prayer circle.

Glenn E. Sauder
Route 1, Lititz, Pa.
Raymond and Margrete Sauder
General
Ask Glenn all about horses . . . ready
for fun . . . able football quarterback . . .
interesting talker.

Janice D. Sauder
New Holland, Pa.
Raymond and Thelma Sauder
General
"Kid!" . . . an asset to the alto section of
chorus . . . double cousin to Delmar . . .
mixes with the crowd.

Warren R. Sauder
Route 1, East Earl, Pa.
Alvin and Mary Sauder
General
Fifty percent of a set of twins . . .
farmhand . . . that quiet look—it's deceiv-
ing . . . interesting personality.

Robert L. Sauder
Route 2, Cochranville, Pa.
Robert and Ruth Sauder
General
Makes people feel at ease . . . joined
the dorm family this year . . . entertaining
table mate . . . unruffled.

CHAPTER 7

Forceful Fifties

FOR MANY YEARS one of Aaron's favorite sayings was, "A weather vane is a small thing, but it shows which way the wind is blowing."

Bishop George R. Brunk read the weather vane in his day. He could discern what was coming even in the 1930s. He could see the advancing Mennonite drift into worldliness and worked as hard as he could to halt it. In desperation George had cried, "Can't we spare at least one congregation even if it results in cleavage in order to keep the faith?"

Many, many years prior, John Wesley had observed, "No church group has been permanently successful." One denomination after another sank under the pressures of the surrounding culture, including John Wesley's Methodists. Because of their adherence to the Biblically distinctive principles of nonresistance and separation from the world, at least some of the Brethren, Mennonites, and Amish have survived centuries of negative social pressures. But even the survivors could not totally escape the assimilating pressures of the worldly American environment.

Aaron had a perspective on history which moved him in 1966 to write his very first article for publication. In response to a request from Paul Reed, Aaron wrote three articles, "Pitfalls Encountered in Missions," "What It Takes to Be Fit for Mission Service," and "How Can We Renew Genuine Mission Zeal?" The first of these was published in abbreviated form in *Youth Messenger*, a publication of Lancaster Conference, of which Paul Reed was editor.[1] A few excerpts from Aaron's manuscript follow.

1 Aaron M. Shank, "Pitfalls in Missions," *Youth Messenger* 3(46) (November 13, 1966):6.

Jesus foretold that the gospel would be preached in all the world before the end comes. Along with worldwide missions, contrary to what one would expect, Jesus also predicted that Christian love would grow cold, and that the larger body of the professed Church would finally be a growing ecclesiastical body of wretchedness ready to be spued [sic] out of His own mouth.[2]

The threat of the pit into which the Church may fall is not a sudden tumble into a dark dungeon, but rather a gradual descent until the Church is unconsciously "wretched, and miserable, and poor, and blind, and naked."[3]

Therefore, we do very well to consider the pitfalls encountered in missions, lest in our worldwide witness we become a part of that great nauseating, lukewarm, and fallen church.

Today we encounter serious organizational pitfalls. We are rapidly moving toward diplomatic relationships with the larger society of worldly Mennonitism and fractional gospel Protestantism—and more recently we are proposing spiritual unity and cooperation with Catholicism.[4] With these tendencies continuing, ere long we will be caught in the unwholesome ecumenical trap that is set as a snare to engulf all Christendom. Jesus prayed for a unity of believers like the unity between Him and His Father, in which unity there is a perfect oneness of doctrine, purity, and purpose. This character of ecumenism we should all pray for and seek to achieve.

Another pitfall is to be zealous of our mission movement—the "go" of the Great Commission,—and neglect the primary cause for missions, which is to preach the gospel and teach the practice of all the gospel standards. A medical ministry, providing educational privileges, relief, and Voluntary Service may contribute to the primary purpose of missions, but when these elements become ends in themselves, the Church becomes, in effect, an "Order of Christian Humanitarian Service"[5] and fails in her primary purpose of "going." This is the social gospel pitfall.

There is always a subtle danger of charting our course by changing circumstances and cultural situations rather than by changeless truth conditioned by eternity and the will of God. Many years ago Bishop George R. Brunk wrote, "I think the gravest danger that confronts us in missions is that of being popularized by exchanging unpopular truth for popular error; the power of God for the influence of men; the last part of the commission for the first instead of holding both; a general compromise such as heathenized the Church of the early centuries instead of Christianizing the heathen..."[6] The same Lord who tells us where to go, also tells us what to teach.

---

2 Matt. 24:12-24; Rev. 3:16

3 Rev. 3:17

4 Denny Weaver, "Protestant-Catholic Dialogue," *Gospel Herald.* August 9, 1966

5 Floyd E. Mallott, *Studies in Brethren History.* p. 244. Brethren Publishing House, Elgin, Illinois.

6 "Editorial," *Missionary Light,* Sept. 1949

Sacrificing Bible principle for numbers become a pitfall for us.

Using results or the lack of results as a basis for Divine approval rather than being guided by the Word is sometimes a real snare. If Noah would have changed his message and methods to win the people, he would have perished with his world. When we do not love and obey the truth, God will send strong delusion upon us, and we will believe the lie of His presence with us long after He has departed from us.

May God spare us from the pitfalls encountered in our personal experience, local church life, and in missions....

Historically the Mennonite Church has drawn distinct denominational lines between herself and other religious bodies.

On the outside cover of Franklin Littell's book on *The Origins of Sectarian Protestantism*[7] referring to the Anabaptists, he says they "broke with all Christendom and attempted under heavy persecution to restore the radical communities of the primitive church."[8]

This line of distinction was drawn because of their full acceptance of the New Testament and their refusal to compromise on its principles. Although they refused to use the sword of blood, they believed in using the "sword" of division between acceptance and rejection of full gospel truth.[9]

...Outstanding on the pages of Church history is the Waldensian movement. Peter Waldo, a merchant of southern France, was converted in the 12th century. He immediately put "evangelical truth into practice and gave himself to the task of spreading it." He is said to have been "the most notable missionary of the primitive gospel in that period." His holy life and mission zeal was contagious. The Waldensians "taught the principle of nonresistance," they "did not permit going to law" or the "swearing of oaths;" they did not allow "worldly amusements and gambling" nor "tolerate immodest clothing." They would "expel such as decline to give ear to our admonitions and persistently refuse obedience." Adhering closely to these and other lofty standards of the gospel, the Waldensian Church moved rapidly over large parts of France and Italy. A contemporary antagonistic writer testified, "There is scarcely any land in which this sect does not exist."[10]

In the early part of the 16th century the Waldenses affiliated with the Reformed Protestant Churches and soon lost their distinctive gospel witness. In 1532 a confession of faith was adopted in which "all points of specifically Waldensian

---

7 Now published under the title *The Anabaptist View of the Church.*—CW.

8 Franklin H. Littell, *The Origins of Sectarian Protestantism*, Paperback ed. The Macmillan Company, New York

9 Matt. 10:34-39

10 John Horsch, *Mennonites in Europe*, pp. 4-14. Mennonite Publishing House, Scottdale, Pa. 1942

teaching are set aside."[11]

May we humbly heed the words of holy writ to "mark" those who teach contrary to the doctrine of the new birth, self denial, separation, washing the saints feet, Christian woman's unshorn hair and veiling, nonconformity, nonresistance, etc., and "avoid" them lest we fail in God's purpose for the Mennonite Church today and become partners with others in disobedience.

...Early Church days were being duplicated in the "Acts of the Anabaptists." "They were practically the only missionaries at that time."[12] Moreover, "Thousands sealed their faith with their blood."[13]

Aaron knew that religious inconsistencies have bred looseness through the centuries. The Church was facing nothing new. Down through the years, as young people have seen their parents and other older people in the church living inconsistent lifestyles, they have tended to discredit the entire church. The hypocrisy turned them off and they began to look elsewhere for meaning and wholeness. In the 1960s the Lancaster Conference was fraught with inconsistencies. Unfortunately, many people were ready to "throw out the baby with the bath water."

The western conferences were the first to succumb to American acculturating pressures. Lancaster Conference held on the longest and had the reputation of being the most conservative conference outside the traditionalist Old Order Mennonites. But powerful and profound changes were underway in the Lancaster Conference of the Mennonite Church by the early 1950's.

Sidney Gingrich reports:

About 1952 there was a continued liberal trend so that three more liberal congregations were started, one at Neffsville, one at Marietta, and one at Monterey. At this point the Conference held firm to where they were for a number of years.

But not many years later there was a constant drift toward more modernism and the Conference gave in to one thing after the other, such as ministry allowed to have radios, sisters cutting their hair, television allowed, divorce and remarriage tolerated, modesty being lost, etc.

While this trend was taking place, the more conservative ones became more

11 Ibid, p. 12

12 Ibid, p. 293

13 Ibid, p. 301

concerned and became more vocal about the direction of travel...[14]

In 1959, Bishop Benjamin Eshbach tried to exercise church discipline with regard to seventeen members in one of his congregations for owning television sets in violation of the Conference standard. Conference stepped in to prevent the threatened expulsion. Conference leadership was fearful of the congregation's reaction to such drastic action. The Conference as a

Ben and Anna Eshbach.

whole was softening, losing its Bible-centeredness, courage, and vision, and was failing to support its own agreed-upon standards.

Spiritual life and vitality, submission, meekness, self-denial, obedience, and practical Christianity (especially nonconformity to the world) were becoming a thing of the past. For example, by 1966 Lancaster Mennonite School girls wore sweaters to hide the despised cape which they were required to wear. Individualism, professionalism, wealth, entertainment, higher education, and material comfort were replacing the older ideals of humility, simplicity, and submission to authority. Many seemed to devalue the separated life and culture forged around New Testament values traditionally held by Mennonites over the centuries. They desired to lay it aside in order to adopt the dominant North American self-centered cultural values surrounding them.

In August 1967, the following appeared as an editorial in the *Sword and Trumpet*. Aaron carried this and another editorial from *Guidelines for Today* (August 1968) in his Bible to be read to listening audiences as evidence of what was happening, completely aside from his own observation.

> One of the characteristics of charity (Christian love) is that it covers the multitude of sins (1 Peter 4:8)....There are differences which reach beyond the problems of personal relationships and which have to do with fundamental

---

14 Sidney Gingerich, interview with author, 1996.

aspects of faith and administration....The presence of error and apostasy cannot be adequately met by simply attempting to cover such with a mantle of charity....When it is difference in belief that brought about division in the first place, the road back to unity must be re-paved by doctrinal understandings.... Recent years have witnessed an increasing fragmentation of thought, so much so that our actual unity now seems in jeopardy.

More recently too, a philosophy of "unity in diversity" has been advanced as the answer to the problem of differences. Its assumption is that there have always been differences, particularly in practice, and that there always will be differences; therefore, we must allow for them and learn to live with them. It assumes that there are some things ... considered essential, while there are other things regarding which there is broadest opinion. It is further assumed that the element of brotherhood is more important than belief, or that brotherhood can exist without regard to a proportional content of faith....

It would seem that a discerning observation of the modern religious world would cause Mennonites to gravitate toward the heart of the faith instead of to fragment...Yet what do we find? [This faith] is being scattered or abandoned on every side for a mess of ecumenical pottage....

As the life of this denomination becomes merged into that of the Protestant world, it loses its real reason to exist. But the faith itself is not lost. [Aaron's emphasis] Here and there it will germinate and flourish in groups of believers who cherish this faith, a company here and a congregation there. It will not be easy. But then, the true faith has always been lived and propagated under difficulties. It had its birth under trial and could well have its rebirth under the same conditions....

More and more it becomes necessary for the faithful concerned to function as a remnant. Let them be assured that insofar as each is personally faithful there is One who never leaves nor forsakes them.

The *Guidelines for Today* editorial stated:

We have just passed, in our denomination, the "Founder's Stage," in which the chief motivation was the preservation of the faith through the training of youth, and are now entering the period where adaptation seems to be the chief motivation. We are out today, it seems, to try to match state programs of education and to help students to become acclimated to the secularized age—to free them from the shackles of traditionalism and old "tribal attachments"...

The wrong trends and emphases have been very divisive as is evidenced in the numerous withdrawals from conferences of churches and groups of churches, and in the falling off of subscriptions of church publications. If modifications could have been made along the way there is no question that we would be far

SPECIAL BIBLE CONFERENCE
Meckville Mennonite Church
AUGUST 8, 9, 1959

Theme: Understanding the Mysteries of God

SAT. 7:30 P.M.—Understanding the Mystery of the Incarnation—
God manifest in the flesh—I Tim. 3:16.

SUN. 9:00 A.M.—S. S. Lesson — Simon G. Bucher

10:00 A.M.—Understanding the Mystery of the Kingdom—
Parables of our Lord—Matt. 13:11.

SUN. 1:45 P.M.—Understanding the Mystery of Iniquity—
The "MARCH" of the Beast—II Thess. 2:7.

SUN. 7:15 P.M.—Understanding the Mystery of Immortality—
The Rapture of the Church—I Cor. 15:51.

Speaker ....J. Irvin Lehman, Chambersburg, Pa.
Moderator ....Simon G. Bucher, Lebanon, Pa.
Song Leader ....Carl Good, Lititz, Pa.

Program for a Special Bible Conference held at Meckville in 1959.

more united today than we presently are. It is not the independent groups that have arisen which are divisive—these are but the fruits of an officially-sponsored program quite oblivious to inherent dangers and divisive elements in the church's ongoing faith and life.

In spite of these astute observations, change continued at a rapid pace. Change was in the air everywhere in Lancaster Conference. The changes seemed irresistible. Some leaders weakly resisted and then joined the changes. Many leaders decided that the best they could do was maintain personal convictions in the midst of the sweeping changes. Some leaders welcomed the changes as a breath of fresh air. For all these leaders, the motto seemed like leadership in reverse: "There go my people; I must follow them." Irvin Kreider, minister at the East Petersburg Mennonite Church, actually said, "Who was I to resist the Holy Ghost?"[15]

A few Conference leaders determined to do otherwise. For them, the Scriptures had not changed, nor had the basic ways of dealing with encroaching worldliness. The surrounding American culture continued to embrace and practice unbiblical values. To these men, a sharp line must always exist between the church and the world. Under pressure from co-laborers to make

15 Statement to author in 1976.

the line fuzzy, their consciences could not cooperate. These men determined to stand by the Lancaster Conference *Discipline* as it was written and which they had promised to uphold faithfully. Aaron Shank was one of them.

The Gingrichs congregation in the Lebanon District had become a case in point. At Gingrichs, plain clothing was departing and capeless dresses were coming in, along with fancy clothing and objectionable hair arrangements. The weather vane was pointing into the wind of worldliness.

Aaron started to work on the problem. He asked the congregation's pastor, Daniel Wert, for several midweek evenings with the congregation to review the basis for Conference standards. Daniel refused, saying, "It wouldn't be profitable. The direction we're going is an indication of maturity; we're able to think for ourselves." The situation became tense.

In preparation for the fall Communion in 1965 Aaron told the Gingrich congregation, "If you cannot agree with the *Discipline*, you should not say that you are in support of the church." Consequently, about half of the group responded with a negative.

Aaron announced that those who desired to be loyal to the Conference could participate in a special Communion service on Sunday afternoon. He did not desire a scene with half of the members not communing.

After the announcement, three or four brethren came to visit Aaron at his home in order to appeal for the regular communion service. They insisted that the people wanted to cooperate. "We don't want a disruption like this," they said.

Aaron replied, "Alright. We will give it another try."

On the Sunday morning designated for Communion, Pastor Daniel Wert rose to conduct the devotional period. Without any advance notice to Aaron, Wert announced, "As a rebuke to the present administration, I will not be communing this morning." With those words he sat down. His wife arose from the front bench, walked back, and seated herself on the rear bench. Some people began to cry.

Aaron rose and stated, "In an atmosphere like this we will not have communion this morning. I would like to announce Communion in two weeks from this afternoon for those who want to commune on the basis of a unified testimony of appreciation for the church's standards."

Daniel Wert (seated, center), minister at Gingrichs, and family, in 1969.

He then proceeded to preach the message he had planned for the morning. At its conclusion he broke down and wept.

He and Daniel walked to the rear door to meet the people as they left. Again, he broke down and wept.

Two weeks later, at the appointed time, thirty-one members—half of the group—presented themselves for Communion.

Simon Bucher was aroused and called for a meeting with the Gingrich congregation. Simon loved the pastor, but he felt that the only thing to do was to silence him. Aaron agreed.

The day of the meeting, January 19, 1966, Aaron spent with Simon. They discussed the matter intensively and prayed fervently. Aaron was sure that silencing the pastor without Conference knowing anything about it would mean deep trouble. Matters would be made worse. Finally, at five o'clock in the evening, Aaron suggested that they resign their responsibility at Gingrichs and request that the congregation seek other bishop help. Simon agreed.

Word had leaked out that the pastor would be silenced that mid-week evening, and some people came to the meeting prepared to fight. The pastor's son, who was influencing his father to change, traveled a distance to be present at the meeting. When Aaron announced that he and Simon had chosen to resign their responsibility and that the congregation should seek other bishop help, it jarred the would-be fighters into meekness.

Aaron proceeded to apologize for not being able to unify the church and help the church along. Resigning seemed to be the only recourse. He then requested forgiveness from the group.

The Lancaster Conference *Discipline* stated, "When difficulties occur in one bishop's district, no other bishop, minister, or deacon shall interfere, but may assist the said bishop if called." Aaron told the group, "On the basis of the *Discipline* you previously did not have the right to call for help but now you do. You are at liberty to call for help."

They did so. The liberal element contacted the Bishop Board appealing for help.

When Aaron discussed the resignation with the Bishop Board, the moderator of conference, David Thomas, said, "I positively could never have agreed to silence the Gingrich pastor."

Paul Landis, secretary of Conference, wrote to Aaron, "Gingrichs desperately wants your leadership."

Aaron wrote back, "They have the opportunity to be under my leadership. I would be glad if they would accept my leadership but they have rejected it."

The appointed committee, David Thomas, Richard Danner, and J. Paul Graybill, smoothed over the problem. Raymond Charles later became the bishop for those dissatisfied with Aaron's administration.

Aaron told the Bishop Board, "The person who wants to be loyal finds himself a victim of displeasure from the Bishop Board while the folks who disrespect the discipline are exonerated and carried along."

About the same time, a couple from the Denver-Myerstown District appeared at Elm Street for Communion one Sunday morning. They had been invited there by the deacon because they were experiencing difficulty in their home congregation. Aaron was suspicious that they were there to commune rather than to commune at their home church. Before sharing the emblems, he announced, "Visitors are welcome to commune if they have made previous arrangements." Immediately, the couple left.

The deacon was very upset. He declared, "Aaron, you should apologize to those folks."

Aaron replied, "I felt led to do that for their good. I just can't apologize."

"You've got to apologize because they were terribly offended," the deacon insisted. Aaron stood his ground.

Aaron's voice represented the voice of other conservatives as well. Benjamin Eshbach, Homer Bomberger, and Isaac Sensenig were facing similar problems. When the offenders and the disobedient complained of restraint to the executives of Conference, Conference sympathized with them instead of the conservative leaders who were trying to maintain a Gospel standard! The complainers knew their Conference leaders were following them!

Later, when the church at Pensacola, Florida, desired to relate with the Eastern Pennsylvania Mennonite Church, Raymond Charles, the bishop who took temporary charge of Lebanon District, wrote to Herbert Ebersole, the pastor, trying to discourage him from doing so. He said in effect, "What

David Thomas, Lancaster Conference Moderator.

a wonderful privilege I have in sharing with the people of the Lebanon District who so much appreciate my administration compared with Aaron and Simon's highly regimented administration....Even Aaron's children are not associating with him in his new church endeavor."[16]

---

16 This was not completely accurate, since Aaron's daughter Louise did associate herself with her father's church leadership.

From the Other Angle

Every issue has several sides. The perspective on the issue determines the angle of view. Even though the Conference was softening with regard to its own discipline, it strongly maintained the right of authority in dealing with issues. One bishop said in response to a question concerning the Bishop Board's fallibility, "Do you think that this board of spiritual men can be wrong?"

From the perspective of the Lancaster Conference leadership, the few conservative dissenting voices were wrong. They honestly and thoroughly believed that. The counsel of the church had to be right. They acknowledged that there were weaknesses in the church and they made efforts to correct them. Furthermore, when they scrutinized the dissenters, the dissenters had flaws. The flaws of the dissenters were magnified into serious problems. From this foundation they were able to deflect attention away from the serious drift into worldliness which the dissenters kept referencing.

Looking at matters from their side, the Lancaster Conference Bishops were not inclined to sympathize with Aaron and the other conservative voices for several reasons.

1. The conservative voices were strident and confrontational.
2. The unity of the Church mattered more than minor Conference infractions.
3. Ruptured unity would lead to more ruptures later.
4. The conservative thrust was not consistent conservatism in that attitudes and improper behavior mattered less than certain externals.
5. The movement embodied a critical spirit.
6. Personalities dominated the movement more than dedication to Biblical truth.
7. The movement could not be flexible enough to work within the existing church structure, nor allow for variations within the Districts.
8. The conservatives tended to irritate those who did not sympathize with them, causing unhealthy reactions on both sides.
9. The conservatives were majoring on minors.

Meeting of Fellowship and Discipleship
Held at Erb's Mennonite Church
September 4-6, 1959

The Apostolic Church	Roy Geigley
The Anabaptist Church	Aaron Shank
Basis of Scriptural Unity	Leroy Stoltzfus
Necessity of Scriptural Discipline	Mervin Baer
Sacrifice and Obedience	Paul M. Landis
Ichabod—Departed Glory	Earl Moseman
The Unequal Yoke—Lost Power	Elmer Showalter
Biblical Holiness	James Siegrist
The Present Crisis; The Call to Repentance	Mervin Baer
The Triumphing Church, Our Vision of Hope	Paul M. Landis

Something needed to be done. No one believed matters could continue as they were. Lancaster Mennonite Conference was divided against itself, and a house divided against itself cannot stand.

Conference had a history of sub-organizations functioning within itself. For example, a Radio Committee promoted radio in Conference even while Conference officially stood against it. (Members could have the radio while the ordained men could not.) If a Radio Committee could exist, why not a conservative sub-organization?

Aaron heard Eli Yutzy, a Midwesterner, repeat the statement, "The drift has been blue-printed by some of the liberal leaders of the western conferences" to a large gathering in the East.

After the service, Aaron approached Eli, saying, "When can some of us get together and organize to reverse the trend? When can we put pressure on the church to reverse the trend?"

Eli responded, "I'm ready for such a meeting even if I must travel to California for it."

These words illustrate the spirit behind the conservative stirring which would follow.

The Rising Conservative Tide

Conscientious members in the Lancaster Conference were already struggling in the 1950s because consistent church discipline was faltering. Elmer Showalter, ordained as minister at Gingrichs in 1954 to replace Herbert Ebersole, who with his family was moving to Florida to help with the Southern mission effort, later refused to participate in the regular communion service because of Conference discipline failure. As a consequence, Simon Bucher and the Conference silenced him. But the matter was larger than Elmer Showalter. Elmer's son Glenn remembers a packed meeting at Erbs Mennonite Church (located near Lititz, Pennsylvania) where listeners stood in the meetinghouse aisles and the "little boys" such as himself sat on the pulpit platform to

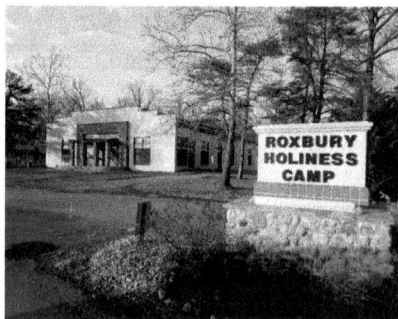

The Roxbury Holiness Campground was the scene of meetings held by conservative Mennonite leaders who eventually helped form the Nationwide Fellowship Churches.

provide room for eager, interested listeners. Hope was stirring the atmosphere; not all was lost after all.

Note the topic titles and the speakers on the 1959 Erbs program (p. 119). Two speakers spoke twice, Mervin Baer and Paul M. Landis; these two men taking major leadership roles in the Mennonite Christian Brotherhood which was about to be born, the actual vote to leave Conference taken at a subsequent meeting at the Sensenig Body Shop a few months later.

Aaron sympathized with these concerns to the point of contributing his voice and influence to the developing response to Conference failure. However, his respect for Conference authority prevented him from joining the movement at the time. How could he simply walk away from the authority which charged him with ministerial responsibilities? Leaving Conference abruptly with a spirit of criticism fell far short of Aaron's concept of how he or anyone else should relate to authority. He appreciated the concerns of the movement and at the same time disagreed with disrespectful attitudes which he saw in the movement. Much later, Aaron mused that his own family would have benefitted from identification with this conservative movement.

Stephen Stoltzfus, who was ordained as minister at Meckville to assist Cletus Doutrich after Aaron was ordained bishop , did identify early with the emerging Mennonite Christian Brotherhood movement. Only two years into his ministry Stephen was ready to abruptly leave Conference. Soon thereafter Stephen moved to Paraguay as part of the colonization effort organized by the Mennonite Christian Brotherhood. That movement itself later became a part of the larger Nationwide Fellowship of churches. The Roxbury Holiness Campgrounds, at Roxbury, Pennsylvania, became the annual rallying point for this group of people who were pulling out of various North American Mennonite conferences.

Aaron felt a strange mix of emotions; on one hand he appreciated and encouraged many of the new developments but on the other hand he did not feel comfortable with the unconventional and undignified manner of operating he observed. However, approximately twenty years later when Stephen Stoltzfus, in Paraguay, invited Aaron Shank and David Wadel, to investigate the possibility of planting an Eastern Pennsylvania Mennonite Church in Paraguay, Aaron consented. The past was past; present opportunities took priority.

And these were not the only voices crying to be heard. Defenders of the Faith, a more local organization, began to hold meetings of their own. Thirteen lay members began to hold prayer meetings each Monday evening in the basement of the Clayton Wenger family home. Elmer Weaver, Sr., Ivan Martin, Sr., and Noah Martin formed a lay-leadership board which approached Conference Bishop Paul Landis with their concerns about church drift. Landis told the group that the Bishops shared their concerns and that they needed their help. But Ivan Martin, Sr., had a son, Galen, who would need to go into I-W work somewhere soon, and he was already unhappy with what was happening in the New York City I-W setting, where his daughter and her husband, Elvin Stauffer, were serving. Ivan Martin, Sr., called the Selective Service Board in Washington D.C., who encouraged him to proceed with some kind of alternative. Next, Martin contacted Bishop Homer Bomberger, who enthusiastically supported the idea as a way to deal with the drift in the church. Word of mouth carried the developments quickly through Lebanon and Lancaster counties. However, local congregational ministers were not eager to allow public meetings in Mennonite churches because they were fearful of a negative Bishop Board response. By this time the concern group had grown so large that their public meetings needed high school auditoriums to accommodate the large crowds of curious

Homer and Naomi Bomberger. Bishop Bomberger was one of the conservative Lancaster Conference bishops who helped form the Mennonite Messianic Mission and was granted an honorable release from Conference.

people. Homer Bomberger had solicited help from Bishops Ben Eshbach, Aaron Shank, and Simon Bucher, thus shifting the movement from lay leadership to ordained leadership, boosting its legitimacy. The Lancaster Conference Bishop Board tried to stop the movement but it had already become too large. Thus the Defenders of the Faith movement stirred up sympathy for the conservative cause which was later represented by the Mennonite Messianic Mission as the leadership of the much more organized group transitioned from lay to ordained

leadership and the Voluntary Service units at Wilmington, Delaware, and Danville, Pennsylvania sprang into existence. It is important to note that the Defenders of the Faith movement did not directly become the Mennonite Messianic Mission. By the time the Messianic Mission began organizationally, the Defenders of the Faith movement had fizzled and a number of its leaders did not transition into the Mennonite Messianic Mission.

In contrast to the 1959 Mennonite Christian Brotherhood movement, referenced above, a sizeable number of Conference leaders were ready to take some kind of action later in the decade. (Mervin Baer, later in life, was amazed to witness how much conservative thought actually remained in southeastern Pennsylvania.[17]) The action taken was *not* an effort to organize a new fellowship. The intended goal of the action was to reverse the trends within the Lancaster Conference. The place to start had already presented itself.

Aaron reported to the Bishop Board that on September 19, 1965, a group of brethren met to plan for an organization to provide for a Voluntary Service and I-W program. The organization called itself Mennonite Messianic Mission. Its objective was "to provide a place for VS services for those who want to stay by the principles and standards as previously held by Conference."

This move alarmed Conference. Fears were shared concerning the "confusive [*sic*] and divisive influence of such a group emerging without conference approval."

On December 22, 1966, the following was read to the Bishop Board as reasons for the developing Mennonite Messianic Mission:

The present interdenominational and ecumenical involvements, the social gospel trends, the loss of conviction and practice of separation of dress on the part of key men and women within the conference, the rapidly increasing number of sisters with cut hair and fashionable hair arrangements who continue in communion relationship with the church, and other situations.

By this time Elmer Weaver Jr., Isaac Sensenig, and Walter Newswanger had contacted the Selective Service as well as the local Lancaster draft board office about prospects for developing a Voluntary Service/I-W program separate from the Peace Section office of the Mennonite Central Committee. This also alarmed Conference because it understood that all clearance with the Selective Service would be made through the Peace Section of the Mennonite Central Committee. Conference stated,

Since the Mennonite Messianic Mission is planning to bypass the procedures established by Selective Service for IW-VS personnel who serve in the program of the Mennonite Church, the Lancaster Conference Peace Committee expresses our deep concern for the potential threat this presents to the present privileges we receive from Selective Service. We are also deeply concerned for the effect this has

17 Mervin Baer to the author in the early 1980s.

on our witness of peace and brotherhood to the world.

Furthermore, it stated,

> We note the proposal that was made by the chairman of the VS and I-W Committee to be a channel for the Mennonite Messianic Mission program. If this proposal is not accepted by the Mennonite Messianic Mission, we stand ready as the Lancaster Conference Peace Committee to channel contacts with Selective Service on the basis requested by Selective Service. We offer this in light of the need to maintain proper relationships with Selective Service.

The situation presented three options: 1) The conservative element could choose to accept the entire Lancaster Conference VS program, 2) Lancaster Conference could choose to cooperate with the Mennonite Messianic Mission in a conjoint VS/I-W effort, or 3) The two groups could take separate paths realizing the potential for division in Conference.

Aaron and the conservatives standing with him chose the third option "to function as a separate organization under the constitution provided by the organization."

In response to a letter from the chairman of the VS/I-W Committee urging that the concerns of the Mennonite Messianic Mission be handled through the Conference program, the MMM responded,

> In consideration of this suggestion our committee unanimously agreed that we believe the most effective means of service we can render to the church today is by the Mennonite Messianic Mission to function as a separate organization under the constitution provided by the organization. (Read by Aaron to the Bishop Board on February 23, 1967)

Aaron was particularly concerned about the convictions and position of the young people in his own Lebanon District. In June 1967, he wrote a letter to them.

> Dear Young People of the Lebanon District Mennonite Churches:
>
> Greetings.
>
> This is a message to our young members who will face the Draft in the next few years or may feel led to donate some time in the Voluntary Service opportunities of today.
>
> I believe that the strength and beauty of our dedicated youth is the most vital

asset of the Church today. I have no greater joy than to know that our youth are remaining unstained and un-wrecked by the corruption of the world and the disobedience and apostasy of unspiritual and unprincipled church members.

It is indeed heart-rending to learn of so many spiritual casualties among the youth of our Church today. There are an alarming number of casualties among our 1W's and VS'ers. A Mennonite minister whose responsibility is to keep close to the 1W boys in a certain area of the Church recently made the statement that "the 1W program is nothing but an embarrassment to me." What a sad commentary on those who profess to be followers of the Prince of Peace--the One who calls us to holiness of life

These young folks are suddenly thrown into new and strange situations. They face tests and temptations that threaten the destruction of their souls--situations like Joseph and Daniel met in their strange new environment. But we thank God that Joseph and Daniel were not victims of destruction and that because they triumphed, we are assured that God's enabling grace is sufficient to bring us through the most severe tests and satanic attacks. We cannot stand in our own strength.

I am sharing with you the questions on the C. O. questionnaire which all our youth -- brethren and sisters -- would do well to study and find intelligent and consistent answers to. It will prepare boys for the day of their registration and have an educational value for the girls. Here are the questions:

1. Do you believe in a Supreme Being?

2. Describe the nature of your belief which is the basis of your claim--and state whether or not your belief in a Supreme Being involves duties which to you are superior to those arising from any human relationship.

3. Explain how, when, and from whom and from what source you received the training and acquired the belief which is the basis of your claim.

4. Give the name and address of the individual upon whom you rely most for religious training.

5. Under what circumstance, if any, do you believe in the use of force?

6. Describe the actions and behavior in your life which in your opinion most conspicuously demonstrate the consistency and depth of your religious convictions.

7. Have you ever given public expression, written or oral, to the views herein expressed as the basis for your claim--? If so, specify when and where.

8. Are you a member of a religious sect or organization? State the name of the sect, and the name and location of its governing body--

When, where and how did you become a member of said sect or organization?

Describe carefully the creed or official statements of said religious sect--

Describe your relationship with and activities in all organizations with which you have been affiliated.

Give here the names and other information indicated of persons who could supply information as to the sincerity of your professed convictions against participation in war.

Some of these questions are searching questions and should challenge us to renewed study and dedication and growth in our Christian life.

I would like to add a few checks which I believe will be helpful to your Christian life and witness in general.

Check up on your Christian experience. Are you really born again?

Check up on your personal convictions. Are you depending on your parents or preacher's convictions to get you through?

Check up on your personal devotional life. Are you reading the Bible and praying daily?

Check up on your Bible knowledge. Are you ready to give an answer for what you claim to believe?

Check up on your attitude toward your Church. Do you really love the Church? Do you enjoy being obedient to her standards more than following world practices?

Check up on your stewardship. Are you giving liberally to the worthy causes of Christ?

Check up on your love for the Lord Jesus Christ. Are you loving Him, living for Him, and looking with joy for His coming again?

To those of you who have written us letters of encouragement, we thank you and the Lord. May God bless you richly.

We are always happy to have you share problems and concerns with us.

We wish God's best to all of you for now and forever.

Devotedly and prayerfully yours,

Your bishop,

Aaron M. Shank

Later in 1967, the Mennonite Messianic Mission contacted Ernest Bontrager from the Messiah Bible School in Ohio and asked him to help

them start their own Bible School. He served for the first two terms at
Numidia, held December 4-22, 1967 and January 1-19, 1968, and returned
the next year. The Bible School was to be a place where conservative values
could be inculcated into the rising generation without the diluting influences
of liberalism. Only solidly conservative teachers would exert influence on
the young minds in attendance. Furthermore, the Bible School would become a tangible rallying point for conservative minds in the East. Aaron was
remembering his own positive experiences with Eastern Mennonite School
in Virginia.

The Breaking Point

The Lancaster Conference Bishop
Board Minutes for March 14-16,
1966 state:

> Benjamin Eshbach reported the efforts
> in his district in the past to work with
> the violations of conference standards.
> Since he cannot continue to serve com-
> munion to those who do not wear capes
> and who have cut hair and long ties, he
> planned to refuse communion to those
> who are in violation and present them-
> selves for communion. The ministry
> requested that this matter be presented
> to the Bishop Board for counsel, he
> planned to refuse communion to those
> who are in violation and present them-
> selves for communion.

David Thomas, diplomatic Lancaster
Conference Moderator who led the
Conference to grant Aaron and his fellow
MMM bishops an honorable release from
Conference in 1968

A committee of four bishops working with the ministry of the Manor
District in which Benjamin Eshbach served presented recommendations
concerning the impasse. As a result, Benjamin reported to the Bishop Board
that he was not able to accept their recommendations.

Ben asked Homer Bomberger, Isaac Sensenig, and Aaron Shank to sit with
him to discuss the problems in his district. The group made a recommendation to the Bishop Board of Conference and also declared that from that
time on, they were committing themselves to give leadership to those who

would honor and respect the authority of Conference. Aaron wrote a letter stating their commitment and presented it to the Bishop Board.

David Thomas, as Moderator of Conference, reacted in alarm, saying, "Let's fall on our knees and pray." The Bishop Board prayed for about a half hour amidst tears.

Rising from prayer, David said, "Now let's analyze this statement."

Richard Danner very calmly said, "Well, Brother Moderator, I don't see any reason why this whole Board shouldn't sign the statement."

The Bishop Board Minutes for September 12-14, 1966 state:

> A letter was read from Homer Bomberger, Aaron Shank, Isaac Sensenig, and Benjamin Eshbach reporting their meeting together at the request of Brother Eshbach and their support of Brother Ben's position and their own position "that after this present communion season we will not be able to serve communion in any congregation in which the Lancaster Conference Discipline cannot be applied for baptism, communion, and daily walk of life." At the request of the moderator we had a season of voluntary prayer of confession and searching for the leading of the Holy Spirit in our midst.

The Lititz congregation considered itself a more urban congregation and thus needed the opportunity to be more progressive in order to make their outreach work more effective.[18] On December 15, 1966, the Bishop Board Minutes include the following concerning the Lititz congregation, served by Bishop Isaac Sensenig. In accord with the other conservative bishops, Isaac could no longer administrate like he had previously, constantly accommodating the worldly trends. He decided to draw a line and in doing so he upset many people.

A letter was read which contained the signatures of 109 members of the Lititz Congregation appealing

> to the Bishop Board for consideration in becoming a part of a district in which it is possible for a congregation to reach out more effectively in evangelism and that these converts can then find acceptable fellowship and participation in the life of the congregation even though of a different cultural background," and further "for consideration in appointing over us until such time as the above appeals can be developed, a bishop who feels he can work with an urban congregation in meeting

---

18 Kenneth Auker, *Keeping the Trust*, 2013, Eastern Mennonite Publications, p. 127.

its needs both in witness and in congregational life. [19]

These appeals were based upon the following:

1) The enforcement of the disciplinary action will eliminate members from our brotherhood who have communed with us for up to 50 years, dressing as they presently do, and have never been denied communion before this time, and is such that only approximately one-third of our members participated.

2) The required commitment is more stringent than that practiced generally in this district and in the districts represented by some of the committee members.

3) There was no indication in the Conference Council report that anything of the magnitude this action indicates was remiss at the Lititz Church. [20]

The Lititz congregation was finally given to another bishop willing to work with them.

The Lititz congregational unrest represents only some of the polarization within the Conference. Significant conservative voices spoke in Juniata County, Cumberland County, and in the Manheim area of Lancaster County. In fact, conservative voices spoke from almost all over Lancaster Conference by 1968. But these voices were in the minority. The majority seemed ready to move along with the continuing drift toward general worldliness.

In desperation, Aaron wrote a significant letter to the Bishop Board in February, 1968. This letter provides a window into Aaron's heart and helps to explain why he said and did what he did. It also offers a window into Bishop Board experience.

Dear Brethren,

Greetings.

For some time I have been feeling that I should put on paper for the Board my interpretation of the reason for some of the rather tense experiences we have had together at times during the past few years.

If I may judge others by myself, surely none of us enjoy the moments of unrest sometimes evident in our sessions.

Doubtless not everyone on this Board, perhaps very few, will agree with my

19 Robert B. Graber, "An Amiable Mennonite Schism: The Origin of the Eastern Pennsylvania Mennonite Church," *Pennsylvania Mennonite Heritage* 7(4) (October 1984), p. 6.

20 Minutes of the Lancaster Conference Bishop Board, December 15, 1966.

observations, but I feel led to present my thinking in hopes that it will help to clear what seems to be a dense fog that hangs over us at times.

These are my personal observations. I have counseled no one in the writing of this letter, nor have the contents been shared with anyone prior to this meeting.

It has appeared to me that our deepest concerns often center around the symptoms rather than around the real cause of our problems. It seems at times that any deviations from the established organization or planned activities of the Conference are looked upon with deeper concern than the basic reasons for the deviations, especially when such deviations are on the part of conservative brethren. To illustrate: when four bishops stated to this Board their intentions to work only with situations wherein our established Conference discipline would be upheld and adhered to, something which I think we all actually promised to do, the statement was looked upon as a very serious dilemma and a threat to Conference, and for about one-half hour we prayed and wept together. This, I am sure, was a very wholesome experience, but would it not have been more consistent, Brethren, and more in order to have expressed some appreciation for this kind of conviction and administration and then to have fallen on our knees in intercession in behalf of the evident spiritual decline and "the process of the great apostasy" that is upon us? Here the symptom, it seems, was our greater concern, and the real cause of the statement was our lesser concern.

When a group of brethren recently withdrew from a given bishop district, and a few bishops responded to a plea from them for help, and this was brought to the attention of our Board, again there was weeping with strong "pleading for a working together" and a period of prayer in behalf of this apparently irregular organizational procedure.[21] But the doctrinal irregularities and/or the irregular doctrinal applications among us have been, at least on certain occasions, taken for granted if not freely justified. We have been told numbers of times that digressions or deviations in one congregation or one part of the Conference need not pose an organizational problem to the rest of the district or Conference. Might it not be that when organizational deviations occur, it is simply an announcement that a far more serious deviation has previously taken place? When a church departs from her own standards of doctrinal unity and purity, does the true and real basis for organizational unity and loyalty continue to exist?

A few pertinent questions may well be asked. These questions are presented for real heart-searching rather than for any purpose of indictment.

Why do we not fall on our faces and weep and pray over the hundreds of sisters with cut hair, fashionable hair dress, objectionably small coverings, and ridiculously immodest attire, along with increasing numbers of brethren in violation, who continue in a communion relationship with the church? If we give up our

---

21 There were several occasions in these years when Lancaster Conference members moved between congregations and even founded new congregations in both conservative and liberal directions in ways which would be considered irregular.

The October 1967 issue of the *Missionary Messenger*, official organ of the Eastern Mennonite Board of Missions and Charities (Lancaster Conference's mission board), carried an editorial by Mahlon Hess which disturbed Aaron. Two excerpts follow:

There is a tool of even greater potential [than the radio] and I personally believe we should take a fresh look at it....With 64 percent of our [United States] population using television as their primary source of world news (with 42 percent credibility rating as compared to 24 percent for newspapers, the second most popular news source), the time may be here when we ought to give consideration to our share in strengthening the Gospel witness on television. Apart from this I believe we ought to begin to help our people to make proper use of this powerful medium.

...As world population spirals, do we limit our efforts at helping increase the world's food supply, or should Christians become involved in problems of population control?

separation dress, is it because the world and its standards have gotten so good that we can now be identified with the world in dress? If we tolerate shorn women in our fellowship, is it because God has changed His mind and lifted the shame on such a practice?

Why do we not weep and pray over a condition which permits divorced and remarried couples to find their way into our fellowship while remaining in their adulterous relationship? Will we go with the masses of professed Christendom and soon come to believe that adultery is respectable in the eyes of man, and acceptable with God when a license [marriage license] is issued for this purpose?

Why do we not weep and pray when a missionary defies Bishop Board action on specific items and then is recommended and reappointed to the Mission Field with honors? When our Mission Board secretary can inform the joint boards that our missionaries on all foreign fields have largely laid aside their separation garb and justifies them in it, why are we not more concerned?

When Amos Horst and Donald Lauver first met our missionaries in Africa dressed in fashionable attire, the Church was shaken and burdened, and a cry of protest went up over the Conference. Last summer when Don Jacobs appeared in the western states in conventional [Western] dress, I was asked to write to him protesting his double standard of dress. He has now returned to Africa, and recent pictures brought back from the field indicate he is freely using the world-designed pattern of dress in favor of our Church-designed pattern. To my knowledge no word of protest or concern has been given to this kind of inconsistency. Has the Church now lost the battle and closed the book on the dress problem with missionaries?

Why do we not weep together over the fact that movie productions provided by both the Church and the movie industry are now being shown in our churches and in halls of entertainment in the name of our Church boards and committees? We have hired and paid an "actor" to assume a character other than his own and "act" for a certain effect it can produce on our people. The word "hypocrite" as used by Christ means "actor" and comes from the stage. Interest in our Church's program on the basis of entertainment now has its foot in our door. Has the manna from heaven lost its appeal and must we now look for quails from the desert to satisfy and motivate our people? Will the showing of key persons of our program who are in violation of our Church standards help to solve or add to our problems?

Why are we not more deeply concerned when there is presented to our constituency through the <u>Missionary Messenger</u>, October, 1967, a powerful editorial in favor of a breakdown of an item in our discipline on which an ultimatum of forfeiture rests [see sidebar above]?

If we become more lax on our position on television, is it because its wicked influence has lessened to the point of Christian acceptance? <u>U. S. News and World Report</u>, November 9, 1964, reports a 200% increase of corruption in ten years, and <u>Time Magazine</u>, November 4, 1964, recommends the non-use of television for children.

Should we not weep and pray together when local pastors are allowed to justify and even encourage their people in disobedience to Conference standards and to cultivate disrespect and insubordination toward Conference and loyal bishops?

For more than five years we endeavored in patience and love and understanding, with our limited abilities, to lead the Gingrich congregation into the kind of spiritual life and experience that could find expression in loving obedience to our Church standards. When the pastor led more than half of the congregation, including the working force of the Church, in a rejection of our leadership and declared that they would not work with a position upholding Conference standards--(and not until then)--we accepted this rejection in the most gracious and humble way we knew under the existing circumstances.

Since that time the Gingrich Church has, in a sense, been exonerated through regular communions now being held on their own terms. This seems to be resulting more and more in unfaithful leaders and disobedient congregations coming into focus who are receiving the recognition they need to continue the course that will lead us on in the "process of the great apostasy." Our Conference discipline, Article II, 9, gives a congregation the right to bring complaint against their bishop in the event that the "bishop should teach unsound doctrine or lead his congregation astray." Have the Gingrich, Lititz, Blainsport, and other congregations who have rejected their bishops and are now receiving favorable recognition from our board brought such complaint, and if so, have the complaints been substantiated? To some of us the contrary seems to be true. Unfaithful pastors leading their congregations astray are vindicated and loyal bishops are being looked upon with some degree of scorn.

The deviations of congregations like the above named ones have a tendency to become the norm of practice for the Church and so the leaven of the elimination of principle continues to spread rapidly over the entire Church. How long can we continue having the disobedient practices of one decade become the standards of practice for the next decade until we find ourselves down the road beyond the point of all probable return. Indeed, some parts of the Church seem to have reached this point already.

I am personally convinced, Brethren, that if there could be at this time, a confessing and repenting and a sharing of blame and responsibility and then "a working together" in correcting these deviations and departures from our Biblical standards, according to our discipline, the symptoms of division and disintegration would quickly disappear--at least on the side of the conservative element of the Church. And the great cause which we have championed together in the past could continue to be championed, rather than to be lost. May God grant us mercy to this end.

Prayerfully and devotedly,

Aaron Shank

The above eloquent appeal fell upon deaf ears. After it was read aloud at the March Bishop Board meeting, there was no discussion, no consideration; the Board simply moved on to the next item on the agenda. The majority on the Bishop Board had decided to embark on a policy of accommodation. (After Aaron had left the Conference, Bishop Richard Danner remembered this eloquent appeal and requested consideration.)

Aaron could not simply sit still. In fact, instead of just decrying the whole situation, he felt that the Lebanon District should make positive efforts to build Biblical conviction. When Lloyd Eby contacted him about the Lebanon District hosting the annual Conference Young People's Institute, Aaron took the request to the District Ministry and issued a reply dated February 3, 1968.

Dear Brother Lloyd,

Christian greetings.

Thank you for your letter of January 29 with the offer from the Christian Education Board to plan for a Young People's Institute in the Lebanon District in August of this year.

At our district Ministerial Meeting on Wednesday, January 31, I presented your letter to our ministry and after considerable discussion there was a motion carried that I respond to your letter and share the decision and sentiment of our board with you.

Some of our brethren feel and have been feeling for some time that our ministry should plan for an institute this summer and so it was decided that we would proceed with plans for an institute on a local level and decline acceptance of your offer at this time.

There are a number of problems we believe we may face in being host to an institute on a Conference basis. Since increasing numbers of our young sisters of the Conference are now cutting their hair, using "whirlwind" type and other fashionable hair arrangement, wearing extremely small coverings, capeless and ridiculously short dresses, etc. -- and since these deviations are spreading through the church like leaven and eating like a canker -- we are reluctant to have this kind of possible influence in our district to add hardship and difficulty to our young people and to us in our efforts towards more loyal support of our Conference standards.

Another possible problem presented was the difficulty we may have in agreeing on speakers for the Institute. We are beginning to observe that we get the most help in maintaining our standards from speakers who are generally frowned upon merely because they do not have what is thought to be the proper organizational relationships.[22]

Personally, I have always enjoyed your splendid arrangements of programs and am indeed sorry that conditions exist that lead us to this action. We recognize that we are human and may err in judgment and procedure but our sincere purpose of heart is to pursue nothing but the very best course for the very best cause.

Thank you again for your kind offer.

With kindest regards and Christian love,

Aaron M. Shank

For Lebanon District Ministry

Plans on a local level matured into the annual Youth Institute. These local Institutes have served the Church well as a positive influence for good among young people for many years since. Aaron possessed none of the mentality "If you can't beat them, join them" that other leaders evidently did.

At a Mennonite Messianic Mission meeting held at the new White Oak Mennonite Church on June 25, 1968, Aaron preached on the subject "Church Issues Facing Us Today." In this message he stated that it is just as

---

22 Aaron is probably referring to conservative leaders from outside Lancaster Conference.

serious to violate a principle of the Bible as interpreted by the Church as it is to violate a clear "Thus saith the Lord." An issue is created when some people justify a discontinuance of a Bible principle or ordinance while others insist that they be continued. The first step toward correcting any problem is to acknowledge that it exists. Refusing to see danger when it exists is self-deception. Then Aaron proceeded to enumerate problems which had become issues between the MMM and the Lancaster Conference.

1. Conference was more interested in activity than orthodoxy.
2. Conference had an unbalanced emphasis on evangelism at the expense of doctrine and holiness of life.
3. Conference was more interested in administrative ability than loyalty to the principles found in the New Testament.
4. Conference valued organizational unity above doctrinal unity.
5. An ever-widening gap was developing between the Conference's doctrinal statement and general Conference practices.
   a. Excellent written statement on weddings, but practice which does not match.
   b. Loss of distinctive modest apparel.
   c. Loss of consistent head coverings for women combined with worldly hair arrangements.
   d. Tolerating cut hair for women and long hair for men.
   e. Adulterous divorce and remarriage relationships tolerated within the membership.
   f. Participation in political campaigns.
6. Conference members were involved in movie productions.
7. Conference was allowing itself to be involved in interdenominational ecumenical efforts.
8. Conference was allowing a gap to develop between the institutions under authority and the agents of authority. Rebellion was being sanctioned.
9. Conference was becoming less and less disciplined as a body of believers.
10. Conference was losing a holy communion among the people of God.

Aaron Shank had a clear understanding of the situation surrounding his family, his church, and his ministry. The question of the hour: How should Aaron and the other conservative leadership who stood with him respond to the enormous pressure that Conference was placing upon them?

"A Document of World Accommodation"

Consistent with the sweeping trend of the times, the Lancaster Mennonite Conference adopted a revised *Discipline* in July of 1968. The new document shifted from stating what "shall" be to what "should" be, making it, in many cases, simply a collection of recommendations. For instance, the new Discipline merely "asked" Lancaster Conference members to abstain from the use of television. The standard was lowered on some specific issues, such as life insurance and dress. Because of these changes, Aaron considered the new *Discipline* to be a document of accommodation. On July 30, 1968, the Lebanon District Ministry responded as a unit to the new Discipline by sending the following out to the Lebanon District Churches.

Statement to the Mennonite Churches of the Lebanon District

**Whereas the Lancaster Mennonite Conference in a special session on July 17, 1968 adopted a revision of the discipline and

**Whereas this revision has been interpreted by the Conference to provide basically a statement of recommendation rather than a statement of requirements for a disciplined Church to adhere to, and

**Whereas we believe that the revised discipline constitutes a document of world accommodation and opens the way for a rapid departure from the Biblical position of the Church on non-conformity, the use of television, and Biblical administration generally, therefore

**We, the ministry of the Lebanon District Churches have agreed in the fear of God to maintain our position and practice for a basis of fellowship.

**We believe our Lord wants the witness of separation and non-conformity maintained in the world and that His blessing will enrich our fellowship as we faithfully yield to His Word and Will.

**A copy of this statement is being sent [to] the Bishop Board of Lancaster Conference.

The Lebanon District Ministry
July 30, 1968

At the same time, Aaron wrote to the Lancaster Conference Board of Bishops the following letter.

Greetings of love in Christ's Name.

I would like to bring a number of items to the attention of this Board.

In 1953 the late J. L. Stauffer wrote to the General Council of General Conference that "It appears we are at the forks of the road on the question of nonconformity to the world. If the Mennonite Church does nothing, the present drift will continue unchecked. Those conservative congregations throughout our conferences will ultimately be smothered out by the increasing tide of worldliness..." He suggests further that one of the great threats to the conservative cause is the associating together of liberal and conservative churches and conferences across the country.

It seems quite clear today that our organizational involvements and associations with General Conference Committees, Elkhart Committees, M.C.C. Boards, E.M.C. Committees, etc., here in the States, and our interdenominational involvements and associations on foreign soil has been rapidly accomplishing that which Bro. Stauffer in his prophetic message warned us against.

We note here a few changes that have taken place the past number of years:

1. Disciplinary action against unfaithful leaders has been largely discarded. In 1945 Amos Rutt and Jacob Miller at Vine Street Mission, Lancaster, PA. were silenced because they would not uphold the discipline of the Church. Today increasing numbers of deacons, ministers, and bishops can no longer support the Church's standards and are vindicated by the highest governing body of the Church. Loyal brethren who at one time were held in esteem are now looked upon with some degree of scorn.

2. Efforts are inadequate to reverse or even halt the shameful practice of sisters cutting their hair. We continue to give communion to increasing numbers of such transgressors.

3. The wearing of jewelry by communicant members is now seen in numbers of our congregations.

4. Sisters in large numbers are unashamedly appearing with dresses well above the knees rather than "well below the knees" as the discipline requires.

5. The present applications of the Christian woman's headship veiling with a proud display type of hair arrangement and a vanity type of covering, or the elimination of the covering altogether is rapidly replacing the "modest combing of the hair," and a covering that "adequately covers the head." The inconsistent application in many cases is now militating against the principle of the ordinance.

6. The production and use of and the justification of questionable films is marching rapidly along. Some of our Executives are now serving on film committees with men like Roy Martin whose appearance, at least at times, would seem to identify him as a first cousin, if not a brother of the beatnik society. In fact, the idea of the V.S. film now being planned for was initiated by this man according to the Gospel Herald report, June 18, 1968. This means of communication seems questionable, if not altogether objectionable. A.W. Tozer in his booklet on The Menace of the Religious Movie writes, "The religious movie is undergoing a period of gestation and seems about to swarm up over the churches like a cloud of locusts out of the earth. The figure is accurate; they are coming from below, not from above."

7. At our board meeting in July we were told that the high majority vote of acceptance of the revised discipline was something to be thankful for. I personally believe that this new discipline will contribute significantly to the present "process of accommodation" and the acceptance of the same is therefore real cause for weeping rather than for thankfulness. From past experience we well know what happens to our church or any other church group where interpretation and regulation of doctrine and discipline is lessened or discarded.

8. To my knowledge I have always been a promoter of the Biblical position of our conference and in the past have devoted my life and energy to promote her written discipline. I have never intentionally lived or taught in violation of her standards. However, since the finalizing and acceptance of the revised discipline, I now find myself, along with a few other faithful brethren, due to our relationship with Mennonite Messianic Mission, in violation of the discipline as set forth in Article I, Section 10. ["Any movement or organization contemplated by and for the brotherhood of the Conference shall have the approval of the district ministry involved or the Bishop Board when Conference implications are involved. Such movements or organizations, if effected, shall be administrated in accordance with objectives and direction of the Conference."] Although we were informed at conference that this section is not intended to be retroactive, I believe this kind of irresponsible attitude toward an accepted discipline weakens rather than strengthens its entire content.

Inasmuch as I believe Mennonite Messianic Mission is more fully carrying out the great principles of Biblical holiness and separation, and is more loyal to the recommended standards of our conference than the conference in general is, I desire to continue devoting my interests and energies in promotion of her worthy objectives.

Furthermore, I now feel that in keeping with good stewardship of my time I must ask to be relieved of my present responsibility on the Foreign Missions Council and the Religious Welfare Committee of Philhaven Hospital.

9. I speak now as a person and not for the MMM organization. It seems to me that inasmuch as the brethren involved organizationally in the MMM are now in

violation of the accepted conference discipline it would become the responsibility of the Bishop Board to approve their work and standards for conference acceptance or define our future relationship to the conference.

I want to express my heartfelt appreciation for the blessings I have derived from the Lancaster Conference as well as for the privilege I have had to use my limited abilities in the promotion of the cause of Christ. By God's grace I shall always maintain a respect for the Conference for what it has been and done over the years.

I have endeavored to serve in all good conscience and this letter is written from a motive of love for the continuance of principles eternal. I keenly recognize that I am human and may therefore err in judgment and procedure. In those areas wherein I may not have understood my own motives and may have caused unnecessary tensions or problems I seek the gracious forgiveness of all involved.

May God grant us the wisdom, the courage, and enabling grace to maintain at all cost a witness of full deliverance from a world fast ripening for the judgments of God. May He save us from the continuous process of accommodation to world culture until we should find ourselves perishing with the world.

Prayerfully and devotedly,

Aaron Shank

The latent tensions of earlier years were quickly coming to a head. It was becoming increasingly apparent that the conservative and liberal elements of the church could not function harmoniously together. Each side was dedicated to its own worldview, which of course created separate trajectories moving forward.

Previously, on July 17, 1968, Bishop Homer Bomberger had written to the Bishop Board that he "will no longer be responsible to any actions of Conference and that I intend to continue to uphold the Old Lancaster Conference Rules and Discipline in teaching and practice." He further requested to be relieved of all his Conference committee responsibilities.

Isaac Sensenig wrote to the same Board on August 10, 1968:

I am therefore resigning from my conference committee appointments which includes the Non-Conformity Committee, Conference Day Planning Committee, Meeting Calendar Committee, and charge of Tellers at Conference. I am also requesting to be relieved from my remaining responsibility in the Hess-Landis Valley District since the ministry there will be minded to work with the new discipline....In the interest of good stewardship of my time and loyalty to Scriptural principles, I plan to continue to uphold the past position of Lancaster Conference Rules and Discipline, and do not intend to support the present conference program in church administration.

In a letter dated August 13, 1968, Benjamin Eshbach wrote that he would "no longer feel responsible to support the actions of Conference" and stated his reasons.

The Mennonite Messianic Mission bishops were trying hard to prevent an explosive situation such as had happened previously. Aaron, especially, had a keen conscience concerning honoring authority, the authority which had placed him in the ministry. Even though he felt his bishop calling was from God, he knew the parent organization which had commissioned him deserved respect and honor. This conviction tempered the events which followed.

The September Conference of 1968 would become historic. On the first day, Monday, tension surfaced concerning the issues facing the Conference. On the evening of the first day, while several concerned bishops were standing together reflecting on the sad state of affairs, Aaron suggested that he would be ready to make a request to the bishop board for an honorable discharge from Conference for the bishops associated with the MMM organization. The others encouraged him to prepare such a statement. The next morning, Aaron brought one which the others agreed he should share with the bishop board. Aaron agreed, but said he would expect one of them to call for it at an appropriate time.

The Bishop Board meeting became tense. The Bishops puzzled over how to help those congregations who were dissatisfied with the Mennonite Messianic Mission bishops' administration and were appealing to the Bishop Board. Finally, Isaac Sensenig said, "Brother Moderator, Aaron has a statement to read that might help us out of our dilemma."

Statement to Lancaster Bishop Board on the organization and work of MMM and implications to Conference relationships.

The MMM as an independent organization has been functioning now for approximately two years. Inasmuch as the objectives and activities of the MMM have been within the scope of the Conference's standard, is there any justifiable reason why the Bishop Board could not look with approval upon the work of this organization? Furthermore, since the MMM is seeking to give leadership to the kind of experience and practical expression which we believe are necessary to maintain Biblical principles plus the fact that there are those in the church who for obvious reasons are increasingly desirous of a more conservative leadership, would there be such a thing as consistently agreeing to disagree without developing and/or harboring ill will toward each other? With this in mind and in view of the sentiments frequently expressed on this board that the Conference may be too large for the most effective operation, could the Bishop Board grant the bishops of the MMM an honorable release from conference relationships for the purpose of functioning within the objectives and activities of the MMM organization?

The Bishop Board meeting became tense. The Bishops puzzled over how to help those congregations who were dissatisfied with the Mennonite Messianic Mission bishops' administration and were appealing to the Bishop Board. Finally, Isaac Sensenig said, "Brother Moderator, Aaron has a statement to read that might help us out of our dilemma."

Aaron read the statement. He broke down in tears several times before he had finished. The whole Board was moved to brokenness and there was humility, consideration, kindness, and warmth that had not been experienced earlier. The extended discussion which followed was carried out in an atmosphere of love and respect.

When someone asked "What will it take to keep us together?" Aaron responded, "There are two ways to leave Conference, 1) doctrinally, and 2) organizationally.

"If Brother _____ who has accepted divorced and remarried persons into several of his congregations, continues to accept them, then he has left Conference doctrinally because Conference states, 'Divorced and remarried people may not be received into the church.'

"Brother _____ said he has dozens of sisters with cut hair presenting themselves for communion and that he can do nothing about it. The Discipline says, 'Hair shall not be cut.' If he continues to share communion with such, he has left Conference.

"Brother _____ said he has members wearing jewelry. If he continues to serve communion to such, he has left Conference because Conference states, 'Jewelry is forbidden according to 1 Peter 3:3,4.'"

"If these matters will be corrected, then there is no reason at all to leave

Conference. We can go on and work together championing the conservative viewpoint." Not another word was said about what to do in order to stay together. From there on, the discussion favored granting the release.

The next morning, mutual love and respect continued. Moderator David Thomas had formulated a statement recognizing the Mennonite Messianic Mission appeal and recommending that the appeal be granted and that the conference honor the new organization.

After editing by Aaron and Conference Secretary Paul G. Landis, David's statement was presented to the Bishop Board for their vote of approval or disapproval of the release. By secret ballot, the Bishop Board voted 22 in favor and 4 not in favor of the release. A statement of explanation was prepared for the Conference body and presented to the Conference on September 19, 1968. The Bishop Board statement was a recommendation to Conference that they honor the Mennonite Messianic Mission request for release.

Statement to Fall Session

of

Lancaster Mennonite Conference

September 19, 1968

The Mennonite Messianic Mission has been functioning as an independent organization within the Lancaster Conference for approximately two years. At the August 15 meeting of the Bishop Board letters from bishops of the Mennonite Messianic Mission were read in which they resigned from all Conference Committees. Action on these letters was deferred until the September meeting.

At the September meeting of the Bishop Board further consideration was given to the resignations of these brethren. By proper action the Bishop Board agreed to recognize these resignations and to elect brethren to fill the unexpired terms. A vote of appreciation was recorded for the faithful services of the brethren on the committees.

At the September meeting the bishops of the Mennonite Messianic Mission presented a statement requesting "release from Conference relationships for the purpose of functioning within the objectives and activities of the Mennonite Messianic Mission organization," and that they be recognized by mutual agreement as an organization separate from Lancaster Conference. After prayerful consideration in an attitude of openness and love the Bishop Board agreed to the release of the bishops of the Mennonite Messianic Mission from Conference relationships and to recognize the organization they feel led to develop.

We do not speak of this as a withdrawal of the bishops of the Mennonite Messianic Mission and of the ministers who choose to serve with them, but as a mutual amiable agreement to have separate organizations.

It was further agreed that several brethren be elected by the Bishop Board and several brethren by the bishops of the Mennonite Messianic Mission to consult together in working out any details involved and to keep communication in working as separate organizations.

It was agreed that the fall communion services proceed as planned and that all details of working as separate organizations be approached carefully and prayerfully with adequate time for counseling members involved.

We are aware that there are difficulties involved in this far-reaching decision. However, it seemed good at this time to mutually agree as brethren to work separately in love and understanding.

Bishop Board of the Lancaster Mennonite Conference

When this statement was presented to Fall Conference, Moderator David Thomas made it clear that if Conference granted the request, there would be two separate organizations. He stated, "We have come to a very important and decisive moment in the experience of our Conference. The decision we make today will be written in large letters on the scroll of church history."[23]

Lengthy discussion followed. (The discussion here is copied from the Lancaster Conference minutes. It is obviously shortened from the actual discussion.)

John Burkholder: "If this is not a withdrawal, what is it?"

David Thomas: "Eight or ten years ago when 13 brethren withdrew, their ministry was relinquished [referring to the events which led up to the formation of the Mennonite Christian Brotherhood]. This is a release from Conference relationships. This is their request but we mutually agreed that this would bring the least frustration to the sheep. We face this with a sense of failure."

Lester Hoover: "Is our vote to agree to divide?"

David Thomas: "Yes. It is not so important where we go but how we go!"

Wilmer Eby: "We do not 'agree to divide' when the request came from one group."

23 Kenneth Auker, *Keeping the Trust*, 2013, Eastern Mennonite Publications, p. 188.

David Thomas: "In our Bishop Board meeting there was deep sharing and openness and we found this way together."

Elvin Herr: "I have a problem. I love these brethren, notice in the bishops a spirit of humility, a spirit I have not noticed before. We need these brethren. They came to this in a deep mellowing. 'How beautiful it is when brethren dwell together in peace.'"

Frank Zeager: "What alternatives are there?"

Mahlon Hess: "Could we work together within the Conference but with separate standards?"

David Thomas: "Some brethren cannot work this way."

Ira D. Landis: "We have leaders. Any group who takes a group backward and not forward are not leaders. If we are following the Word, why must we divide? Wood never splits the way we want it to split. The meetinghouses belong to Lancaster Conference. (Never in history have we sanctioned any seceding group.)"

David Thomas: "In the Bishop Board, 22 votes were 'yes;' 4 voted 'no' to this separation."

Homer Bomberger was called by David Thomas to the pulpit. Homer spoke: "We shared with appreciation of my bishop brethren as we worked together to resolve this. This is different from any period of past history. We only want to try to maintain Bible principles. As far as we are concerned, this action we take toward this is very important. We can either heal or harm. We are not here to judge but we have a conscience. The support of this is unanimous as far as we [the 3-M bishops] are concerned."

David Thomas: "I have had to repent because of injury to personal pride because of failure as moderator."

Lewis Coss: "Abraham Lincoln said, 'The Union must be preserved at every cost.' Has everything been done to be a balm to this? ...History spoke of Brethren Church-German Baptist division, 'After the division neither group had any more to offer to the world.'"

David Thomas: "We concluded yesterday with a prayer that God would overrule if this is not God's will."

James Martin: "If we vote no, what then?"

Arthur Histand: "I want to be enlightened. We are ill prepared to make a decision. This should bring all of us to repentance before God."

Jacob Musser: "What will be the responsibility of this committee?"

David Thomas: "To rise above the legal and try to find God's answer. We are not interested in fighting over buildings."

Russel Baer: "I appreciate the Mennonite Church. This can be decided only after prayer. I want my children to appreciate the Mennonite Church."

Raymond Charles: "Could we ask Aaron Shank to speak?"

Aaron Shank: "The Moderator is clarifying things well for us. We have been facing situations for some time. Folks have been suspicious of divisions. Becoming a Christian brings divisions. In our local situations we tell people to rest, as there will be no fighting over territory, buildings, etc. This will be a voluntary response. If others do not want to go with us, we will help them find the way. Differences do exist, and we must face these. I felt a sense of direction these past days that blessed and rested my own soul. If we maintain the Spirit of Christ and avoid being explosive, the blessings of the Lord should rest upon us."

Melvin Lauver: "Various areas will be affected in different ways. The very thing asked for was denied by those now involved. There must be mutual repentance."

Isaac Baer[24]: "Allow no barricades to be thrown across our route. I was with this movement from its conception. History shows us that in separation we must do so in a Christlike way in the love of God. Maintain proper attitudes. Similar movement in the Pacific Conference. Told to put down on paper. [He read the dissenting group's position.] We are in the end times when there is much apostasy. No power can keep us from following the Lord. We are losing confidence in the leadership of the Mennonite Church from coast to coast. I love and want to forgive everybody. We do not condemn any irregularities or inconsistency. The Word of God has the solution to every problem we face. The issue is not Conference rules."

Maurice Lehman: "Four hours ago we received this paper. I recommend that we wait until next Conference and give everybody time to repent."

Isaac Sensenig from pulpit: "I can feel for the audience. This is not new. I

---

24 Isaac Baer is credited for inserting the word *Messianic* in the organizational name *Mennonite Messianic Mission*. Isaac Baer was involved with Jewish evangelism at Peabody Street in Washington D.C.

sensed something in last three days that I never sensed before—a baring and openness together. There are no personality clashes involved with any bishop brethren. It is a new way to approach a problem in this way. Can we not be open to the Spirit to a new way? I feel there is a holy dignity to the way this is being handled. If this is accepted, I personally will accept it as the will of God. If it is not accepted, we will face difficulty in the days ahead. We want our people to be at ease. They will have sufficient time to decide where they go. We believe this is God's will for the hour."

Larry Wenger: "One alternative would be to table the action. What would this mean?"

Edwin Gehman: "If every district lived up to the discipline this would not be happening."

David Thomas: "This is right."

Walter Shank: "We live in a world of tension. The world looks on with horror at Russia [handling] Czechoslovakia to keep peace at any cost. If this is voted down to have peace at any cost, we are voting against our bishops."

David Thomas: "I want to be a peacemaker and devote myself anew to my call."

Noah Good: "We have watched this movement. There are equally sincere brethren on both sides. They have moved together patiently, some persistently. We have not spoiled relationships so you can come back."

H. Raymond Charles served on the Coordinating Committee and also served as temporary bishop of the Lebanon District in the days after the Eastern/Lancaster separation.

John Rohrer: "Would these brethren be welcome to share in programs?"

David Thomas: "Yes."

Frank Shirk: "At Conference meeting in the spring, it was announced that Mennonite Messianic Mission have not organized congregations. Would this mean another organization?"

David Thomas: "The new organization would not necessarily be Mennonite Messianic Mission."

Aaron Shank: "There are thirteen brethren in the Mennonite Messianic Mission. There are other people interested. The churches are not organized under Mennonite Messianic Mission."

Lester Wenger: "This is a very humiliating time. Could we come before the Lord in prayer before anything is done?"

Howard Witmer: "The purpose of the committee will be to work out any potential problems that may develop."

Pastor Nashon [from Africa]: "I have three words to say. The first—If my people pray and search my face, I will hear from heaven and heal their land. If we pray, He'll hear from heaven and help us. There are no perfect persons. God is merciful to all of us. Nobody can say they are more worthy than others. All received mercy—bishops and pastors. We are the people of God because of His mercy. When the temple was built, there were no hammers or saws. He built the House of God in silence. God help us to build the temple of God without hammers and saws. In Africa, I trembled when I heard of dividing because division is breaking much of Africa today."

Elam Stauffer: "I would request silent prayer. The issue is not if we stay together or separate, but what our <u>attitudes</u> are. What will they be if we stay together? 'By this shall all men know that ye are my disciples if ye have love for one another.'"

After a period of silent prayer, the group sang "Have Thine Own Way, Lord." Secret ballots were cast with the result of 281 votes agreeing to the honorable release and 32 against it.

The following statement was released to the *Gospel Herald, Mennonite Weekly Review,* and *Sugar Creek Budget.*

The Fall Session of Lancaster Mennonite Conference held at Mellingers Church on September 19, 1968 was a very significant Conference in the history of the church.

The bishops who are associated with the Mennonite Messianic Mission had previously requested consideration of a release from relationships to Lancaster Conference. The Bishop Board after prayerful consideration in an attitude of openness and love agreed to the release of these bishops from relationships to Lancaster Conference and to recognize the organization they feel led to develop.

The Conference in an atmosphere of serious searching and prayer took action to accept the proposal from the Bishop Board to recognize the release from relations to Lancaster Conference by these brethren.

This means that there has been a separation from Lancaster Conference and that these bishops as well as other ministers who choose to serve with them are no longer a part of Lancaster Conference but will be recognized as another group by a mutual, amiable agreement. Several bishops selected by each group will consult together in working out any details involved and to keep open communication between the separate organizations.

It was important to Aaron that his part of the separation be conducted with a nonresistant spirit. Beginning with requesting an official honorable release from Conference all the way through the process of forming a new group, a sweet, nonresistant spirit would need to prevail. He would not sanction petty disputes or infighting. That carnal spirit existed in both camps in the days following, but not in Aaron's heart. To Aaron belongs a large share of the credit for the amiable separation from Lancaster Conference. It could have been different.

On October 17, 1968, David Thomas, J. Paul Graybill, Clarence Lutz, and H. Raymond Charles were elected by the Lancaster Conference Bishop Board to work with Homer Bomberger, Ben Eshbach, Aaron Shank, and Isaac Sensenig. This eight-man group, known as the Coordinating Committee, held their first meeting at the Lancaster Conference Historical Society Building on October 29, 1968, to begin the process of working out the details of separation. David Thomas, as Moderator of Conference, served as Chairman and Raymond Charles was elected by the committee to serve as secretary.

The proposed agenda was extensive.

1) Working relations
2) Guidelines for working
3) Meeting calendar listings
4) Transfer letters
5) Specific areas needing attention
    a) Orrville Home
    b) Wisconsin
    c) Myerstown
    d) Lebanon County
    e) Weaverland District

6) *Youth Messenger*

7) Relation to World Council of Churches

During this first meeting several items were decided. First, all congregations and buildings would continue to be a part of Conference until there would be a decision otherwise. Questionable situations would be referred to the Committee for study. Second, plans for new buildings or relocating congregations would be referred to the Committee. Third, membership transfers would be made from one congregation and conference to the other. Fourth, a class action choice by ministers and deacons to associate with the conservative bishops would be recognized by Conference. Similar individual choices would be transferred individually by letter as they arose.

Later meetings included the following decisions: Public meetings held in Conference churches for approving the 3M proposed discipline needed to be cleared by the Committee. A deacon ordination at Churchtown/Mountain View by Ben Eshbach instead of the District bishop Clarence Lutz was approved. (Noah Rudolph was ordained November 30, 1968, and can be considered the first individual to be ordained under the jurisdiction of the new group.)

The fourth meeting of the Committee, held on December 27, 1968, took the following action:

> It was agreed that this committee arrange for councils to be held in the Lancaster Conference congregations where the 3M brethren are in charge. A questionnaire should be prepared by this committee to be given to each member for the purpose of discovering his relationship, whether to Lancaster Conference or to the Eastern Pennsylvania Mennonite Church. These questionnaires shall be distributed in the February 9, [1969] Sunday morning service and a mid-week meeting planned by this committee to be held within the district for the purpose of returning it. The mid-week meeting shall be led by a representative of the Lancaster Conference and the local Eastern Pennsylvania Mennonite Church bishop. Committee members are requested to give careful thought to the contents of this questionnaire. The questionnaire shall be prepared by this committee in its next meeting.

The questionnaire turned into a "council statement" which included one question, "With which group do you choose to identify?" All other questions would be decided later. The Committee meeting on January 24, 1969, issued the following:

Dear Brethren and Sisters:

At the 1968 Fall session of Conference held at the Mellinger Church on September 19, after careful consideration and prayer the Conference agreed to release the bishops associated with the Mennonite Messianic Mission from their relation to the Lancaster Conference and to officially recognize the organization they feel led to develop.

It was also agreed that several brethren be elected by the Bishop Board and several by the bishops of the Mennonite Messianic Mission to consult together in working out any details involved and to keep communication in working as separate organizations. A joint committee has been formed. The Brethren Homer Bomberger, Isaac Sensenig, Aaron Shank, and Benjamin Eshbach have been named to represent the Mennonite Messianic Mission, and J. Paul Graybill, Clarence Lutz, H. Raymond Charles, and David Thomas by the Bishop Board. The committee met several times to seek the Lord's will in working out the details.

It was further agreed that the Fall communion services proceed as planned and that all details of working together as separate organizations be approached carefully and prayerfully with adequate time for counseling members involved.

At a meeting of the joint committee on December 29, it was agreed that a statement be prepared to be given to each member in the Lancaster Conference churches where the Mennonite Messianic Mission bishops are in charge. This statement is to be given on Sunday morning, February 9. The following week meetings will be held at 7:30 p.m.: Monday, February 10, at Denver, and Tuesday, February 11, at Myerstown. Representatives of the Joint Committee will be present at these meetings. It is our concern as a Joint Committee to give members an opportunity for expression and counsel.

The new organization has chosen the name, "The Eastern Pennsylvania Mennonite Church." At these meetings your counsel will be taken on the question, "Do you desire to continue as a member in the Lancaster Conference or do you desire to be a part of the Eastern Pennsylvania Mennonite Church?" Those who cannot be present in the midweek meeting shall return their ballots to one of the bishops by Sunday morning, February 16.

The Joint Committee feels deeply that we should not decide the matter of church buildings and property deeds at this time, but hold this decision for a later time. We feel at this time we should discuss and seek to find the Lord's will as it relates to organization and relationship.

We call every member to prayer and participation in seeking the will of the Lord for the building of His church.

The Joint Committee

By meeting number 6, held on February 21, 1969, the vote was tabulated. The numbers were as follows for the Lebanon County congregations.

Yearbook Membership Listing	Congregation	Lancaster Conference	Eastern	Total Votes
52	Miner's Village	7	42	49
135	Denver	6	120	126
48	Bernville	13	22	35
63	Texter Mt.	4	50	54
130	Myerstown	55	67	122
51	Dohners	18	33	51
29	Elm Street	6	17	23
4	Grand Avenue	0	3	3
57	Kralls	26	29	45
110	Meckville	37	43	80
0	Schubert	0	4	4
69	Shirksville	6	37	43

At a later members' meeting held at Churchtown/Mountain View, all 29 members present voted to relate to the Eastern Pennsylvania Mennonite Church.

Based on the voting, separate council and communion services were held at various locations, giving members in the involved congregations the privilege to participate according to their church preference.

The following list of ordained men associated themselves with the Eastern Pennsylvania Mennonite Church at its inception. Because the movement was a release from Conference, the offices of each of these men remained intact and was transferred to the Eastern Pennsylvania Mennonite Church.

Bishops

Homer Bomberger

Simon Bucher

Benjamin Eshbach

Isaac Sensenig

Aaron Shank

Ministers	Deacons
Noah Boll	Joseph B. Boll
Paul Ebersole	Eli Burkholder
Sidney Gingrich	Eli Gehman
Earl Horst	Henry Hertzler
Amos N. Hostetter	David Lapp
Daniel Kraybill	[Noah Rudolph]
Amos W. Martin	John K. Sensenig
Edwin W. Martin	Jacob Shaub
Phares W. Martin	Samuel S. Sweigart
Wilmer Myer	Arthur Torkelson
Clyde Mellinger	Joseph Wadel
Jesse Neuenschwander	Martin M. Weaver
Walter Newswanger	Norman Wine
Aaron Sensenig	
Ralph Shank	
Landis Shertzer	
Lester Shirk	
M. S. Stoltzfus	
Roy Ulrich	
David Wadel	
W. Banks Weaver	
Henry M. Weaver	
Martin E. Weaver	
Paul M. Weaver	
Paul R. Weaver	
Paul L. Witmer	

The thorny problem of settling which group gets their respective buildings needed to be faced squarely after the spring communion season of 1969. The earlier voting had made it fairly clear that certain congregations would naturally use certain buildings. But two congregations were in question and they were large ones: Meckville and Myerstown.

The Coordinating Committee understood that the members meeting in both locations desired to remain intact as a congregation rather than be assimilated into a neighboring congregation. They also recognized that each group at both places would be considerably smaller than it had been previously.

The Committee decided that meetings should be held at Meckville and Myerstown, with Committee members from both organizations present at each meeting. In the interim, the Committee would carefully consider the matter of each congregation's identification. By April 15, 1969, the Coordinating Committee had decided on the following recommendation:

Lebanon County

Lancaster Conference	*EPMC*
Gingrich	Shirksville
Kralls	Dohners
Meckville	Elm Street
Shubert	Tower City

Denver-Myerstown

Lancaster Conference	*EPMC*
Blainsport	Denver
Green Terrace	Myerstown
	Texter Mountain
	Bernville

The work at Shubert had begun a few years prior when Walter Newswanger had bought the building. The Lebanon District wrote to Ralph Shank requesting that he move to Pennsylvania from Florida to pastor the Shubert congregation.

Prior to the scheduled meeting on April 29, 1969, at Meckville, the Eastern group had already withdrawn from the building and rented the Zeigler meetinghouse, later called Rehrersburg (now known as Little Swatara Meetinghouse of the Old German Baptist Brethren), for their activities. Aaron had written the Committee a letter stating these facts and informing the Committee that they would not contest the recommendation. To Aaron, the meeting did not need to be held. The Committee members turned the meeting into plans on how to proceed from where they were. On May 11, 1969, Meckville, the place where Aaron had expended so much time, energy, and preaching, was turned over to Lancaster Conference administration. Aaron's son, Milford, despite the fact that he would not identify with the Eastern group, could not appreciate the group which had rejected his father. He chose to make Blainsport Mennonite Church his new church home.

While the decision to keep the Meckville meetinghouse under the jurisdiction of the Lancaster Conference had been completed peaceably, the May 1, 1969 meeting at Myerstown was different. The Coordinating Committee had recommended that Myerstown go with the Eastern group, but this idea upset many Myerstown people. Petty issues were raised, such as who donated the land for the meetinghouse. During the first meeting, repeated comments were made that it was not fair for the Eastern group "to have complete control of a Lancaster Conference Church." The dismissal of Lancaster Conference Sunday School teachers hurt. Furthermore, some Lancaster Conference members felt "unwelcome by Eastern members and struggled with messages being preached…" Some Myerstown members felt that Lancaster Conference was deserting them even though they had chosen to stay with Conference.

The second meeting climaxed with a motion to "ask Lancaster Conference to hold services every other Sunday morning and alternating Sunday evenings." The motion passed with 34 in favor and 8 not in favor.

When the same motion was presented to the Eastern segment, there was a unanimous

Meckville members who chose to affiliate with the Eastern group gathered at the Ziegler meetinghouse, renamed Rehrersburg. It was rented from May to September, then purchased from the Ziegler family in October 1969.

vote against the arrangement. Some felt that a sum of money should be offered to the Conference group to help them accept the Coordinating Committee's recommendation. A motion was passed to that effect, with the added provision that the Conference group could offer the Eastern group the same sum and they would leave. There was unanimous support for this counter-proposal.

Another meeting was planned for each group by the Coordinating Committee. During their scheduled meeting, held June 24, 1969, the Eastern group decided to relinquish the building. In their letter to the Coordinating Committee they stated:

> At this juncture, however, there is much dissatisfaction expressed about the arrangement on the part of Lancaster Conference members of the Coordinating Committee and the Lancaster Conference members involved as related to Myerstown.
>
> An official request was presented [to]... share the use of the house at Myerstown....
>
> This would hinder the effectiveness of either group in church life and outreach for the congregation. It also changes the original agreement on the recommendations based on the afore-mentioned facts. We, nevertheless, are experiencing peace and a consciousness of God's blessing upon us in the midst of it all.
>
> We, therefore, the members of the Eastern Pennsylvania Mennonite Church at Myerstown, will for the sake of peace and healing relinquish our privilege to use the Myerstown Mennonite Church building in its entirety and plan to vacate it by Sunday morning, August 10, 1969...

The Committee had reasoned that if the Meckville building stayed with Conference, the Myerstown building would not. J. Paul Graybill had said earlier, "For the blessing of God to be upon the work, the Myerstown building should be a part of the Lebanon District. The people of the Myerstown Church moved into the area from elsewhere and built that building. Geographically, that building belongs to the Lebanon District."

The ready surrender of those two buildings by the Eastern group stood as a witness of practical nonresistance to those involved at that time.

In response to the meetinghouse question, Aaron included the following article titled "Church Properties" written by Jesse Neuenschwander in the October 1969 issue of the *Eastern Mennonite Testimony.*

> In times of transition and regrouping as we are experiencing today the question is frequently raised, "Who owns the church buildings?" This question usually receives a variety of answers which are dependent upon the person's vantage point or how it appears to him.

One reads and hears of church groups in conflict over meetinghouses. The situations may vary but it usually narrows down to one basic difficulty. A group of people having found themselves in disunity to the extent where continued working together is unlikely, owns a property in the form of church buildings, which, in the light of "moral propriety" belongs to everyone who is a part of the group at that point.

This is a crucial point because of many different aspects to the problem. Some will say that they hold to the original beliefs, therefore they should have priority. Others say they are the larger group, therefore they have more rights. Still others claim that they had contributed more and therefore should receive some remuneration.

Statements like these are dry tinder for the fires of conflict. There is truth in each of these statements but they simply do not arrive at the standard that is given by the "Prince of Truth."

In the recent dissolving process through which we have recently passed, and through which some are still passing, there have been some disappointments. Some of these disappointments have been due to the decisions regarding a few meetinghouses. In order to evaluate the grounds upon which such feelings prevail we must consider several facts.

In September of 1968 when sanction was given by Lancaster Mennonite Conference for the Eastern Pennsylvania Mennonite Church to exist, it looked as if finally the Mennonites could peacefully come to an agreement to take separate ways.

The spirit that prevailed at that conference session was one of peace, at least on the part of most people that were present. The idea was projected that this was not a division but a mutual agreement to have a separate organization and church program. In our minds this was a Christian approach to the problem by both parties involved.

Now after a year has passed and the meetinghouse problems have about all been settled we look over these affairs and ask ourselves a few questions.

Have those responsible to oversee the transition of property acted in the spirit of the 1968 fall conference? Have the Eastern Pennsylvania Mennonite Church brethren been regarded as secessionists or as those separated by mutual agreement? Have those congregations who found themselves in a situation where an additional building was needed been given consideration in the spirit of mutual agreement and gospel principles?

These are questions that should not be too difficult to answer. And, regardless of the answer, we wish to urge our people to accept the inconvenience of establishing a new place of worship as that which can work out for our spiritual good.

If any are disappointed, it may by good to consider the patriarch Isaac who was willing to dig another well rather than quarrel over one which someone else claimed.

Also we would remind ourselves that contending over church buildings has never brought spiritual vigor to those who were so engaged regardless of whether they won or lost.

Finally, let us prove our claim of nonresistance by accepting joyfully the loss or spoiling of our goods knowing that in heaven we have an enduring substance.

No congregation has ever suffered permanent loss by needing to build or purchase a place of worship.

The passing of time has provided some perspective regarding the bishop work of Aaron Shank and Simon Bucher. First of all, Aaron and Simon retained more of the Conference structure than the other separating Eastern bishops. Simon and Aaron continued to administrate in Eastern as they had in Lancaster Conference because so much of their work accompanied them into Eastern. They continued administrating as they had been administrating because the Lebanon District did not need to start over. They worked with many of the same people, who saw themselves as retaining the Faith as they had known it. These people were not venturing out in a more conservative direction, or returning to Old Order practices they had known from their childhood, because most of them had been raised to appreciate the standard that Lancaster Conference had seen as ideal. Furthermore, they wanted to make the conservative ideal appealing to family members whose churches were rapidly replacing Biblical obedience with worldly values. No other bishop kept as many church buildings, which tended to keep the district intact.

Aaron was the only separating bishop to have a Virginia connection. This Virginia connection, as learned first from his father John and reinforced at the feet of Bishop George Brunk I, introduced a different kind of influence as compared with the traditional Lancaster influence. This influence was positive in that it insisted upon consistency throughout, rather than satisfaction with tradition. Probably the best example of this was the tobacco issue. While Aaron never had any tolerance of tobacco growing or use, the Lancaster tradition as a whole tolerated it.

Aaron's break with Lancaster County tradition was not only in the tobacco issue. As mentioned before, his strong Biblical preaching came from vigorous study habits and the use of notes. Aaron kept careful record of where he had preached a sermon before, and kept using a sermon in order to perfect the content. Another area of break was the banning of basins in the pulpit. Traditionally, during the feetwashing service, the ministry would wash each others' feet while the membership washed each others' feet. Aaron saw this as a violation of Jesus' example of washing His disciples' feet, so he changed the tradition to the ministry mingling with the brothers when feet were washed.

Furthermore, Aaron's Virginia connection offered him a broader horizon, a broad spectrum of personal knowledge that none of the other Eastern bishops had. This broad horizon brought him in touch with many people outside Lancaster Conference. Being a Virginian by birth, and having a respected Virginia father, he was accepted by the Virginia Mennonites and naturally enjoyed a rapport with them.

One of Aaron's largest contributions to the new Eastern movement was his clear doctrinal writing and preaching. This dynamic doctrinal emphasis became a strong rallying point for others who associated with the movement at the beginning and for those joining the movement later. As an example, Richard Mummau was impressed in 1975 with Aaron's ability to interpret the Scriptures, explaining them clearly in a way that made sense. Instead of just reciting platitudes or ideas which listeners were supposed to accept because the preacher said them, Aaron put a listener's mind in gear and appealed for a response based on reasoning from the Scripture. A listener needed to think to follow Aaron's messages. His thoughts were clear in his own mind, his words were carefully chosen, and his constant reference to Biblical illustrations naturally impressed any listener. Furthermore, the messages were so dynamic and passionate that listeners could hardly resist the spiritual impact.

For Aaron there was no "fear of faces." When the Bible spoke on a matter it spoke to everyone, without partiality. Aaron would preach the same way regardless of who was in the audience. He cared more about being Scripturally right than about being diplomatic.

For years before and after Eastern began, people drove distances to hear his passionate doctrinal preaching. Many were starving for this kind of preaching. Once they got a taste of it, they hungered for more and more. Aaron was always ready to share it. While some people did not appreciate how lively and passionate Aaron could become in the pulpit, many more appreciated the life and the content of his preaching. Many people of that era owe a spiritual debt to Aaron, as the one man more than any other who helped them form a solid Scriptural base for their belief system. Preachers became better preachers under his influence. To this day people still drop comments of Aaron's words and wisdom. His legacy continues to live on.

One outgrowth of his strong emphasis on doctrine both rallied some people and alienated others—his strong premillennial position. Traditionally, Mennonites have held an amillennial eschatology and have considered premillennialism as a non-Anabaptist innovation. Areas of the church that appreciated Aaron's strong conservative emphasis because of his desire to be Biblical sometimes feared the premillennial aspects of his teaching. These ministers were less ready to expose their congregations to Aaron's preaching lest premillennial "heresy" infect the local flocks. In his zeal and with his keen intellect, he could make amillennial weaknesses look inconsistent.

Aaron's Biblical literalism naturally translated into a premillennial eschatology. He grew up under the influence of the strongly premillennial George R. Brunk I, and his family was oriented to seeing Bible prophecy from a literal standpoint. Furthermore, he lived in an era when, seemingly against great odds, Israel became a nation among the nations of the world. For many, it seemed that Bible prophecies were being fulfilled almost every day.

However, Aaron did not subscribe to all flavors of premillennialism. He refuted the errors of C. I. Scofield, whose version of premillennialism effectively canceled out the teachings of the Sermon on the Mount. Aaron believed Jesus' teaching on nonresistance was consistent with Jesus' giving Himself to die on the cross at the hands of His enemies. Likewise, when late in his life, zealous premillennialists set dates to coincide with the passing of a generation, Aaron resisted any movement that would counter the doctrine of the imminent return of Christ.

Similar to his other doctrinal positions, Aaron had thought through his premillennialism and could ably defend his understanding. To him, premillennialism was the way the future would unfold, including a place for the Jewish people to be restored to a prominent place in God's program. He maintained that if "the literal sense makes sense, it is nonsense to make any other sense." Listeners loved Aaron's clarity, passion, and the force of his presentations, deeply impressed by the breadth of his knowledge and his comprehensive understanding.

Since many of his listeners felt rather ignorant about eschatology, they naturally received his well-defined eschatology and made it their own. Even today, many people still remember Aaron in terms of his memorable pre-millennial teaching.

However, some listeners found this viewpoint difficult to receive, let alone adopt as their own. In one setting, several potential listeners refused to subject themselves to his teaching by simply refusing to attend his lectures. Others struggled when his strong statements against allegorical interpretations of the Bible made others' positions look ridiculous. There was a generation of Bible scholars in Aaron's day that tended toward vehement statements about prophecy. When time passed and proved there was too much speculation involved, the subject of prophecy began to be regarded much more objectively.

Aaron's gift to the conservative Mennonite church was his strong doctrinal preaching and conservative stand. While he was not handicapped as an organizer, he left the organizational aspects of church life to others more gifted in that respect. His doctrinal preaching and firm convictions needed the practical organization and structure that his coworkers offered. The organization offered a tangible dwelling place and rallying point for his more intangible efforts. He would often mention his appreciation for the organizational input that Isaac Sensenig, as a fellow bishop, and Jesse Neuenschwander, first as minister and then as bishop, contributed to the Eastern structure. He did not feel that because he had contributed so much to the birth of this movement that he had to continue to be the center of influence.

There is irony in Aaron's organizational abilities. From his preaching, one would assume Aaron to be one of the most personally organized men around. He was not. His memory was organized and very sharp. His files were not. His wife was organized with her matters, but he was not. Aaron considered himself to be one of the sloppiest filers around and was embarrassed by the fact.

The beginning of the Eastern movement was a precarious undertaking. The bishops involved had little history of working together other than as a part of the much larger conference body. Could these strong-minded men exercise themselves with the give-and-take necessary for the long-term survival of a new group? Observers of the emerging conservative movement could have easily wondered whether the movement would survive without fragmenting. Strong-minded men are often inflexible. Negative feelings about Lancaster Conference united these men, but negative feelings are not very constructive.

The developing Mennonite Messianic Mission movement forced the four bishops to be constructive. The voluntary service program required much positive and constructive thought and energy. This period of constructive energy took place while the bishops were still a part of Conference. Membership in Conference placed confines upon them which prevented independence. The Mennonite Messianic Mission concerns motivated action. The dual situation of conservative motivation along with Conference confines provided a firm footing for the bishops later when they were out of Conference and establishing the Eastern Pennsylvania Mennonite Church.

Furthermore, Aaron's insistence upon an honorable release from Conference, rather than recklessly and dishonorably pulling away, also offered a strong stabilizing influence for the new group. Aaron understood that once authority is disregarded, it is easily disregarded again later when new authorities are in charge. By granting an honorable release, the Conference authority granted permission and offered a blessing to the new group. From its inception, the Eastern Pennsylvania Mennonite Church was blessed with an intact sense of continuing authority. No new authority needed to be established.

This respect for authority is all the more amazing when one considers the disrespect for their own authority that the original bishops suffered. Aaron had felt mistreated by the Gingrich situation. Others observing the situation also felt that he was mistreated. But Aaron realized that he had nothing to gain by broadcasting the Gingrich situation and crying, "Foul play!" Instead, his respect for authority kept his mouth shut while he felt mistreated inside. In this case he demonstrated that issues of right are more important than personal vindication. He would demonstrate more of this same quality later.

Aaron inherited a quality of his father which bolstered respect for him as an authority figure. Like his father, he was sensitive to his own failures and mistakes. On the bishop level, he was most conscientious and ready to apologize for his mistakes or to clear offenses. This quality made it difficult for him to understand why his peers were less ready to do so. If he discovered he was wrong, he would not gloss over the matter or dismiss it, but would rather take measures to correct the wrong. He could not understand why other leaders, who were supposed to be examples to the flock, would neglect or refuse to do the same. It troubled him deeply to see his peers fail to be honest with facts and with people. Finally, he decided to do what he needed to do to clear his own conscience and leave the rest to God.

This kind of humility and refusal of "executive privilege" endeared him to many, in leadership and otherwise. Those closest to him highly respected his integrity. Those more distant were more ready to spread rumors or false charges. The distant critics did not realize the charges would fall on deaf ears because of his reputation for scrupulous honesty. One peer felt so strongly about this that he refused to take issue with Aaron on a matter because he knew Aaron would have made it right if he had actually been wrong.

Aaron was slow to speak at Board meetings. In the pulpit he tended to dominate a meeting by his keen intellect, carefully chosen words, and

Numidia Bible School teachers, c. 1989. L to R, back row: Aaron Weaver, Philip Ebersole, Isaac Sensenig; front row: Harlan Martin, Stanley Wine.

passionate delivery. Not so at Board meetings. At Bishop Board meetings he heard everything said, but he did not dominate the discussion. There he only spoke when he felt it was necessary. He never thought out loud.

Back at Meckville

On the human side, Aaron was sensitive to people moving into the Lebanon area and refusing to become part of the Lebanon District. For him, the geography should determine the church district. When newcomers came to the area unacquainted with Lebanon District administration and insisted upon another kind of administration, joint projects like the Myerstown School suffered some disjointedness.

While the Lancaster Conference-Eastern Pennsylvania Mennonite Church separation was an action of two organizations, church life is largely experienced by individuals relating to one another. The pivotal separation caused individual stories to develop in response to the group action.

One Sunday morning in 1966, Meckville Pastor Cletus Doutrich had called Aaron to ask if he could read a statement to the congregation. Aaron assumed that it was of a personal nature and told him that he could. He later realized that he should have asked the pastor to read the statement to him first.

J. Paul Graybill, a staunchly conservative Lancaster Conference bishop, did not join the Eastern group but appreciated the reasons for its formation. He called the separation "a division based on doctrine."

That morning Cletus preached about the disciples toiling all night with their fishing but catching nothing. He applied that to himself; he was "catching nothing." At the close of the message he read his prepared statement to the effect that he felt it was God's will that he resign his ministry. Then he led a benedictory prayer.

While he was praying, Aaron moved to the speaker's stand. At the close

of the prayer Aaron said to the congregation, "This is a total surprise to me. But since our brother feels like this is the will of the Lord, we will need to accept that."

Cletus continued to attend Meckville after his resignation. He attended some of the Mennonite Messianic Mission meetings, but did not like the spirit he sensed there. Meckville needed a minister; therefore a vote was taken at Meckville as to whether or not to restore Cletus's ministry. The vote did not carry.

Early in 1968, Amos W. Martin was ordained to replace Cletus. Amos chose to identify with Eastern when Meckville divided, whereas Cletus stayed with Meckville. With his ministry eventually restored, Cletus left Meckville several years later to identify with the Mid-Atlantic Fellowship.

Deacon Steve Olesh at Meckville told Aaron one day, "You are changing. We need good evangelical preaching. People get tired of hearing rules and discipline all the time." Personally, Steve no longer enjoyed Aaron's preaching, and he felt that messages like Aaron's message titled "The Danger of the Neutral Position" were reactionary in nature. He did not believe the threat was as serious as Aaron was making it. Steve felt like he was growing in his spiritual walk, but that an appropriate spiritual emphasis was missing at Meckville.

These differences between Steve and Aaron were honest differences, coming from two very different backgrounds. Steve was concerned about people in the church who gave little evidence of the New Birth but who kept the forms of the church very well. In Steve's mind, Aaron was less concerned about such conditions. He perceived Aaron to have the mentality "This is the way you must be or you are not my brother." Aaron's emphases on obedience and loyalty caused him to believe that Aaron was lacking in real spiritual interest. So he asked Aaron, "Are people who are not Mennonites Christians?"

"Yes, depending on how well they live up to the light they have."

"Are they your brothers then?"

"Well, yes, but we must maintain what we know the Bible teaches."

The deacon honestly wondered if a Christian could be that narrow and Aaron honestly wondered if a Christian could be that broad.

When Aaron moved out of Steve's life, something significant for the deacon moved out too. It troubled him somewhat. Much later, in 1996, he admitted, "Maybe we should have rallied around Aaron and stood with him. His prophecy of the church drift has proven true. I didn't think it would go the way it did."

Aaron had told his congregation publicly that if some members want a more liberal church, they ought to go to one. "We're going to maintain a conservative congregation here. Church membership is voluntary. We are not compelled to come in nor compelled to stay in. We don't enjoy seeing people leave, but if people are unhappy with their church life, they can hardly receive the benefits needed for spiritual life." Aaron believed that churches have both a front door, to welcome newcomers, and a back door, through which the dissatisfied are permitted to leave.

Some did leave. Some could not accept Aaron's administration and left. They felt that Aaron's discipline was harsh and unsympathetic. After Aaron left Meckville, they returned to Meckville. Others came from the other district churches when they had chosen not to relate to the new group. Before long Meckville had returned to its previous size in numbers.

At home, Aaron's children suffered from the fallout of church stress. Richard had left before the church stresses got heavy. Milford married in early 1965, still struggling with the issues of his own heart. About the time the Mennonite Messianic Mission got under way, Ruth suddenly turned away contrary to her parents' wishes. Louise was struggling with the pull of her peers.

Milford continued to work for his father after he was married. He saw him bear an enormous load of stress. In Milford's eyes, his father was "waging war" against worldly trends in the church. Both he and the family doctor were concerned about Aaron's physical and emotional health.

Afterward

Time and change marched on. The gap between the new Eastern Pennsylvania Mennonite Church and the Lancaster Conference rapidly widened. The conservatives were no longer exerting their influence for practical nonconformity and loyalty to the Discipline. J. Paul Graybill, who opposed the separation but who had an appreciation for the basic reasons for it, one day at a Bishop meeting called upon his fellow bishops to consider Aaron's eloquent February, 1968, statement to the Bishop Board. Graybill's statement to the rest of the Bishop Board has become classic in its own right: "This is a division based on doctrine."

In 1963 Aaron preached at the Warwick River congregation in Virginia, the former strong conservative congregation that had been home to his parents before they moved to Harrisonburg. After the benediction, Aaron said to the pastor, "For all practical purposes the headship covering here is gone."

"I did not like Aaron's preaching when I was young. Now I realize how right he was"

—Ann(a) (Olesh) Showalter, 2019

Granddaughter of John and Anna Olesh

Member at Meckville in her youth

The pastor looked Aaron in the face and said, "And if that is true, you will write it off too within the next ten years." The Warwick River pastor did not know this Warwick River son, a man willing to pay the price for conviction, stability, and loyalty to the Word of God.

Editor of the *Eastern Mennonite Testimony*

The newly-formed Eastern Pennsylvania Mennonite Church decided to launch its own periodical and chose Aaron Shank as its first editor. *The Eastern Mennonite Testimony* issued its first number in July 1969. The introduction reported:

> On November 22, 1968 at the Mennonite Messianic Mission Informative Meeting at Denver, Pennsylvania, there was a vote taken to see if the supporting group would favor such a work. There were 106 votes in favor of the periodical and none opposing it...

Our aim is to produce a publication that will inform us of each other's activities, give technical cohesion to the group, and provide a historical record from this point on.

There will be articles and editorials which will reflect our basic faith as well as a proper and practical practice.

Aaron M. Shank has consented to serve as editor of the publication. Associate editors are Isaac Sensenig and Paul R. Weaver...

His very first editorial in the July 1969 issue illustrates well the way Aaron approached his assignment. His one point was well developed with Scripture and history and yet included wit, vigor, and freshness.

IN THE BEGINNING

This issue of The <u>Eastern Mennonite Testimony</u> is the beginning of a new paper the Eastern Pennsylvania Mennonite Church plans to publish in the interest of the Christ and the Church it represents.

The title of this article is a quotation of the first three words of the Book of God. God Himself was not now just beginning, but He was beginning to take action on the decisions of the Triune Committee of eternity.

These words also represent the beginning of God's Publication of His activities and His never-dying message to mankind. God wanted to share this information with His creatures and so He published a Book.

Age-wise, this message from God may be considered old because it has long ago been given to man. However, in character it is always young and fresh because that which cannot die cannot grow old either.

Since the beginning of the "very good" work of God recorded in Genesis 1, there have been many beginnings designed by God to accomplish His purposes in the world.

Following the failure of Adam's sinful race and the destruction of the world of sinful man by the flood, God effected a new beginning with Noah and his family.

God found it necessary again to establish a new beginning in Abraham and called him out of his idolatrous environment to keep His remembrance and His mercy alive on the earth.

The Gospels are a record of another great new beginning. St. Mark calls it "the beginning of the Gospel of Jesus Christ."

Pentecost marked the beginning of a new experience and power given to man.

Peter said, "The Holy Ghost fell on them as on us 'at the beginning.'"

Doubtless the 16th century Anabaptist testimony was another beginning in the good providence of God to bring light to the long night of a thousand years of religious corruption.

In this 20th century with the darkness of the end-time increasing in intensity may we humbly pray that on the "Eastern" horizon there may again be seen a new beginning that is directed and blessed of God for our day.

"In the beginning" of this publication and as long as our Lord shall grant us mercy to continue its publication, it shall be our purpose to share the kind of Testimony that will inspire the practice of that which is as old as the beginningless eternity, and just as fresh and young because truth is immortal.

Aaron's imprint and impact are readily discerned in the *Testimony*. His thirty-eight editorials during his five-year tenure reflect his spoken word. So do his eleven other articles. Still respecting his father at age fifty-eight, he included an unfinished article by his father in the April 1973 issue. He also included twelve articles by his brother Ralph. He frequently used quotes from his former mentor, George R. Brunk. News and details from the Lebanon District were sure to be included.

Aaron's gifts are also illustrated by the cover design of the *Testimony*. Aaron insisted that the two verses that are still on the front cover be included. "Be not thou therefore ashamed of the testimony of our Lord" (2 Timothy 1:8) and "To the law and to the testimony: if they speak not according to this word, it is because there is no light in them" (Isaiah 8:20). These verses still communicate Aaron's legacy.

Aaron discussed his assignment as editor in his final editorial in June 1974.

FIVE YEARS AS EDITOR

With this issue of the <u>Eastern Mennonite Testimony</u> we conclude five years of monthly releases. The <u>Testimony</u> is published by the Publication Board of the Eastern Pennsylvania Mennonite Church and Related Areas. For this publication the editor was first appointed for a two-year term and since that time has been appointed annually. At the appointment a year ago the editor committed himself for the coming year with a request to be relieved at the end of the year. The end of this fiscal year is now here. The board honored this request and has asked Brother Daniel N. Kraybill, Route 2, Dillsburg, Pennsylvania 17019 to assume this responsibility....

The Publication Board has eased the editor's work considerably by helping to decide on subjects for articles and assigning them to different writers. This has helped to broaden the scope of The Testimony and keep it well balanced....

One of the Mennonite editors of the past is said to have rewritten his first editorial twenty-five times. This editor has had similar experiences....

Editors are responsible to see that articles are easy to read, easy to understand, and that they make a spiritual contribution to the cause. They have the tremendous responsibility in having the last word in what may or may not be published. Obviously, like bishops and janitors, they can't please everybody.

During these short five years of editing, the responses in general to the editorial changes that were made have been appreciative. Editors must run the risk of resentful reaction toward them for changes they feel need to be made.

The editor needs your prayers. If you neglected to pray for the editor of the past, ask God to forgive you and pledge yourself to faithfulness in remembering the new editor.

May the Eastern Mennonite Testimony continue to fill a need in the Church and be the stabilizing witness needed in these days of extremism and negligence.

AMS

P.S. Editors need editing sometimes too. This is the publication board's responsibility.

Homer Bomberger

After the Eastern church was formed, not everything functioned smoothly. Some disturbances soon developed in relation to Homer Bomberger, one of the founding bishops.

In contrast to the organizational skills of other bishops, Homer used his relational skills to lead his flock. While Homer's "pastoral" style of leadership was appreciated by his church members, his broader responsibilities demanded an administrative style that was able to keep abreast of the wide variety of issues facing the church. Some did not feel that he was able to do that.

Frustrations soon developed on the administrative level. Homer placed a high value on the need for consensus among those under his leadership. Discussion of issues was welcomed and input would come from a wide variety of sources. While this offered Homer a broad view of any one particular issue, some felt that he was slow to bring the matter to a definitive conclusion. Homer would be satisfied with an acknowledgment of general support from the group and would consider the matter at rest.

Homer was not viewed as being "strongly conservative" by most of those within Eastern's leadership. In general, the two ministers at White Oak were perceived as being more aggressive in maintaining a conservative position. Aaron reminded the White Oak ministry that Homer held the same convictions as he did when he came out of Conference.

When Homer and the White Oak ministry requested help, Aaron and Ben Eshbach were appointed to assist Homer in the White Oak District. This arrangement also frustrated Homer. He said, "You can't have two queens in one hive." With the support of his family, Homer considered resigning. When he suggested the possibility of resigning, Aaron discounted the idea. When he presented Homer's resignation to the Bishops and the White Oak District, Aaron assumed neither body would accept it. To his surprise, they did.

A meeting was held at White Oak to consider Homer's resignation. The discussion became heated. Aaron tried to assist Homer in obtaining an honorable resignation. At first Homer's supporters desired to work with him within the Eastern Pennsylvania Mennonite Church. Elmer Snavely, the deacon at Miners Village, along with twenty-five brethren, had signed a petition requesting the Miners Village meetinghouse and Homer as bishop. The bishops refused this request.

As the matter drew to a close, Homer was clearly disappointed in Aaron. Later, in an apology written to Homer, Aaron shared his feeling that there should have been a "more redemptive way to deal with the whole situation." The May issue of *The Eastern Mennonite Testimony* presented an open written statement concerning the problem.

Statement of Proceedings Regarding Brother Homer Bomberger's Status

in the Eastern Pennsylvania Mennonite Church

On October 6, 1971 the Eastern Pennsylvania Mennonite Church bishops received a letter of appeal from the White Oak Ministry asking for some administrative help due to some unrest that existed within the district.

Accordingly, on October 20, 1971 the bishops met with the White Oak District Ministry at which time there was a unanimous vote from the White Oak District Ministry to recommend to the membership of the White Oak District that two bishops be asked to assist in some of the administrative work of the district. The following statement outlining procedures was also agreed upon to recommend to the membership of the district at a members' meeting called for on November 1, 1971:

We recommend that two bishops serve with Brother Homer Bomberger in the bishop responsibility of the district. Their term of service shall be for two years.

Their responsibility shall be as follows:

1. Brother Homer Bomberger shall have charge of moderating the District Minister's meetings.

2. Brother Homer shall continue to have charge of the marriage ceremonies in the district.

3. Applicant instruction and baptism shall be in charge of Brother Homer in consultation with the bishop helpers.

4. One of the bishops shall assist Brother Homer in the Councils and Communions.

5. Any other details shall be worked out as the need arises.

After considerable discussion in the members' meeting there was a motion made and seconded that this recommendation be accepted. By ballot vote the recommendation was approved. The brethren Benjamin Eshbach and Aaron M. Shank were elected by the bishops to serve with Brother Bomberger in the capacity outlined above.

At a later meeting of the bishops held December 10, 1971 Brother Homer presented a request that he be given a bishop retirement status in the Eastern Pennsylvania Mennonite Church. Upon this request the bishops agreed to release Bro. Bomberger of his administrative responsibilities for an indefinite period of time.

We wish to express our appreciation for the untiring efforts Brother Bomberger has given to the work of the Church in the past. We regret that some misunderstandings and misrepresentations have been circulated about this matter, which, as usual, has given the enemy occasion to reproach the worthy name and cause of Christ. May we all pray for each other that the purposes of God might be fulfilled in us.

Eastern Pennsylvania Mennonite Church Bishops

Even before this announcement appeared in print, new developments were taking place.

The very next issue (June 1972) of *The Eastern Pennsylvania Mennonite Testimony* announced:

> Inasmuch as there has been a refusal on the part of a number of members of the White Oak District to hear the voice of the church in relation to the current problems of the district, and
>
> Inasmuch as this group has now formed a new church organization, and
>
> Inasmuch as Homer Bomberger, Samuel Miller, and Elmer Snavely have supported those members of the White Oak District who have refused to accept the church's action, their membership in the Eastern Pennsylvania Mennonite Church, in keeping with the teaching of Matthew 18:17 and the discipline of the Church, is now terminated.
>
> The Eastern Pennsylvania Mennonite Church door remains open with an invitation to any such who at any time would desire to return to their former church fellowship.
>
> Eastern Pennsylvania Mennonite Church Bishops

Six years later, in 1978, Homer helped found the Mid-Atlantic Mennonite Fellowship.

Dublin, Georgia

In 1969, Wilmer Shenk was ordained as deacon in the newly formed Rehrersburg congregation. He served a few years there, performing well in his office. Aaron enjoyed working with him.

Before long, he claimed that cold weather was bothering his leg in which he had suffered blood poisoning as a child. He began scouting around in the South for a new location to live. He found what he was searching for in Dublin, Georgia, convincing him that the Lord was calling him there. Without informing the local ministry or his bishop, Wilmer agreed to purchase the Dublin property.

Sensing that Wilmer was a bit secretive, Aaron opened the subject by stating, "I sense a secretiveness about your interest in going south that gives me some concern."

Wilmer responded, "I need to move south. The Lord opened the way by having everything fall into place. We looked other places but nothing opened for us until we found the Dublin property. We have salted down the land."

The statement implied that a reversal of course was no longer possible.

Wilmer moved his family to Dublin and asked Aaron for assistance in starting a church there. Aaron was ready to assist Wilmer, even though the move to Dublin was a bit irregular. The other bishops were much more cautious in their view of the situation. In response to Aaron's request, Wilmer wrote an apology to the church at Rehrersburg as well as to the bishops. Aaron felt that his apology should be accepted. Not everyone was ready to do so.

In the end, the bishops agreed that he should retain his deacon office and that the Lebanon District could help Wilmer establish a church at Dublin, Georgia. The first service was held in July 1974.

The fifth decade of Aaron's life was marked by rapid change and organizational uncertainties. The passing of time also removed Simon Bucher from the earthly scene. A slow deterioration of health finally culminated in an incapacitating stroke. Simon "slipped away" on July 5, 1972, aged 85 years. Aaron always felt that Simon "was a man sent by God" who brought a new vitality and spiritual dynamic to the Lebanon District.

The calendar read 1975. Aaron Shank was sixty years old.

Overleaf: Aaron's premillennial eschatology found visual form in this chart. It is based closely on one made by Aaron Shank; references added by Steve Ebersole.

Time is a Parenthesis Within Eternity
2 Pt. 3:8; 1Cor. 15:19,28
Time Came out of Eternity
and Will Move Back Into Eternity

Eternity Past
Psalm 90:2
John 1:1-3

Creation
Gen 1:2
Heb 1:10
Col 1:16
Job 38:4-8

Innocence

Adam to Abram

Conscience

Earth

O.T. Paradise
Isa 5:14; Pro 27:20
Rev 9:2-3; 11:7
Bottomless Pit
Num 16:33

Earth

Place of Comfort

Paradise

OT & NT Saints
"My Father's House," John 14:2
"Depart and Be With Christ," Php 1:23

The Indignation Sear of Christ
2 Cor. 5:8-11 ; Rom 4:10-15

The Marriage Supper of the Lamb
Rev 19:1-10

RAPTURE
1Th 4:13-18
1Th 2:1

REVELATION

Satan and his host
cast out of Heaven

70th Week - Dan 9:24 & 27

The Great Tribulation

Armageddon

Satan Bound
Rev 20:1-3

Final
Defeat
of Satan
Rev 20:10

Wicked judged
and cast into
the Lake of Fire

Eternity Future
Dan 12:3
1 Cor 15:24-28
Eph 2:7
1 Th 4:17

A New Earth

A New Heavens

Lake of Fire

Satan bound and cast into
the pit for a thousand years.
REV 20:1-3,7

Beast and False
Prophets cast
alive into the
Lake of Fire
Rev 19:20; 20:10

Original Chart by Aaron M. Shenk
Revised by H. Stephen Ebersole
Drawn by Justin M. Ebersole
February 2006

CHAPTER 8

Serious Sixties

THE DECADE FROM 1975 to 1985 can be characterized as Aaron's restful, golden years. For nearly all his married life he had been a church leader. By taking upon himself the responsibility to arrest the drift in the Lancaster Conference, he bore the rigor of many battles in defense of Biblical conservatism. The decade just past, 1965 to 1975, was the scene of the most heated battles.

With the honorable release from Conference, Aaron entered a phase of life that he had never experienced before. Instead of ministerial meetings bristling with conflict, the ministerial meetings were restful. The District ministry was united in its goals, outlook, and methods of operation. The church was at peace and it was growing.

From a total membership of about 200 at Rehrersburg, Dohner, Shirksville, Elm Street, and Tower City combined when the Eastern Pennsylvania Mennonite Church formed, the Lebanon District membership had climbed to almost 600 by 1985. The five congregations had doubled to ten.

Once again Aaron was working as a team partner with Sidney Gingrich, ordained bishop in 1972 to assist him. Aaron had loved the team arrangement he had learned from Simon Bucher and he always had the deepest appreciation for his working relationship with Sidney. While Sidney said that he always felt like Aaron's "little boy" in comparison to Aaron's doctrinal understanding, he also testified that Aaron always respected him.

Furthermore, in 1980 Alvin Snyder was ordained to assist in the administration of Tower City, Hartleton, and Danville. Here again the teamwork concept came into practice. Alvin assisted Aaron for a number of years with the understanding that gradually Alvin would shoulder more of the load with the intent of a separate district growing out of this arrangement.

The later 1985 ordination of a successor to Aaron did not include the churches Alvin Snyder shepherded. This arrangement was tailored as part of the effort at creating a northern district.

On the overall church scene, Aaron served as Chairman of the Bishop Board from its beginning as a distinct entity in 1978 until 1989. Prior to that there were no separate Bishop Board meetings; Mennonite Messianic Mission committee meetings filled that executive role. Homer Bomberger had been the first chairman and when he resigned, Aaron filled that role. After the Mennonite Messianic Mission committee meetings were separate from the Bishop Board meetings, Aaron served as chairman of both boards. In 1989, when stress was developing relative to

Aaron and Marjorie on their 42nd anniversary, 1982.

the Lebanon District, Aaron requested that he would not be re-nominated to the chairmanship of the Bishop Board.

Disturbing Winds

Already by 1975, something was in the air which bothered Aaron. The Lebanon District was largely at rest and the disturbing aspects entered the air from outside the district. The following letter from the neighboring Richland District disturbed and challenged Aaron.

TO THE BISHOP BRETHREN OF THE EASTERN PENNSYLVANIA MENNONITE CHURCH AND RELATED AREAS

Dear Brethren,

Greetings in the Name of our Lord and Savior.

At a meeting of the ordained brethren of the Richland, Texter, Bernville, and New England Valley congregations, held on January 17, 1976 at the Richland Meetinghouse, it was decided to present a written appeal to you, the bishops, for consideration in the near future.

We are appealing for a placing of confidence that will make our continued working together not only possible but also a joy and a blessing. The spiritual welfare of our congregations demands "that ye all speak the same thing, and that there be no divisions among you, but that ye be perfectly joined together in the same mind and in the same judgment." (1 Cor. 1:10)

In efforts to help a number of members to an attitude of loyalty and full support of the church, difficulties were encountered which we believe are traceable, in part, to a lack of unity between the Lebanon and Richland Districts in the administration of the discipline of the Church. A matter of special concern to us is the influence of Bro. _____ in relation to members who are under church censure in the Richland congregation. Expressing a lack of confidence in disciplinary measures taken by properly authorized brethren serves to give encouragement to rebellious attitudes and blocks the road to spiritual help for those who need it.

Dear Brethren, it is with confidence, that you as well as we, desire the very best in spiritual care for the church. It is our desire to fulfill our obligations as ordained brethren to work in harmony with the discipline of the church, both in principle and in spirit. We also desire to grow in effectiveness as servants of Christ and the Church and invite correction if error on our part has been discerned.

May the God and Father of our Lord Jesus Christ hear our prayer to frustrate the efforts of the Devil to accomplish our ruin and give us grace to stand together as leaders of the Church in the task of winning and feeding souls for His glory and praise.

Sincerely,

The Richland District Ministry

Aaron responded to the letter by writing a letter of his own to the Bishop Board the following month. His letter clearly portrays the non-divisive, yet perceptive, perspective from which he administrated in the Lebanon District.

Bishops of the Eastern Pennsylvania Mennonite Church

Dear Brethren:

Greetings.

This letter is a personal observation of, and response to, the letter from the Richland District Ministry addressed and read to the bishops at White Oak on January 21, 1976. That letter, I believe, expresses a sincere desire on the part of those presenting it for peace and unity and loyalty.

When Bro. Isaac said he told the Richland ministry, in connection with their concerns, that we do not want to think in terms of division and that he is sure Aaron is not interested in division, he was speaking the truth, not only for me but for our Lebanon District as a whole.

The letter, however, I feel is highly suggestive that the Richland brethren must have been thinking in these terms. The statement at least implies that the Lebanon District is not working with the discipline and that a continuing working together will not be possible unless the Lebanon District will employ the same wholesome methods of discipline that the Richland District employs.

It is not my intention to justify any weaknesses or failures on the part of the Lebanon District. God knows, and we humbly confess, that we have plenty of them. We have lots of room for improvement both as shepherds and as disciplinarians.

Neither is it my intention to justify the one personality that is brought into focus and is indicted in the letter. God knows, and that person knows, that he has human tendencies and weaknesses. However, I do believe that if those his accusers were to look carefully into their own past procedures, I doubt they could cast a single stone....

Since the withdrawal of the Richland District from our school came into focus at our meeting on January 21, I would like to present a few questions. In presenting these questions I want it understood that we are not prejudiced in any way against the Milbach School. We need this school and are thankful for its existence.....

In spite of faulty procedures related to the writing of the Myerstown School Constitution, which we humbly confessed and asked forgiveness for, was it wrong for the Lebanon District as the owners and the parent of the Myerstown School to assume the responsibility of drawing up a Constitution for their own school?...

Was it consistent for the Milbach School to indict the Myerstown School operation on a number of points and then proceed to do the same things in their own school? One of their ministry told me that he told the Milbach Board that they are doing everything in the Milbach School that they condemned in the Myerstown School....

It seems to us that it goes without question that in spite of our Lebanon District weaknesses, undue prejudices have been building up against the Lebanon District for years on the part of the Richland District and perhaps in a lesser degree on the part of most of the Eastern Pennsylvania Mennonite Church....

Bro. Herbert Ebersole has told me more than once that the Lebanon District is being repeatedly stigmatized to his son Stephen in the Honeybrook area....

I am sure I speak for the Lebanon District as a whole when I say that we appreciate the Eastern Pennsylvania Mennonite Church and we desire to be an integral and faithful part of it. If, however, we have done anything worthy of death, we "refuse not to die."

Maybe the Church needs the critical and competitive aspects that this letter represents, but it seems to me that it is an indication of deterioration rather than of strength. It may be good for us at times to suffer at the hands of each other, but if this thing continues too long, the fellowship will cool off and our Church structure will crumble. I believe that the Eastern Pennsylvania Mennonite Church stands today as a miracle and monument of Divine grace. May we humbly appreciate what God has wrought among us and exercise the spirit, love, and loyalty that will keep us in His love.

Perhaps the most imperative need of our fellowship today is a renewal of our first love, warmth, and devotion to our Lord and to the brotherhood which we had experienced at the time of the inception of the Eastern Pennsylvania Mennonite Church. Remember?

If we cannot allow for some variation or applications without gossiping about, labeling, stigmatizing, and branding each other, and threatening a break in fellowship, I see little hope for the future of our Church....

In Christian love,

Aaron M. Shank

The matters at Richland did not rest. Letters came to the Bishop Board in late 1980 expressing concern that Bishop Earl Horst was too tolerant in his bishop administration. One letter from a minister encouraged Earl's removal from the Bishop Board. While the Bishop Board grappled with the dissatisfaction in the Richland District, Aaron pled for tolerance and unity. Aaron was unwilling to be divisive and heavy-handed when dealing with Earl.

**FIRST
TERM
TEACHERS**

**SECOND
TERM
TEACHERS**

**THIRD
TERM
TEACHERS**

Numidia Mennonite Bible School teachers and cooks, 1977.

**FOURTH
TERM
TEACHERS**

COOKS

COOKS

From the Bishop Board meeting held on March 12, 1981, the minutes state:

> There was a lengthy discussion on the problem and what we should be doing now as a bishop group to help matters. The following approach was decided upon:
>
> A. By ballot voting the following bishops were appointed: David Wadel and Jesse Neuenschwander. They will be responsible to work as the following statement reads. This statement shall be read in the Richland Congregation.
>
> B. In light of appeals that have come to the bishop group and since there are some problems and disunity and since there is some feeling of uncertainty about Bro. Isaac Sensenig's role in the Richland District, we state the following:
>
> 1. That we ask Bro. Isaac to work directly with the Richland District and be in charge. Bro. Earl and Bro. Carl will assist him. He will continue taking the leading role until such a time as things are cleared to go on. We come to this conclusion because of the steps that were taken when the separate districts were formed, Richland and Denver, and the place that Bro. Isaac had in that.
>
> 2. We are asking two bishops to meet with the Richland District Ministry in an effort to adjust the points of dissatisfaction and recommend corrections that may be needed among the ministry in order to establish the confidence that is needed to work together harmoniously. By ballot voting the following brethren, David Wadel and Jesse Neuenschwander, were appointed.
>
> These two bishops will report this communication to the Richland District and will also bring recommendations back to the bishops where further action may be needed.

The Bishop Board minutes for August 25, 1981 state:

> There was a question on the situation with Earl Horst and Edwin Gehman. At the present it is obvious that Earl Horst and Edwin Gehman and the group with them have interests that are not with our church group. Earl Horst has officially withdrawn from our church and Edwin has been working with him. So we are herewith recognizing the fact that they are no longer a part of our church group.

To Earl Horst, the matter looked differently. He was the second bishop to lose his place on the Bishop Board. He was grateful for Aaron's effort to grant him an honorable release, even though it was not forthcoming.

In a letter to the Lebanon District Ministry written much later, Aaron tried to analyze what he was sensing back in the period of 1975 to 1985.

> For this survey I have depended on minutes, on memory, and on notes taken in

our meetings in bygone years. Since minutes are not infallible and memory is sometimes faulty and notes taken in a hurry may at times be unduly slanted or biased in a certain direction, this report is not claimed to be infallibly accurate. It is, however, an honest effort to give an accurate account of happenings over the past year and beyond.

In sharing this information and analysis I do not mean to be unduly critical of my fellow workers in the vineyard of the Lord. This information therefore is not intended to label or stigmatize any group, person, or church activity. The Apostle Paul did at times share his experiences of mistreatment. However, at the close of his life, in speaking of mistreatment he declared "not that I had ought to accuse my nation of." Although he did share some of his abuses and mistreatment, he was careful not to pass judgment on his accusers. I want to use that same kind of carefulness. I would say, further, that I believe some or many of the accusations against me or against the District have been valid and helpful. I would be the first person to confess being in need of help from my brethren. It is the continued stress and strained relationships that keep surfacing and focusing on the district, and the judgmental and apparent unforgiving spirit which concerns us most. What we can do to be assured of the blessing of God is therefore the burden of this message and our meeting today.

Hence, the information and evaluations shared herewith are to help us ascertain what would be the best for us as we face the future. We want to again lay ourselves and our needs before the Lord and seek His direction and blessing for the few remaining moments we may have yet to serve Him here in this world.

From the inception of our Eastern Pennsylvania Mennonite Church fellowship the Lebanon District has been looked upon by an element in the church with a degree of suspicion and as somewhat of an inferior, unsafe part of our fellowship. At one time I told the bishops that if we must be looked upon as the black sheep of the E.P.M.C. we want to be the very best little black sheep possible.

In a letter to _____ by a brother from another district, whose name we prefer not to share, the writer gives some rather interesting observations in relation to the above concepts, and I quote in part:

'...It seems that this friction or problem has come, not so much because we do not believe alike, but rather because the leadership and people of the Lebanon District as a whole have been more tolerant and considerate....

Part of this can be explained by the fact that to a large extent the Lebanon District likely has the largest concentration of Lancaster Conference people, whereas most of the other districts are made up of people who come from Horning or Old Order background. So you have people with differing backgrounds and teaching coming up with differing conclusions and applications....

As I study church history and observe people, I am made painfully aware that as a conservative people we often tend to become very intolerant toward other church groups or even within our own brotherhood when in reality we are nearly alike in faith and practice. I am not necessarily favoring a conservative ecumenical movement, but at least we should have mutual respect for one another....'

It was only a few years after our church was formed that the White Oak Ministry became seriously dissatisfied with Bro. Homer Bomberger's bishop administration. As the going became more difficult for Bro. Homer, to the point where he felt like resigning, he and his wife Naomi told me repeatedly that when they are out of the way, judging from what they have heard, I would be the next target for extinction. Bro. Homer resigned from his bishop responsibility in the E.P.M.C. about three years after its inception. The Bishop Board accepted his resignation. Bro. Homer was not dealt with by the Bishop Board but shortly after his resignation of bishop responsibility a group of brethren appealed to him for leadership. Bro. Homer responded and the Mid-Atlantic Fellowship was thus begun.

When Bro. Earl Horst withdrew from E.P.M.C. he made predictions similar to those of Bro. Homer and Sis. Naomi.

About [1979] my relationship with the church was severely threatened over the maternity cape issue. I was told at one of our bishop meetings that the honorable thing for me to do would be to resign. Another bishop followed saying that we might as well finalize this thing right now. A third bishop squelched the thing by telling them that we are not parting ways today and that they were to get that out of their heads [immediately]. Other threats could be cited. These examples are not cited to cast reflection on anyone but rather to illustrate a perpetual situation that continues to exist among us today....

Why do these problems exist in a Christian brotherhood? The answers are not easy. We should perhaps first of all and most of all examine and censure ourselves. It is very rare indeed that in conflict and stress one side is altogether to blame and the other side is altogether blameless (except in the conflict between God and Satan), but many times it is true that one side is basically at fault. In the case of Job and his critics, Job was basically right and his critics were basically wrong. It seems, however, in his defense Job may have become overly defensive of his integrity and God had to deal with him for it. If, indeed, we know how to do it we should be very humble when criticized and careful not to be too justifying of ourselves. Perhaps the easiest thing for us to do when we are criticized is to quickly look for something to criticize the criticizer until it becomes a vicious back and forth fault-finding process. We may then bite and devour one another until we be consumed one of another. God forbid!

In reality, I think we must agree that there are "differences of administration" and "diversities of operations" from district to district.

Sometimes stresses develop over a slight variation of application of principles and a lack of tolerance for differences of opinion on application.

As I understand the purpose of our church discipline, it is not to replace or add to the Bible, but is rather to help us to have a reasonable degree of uniformity in applying and practicing the principles of the Bible.

Our discipline is our church's formula for successfully practicing and maintaining Bible truth. It is our interpretation and application of a practical way of expressing and keeping alive principles whose application is not specifically outlined in the Scriptures. How often to hold communion services, a consistent veiling pattern and modesty in dress would be a few examples where the Bible gives the principle without spelling out practice. In our applying and in our promotion of the discipline we often refer to the spirit of the discipline as a basis for regulating on items not specifically spelled out in the Bible or in the discipline. Our social activities and hair arrangements would be a few examples.

It seems it is in the area of districts making their own applications to the E.P.M.C. Discipline's application of the Word that we find ourselves in a slight degree of differing emphases from time to time. It is not in the area of working with and applying the written discipline that there is any conflict.

Another area of stress grows out of the consensus that is sometimes taken at our Church-wide Ministerial Meetings. For some of the bishops and ministers the concepts embodied in a consensus vote is considered authentic and binding. Any hesitation to promote or administer consensus items is looked upon with disapproval. However, the Guidelines for the Church-wide Ministers Meeting states that 'this group does not...have equal or superior authority to the District Ministry.'

In Article VIII, Number 1 the discipline states: 'This statement of Christian doctrine and rules and discipline shall be the working standard of the congregations and ordained Brethren of the Eastern Pennsylvania Mennonite Church and Related Areas. This is considered the minimum standard.'

Sometimes when our administration has been criticized on the Bishop Board we have asked our fellow bishops to show us where we are not living up to and administering the discipline. In response 'the spirit of the discipline' and the 'consensus of the ministerial body' is sometimes referred to as not being respected as readily as it should be. Once to prove our failure to adhere to the discipline we were reminded that our brethren don't always wear their hats. The district ministry and bishop meeting held at Elm Street ... was cited as an example of our ministers coming to a meeting without wearing hats. (This was a mid-summer meeting.)

We believe it may be necessary to consider the spirit of the discipline in administration but if each district takes too much liberty in having their own private interpretation of the church discipline we could in time seriously weaken the discipline....

The analysis mentions that Aaron's relationship with the Eastern Church was severely threatened over the maternity cape issue. This story is told in the next chapter.

Radio

When the Eastern Church took a position to eliminate the radio from among its membership in the early 1970's, Aaron's critics looked at his mother, who owned a radio. "Whatcha gonna do with your mom?" In an action that spoke volumes about the foundations of church life she and her husband had laid for their children over the previous decades, Mary responded sweetly, "If that is what the church wants, I'll get rid of it."

The older Mary got, the finer her disposition became. At ninety-four years of age her mind was still sharp and supple. Finally, on September 17, 1975 she succumbed to congestive heart failure. She had been a widow almost thirty years.

Unlike Aaron's mother, Lester Shirk, pastor of the Shirksville congregation, did not agree with the church's position on the radio. He thought it should be permitted. In October 1979, he withdrew from the Eastern Pennsylvania Mennonite Church.

Mary Shank, Aaron's mother, in her later years.

When Lester withdrew, he thought the Shirksville meetinghouse should accompany the withdrawing group. Others did not feel that way. The matter was quickly settled by agreeing that the building was worth $60,000.00. Since one-fourth of the congregation withdrew, the group received one-fourth part of the value of the building or $15,000.00. Lester and his group became a part of the Mid-Atlantic Fellowship. The stress related to this departure was minimal.

"The Lord sent you"

On his way home from Danville one day Aaron stopped to visit Lester Martin, bishop in Lancaster Conference. When he got inside the house, Lester's wife Doris said, "The Lord sent you here today."

Tombstone of John and Mary Shank.

Aaron knew that the Martins were dissatisfied with conditions in the Lancaster Conference. He forthrightly said, "I understand you are facing some stresses. I think you would benefit from relating to us."

Lester was discouraged. He had been ordained as minister of the Roedersville congregation (east of Pine Grove) late in 1964 and as bishop of the Hammer Creek District in 1966. When he became a part of the Bishop Board, he was shocked with the lack of conservative leadership at that level. But he did feel responsible for the work he was called to. He asked Aaron, "What am I to do with my ordination charge? I can't feel right to leave my ordination charge."

Aaron responded, "Were you ordained to give communion to sisters with cut hair, etc.? Did you promise that?"

This reasoning brought a new perspective on Lester's predicament. By the end of 1971, he submitted his resignation as Bishop in the Lancaster Conference. He continued to preach at his home congregation at Roedersville until he and his family were received as members at Rehrersburg in June of 1972. Even before he was a member at Rehrersburg, he preached there occasionally.

Lester was received as a minister at Rehrersburg with assisting bishop status by March of 1973. He was to assist the Lebanon District bishops as he was called to do so. He did not have bishop administrative responsibility.

As part of the Lebanon District, Lester found Rehrersburg to be a church home and Aaron to be a spiritual father to him. He felt accepted and he felt at home. Aaron's strong doctrinal teaching enabled him to develop areas of his understanding and to grow in practical applications.

Auto Insurance

When auto insurance became compulsory in Pennsylvania, the Eastern Pennsylvania Mennonite Church sent Jesse Neuenschwander, Isaac Sensenig, and Aaron Shank to Harrisburg to appeal for exemption. There this committee met with Herbert Dennenberg, an atheistic Jew, who was Secretary of Highways at the time. Mr. Dennenberg had no sympathy whatever for the Eastern position.

Aaron told him, "We trust the Lord. We believe He may allow some difficulties to come into our experience but not more than what we can take care of."

Mr. Dennenberg replied, "You fellows don't know what you are asking for. You simply don't know what you are asking for."

Aaron opened his Bible and read Isaiah 57:13, "When thou criest, let thy companies deliver thee; but the wind shall carry them all away; vanity shall take them: but he that putteth his trust in me shall possess the land, and shall inherit my holy mountain."

Mr. Dennenberg was unimpressed. "Yeah, but your God doesn't have a very good record. Look at what happened in Hitler's Nazi Germany."

At that point another man in Mr. Dennenberg's office spoke up saying, "I presented an accident claim to a company and they were never paid."

Mr. Dennenberg asked, "What company was that?"

The man gave the company name.

Mr. Dennenberg said, "They went bankrupt. I understand that."

One of the committee saw his opportunity and said, "The wind carried them away."

Mr. Dennenberg did not hold his position very long. He was replaced by a man who was sympathetic to the church's appeal.

From Fill-in to Nineteen Years

Marjorie taught at the Myerstown Mennonite School for nineteen successive terms. Three of those she taught in company with her daughter Ruth. To become better prepared as teachers, both Ruth and Marjorie attended Millersville State College for two summer terms, Marjorie already in her fifties. She took the most difficult classes and received A's for her work.

Marjorie Shank, teacher.

Marjorie's school teaching terms ran from 1963/64 through 1981/82. Near the close of her last term, on May 1, 1982, the school held a reunion for the 331 students she had taught during her tenure. On that day, 400 people attended the reunion and a set of five scrapbooks was presented to her. The 376 pages in the scrapbooks were completed by the students she had taught during those years.

Reading the scrapbooks today presents the distinct impression of a quality teacher at work, investing her life in the many lives she touched in her classroom. They have become a memorial of her life and work at the Myerstown Mennonite School. Through Marjorie, Aaron touched many homes quite apart from the pulpit and general church administration. Following is a compilation of some of the comments her former students offered in the scrapbook.

"Another thing I remember was the welcome sight of that 1964 Chevy ... when you took us to school. And, the good part of that was I was lucky enough to be with my teacher an extra fifteen minutes a day!"

Glen Kilmer

"You were never too busy to help if anyone had a problem...."

Jay Paul Gingrich

"I also appreciated all the Bible Memory work you had us learn. Sometimes we had to write the passage by memory, plus the punctuation had to be correct...."

Linda Martin

"In my teaching years I have often thought of you because in my eyes you were an ideal teacher...."

Ruth Martin

"I recall being called into Sister Marjorie's room. Not knowing why made me rather nervous. She wanted to know if I ever considered teaching school. That was far from my mind then but that little talk I didn't forget. Six years later found me behind the teacher's desk instead of Sister Marjorie!"

Rhoda (Martin) Weaver

"One time for memory work you had us memorize Luke 2. We were allowed to come up to your desk one at a time to say it to you. I remember well how humiliated I felt because you laughed and laughed at me. When I got to verse 19, 'But Mary kept all these things and pondered them in her heart,' I said, 'Pounded them in her heart.' So whenever I read or hear that verse I think of school and you.

Myerstown Mennonite School. The car next to the building is Marjorie's.

"Another incident was on a regular school day. Everything was going on in the usual way when ... there was a bump....No teacher. What happened? And then Mrs. Shank's laughter. You had tipped your chair in getting something from your lower desk drawer. For a couple seconds the schoolroom was so quiet you could have heard a pin drop. But afterwards it was in an uproar."

Verna Martin

"I will probably never fully realize everything those years did for me. But I thank God for directing my footsteps into this classroom and I thank you,

Betty Weaver   Miriam Landis
Ruth Baugher   Marjorie Shank
Lorene Mast   Ivan Martin   Rosa Mast

Myerstown school teachers, c. 1980, near the end of Marjorie's tenure.

Sister Marjorie, for using your influence to point me God-ward."

Clifford Weaver

"I remember the time we memorized 26 Bible verses each beginning with a letter of the alphabet...."

Eunice Sensenig

"I always enjoyed the stories you read to us after the noon recess, too. A chapter each day from books such as The Broken Bottle. I really enjoyed having you as a teacher and always felt free to ask you any question. Thank you so much for all the help you gave me and all the patience you had with me. I really appreciate everything."

Miriam Martin

"First of all I want to thank you for being my teacher and all the happy memories of school in seventh and eighth grades. I appreciate all you've done for me maybe now more than I did when in school. Some of the things you said and taught and your attitude toward lessons and studying had great influence on me....Also the spiritual help you often gave me and others. I remember you saying sometimes when someone would complain about lessons being too hard, that they are intended to be hard or else we wouldn't keep learning more. I often have to think of that and it can apply to our everyday trials and challenges....Trials of our lives make us grow in patience and faith."

Arlene Sensenig

"I, of course, remember more of you than teaching, as you have always been a dear friend to my mother and the family. I will always remember your gentle and generous ways. I know you will be greatly rewarded, even though you have not lived your life for rewards...."

Scott Ellison

"One of the most outstanding memories I have of eighth grade is Public Speaking Class. We had this class instead of English every Wednesday, seventh and eighth graders taking turns giving oral speeches one week and written essays the next.

"The thing that amuses me so very much is how 'mad' we were when the suggestion was brought up to have the class and then how we ended up enjoying it so much. We enjoyed it so much, in fact, that when the first semester was over and the teacher decided to drop speech class for the remainder of the year, we all protested!...It's the number one thing that I give you credit for helping me develop self-confidence..."

Esther Mae (Faus) Mast

"Happy, happy school days!...It all was two wonderful years learning together. We learned our reading, writing, and arithmetic (somehow)! But, oh, so much more was caught and stuck in those years. Sister Marjorie was a terrific example of kindness, forgiveness, love, patience, and so forth.... When a person broke a rule, just punishment was given—then true love and patience was shown by never bringing up that experience again...."

Erma (Martin) Graybill

"I have happy memories of my years in your room....One thing I remember well is that good behavior was always required, especially on school trips.

Upon returning, you would encourage us with reports of what the guides at the places we visited thought of us. It was usually something like this, 'This was the most well-behaved group we ever had here!'

"You kept us from getting bored by giving lots of interesting illustrations as you taught....

"Also I remember receiving a little note from you when I accepted Christ, saying how happy you were that I had made this decision...."

Eileen (Martin) Stahl

"I wrote a composition on heating systems for science class. All the way through I spelled duct work, duck work. Needless to say through that composition I learned that ducks quack and that ducts are used to heat homes...."

Nevin Martin

"The first thing that comes to my mind about Sister Marjorie is the way she laughed. She would sit in her chair and start with a giggle. And that alone was enough to make you yourself laugh. Then when she saw you laughing, she would start to roll and bounce. Then she would turn red in the face and bounce some more...."

J. Mark Stonesifer

"I was taking my turn at talking and I was saying something about going straight down Route 501 to the place I lived. I remember how you all of a sudden said, 'You know I've tried many times to go straight down 501 and you just can't do it....'"

Chris R. Craft

"When you left the schoolroom and before you'd come in again, you'd peek through the window in the door to see if we're behaving. One time you caught me talking...."

Lamar Lehman

"When I think of Grade School days, I consider you my favorite teacher. You often talked to us as friend to friend, not teacher to just a mere student.

"Speaking of weekend events, message gleanings, interesting happenings, etc. proved to us you really enjoyed teaching. Also the inspiring Pep Talks showed concern for our souls.

"As for compositions, the most challenging article we were asked to write was on what we would do if we knew this was the last day of our lives...."

Mary Ann (Boll) Gehman

"I remember so well when in Reading Class Sister Marjorie corrected me on my <u>V</u> and <u>W</u> pronunciation. I had to repeat the word till I had it correct...."

Grace (Martin) Zimmerman

"I want to thank you for making my school days pleasant. I know at times I thought things were too hard, but I can say I have enjoyed school with you as my teacher...."

Myron Martin

"Eighth grade (my first in a Christian school) was by far my happiest school year!"

Carolyn (Wenger) Schrock

"I believe your personality helped your success in the classroom. I feel you had control in the classroom and the respect of the pupils while I was your student...."

Mark Weaver

"I was sorry to leave school at the end of my eighth grade."

Mary Jane (Weaver) Martin

"I especially remember the singing we'd do in your class. It was most enjoyable...."

Rebecca (Hess) Bontrager

"Something I'll never forget that took place while I was in eighth grade is our memorization of the book of 1 Peter. It was a real challenge to say all five chapters at once and I've been thankful many times since that we had that challenge...."

Marvin Weaver

"I remember [Sister Marjorie] eating raw cucumbers for her diet. Only later did we discover how good they do taste and now my husband considers them a real treat....

"Another interesting finding occurred when the word meticulous was written beneath my grade on my corrected paper. Since we didn't know what it meant we used the dictionary and learned a new word...."

Marie (Ebersole) Wentz

"One remembrance I have of Mrs. Shank is she often ate a head of raw cabbage with her lunch. This was outstanding to me because of my dislike of cabbage...."

Delmar Lehman

Not only did her students commend her work, but so did John Kraybill, who visited the Lancaster Conference schools to evaluate them, encourage them, and give suggestions for improvement. Many of his reports commended her work.

Standards and the Truth

A family from the Metzler congregation had moved into the area and attended Shirksville on Sunday mornings. The husband was an outspoken sort of man. Aaron was present for the Council service to be held that morning.

In the Sunday School discussion, the man waxed eloquent against church standards, referring to the passage "Not giving heed to the commandments of men." He made it clear that the Bible taught that Christians were not to give heed to the commandments of men and applied the text to the regulations of the church.

Sitting there listening to the discussion, Aaron did not reply, but he did decide to change his message for the morning. He decided to use the very same verse the visitor used against church standards, "Not giving heed to Jewish fables and commandments of men, that turn from the truth" (Titus 1:14).

In the message he went down through the Discipline statement. At each standard he asked, "Does this standard turn from the truth or does it help us put truth into practice?"

The visiting family left before the service was over.

No News!

About 1976, the son of Harvey and Ann Hershberger was touring South America along with his girlfriend. The two disappeared and were never heard from again. CBS News wanted to make a news item out of the incident, incriminating the United States for not taking better care of its own citizens in foreign countries.

Not satisfied that they were handling the situation correctly, the Hershbergers referred CBS News to Aaron.

One day Aaron picked up the phone to hear, "Mr. Shank, this is CBS News from New York."

A lengthy conversation followed, including Aaron stating, "We do not want to be on television and we do not want to incriminate the government." Aaron tried to explain the principles of separation from the world, nonresistance, and the principle of willingness to suffer unjustly.

CBS News was not so easily convinced. "It would certainly be a Christian duty to do something about a matter to offset things like this. This isn't right that you won't let us do things like this."

Aaron held his ground.

Suddenly CBS News said, "Mr. Shank, it's been very depressing to talk with you!" and hung up.

No more was heard of the matter.

Not Suing

In 1978 Aaron helped _____ work through a threatened lawsuit. In the case, a company was using _____, one of Aaron's members, as plaintiffs to obtain money from another company.

In working with the case, Aaron rephrased their statement to be consistent with nonresistant principles.

The lawyer called Aaron saying, "We all know _____ are not suing but it must be said that way. There is no way we can collect anything unless we sue. _____ has got to sue."

Aaron replied, "They're not suing."

The lawyer was not satisfied. "They're not suing. They are just saying it that way."

Now Aaron was not satisfied. "_____ are just as concerned to say it Scripturally as to do it Scripturally. They will not sue. I have a statement here that you *can* use." He read the statement.

The lawyer responded, "That won't work."

Aaron said, "There is no other way. We will not accept any remuneration if it has to say that _____ are suing. _____ will be taken care of regardless, without a suit."

The lawyer replied, "Alright, let me talk with the other lawyers."

A few days later he called back saying, "We've accepted your statement the way it is written with a few minor changes."

The final settlement netted the lawyers 66% of the settlement figure.

Laying Hands

One of Marjorie's own sisters married a Mennonite man, but as the years passed, the couple dropped their conservative Mennonite ways and became strongly charismatic.

One day when Aaron and Marjorie were visiting with them, Marjorie's sister said, "Aaron, wouldn't you like us to pray over you and have your back healed?"

Aaron replied, "I was anointed one time and prayed over for my back condition. I believe the Lord gave me the same answer he gave Apostle Paul, 'My grace is sufficient for thee.' I understand Him to be saying to me that it will be to my benefit to live with the handicap. _____, I want to tell you one thing. I wouldn't want to have a bobbed-haired woman, a jewelry-wearing woman, an immodestly dressed woman lay hands on me for anything."

They responded saying, "That's terrible. We have the witness of the Spirit. Wouldn't you let us share communion with you either?"

Aaron said, "No. We would not have a communing relationship with the differences between your beliefs and our beliefs."

To them, such a position was unfortunate and misguided.

Brunk Brothers Tent Revival in Lancaster County.

George R. Brunk II

When the Fellowship of Concerned Mennonites developed in the 1970's, Aaron wrote to his old acquaintance George R. Brunk II. "I appreciate your loud voice against modernism and the drift. It would do your cause a lot of good if you would not use speakers who appear in fashionable attire or whose group does not practice the Christian woman's headship covering."

George wrote back saying, "You need to be more definite and clear."

Aaron wrote again. "Your movement would gain a great deal of momentum and influence if you would have a distinct group of people that are representing your crusade against the drift."

When George began his tent crusade in 1951, Aaron thought it was a great work for God. He encouraged attendance and himself transported friends and relatives from Lebanon County down to Lancaster. He loved the dynamic preaching in defense of conservatism. At that time, George considered Aaron a devout supporter of the crusades.

The Brunks had set up a tent across from the East Chestnut Street church in Lancaster for a two-week series of meetings. When crowd size forced the relocation of the meetings, he moved out into the countryside and extended the meetings for six weeks. His tent revival campaign took off from there.

As the tent revivals toured the nation, the kind of people who attended and supported them shifted from conservatives at the beginning to liberals at the end. This was a disappointment to Aaron, and he withdrew his avid support.

But Aaron did recognize George's defense of Biblical values by way of the Fellowship of Concerned Mennonites. The recognition was mutual. In 1996 George said of Aaron, "I was impressed with the pungency and clarity of his messages which were Biblical and sound. You could be confident that the teaching Aaron gave was correct and Scriptural."

George's brother Menno, another of Aaron's long acquaintances, wrote of Aaron,

"Let the elders that rule well be counted worthy of double honor, especially they who labor in the Word and doctrine." (I Timothy 5:17) Brother Aaron did that.

Apostle Paul writes [in] Philippians 1:17, 'I am set for the defense of the Gospel.' Those who heard Bro. Aaron preach had good reason to believe that was his aim and purpose in the ministry.

I remember Bro. Aaron's boldness for the truth as a meek and humble man as he went about the responsibilities the Lord and [the] church placed upon him.

Some years ago Bro. Aaron was given a topic to speak on at Numidia Minister's Week. He asked some one else to take it. Soon after that session a brother came to the one who preached on the topic and asked him, 'Why didn't Aaron do it?' I think Brother Aaron did that in order to involve others; which was another example of Aaron's good traits.

Also I consider Brother Aaron and his wife examples of Christian hospitality...

Memories

A former deacon wrote of Aaron's work and ministry during the decade 1975 to 1985, "His wisdom and humility in helping our local bishop in resolving problems in ... our congregations ... I appreciated his peace-making role."

Another observer wrote:

I never belonged to Aaron's local congregation, but I've been close by ... and my impression of his role and contribution has been favorable. I've seen growth in membership and Bible-based convictions. He consults with others in leadership and tries to work together with them in making decisions. He has sometimes had to disagree, and some did not like it, but usually I believe he was right.

Those in the church under Aaron's oversight, generally speaking, loved him and appreciated his leadership. I've heard this in relation to his humility and honesty. I know he tried not to speak too quickly. He was a good listener. I felt I could safely express my thinking, and when he thought otherwise, he would kindly and frankly tell me why....

Aaron's leadership has been effective, generally speaking, but he met with plenty of opposition. I think most of that has been unfair. He withstood and tried to correct some of his associates in the ministry, in the Lancaster Conference and in the Eastern Church, some who taught Calvinistic doctrine, and some who over-looked even gross evidence of worldliness. He also stood against dead formalism and legalism. He would emphasize that spirituality must be from the inside and [work] outwardly....

Aaron has sometimes been too slow and weak, maybe because he is kind and very considerate of how people can be adversely moved by well-meant but unwise discipline; he wants to help and not hurt, and that is not weakness, but at times he may be cautious and hesitate when he needs to act. I sometimes have thought he should be more decisive, but I also realize that premature action can be worse....

I know Aaron has been a spiritual father to many others who evidently are keeping the faith. He tried hard but failed to keep others in the right way, I think because of their stubborn refusal to walk therein.

In relation to personal encounters with Aaron, I've met with rebukes from him, but never was he unkind or unreasonable. He also has given me a lot of encour-agement....In each encounter with Aaron, he always has been unselfish, and I've liked his frankness. I've never had to guess at what he meant.

Aaron has often mentioned some of his memories. When he first gets up to preach, he often leads the people in singing, "My Faith Looks Up to Thee" or "Before Jehovah's Awful Throne" or "Above the Trembling Elements" or "Jesus Lover of my Soul." He leads in singing those and other hymns without the book, and says we should have the prayer hymns memorized. Aaron has learned to worship God, and he inspires others to worship.

I've been impressed by his wisdom in keeping the confidence entrusted to him. Aaron does not gossip or speak to slander people. I've been impressed also by his humility; he talks to common men as equals, and I feel comfortable in being with him. He often has patiently waited to speak his mind until the others have finished, and then he spoke to relieve the tension and bring the right agreement....

Bishop David Wadel's encounters with Aaron span quite a few years. He wrote:

I have many pleasant memories of Bro. Aaron's input in the formative years of the Mennonite Messianic Mission during the late sixties and early seventies. When I was ordained bishop in 1975, the relationship was intensified as we were often together. His role as a respected leader in the Lancaster Conference was a definite asset in charting a safer course for an emerging group.

The following quote I picked up along the way and wrote it on the inside of the Bible I used at the time. Bro. Aaron said, "The division of 1968 is the first in Mennonite history that was based on doctrinal issues. Divorce and remarriage, the Christian woman's veiling, cut hair for women, nonconformity, the unequal yoke, [and the wearing of] jewelry are doctrinal issues."

His dynamic preaching and humble leadership had blessed many even though it seemed that he was slower in firm disciplinary action at times.

One event in more recent years comes to mind. In 1980 Bro. Aaron and I were sent to Paraguay to investigate a request for our mission board to start an outreach in that country.

We were traveling by bus through the countryside when we ran into a rain shower which made the road very slippery. The bus slid toward a big ditch along the side of the road, and the driver told all the men to get out and man the ropes. One rope was tied to the front of the bus and a group pulled it forward. The other rope was tied to the back bumper to pull sideways to keep it out of the ditch.

Bro. Aaron's back was bothering him at the time and he did not get out. Some of the men complained rather loudly that this man should get out and help or drive the bus.

Bro. Aaron saved the day by digging into his pocket and coming up with a handful of U.S. coins. He passed them out and the men were elated to have U.S. money and their gripes were soon forgotten. Bro. Aaron said that he often took US coins along when traveling in foreign countries.

Perhaps my greatest reflection of appreciation for Bro. Aaron goes back to the early 1950's. I was a teenager and Bro. Aaron was an instructor at the Millwood Mennonite Bible School, Gap, Pennsylvania for a number of years. For some reason he stood out, although men like Jacob Rittenhouse, Clarence Fretz, J. Irvin Lehman, Norman Bechtel, and Elias Kulp also were deeply appreciated as instructors there.

These brethren filled a very important place in the solidifying of convictions and goals in my life. Bro. Aaron's enthusiastic manner of presenting truth and his ability to make it practical in life has inspired my life many times.

To God be the glory.

Bishop Amos Sauder writes of Aaron before the Eastern division of 1968:

He was a song leader, preacher, and was not easily intimidated. Sometimes he appeared to be too arrogant by those who did not know him intimately....He was a conservative and spoke frequently about the Christian's dress.

The Methodist and the Mennonite

In 1979, at age seventeen, Darlene Herman responded during revival meetings at Numidia Mennonite Bible School. Her experience among the Mennonites influenced her to develop Biblical convictions and created within her the desire to leave her parental home at age eighteen. The Mennonites readily received her.

But her parents and Methodist pastor did not approve of the move at all. They thought she was joining a cult. Consequently, her pastor, Richard Bardo, wrote a scathing letter to Aaron on October 23, 1980, expressing his concern.

Dear Mr. Shank,

I am writing as the pastor of Darlene Herman and her parents, Mr. and Mrs. Reuben Herman. Darlene's mother Ruth wrote to you on September 15, 1980 and she has shared with me your response of October 20, 1980.

Having known Darlene for three years I would agree with you that she appears to be very conscientious in her desire to do God's will and it appears on the surface that her choice to be a part of the Mennonite community is by her free will. Having known Darlene for three years, however, we are convinced that these things only appear to be so and are not in reality.

Religious freedom is indeed the point and the question here. The real question is whether Darlene has been truly free from constraint or from sub-conscious suggestion or subtle mind-control in making her choice. We think not. We firmly believe that her decision was not made freely.

It is clear that Darlene was openly encouraged to disobey and deceive her parents.

It is clear that Darlene was informed as to questions she was to ask her parents and statements she was to use to respond to them. It is also clear that Darlene's naivete was courted [for] the advantage of those who would pull her from her family and established church home....

Our congregation concentrates its efforts on those who do not know Christ rather than stealing sheep from Christian groups whose practices differ from ours. Your own people on the day they took Darlene clearly agreed that we were unified in our faith and differed only in our practice...

It is not your public worship which leads us to the conclusion that this group is cultic. It is their practices and recruitment techniques which are so similar to groups which, on the basis of claims for religious freedom, are the very destruction of it. You are a people known to emphasize the externals as a sign of the place of your hearts. Having seen the practice of your lives can we conclude anything else except that the outer appearance of the cup belies the inner corruption (Matthew 23:25-28)?...

I was present the day your people took Darlene.

Darlene Herman left the Methodists and joined the Mennonite church.

They came on false pretenses and did not reveal their previously darkly-hatched plan for three and one-half hours. They took advantage of the home and hospitality of Christian people, who even after the plan was revealed allowed your people the continued hospitality of their home.... You have caused a young one to sin and are calling down the millstone upon your necks (Matthew 18:5-9).

I would hope that you would exercise your authority as bishop over this group to reestablish what are clearly the biblical norms and priorities in dealing with one's neighbors. The clear basis of final judgment is not matters of outward appearance nor of doctrine, but matters of how we have dealt with even the least important of our fellow men (Matthew 25).

We pray for a swift resolution of this unfortunate incident, for the return of Darlene to her home, and for the conviction of the Holy Spirit upon those who have practiced deceit with others and have dealt treacherously with God's Word.

Respectfully,

Richard Bardo, pastor

The above accusations were not facts. Aaron knew that. But he did not argue over the situation. He wrote back on November 3, 1980, with a letter characteristic of how he dealt with such situations.

Dear Pastor Bardo:

Your correspondence of October 23, 1980 has been received and the contents carefully noted. The letter provides a challenge to us to examine again our position and the consistency of our doctrinal beliefs and practices. It is always our aim to be perfectly consistent in our profession and practice as well as in our relationship with God and our fellow men. At the same time we also realize that the greatest room in the world is the room for improvement, and it is our desire to live in that room for improvement.

In all due respect, however, I believe your letter involves some misunderstandings, some misrepresentations, and some unfair indictments against our people.

I can assure you that we are sympathetic with your deep feelings in relation to the Herman family in their present experiences regarding Darlene's recent choices in Christian experience. We surely would not expect either you nor her parents to be totally disinterested. We have also had experiences when individuals of our fellowship chose to leave their home and church background, and, while we have deep feeling and discourage folks in making a move from our church group to another religious profession, we usually make it clear to them that we believe that church membership must be voluntary, and if they cannot be happy where they are, it may be better for them to go where they believe their spiritual needs can be better met.

I have never entered into religious controversy or issued judgmental indictments to leaders of groups who received folks moving from our ranks.

You suggest that, rather than making a voluntary choice, Darlene was under "subtle mind-control" by our people which influenced her decisions in her present move. If such is the case, we evidently possess a power of which we are totally unaware. We do not knowingly or intentionally bring people under "subtle mind-control." We do believe, however, that the Holy Spirit will activate one's Christian witness and take possession of and give guidance and courage to a mind yielded to Him in a sincere desire for the truth.

It is our understanding, and Darlene's understanding, that she has not been under any compulsory constraints in her present experience and pursuits. Our brethren who visited Darlene's home and provided transportation for her did so at her own request, and should she, at any time, request to return home, her request will be granted.

Perhaps you should appreciate that our people were open enough and noble enough to go to Darlene's home and face her parents in appreciation of Darlene's interests rather than to provide another home for her without the parents knowing anything about her move. I do not consider their responding to Darlene's request as stealth, trickery, and dishonesty as you so strongly infer in your letter. I believe it was a consistent Christian approach to the need.

We are in agreement with you that the Bible enjoins upon children respect and honor for parental authority. However, parental authority, church authority, and all other earthly authority is a delegated authority rather than an absolute authority. When one believes that to respect delegated authority hinders his respect and obedience to the absolute authority of God, he is under obligation to obey God rather than man. (Acts 5:29) When delegated authority is misused, it forfeits its right of authority. If this were not true there would be no justification for Mennonitism, Methodism, or any other church formation outside the Roman Catholic Church.

It is, of course, our belief, that our practices find their bases in biblical principles; and a principle, if believed in, must find outward expression in order to exist. An unexpressed principle is dead or dying. In the area of dress and the Christian Woman's Veiling which are usually thought of as some of our "pet points" our practices are in keeping with the concerns of the founder of your Methodist brotherhood, as well as of many, many other religious leaders of the past.

In his sermon "Causes of Inefficacy of Christianity" preached two years before his death John Wesley lamented:

"I am distressed. I know not what to do. I see what I might have done once. I might have said peremptorily and expressly, 'Here I am: I and my Bible. I will not, I dare not vary from this Book, either in great things or small. I have no power to dispense with one jot or tittle of what is contained therein. I am determined to be a Bible Christian, not almost, but altogether. Who will meet me on this ground? Join me on this or not at all.' With regards to dress in particular, I might have been as firm (and now see it would have been far better,) as either the people called Quakers or the Moravian brethren; -- I might have said, 'This is our manner of dress, which we know is both Scriptural and rational. If you join us, you are to dress as we do; but you need not join us unless you please.' But alas! the time is now past; and what I can do now, I cannot tell."

--From Sermons Vol. II p.439 The Works of the Rev. John Wesley

In his "Sermon XCIII on Dress" taken from Sermons on Several Occasions Vol. II Wesley gives the following admonition to parents and others:

"I beseech you, oh ye parents, do not hinder your children from following their own convictions, even though you might think they would look prettier if they were adorned with such gewgaws as other children wear!...Above all, I adjure you, ye half Methodists, you that trim between us and the world...whatever ye do yourselves, do not say one word to hinder others from recovering and practicing the advice which has now been given...."

We believe that rather than discouraging Darlene you should appreciate her courageous step, her manifest deliverance from a fashion-enslaved world, and her readiness to suffer reproaches and misunderstandings for Christ's sake.

Rest assured of our continued prayers in behalf of all those needing special grace and wisdom from above for these experiences. It shall be our aim to do nothing but what we believe will be to the glory of God and the best interests of His worthy cause.

Should we at any time be convicted of error or wrong-doing, our apologies and any necessary corrections will be forthcoming.

With kindest regards,

Aaron Shank, Bishop

Lebanon District Churches of the

Eastern Pennsylvania Mennonite Church

In leaving her parental home, Darlene went to live with Dorothy Newswanger for two years. There she found the spiritual rest which she sought. She concluded her stay with Dorothy because at age twenty, she married Ervin Martin. Fourteen years later, Dorothy Newswanger would become Aaron's second wife.

Farm Stress

Aaron needed to deal with stress on the farm in addition to all the other stresses he faced. His chickens provided their own kind of stress. Regardless of the kind of stress faced, he graciously faced straight into the wind. When they had problems with dying chickens and their purchaser cancelled their contract, Aaron wrote to the Broiler Grow-Out Manager:

I doubt whether you have a grower anywhere that has tried harder or cooperated better with the Doctor's suggestion than Milford has. It may not be out of order to remind you that over the years of our involvement with Pennfield, the Company has not always lived up to their end of the contract. We have been shorted on chicks again and again. On a number of occasions we were not given the full weight of our birds. Again and again we were assured that we will surely get a bonus on this lot, but those settlements repeatedly came through with a deduction. It was only when we called attention to the fact that some truck loads of broilers out of the same house and from the same floor too, yielded as much as 1/2 pound average less than other loads, that the illegally-used scales problem was revealed. Since it was not our responsibility to weigh the poultry, surely that loss should not have been ours.

The Shank chicken barn.

We herewith accept your termination verdict graciously. We do not intend to retaliate in any way at all. We thank you very kindly for the help you gave us in the broiler business over the years. We want to finalize our relationship with Pennfield Poultry, Inc. as honorably as possible, and wish you continued success in the future...

Respectfully yours,

Aaron M. Shank

Aaron Shank, Farmer.

Marjorie's brother, Leonard Showalter from Springdale, Virginia, boarded with the Shank family and helped on the farm since Aaron was gone so much of the time. He married John Olesh's granddaughter, Ann(a) Olesh.

No change

In July of 1982, Aaron was asked to share in the funeral service of Bishop Richard Danner. In his testimony he made reference to the agreement which he and three other bishops made in 1966 that from that point on they would only give leadership to church members who would honor and respect the authority of Conference. When that statement was read to the Bishop Board, Richard Danner had said to Moderator David Thomas, "Brother Moderator,

I don't see any reason why this whole Board shouldn't sign the statement." Aaron repeated Richard's comment as a tribute to Richard's conservative position in Conference and which he continued to hold sixteen years later.

Two Lancaster Conference bishops were present at the funeral and heard what Aaron said. After the service Aaron met them. One of them said, "We were just talking about you. I said, 'Aaron is a man that just does not change.'" The statement characterized Aaron well.

Responding to History

In October of 1984, the *Pennsylvania Mennonite Heritage* published an article entitled "An Amiable Mennonite Schism" written by Robert B. Graber. Aaron read the article with great interest. How did the outside observing public interpret the separation from Lancaster Conference fifteen years prior? Aaron responded to the nine-page article with three pages of his own, mostly minor clarifications. Whereas the article listed three contributing factors to the schism, Aaron added a fourth: The inconsistency of having an established statement of standards, but having administrators justifying and promoting those who were defying and deviating from those standards.

He also wanted make it clear that the Mennonite Messianic Mission was not a subgroup to or the successor of the Defenders of the Faith, as the article portrayed. In all, he made about eight separate clarifications. Aaron was concerned that accurate information be passed on to anyone who might investigate the story.

The next generation

At age seventy, Aaron decided that his three-score years and ten merited plans for the next generation in the bishop office in the Lebanon District. Frederick Kauffman, who had been born in 1709, migrated to America in 1742, and died in 1789 had been the first resident bishop. Michael Gingrich was next (1792-1860). Jacob Dohner (1805-1881), Isaac Gingrich (1822-1892), and David Westenberger (1857-1933), who baptized Aaron, had preceded Simon Bucher (1887-1972). Aaron had appreciated his bishop teamwork with Simon Bucher so much that just before Simon died in

1972, Sidney Gingrich was ordained to serve with Aaron as a teammate. Aaron and Sidney worked together as the sixth generation of Bishops for the District.

Aaron approached the Bishop Board concerning the possibility of Bishop Lester Martin serving the District. Lester was considerably younger (age 56) than both Aaron (age 70) and Sidney (age 68) at that time. The Bishop Board felt that Lester should continue to serve as an assisting bishop for the district. They did give clearance for beginning the normal procedures of preparing for a bishop ordination.

The plan was to include the Southern churches (Dublin, Georgia and Pensacola, Florida) in the voting area, with the understanding that if a brother from the South was nominated and chosen for the work, he would be expected to relocate to the North.

As a result of the voting that followed, three ministers received sufficient nominations: Harry Erb from the Elm Street congregation, Wayne Rudolph from the Dohner congregation, and H. Stephen Ebersole from the Pensacola, Florida congregation.

Sidney & Mabel Gingerich. Sidney was a fellow-bishop in the Lebanon District.

After the nominations were announced, there was considerable reaction to Stephen being included in the class. With Stephen's upbringing in an outlying area and then years of being pastor in a non-Mennonite community, he naturally tested issues from the Scriptures rather than to assume the group thinking was correct. Furthermore, by nature he tended to be outspoken, especially when he felt Bible principle was being compromised. He had supported Aaron's principled way of reasoning about issues and did not display the loyalty for tradition which some of the Eastern bishops desired. Some of the bishops put pressure on Stephen to withdraw from the class. While he personally felt he would rather not move to the North and face the friction that he knew existed, Stephen could not conscientiously run away from the Lord's call. He would rather have the lot reveal God's will.

There was talk of canceling the ordination. Aaron offered to submit to this and have Alvin Snyder, who had been previously ordained for the three Northern churches of the district, to be given responsibility for the entire district. He had confidence that Alvin would be a suitable bishop for the entire district. It was decided to proceed with the ordination as planned, with the three nominees sharing the lot.

On the ordination day, July 10, 1985, a full house at Rehrersburg waited expectantly. Aaron explained that the man to be ordained that day would be the next generation bishop. After a message preached by Harold Good, three Bibles were taken to a private room, the lot slip placed, and the Bibles shuffled so that no one knew which book contained the lot, and returned to the pulpit.

Sidney Gingrich placed the first Bible next to the speaker's podium, placed the next book at the end, and set the last book in between the other two. Harry Erb rose and took the first book next to the podium. Wayne Rudolph chose the last book. The only book remaining was the middle one. Stephen took it.

The lot was found in Stephen Ebersole's book. When it was discovered there, one bishop on the platform whispered to his fellow bishop, "If this works, anything can work."

The individuals involved in the ordination felt they had some unusual confirmations that God was working in this ordination. Before the ordination, Wayne had a dream that left a strong impression on him. From the dream he felt he had clear direction that he was to take the last book in the line. Stephen also had a dream, even before the nominations were announced. In his dream he saw three books and the middle one was left standing. The next morning, he shared with his wife Sandra that if the dream was from the Lord, there would be three brethren in the lot, and if he was the last one, he would be taking the middle book. While both brethren shared their dreams with their wives, they did not share them with each other or anyone else until after the ordination was over. During the ordination, Sidney had planned to place the books in the natural order they were given to him. But

Steve Ebersole family in front of their Pensacola, Florida, home in February 1986, before they moved north.

when the time came, he felt moved to mix the arrangement.

A keen observer commented afterward, "If the books had been put in the order they came, and the brethren had taken the books in that order, the lot would have been in the last book. Either way, the last book was Stephen's book, the lot book."

These confirmations gave Aaron much encouragement. He knew too well the distrust that was evident in a few sectors of the church. In his older years, he longed for peaceful church life. But he knew that with Stephen's ordination, things were set for more trouble to come.

Six years later, Aaron wrote the following letter.

Dear Bro. _____

There is something that is troubling me rather deeply that I seem not to be able to shake off. You may feel that this is simply the evidence of a confused mind or the evidence of a fallen brother. If so, I will not argue the point. I realize perhaps as no one else does, my own inabilities and limitations. I hesitate to even approach you with my concerns.

In a letter presented to the bishops recently (not dated) entitled "An Effort to Understand Our Present Need" on page 2 it is implied that the judgment of God is upon us for allowing the ordination of Bro. Stephen to take place.

At our last bishop meeting it was rather strongly stated that our present church dilemma is the judgment of God on us "for ordaining a man we all knew should not have been ordained."

Now it may be that some of our board are living in close enough communication with God to be able to make such bold confident pronouncements and know they are in the will of the Lord doing so. However, when we make an observation like that, are we not rather strongly implying that the devil was in control of the ordination? How else could we have done something that brings us under the judgment of God?

Some of us felt that our proceedings in the ordination were altogether within the confines of consistency and felt we did experience the leading of the Lord in the proceedings. You may not remember but when there were concerns registered about Bro. Stephen's involvement, I offered to cancel out the plans and consider having Bro. Alvin Snyder assume a bishop role over the entire district. That suggestion was given no further consideration. I also asked board counsel regarding Bro. Lester Martin being eligible for the work. It was board action that he should not be considered but that he remain in his previous status. I now wonder, were these decisions a result of the leading of the Lord?

My problem—just suppose that Bro. Stephen was made overseer by the Holy Ghost (Acts 20:28) and by our declaration that the judgment of God is upon us for "ordaining a man we knew should not have been ordained" and by such an assertion we imply that we were under Satanic influence in the ordination—then what?

That "his ordination was a mistake" has been freely stated numbers of times even in his very presence. If indeed our church wide confusion is related to Brother Stephen's ordination, is there no possibility that it is caused by our fighting against God's calling and placement of him to this office and work?

The 1975-1985 decade with its restful golden years was ending with dark clouds upon the horizon. At the age of "three score and ten," Aaron Shank was now an old man.

CHAPTER 9

Sacred Seventies

THE MINUTES OF the January 2, 1985 Eastern Bishop Board meeting include the following:

> In our last Church wide Ministerial Meeting there was a consensus vote that the Bishops take a look at the maternity dress issue and give some more clear direction and seek a greater unity among us as to what is acceptable.

Back in Lancaster Conference, maternity dresses were generally purchased commercially. Obviously, those dresses were made without Biblical concern for modesty. Some of the more conscientious and spiritual sisters developed a pattern of their own, which was a sincere attempt at applying Biblical modesty in a maternity dress. The pattern they began to use was a separate sleeveless top cape draped over the dress below, similar to what some of the Nationwide Fellowship churches had adopted. This top piece reached below the waist and effectively functioned as a long cape. It satisfied the principle of modesty very well, and Aaron was pleased with the pattern.

The use of this style of maternity dress became the norm in the Lebanon District. It tended to spill over into other districts as well. But this did not please the administrators in a few other districts. They considered the larger caped dress as a threat to the normal caped dress. In fact, they termed the Lebanon District practice an "apostate carryover from Conference."

The other districts promoted a maternity dress made by extending the length of the usual cape. Like the regular cape, it remained open on the sides.

To some of the other districts, deviating from the traditional cape in favor of the more modest draped cape was more of a problem than the modesty issue. They felt that the entire practice of caped dresses would be threatened by allowing a deviation. To them, changing at all was the first step to losing the practice altogether.

In private, Aaron was repulsed by the less-modest caped maternity dresses which showed up in his jurisdiction at times. Those deviations from the Lebanon District norm became more evidence to him of the appropriateness of the Lebanon District practice. He even pointed out an example of a more-modest maternity dress in his district to a fellow bishop after a service one day. The other bishop responded, "Yes I like that too. I could go along with that but I must work with my ministry." In other words, even though he considered the flowing, draped-style maternity dress appropriately modest, he needed to yield to the clamor of his own district ministry's demand for the traditional caped maternity dress,

This drawing from a 1992 Pilgrim Conference bishop letter illustrates the style of maternity dress typical of Lebanon District.

even though he agreed that Lebanon's pattern was more modest for the expectant mother.

This issue had been debated for some time. The following letter, signed by the Lebanon District bishops, is dated April 1976.

Bishops of the Eastern Pennsylvania Mennonite church

Dear brethren: Greetings.

At a recent ministerial meeting of the Lebanon district, there was an action taken to present to you a concern that many of our brothers have concerning the dress practice of our expectant mothers.

Our church discipline states, page 19, 1974 printing, that "Inasmuch as... spiritual growth may lead to more scriptural forms of applying principles of the gospel, this... discipline shall be reviewed approximately every three years for the purpose of strengthening the church in her expressions of biblical principles."

It is a sincere conviction of many of us that it was due to spiritual growth that many of our expectant mothers had difficulty feeling comfortable and modest in the conventional open sided, belted cape and had arrived at a comfortable, modest expression in the design and use of the maternity cape. Some of our more conservative ordained brothers were also encouraging their wives to use a more consistent and practical expression of modesty during this experience.

This pattern, we believe, was not a copy of the world nor a carry-over from conference. It was not an act of worldliness nor of rebellion against the discipline. Rather, it was a sincere effort on the part of many to fulfill the true spirit of the discipline. If the influence came from any outside source, it was probably from a number of Conservative Fellowship groups who have adopted something similar to what our sisters were wearing.

It is our observation and opinion that at least some of our sisters who were previously wearing the maternity cape, and are now trying to conform to the conventional cape, have deteriorated somewhat in modesty. In at least a number of our districts there is some variation of application, including some shift dresses with some type of makeshift, legally acceptable capes attached to them. A few sisters are wearing the open-sided, belted conventional cape and wearing a maternity cape or something else over it in order to feel modestly dressed. In other words, they feel that they're being asked to wear something that they must cover up in order to be modest.

An ordained brother outside the Eastern church testified some time ago that since his church group requires a conventional cape during all of pregnancy, his wife needs to stay at home about three months before delivery time, a time when he felt she especially needed the benefits of Christian fellowship. When she was wearing a maternity cape she felt free to attend services close to the time of delivery.

We realize that many in our Brotherhood have little appreciation or sympathy for those who have a problem wearing the conventional cape during pregnancy. We realize too, and are very sensitive to the fact, that the church does have a voice of authority (within certain limits) to legislate and regulate her constituency. We are also conscious of the fact that the larger part of our constituency understood that they were voting to require the wearing of the conventional cape during all of pregnancy.

Recently an ordained brother of our Eastern Church spent considerable time arguing in favor of the exclusive use of the conventional cape. In his argument against the use of the maternity cape, he stated a number of times that he believes that the maternity cape does simplify modesty and is generally an improvement over the conventional cape, and that he personally would favor it, but that the church has spoken and therefore the conventional cape must be required regardless of the ensuing immodesty or hardship it may impose on those already in an abnormal situation.

This type of argumentation presents what seems to us to be a questionable concept of church authority. If we must argue, as this brother did, that the voice of the church has the power to hinder one from an improvement in any given biblical principle, then we have given to a fallible church an authority which is over and above the infallible Scripture itself. To be sure, not everyone believes that the maternity cape is an improvement, but for those who do feel this way, could they not have the privilege of giving God and the Scriptures the highest place of authority in their practice?

Technically and obviously the present statement does allow for some variation of application. The fact that a separate paragraph speaks to the maternity dress, suggests some adaptations are expected and acceptable. Even though the discipline statement is interpreted to mean the conventional cape, most of us can doubtless recall that such terms as "the regular cape dress" or "the conventional cape" etc., were purposely avoided by the discipline reviewing committee in order to allow for some variation in application and to make the statement more readily acceptable.

Since we believe that the conventional cape dress complicates the problem of modesty for some sisters during pregnancy, and that the maternity cape does simplify modesty for many sisters, we find ourselves unable to discipline any sisters for an improvement in modesty. Another problem we face is how to be true to the highest authority of God and still respect the authority of the church? As we see it, the only way that this can consistently be done is to allow an interpretation of the statement, which was originally worded to allow for some flexibility, to include the use of the maternity cape. If this cannot be done, could we allow individuals to be obedient to what they believe to be the best application of the principle of the word of God which we as a church declared to be "the only infallible rule of faith and practice," without being classified as liberal and rebellious? If one must be considered liberal or rebellious in his interest in what he believes to be the best application of biblical modesty, it will be difficult to maintain the high degree of respect for the discipline which is necessary for the most effective and fruitful church administration. On the other hand, if from the highest level of church administration folks can simply be assured that we do allow for flexibility within the realms of modesty during the special period, and that, in spite of variations which appear, we are all doing our conscientious best to preserve biblical modesty, the seeds of misapprehension and distrust will be replaced with confidence and renewed strength within our Brotherhood.

Lebanon district bishops

While the issue of maternity wear was important in its own right, it became the lightning rod for a deeper issue. The issue simply stated was, "Which shall prevail, tradition or principle?"

For many years, Aaron had worked from the premise that Biblical principle should always prevail. Even though tobacco farming was traditional in Lancaster Conference, it needed to surrender to the higher Biblical principle of respecting the human body as the temple of the Holy Spirit. Even though traditionally the ministers only washed feet with each other, the practice needed to surrender to the higher principle of equality in the brotherhood. Even though the bow tie was the traditional practice, it needed to surrender to the higher principle of not adorning the body.

When conflicts arose, it became easy to feel like there were two different goals in focus for the church. Each side felt the other had inferior goals. From the Lebanon perspective, it seemed this way: As more and more people who had roots in Old Order Mennonite settings became members of the Eastern Church, the sentiment more and more shifted in favor of tradition. These people had a strong base in tradition and were not accustomed to evaluating issues in terms of Biblical principles alone. Instead, they tended to evaluate issues in terms of their traditional background. The old traditions could not be wrong. New situations needed traditional answers, not necessarily Biblical answers. Of course, other Eastern districts had a different perspective and saw the issues differently.

By 1985, Aaron found himself in the minority on the tradition versus principle issue. He stood his ground under pressure just as he always had. The Bishop Board minutes indicate that lengthy maternity dress discussions occupied the Board.

Furthermore, the Eastern church was not ready to allow the district variations in practice. Many administrators felt that once district variations were accepted, the Eastern church would lose its authority. The only alternative was, "Either we all do it, or none of us do it."

Without naming anyone, the July 1985 issue of *The Eastern Mennonite Testimony* attacked Aaron and the Lebanon District in an editorial entitled "Maintaining District and Church wide Coherence."

> The form of church government employed by our church group obligates individual congregations and districts to a broader church fellowship. This coherent

relationship is Biblically based and contributes to the spiritual life of the church when the church setting is otherwise Scriptural.

A number of factors are involved in keeping the broader church relationship intact and beneficial. Presently, we will consider the place bishops fill in this area. If a deficiency develops on this level, all other efforts will be greatly hindered.

On a district level, a bishop is responsible to promote unity of conviction and administration among the district ministry. Meaningful district ministers' meetings are an asset in accomplishing this goal. Here issues such as clothing and car standards, social activities, and other current concerns must be openly and honestly discussed. The bishop may not serve as a moderator of the discussion, but he must rather see that the issues are properly clarified and concluded. He should encourage the district ministry to remain alert to trends and violations in other congregations of the district.

A bishop must be careful that one or more of the district congregations does not become the gathering place for substandard and liberal-minded members. Momentarily, this may seem like a way to avoid conflict, but the seeds of disloyalty and disunity will eventually spring forth and bear fruit in open dissension and division. To avoid this and to enhance district unity, issues and problems may not be ignored.

On a church wide level, bishops must respect the church wide conviction and consensus and seek to direct the district ministry and members into that channel. Church wide consensus is determined by the written church discipline and by the discussions and actions at the bishop meetings and the church wide ministers' meetings.

When members desire to transfer from one congregation to another, the bishops involved must be sure the reasons are valid and the motives are sanctified. If members have been restricted or excommunicated, they may not be received into other churches without proper clearance from the former setting. Church authority and unity will be quickly destroyed if the administrative actions of the other districts are not honored.

Bishops must be open and honest with each other. They must value mutual advice and admonition and may not feel suspicious or distrustful of each other. No issue should be so delicate that it cannot be discussed either person to person or together at the bishop meetings...

The writer of the editorial above was a deacon, not a bishop. However, the editorial message expressed a growing sentiment of disfavor toward Aaron and the Lebanon District. This kind of outspoken sentiment was forming an unofficial "party line." Others who did not want to fall into disfavor, parroted the "party line." Anyone who dared question the growing sentiment was considered dangerous and disloyal.

Aaron was associate editor of the *Testimony* when the above editorial was written. He knew that he dared not make an issue of the matters. He chose to remain silent and be non-divisive. He had convictions and experience of his own which he knew was not welcome on an official level at the time. He knew that the various bishops and ministers from other districts who had given him private support would not dare to speak their thoughts in public.

On the maternity dress issue, the majority of the Eastern Church stood ready to take the traditional route. Knowing this, there was pressure on the Bishop Board to threaten Aaron's relationship with the Eastern Church. Some level-headedness on the Bishop Board prevented open schism.

The final wording from the bishops on the maternity dress issue was issued in March 1986 after more than a year of discussing the issue. The Bishop statement was entitled "Approved Maternity Dress Patterns."

> For some situations, extending and enlarging the conventional cape is suitable and adequate. For others, modesty is enhanced if the cape is adapted as illustrated. Adaptations shall be within these guidelines.
>
> The cape is to be made with open sides. The front and back pieces may not come together above the normal waistline. An upside-down tear drop opening is acceptable or the sides may be open a few inches at the normal waist. The sides of the cape below the normal waistline shall be closed.
>
> The cape and dress shall be loose enough so it is not form fitting.
>
> Simple gathering in the front piece for fullness is acceptable but shall be inconspicuous. The material for the entire cape shall be of the same material and run the same direction.
>
> A belt effect is to be maintained around the bottom of the cape. This can be done by folding and sewing as illustrated on the left.

The above statement represented a compromise to which Aaron could agree. In it, the traditional cape and modesty came together in an acceptable maternity dress.

However, the basic issue of tradition versus principle was far from settled. It surfaced in the bishop ordinations conducted during the summer of 1985.

Bishop Isaac Sensenig wrote prior to those ordinations:

> The church is again preparing for the important work of ordaining bishops. In light of the far-reaching influence that is represented in the bishop office, our brotherhood is called to prayer and fasting in behalf of this great work.
>
> The work of the bishop is recognized with prominence in the New Testament Scriptures. While the apostolic office ceased to exist with the death of the apostles, the principles of church administration represented in the apostolic office continue to function. Therefore, it is proper to say that the bishop office was inherent in the apostolic office...
>
> The foregoing principles were historically embraced by the Anabaptist-Mennonite Church...

In July 1985, two bishop ordinations took place. Stephen Ebersole was ordained as the next-generation bishop for the Lebanon District and Lynn Martin to serve the western end of the Denver District.

Of Aaron's new junior bishop, the Bishop minutes state, "Bro. Stephen Ebersole is now a part of our bishop group as a bishop in the Lebanon District since the ordination held at Rehrersburg on July 10, 1985." The story of that ordination can be found in the previous chapter.

Of Lynn Martin the Bishop minutes state, "Bro. Lynn Martin was welcomed as a new member of this bishop group by virtue of his having been ordained as a bishop on July 31, 1985 at Culbertson to serve in the Antrim, Culbertson, and Woodbury congregations of the Denver District."

Criticism of Lebanon District

The Stephen Ebersole family moved to Pennsylvania in April 1986. In November 1987, they moved into a house built on the land Aaron provided to them for their homestead. The two became close working companions. Though they were very different in nature, they saw eye to eye on Bible doctrine, especially on the issue of honoring Bible principle before Mennonite traditions. Even as Simon had told Aaron years before, so Aaron told Stephen, "First, I will walk ahead and you may follow. Then we will walk together, side by side. Then you will walk ahead and I will follow until one day I will slip away." They served together in this changing relationship for over seventeen years.

Aaron and Sidney knew they were under criticism from some sectors of the church for not "doing their homework." When Stephen moved to Pennsylvania, Aaron and Sidney both told him that they would like him to feel free to move ahead with disciplinary activities. But Stephen had woefully little experience in such matters. He had served as minister in Pensacola, Florida, for nearly seven years, but had needed to do very little correctional work.

Stephen realized the members in the Lebanon District churches had far more respect for Sidney and Aaron than they would have for him, an unproven newcomer. He chose to endeavor to strengthen the efforts of his senior bishops rather than to take a different approach.

There were several issues that had been hanging between some of the districts for some time. For a while it seemed the new face in bishop work was a help as the bishops worked through a number of these issues. The maternity cape issue was one of these, and a difficult membership transfer was another.

The Lebanon District bishop team sensed that there was an effort to divide them. As time progressed, they developed a closer cohesion and appreciation for each other. As their cohesion developed, they sensed the old criticisms return.

Back in the Lancaster Conference, Aaron had the reputation for insisting upon religious practices as expressions of Biblical principles. The Biblical principles needed to be living principles, expressing themselves in glad obedience. The Lancaster Conference lost so many right practices (traditions) because the principles behind the traditions were not firmly grounded in the hearts of the practitioners. Aaron recognized that meaningful traditional practice has a short life unless it is undergirded and motivated by Bible principle. He knew that the only other way for lifeless traditions to continue was as lifeless cultural formalism. Once again, Aaron was set for the defense of the Gospel.

Another clash resulted over whether Social Security withholdings were considered a tax or insurance premiums administrated by the federal government. Some felt that Social Security taxes paid by church workers became insurance premiums and thus were a violation of the Scriptures. These same people felt that payment of these taxes (insurance premiums) would undermine the non-insurance approach to life and that church/state issues would become clouded. The other side maintained simply that taxes should be paid to the government.

The one side perceived that the Mennonite lifestyle was threatened and was ready to violate the law of the land to preserve the lifestyle. The Lebanon District believed obedience to the laws of the nation was mandated by the New Testament.

The issue faded when the laws of the land changed to allow plain people exemption from the Social Security tax. The Eastern Church leadership issued a statement to the church (printed in the January 1989 issue of *The Eastern Mennonite Testimony*) urging the members to waive the benefits. The statement urged members to opt out of the socialistic system.

On another front, the Lebanon District was taken to task for permitting too much game playing by young people. An agreement was reached among the bishops which stated:

1. That playing is a normal part of a child's life. Playing at home and at school with proper parental and teacher direction is considered a part of a young person's normal development.

2. When a young person becomes a Christian then the playing should begin to taper off.

3. By the time they are old enough to date the playing should be about over except such situations that they play with students or younger brothers and sisters.

4. Playing among upper teenagers should be limited to a home experience or where families visit each other.

5. Where groups of young people gather from various areas to attend a service and then go to a home afterward for social life is not viewed as a good thing.

6. Young people of the church meeting primarily for play activities is not considered acceptable.

7. We see that it is best for the mid-teenager and younger to be with their families and not be left to roam too freely.

8. That we work toward these goals and to keep social interest from becoming predominant.

The hat-wearing for the brethren became another focus in the increasing polarization. While the Lebanon District held the position that a man wearing a hat should use a plain hat, the other districts felt that plain hat-wearing was a symbol of nonconformity to the world and identification with the Mennonite heritage. The Lebanon District felt that making a religious issue over the hat converted the hat from being simple weather protection to a symbol of religious significance, which is forbidden to men in 1 Corinthians 11. One of the outward signs of a Christian man is his uncovered head.

On still another front, changes made in the 1987 discipline review affected Aaron and the Lebanon District directly. The following item was added in its entirety under Article VII, Restrictions.

8. Recorded music should build appreciation for the worship hymns of the church, and for congregational-type singing. We believe that a capella singing is the form that most accurately represents New Testament principles as well as the historic Anabaptist, Mennonite faith.

Because of the highly emotional appeal of stringed instruments, and their prominent place in modern sensual music, they are not permitted for actual use or in recorded selections. Electronic keyboard instruments which can automatically simulate the rhythm and tempo of secular music are also objectionable, and are not permitted. We also sense the possible conditioning effect of the traditional keyboard instruments.

A capella singing and recorded selections that reflect the emphasis of modern "gospel song" performers with their entertaining appeal should be eliminated. The songs we sing and to which we listen should be Biblically sound in content, and sung in a manner that glorifies God rather than man. Ps. 40:3; 1 Cor. 14:15; Eph. 5:19; Col. 3:16.

It was no secret that the Lebanon District ministry were largely opposed to forbidding certain types of musical instruments, such as organs and pianos, for personal use. While the issue was being decided, they endeavored to use their influence to prevent such a ruling from coming into existence. But when the vote was taken, the proposed standard was adopted. They never even considered resisting the new standard.

The Lebanon District bishops and ministry wrote a letter to the members of the District in response. They were ready to lay down their preferences out of loyalty for the larger church body and in an effort to minimize the differences between them. Aaron was grieved when rumors later went out that he had not used his influence to help his district accept the ruling. He not only accepted it; he was ready to exercise discipline if there were members who refused to comply. The Lebanon District did lose some members over this issue.

> Greetings of love and peace in the Name of Jesus, the Prince of Peace. We thank our God often for your sincere desire to wholeheartedly follow the doctrines of Christ and the applications of the church.
>
> This letter is a response to the new disciplinary ruling on music interests and the deep feelings some of you have experienced in relation to it.
>
> We believe this statement has come in the interest of eliminating worldly influences in our music. Sensing the direction worldly music is traveling and the increasing interest on the part of some in unwholesome music we consider this concern to be valid and legitimate.
>
> We recognize that this statement does call for the disposing of some music that had been considered legitimate and the elimination of some previously accepted musical instruments. We also recognize that the Scripture's teaching concerning personal praise and worship and the use of musical instruments cannot be changed. We consider the current ruling to be an effort to eliminate worldly influences in music and not an effort to make some instruments moral and others immoral.
>
> Therefore, for the sake of Brotherhood unity (Psalm 122:6-9) and since in our opinion conforming to this standard will not force anyone to disobey the Scripture, we ask our membership to comply by Spring Council and Communion.
>
> To those who are especially dissatisfied with this statement we enlist your support. Rather than leave our fellowship, or grow disillusioned while remaining in our midst we beseech you to remain with us and throw your energies into Christian growth and service.
>
> In these remaining days on the earth, let us not be among those who begin to smite their fellow-servants, but continue to watch for our Lord's coming, and serve Him faithfully.

The Lightning Rod Message

On October 26, 1989, Stephen Ebersole preached a message at Shirksville which reflected against the church administration of leaders in other parts of the church. Interestingly, the reverse had been happening every so often across the church with silent sanction. While the editorial above named no person or district, most people in the Eastern Church knew who was being referred to. Some visiting preachers even reflected against the Lebanon District administration while preaching in Lebanon District pulpits. Reflection one way was sanctioned; reflection the other way was totally unacceptable.

Aaron agreed with some of the concerns and shared these concerns with Stephen. He disagreed with making a public response to what everyone knew was obvious: that there was discord in the church.

He saw what the perceived ostracism and stigmatizing was doing to his district. Rather than producing a respect for the conservative viewpoint, there was an increased groundswell of resentment against not only the antagonists, but more and more for what they stood for. Aaron had enough experience resisting apostasy in the Lancaster Conference. Now he saw his constituency being prejudiced against conservatives. He did not believe making a public response would help hold together the church that he loved. Aaron understood that even though he had invested so much energy into it, the Church still belonged to Jesus Christ.

Aaron was concerned that an effort to confront traditionalism would result in a reaction against conservatism. "A thing over done is a thing undone." He felt if a position against traditions was too forceful, then people would disregard the good traditions of the Mennonite church. Indeed, a few of the Lebanon District families had already left and were attending Charity Christian Fellowship in Leola, Pennsylvania, an Anabaptist/Pietist-type movement with strong rhetoric against church standards and against Amish/Mennonite traditions.

Stephen Ebersole's sermon at Shirksville opened the floodgates of pent-up criticism in parts of the Eastern Church. To help deal constructively with the situation, four bishops were assigned to work with Stephen on his perceived weakness. At a meeting in Aaron's home on September 23, 1989, Stephen was presented with three questions he needed to answer. 1) What is your view of tradition and culture? 2) What is your view of church authority? 3) How do you view your relationship to the church and particularly to the bishop group of which you are a part?

Stephen gave his answers in the presence of the four bishops. Aaron took comfort in the statement made by the most experienced leader of the bishop committee. "I see nothing here that would call for drastic action against

Brother Stephen." Furthermore, he then asked each member of the committee personally, and each one gave a favorable response to this conclusion. It was agreed to present an acknowledgment to the bishop board and then read the statement to the Eastern ministry.

When the committee's conclusions were reported to the bishop board, some of the bishops were not at all satisfied and a lengthy discussion followed.

On February 6, 1990, while the Lebanon District bishops were excused, the rest of the Bishop Board formulated a plan as to how to deal with the situation.

1. That a statement be made at Shirksville involving Bro. Stephen Ebersole.

"Regarding the message on October 26, 1989. In whatever way my statements were undermining the church, I am sorry and I am herewith submitting myself to work in harmony with the rest of the bishops and I intend to continue to uphold the discipline of the church."

2. That the four bishops presently appointed continue to give Bro. Stephen some help in his thinking and in relation to his responsibilities as well as his companion's [wife's] attitude.

3. That two bishops be asked to give some counsel and direction to the administration of Shirksville and Elm St. Congregations. By voting it was decided that Bro. Alvin Snyder and Bro. Lynn Martin shall do this.

4. For Bro. Stephen's continued services as a bishop we are waiting to see what can be accomplished in the immediate future in helping him find his way through this matter. But as a bishop body we are feeling that his involvement in bishop work should be limited and Bro. Alvin fill in for him.

The response to the four points brought further unrest. On March 16, 1990, while Stephen was in the South holding counsel and communion services, the non-Lebanon bishops decided that Stephen should be silenced. The Bishop Board minutes state that

There was a long discussion on how to meet this problem and how to help Bro. Stephen find his way. We agreed to ask Bro. Stephen to limit himself in the following way...

1. Bro. Stephen would not exercise his ministerial-bishop office for 5 months— April 1-September 1, 1990.

2. After September 1, 1990 he will be preaching again in the district and exercise

his office and after January 1, 1991 he will return to normal duties if the situation is brought to a satisfactory rest.

This move by the Bishop Board deeply disturbed Aaron and most of the Lebanon District. Stephen himself wrote a three-page letter addressed to the Bishops "and all concerned" in response. In the letter he says:

I must confess I have been reeling in shock at the action taken at the last bishop meeting restricting my service in the church. This letter is an attempt to reply to that action, and is an open letter for whomever may have an interest in the issues in the church at this time.

As I reflect over the past events that have led up to the more recent past, I continue to ask, what are the issues, what are the charges that have prompted such a drastic action? Are there really theological or ideological differences? Are there specific events or actions in focus?

About the time I feel that I understand the situation, and analyze it and share it, I find out some of my fellow bishops maintain to others that we don't disagree when we discuss issues, the action is therapeutic, but if we agree, why the action?....

Another answer to "Why the action?" might be that apparently much of the emphasis to restrict me originates or comes from church-wide reaction and a desire to appease the masses. The excuse is given, we must do this for therapeutic results. My question is "What are people being told that stirs them up so?" I am again made keenly aware of the amazing ability of the human heart to believe and accept as truth, rumors and tales that are far from the truth and never bother to verify them. To use the reaction of the group to determine the guilt and sentence of an individual can lead to serious error. Is that not what gave the momentum to the horrible crucifixion of our Lord? Where guilt is established, punishment may be meted out to criminals. Where guilt is not established, the result is a martyr.

The question comes to me, "Can I accept the restriction placed upon me? Can I submit?" According to 1 Peter 4, suffering patiently is always thankworthy and glory will go to the Father. It would be very hard to accept the stigma and the restriction for I enjoy my calling, but the restriction could be beneficial in the struggle of my new nature to overcome the old man. I can bow my heart to this as permitted by the Father's will and become better through it all...

The Lebanon District met together to discuss how to relate to this action. There was widespread speculation that the district ministry would take the normal route and divide the church. Some of the ministry had written letters encouraging division, and there was a strong push to move on.

In the end, the Lebanon District ministry chose to submit to Stephen's silencing rather than to divide, for several reasons. Aaron emphasized the need to recognize and submit to God-ordained authority. He often reflected back on the amiable division from Lancaster Conference and wished that if there must be a separating of ways, it could be done with the mother group's blessing. Also, he loathed to leave the church that he had helped to bring to birth and had labored for so diligently. Aaron and Stephen understood that the Scriptures do not teach using division as a means of solving problems in the church, and urged the district to respond with patience.

This counsel carried the day. The Eastern Pennsylvania Mennonite Church remained organizationally intact.

Aaron and his co-bishops, Sidney Gingrich, Lester Martin, and Stephen Ebersole wrote a letter to the Lebanon District Churches dated March 28, 1990.

> Your district ministry has been together in several sessions with almost 100% attendance. Our brethren came from Grays Prairie, Dublin, Pensacola, and the Bahamas (Wilmer Shenk) to share in our deliberations and discussions...
>
> After several hours of careful, prayerful consideration, with Bro. Stephen's encouragement we agreed on the following statement to present to the bishops:
>
> "With regard to the bishop action of 3/16/90 concerning Bro. Stephen Ebersole, we as a district ministry continue to have reservations about the restrictions, the validity of the charges, and the procedure taken that resulted in this action.
>
> "Furthermore, we would welcome calling a committee of bishops who are unrelated to the problem to help us resolve this difficulty. (The bishop group would choose one member, the Lebanon District Ministry would choose a second member, and these two appointed ones would choose a third member. These three brethren would comprise this committee.)
>
> "Nevertheless, if the bishop board decrees that Bro. Stephen shall be inactive until September 1, 1990, we will not resist the temporary restriction."
>
> ....We would again urge that we all exercise ourselves in prayer and fasting, in love, and in patience and faith in our unchanging, Almighty God...

Aaron himself wrote a letter to the bishops appealing for consideration.

> The part of the statement that Bro. Stephen gave particular encouragement to is ... "we will not resist the temporary restriction." The district ministry as a whole

does not yet feel that the charges warrant the measure of discipline taken against Bro. Stephen. We do not therefore believe he should voluntarily limit himself as requested. Neither do we believe that the district ministry's counsels and recommendations can legitimately be by-passed or simply brushed aside.

We have agreed, however, that we will not resist but rather submit to the action of the bishops for his temporary inactivity. We are indeed sorry that there need to be divided viewpoints on how to resolve the difficulties we find ourselves in....

In light of what has been termed by people across the church as carnal and un-Christian reactions to the concerns of the past few months, could the bishops consider rolling back the record and calling our people as a whole to repentance and revival?

There have been so many hear-says, judgmental attitudes and expressions, imaginations and surmising, rashness and unwholesome reactionary responses, etc. embodied in our brotherhood that perhaps nothing but revival will heal the hurts and wounds among us.

Neither have we bishops been altogether free (perhaps unintentionally) of misunderstandings, some hard speeches and hurtful insults.

Not only in our brotherhood but all over the nation as well as across the borders of our nation people of many church groups are focusing their attention on what is happening in the Eastern Pennsylvania Mennonite Church. They are evaluating, passing judgment, making predictions, and taking sides. It would seem that the greatest challenge we could give to the religious world of currently interested folks and the greatest and most effective witness to the cause of consistent conservativism would be realized if we could experience a revival that would melt us and mold us together in the cause that we have paid a high price for the last quarter of a century.

In the words of the song writer my heart cries out; "O Lord, send a revival and let it begin in me." I do not hesitate to identify myself as one who needs revival. I have had a tendency to lose confidence and courage. I have reacted to disappointment in others by sharing things that although they may have been the truth would not have needed to be said and certainly did not contribute to love and unity among us. For this I seek forgiveness and forbearance from God and from all of you.

Israel's experience of renewal after 70 years of captivity was preluded by a man of God humbling himself before God and identifying himself with a people who were desperately in need of the mercy and delivering power of God. Daniel gives his testimony in chapter 9, verse 4. "I prayed unto the Lord my God and made my confession." And then in a long confession he identified himself with the sins and needs of his people through the use of the plural pronouns "we", "us", "our" more than a dozen and a half times. He then concludes his prayer of confession with, "O Lord, hear; O Lord forgive; O Lord hearken and do; defer not, for thine own sake, O my God, for thy city and thy people are called by thy name."

For our Lord's sake, and because of the church of Christ which we represent, and because we are called the people of God, may we yield ourselves to the work of revival that will bring healing to our hurts and glorify our Lord and bring added souls into the kingdom before our candlestick is removed and darkness descends upon us.

In Christian love and hope,

Your fellow brother and companion in need of the mercy of our Lord Jesus Christ.

Aaron M. Shank

No clemency was forthcoming. On April 9, 1990 the bishop board took action "to ask that Bro. Stephen Ebersole submit to a period of inactivity in public ministry."

The Bishop Board minutes state, "Bro. Stephen gave a response that while he is not able to see into the propriety of this action he is willing to submit to it."

The four bishops in the Lebanon District consequently wrote a letter to the Lebanon District churches dated April 15, 1990.

The following is Bro. Stephen's testimony to our district churches in regards to this action:

"The Holy Scriptures have much to say as to what the believer's response is to be to buffeting and reproof. While I do not understand why this action has been taken, I nevertheless choose to 'count it all joy' knowing 'that this shall turn to my salvation through your prayer and the supply of the spirit of Jesus Christ.' (Phil.1:19)

"If this action is just, I want to profit by it. If it is unfair, a wrong response will not rectify the situation.

"My heart goes out to you my brethren in this struggle and my prayer is that you become not bitter, but better in Him, knowing 'the love of Christ which passeth knowledge, that ye may be filled with all the fulness of God.' (Eph. 3:19) I would also appeal to you that 'we continue to strive together for the sake of the gospel.'

"As in the past we have sought the will of the Lord Jesus Christ through His Holy Word, let us continue to do so, and exalt His power and seek His blessing by bowing our hearts before Him in submission and worship."

Your Lebanon district bishops and ministry have found this to be a very humbling and testing experience. It has placed many questions on our minds that are not easy to answer. We are herewith recommending that we identify with Bro. Stephen's testimony in our personal response and submission....

The following unofficial statement was privately handed by Bishop Alvin Snyder to Aaron on April 11, 1990 as an answer to the Lebanon District Ministry on why the action was taken against Bro. Stephen Ebersole's bishop-ministry work.

> We feel that the sentiments expressed by Bro. Stephen in the sermon and otherwise are not in harmony with the burden of the founding of the Eastern Church and will undermine the church as we presently know it.

> We sense some confusion in the mind of Bro. Stephen as to his loyalties to the church and as to his belief regarding the place of the church and church discipline. We sense a tendency to depreciate the necessary place of standards and church regulation. This influences towards exercising excommunication only when Scriptures are directly violated, and undermines the right of the church to make applications in harmony with the spirit of the Scriptures.

> We see a tendency to be independent in his thinking and outlook. He has on occasions openly challenged church positions and the work of his fellow bishops. He tends to hold his personal view of the Scriptures over the collective church's view of the Scripture and has been slow at times to give himself to bishop board feeling and consensus.

> In light of the above, the action of April 9, 1990 was taken to settle disruption across the church and to check the influence of the areas of concern above. Also, this will give Bro. Stephen time to sort and correct his thinking and to show whether or not he can move with the rest of the bishops.

Aaron wrote back to Alvin on April 17, 1990.

> What will people conclude now who see or hear these "we feel" and "we sense" and "we see a tendency" indictments and compare them with Stephen's clear-cut statement of his beliefs in the letter he shared at our bishop-ministers' meeting at Elm Street on March 27, 1990.

> If you were a person unrelated or uninvolved in the conflict and would compare the two statements, which side do you think you might come out on?

> I did not talk to Bro. Stephen yet about your statement. However, having worked with him in administrative and disciplinary work, I must say I do not believe your statement represents clear-cut truth. The second paragraph is particularly untruthful in relation to his administrative performance as well as his own declaration of his position in his letter.

> Whether the action of April 9, 1990 will "settle disruption across the church" or increase disruption remains to be seen. Whether the blessing of the Lord can be upon it or not also remains to be seen.

May the God of all grace and the Father of mercies be gracious unto us.

Prayerfully yours,

Aaron

Aaron insisted upon protocol in formal meetings. At a ministerial meeting held at Rehrersburg the previous January 24, a disruption occurred when some ministers overrode the authority of the bishops. Aaron was moderating this special church-wide ministers' meeting. After the first point on the agenda was discussed in a wholesome manner, Aaron moved on to the second point—formulating a church statement on the issue of divorce and remarriage.

Several of the ministerial body stood to their feet, evidently speaking on behalf of others, and stated that until the issues among the bishops get resolved they are unwilling to consider the issue at hand. By doing so the protesting ministers boycotted the purpose of the meeting.

Aaron explained to them that a committee of bishops had been appointed and were working with the problem. A number of ministers were not satisfied with this explanation and requested that the bishops adjourn for a special session and return with a proposal more definite and satisfactory to the group.

The bishops went to the basement and reviewed a statement that Jesse Neuenschwander and Stephen Ebersole had previously worked out and agreed could be shared should opportunity arise that evening. When the statement was shared with the bishops, the majority of the bishops nodded consent. However, at least two had a serious reaction, maintaining that the ministerial body would not accept it. These bishops asserted that only Bishop Board action against Stephen's ordination would satisfy the ministerial body.

Half an hour later, Jesse Neuenschwander appeased the ministerial body with an explanation.

Characteristically, Aaron would not let the matter rest when guidelines were violated. He wrote:

Dear Brethren,

We believe that the Guidelines for the Church-wide Ministers' Meeting were seriously violated in the January 24, 1990 meeting at Rehrersburg.

Guideline #3 states "That this group does not...have equal or superior authority to the district ministry or the bishop group." In as much as our bishops are responsible to plan for the church wide ministers meetings "as the need arises" and in as much as the January 24 meeting had been planned for by the bishops and in as much as the agenda had been mailed out to the ministry inviting them to come and share in a discussion on the items of the agenda, was it not an act of "superior authority over the bishops" for the ministry to disrupt the meeting and defy the moderator's efforts to fulfill the purpose of the planned agenda for the evening?

Number 5 of the Guidelines states that "This group shall not have authority to deal with individual members of the ordained group." Was it not an action of "superior authority" over the bishops, for brethren who knew that the bishops had an appointed bishop committee working on a particular issue involving an ordained brother, to disrupt and boycott the purpose of the meeting in order to bring pressure on the bishops for action against an ordained brother according to their concepts of the issue at stake.

To add to the seriousness of this type of boycotting, it is commonly reported that some of our bishops were encouraging our ministry in this type of action. Could an appeal be made to our ministry that we do not resort to the world's method of boycotting a bishop-planned meeting in order to bring pressure on the bishops for any cause? If, as leaders, we cannot honor our own Guidelines and standards, can we expect, or have any right to expect, our people to respect them, whenever the standards run counter to what they believe to be consistent and right?

We believe the proper order for the January 24 meeting, as well as any other meeting—especially when the agenda is previously arranged and called for by the bishops, would be to carry through the basic purpose of the meeting and then to give opportunity for additional items for consideration. If concerns are raised that are worthy of consideration and there is not sufficient time for discussion, another meeting could be called for.

At the Rehrersburg meeting there were brethren from out of state who came nearly 800 miles especially in the interest of the divorce and remarriage discussion. They had to turn around and leave for home, not only embarrassed, but greatly disappointed. Is there any way for such a situation to be justified?

Lebanon District Ministry

On April 11, 1990 at the Ministerial Conferring Meeting, the bishops shared the following concern.

The bishops are appealing to the ordained body that we use charity and good judgment in bringing items to the floor and respect the guidelines outlined for this work.

We regret the lack of order in the January 24 meeting wherein some traveled far to come to the meeting and then were not able to discuss the issues intended.

The bishops also are appealing to the ordained body that we exercise care in the statements we make about each other and in a discriminatory way refer to each other and to each other's districts. Also, that we speak the truth in love and not be too ready to believe and pass on rumors that only bring more stress.

Nor would Aaron allow another irregularity to rest. At the next Bishop Board meeting following the ministerial boycott, February 6, 1990, the Lebanon District bishops were dismissed from the meeting while the rest of the bishops discussed a solution to the problem facing them. This left 62% of the bishops to decide on a recommended procedure while the discipline calls for 75% affirmative vote of the bishops to consider a matter passed. Aaron commented:

This ... was a questionable procedure on at least two counts. 1) It reduced the number of bishops to where it was illegal to do business and 2) Bishops have never been dismissed from a meeting without rivals or opposing sides being sent out together. While the action to silence Bro. Stephen was not sealed at that meeting, the minutes state that the proposed silencing was voted on and passed in the absence of the Lebanon District bishops. After the recommended action was passed ... the bishop minutes state that the Lebanon District bishops were called back to the meeting and "the decision was read and shared." The meeting was then dismissed....

At no time was Bro. Stephen examined in relation to his personal life and found to be unfaithful, at no time was his doctrinal position examined and proven to be false, and at no time was he blamed for and found guilty of refusing to accept the counsel of the bishops and the district ministry. He even accepted and recommended that his ministry accept his period of silencing.

As it relates to the discipline's outline for dealing with an ordained brother the bishops argued, and continue to argue, that this statement of procedure does not apply in the current situation. It is argued that the bishops have the authority and "are responsible to make final disposition in correcting matters."

It is very true that the bishops constitute the highest authority in the organization of the church and that "The bishops are responsible to make final disposition in correcting matters." However, when or where ever law makers have established laws and guidelines is it not true that the highest authorized agents need to find their basis for an authoritative voice in their established rules and guidelines? Can any governing body ignore or detour around their own established laws on any given item or issue without rendering void their right of authority on any other items of the established laws of their organization? The Scripture declares that even God has magnified His Word above all His name. If God were not to work consistently with His laws, His name would be meaningless. This method, to some of us, seems like another irregularity of procedure in dealing with the problem. The fact is, the outline in our discipline for dealing with an ordained brother was never even considered in the action that was taken.

Another thing that seemed irregular and unfair was the fact that the action was taken without any advance clear-cut statement as to the basis for the action. Since the action was taken, there have been a number of attempts to provide a written statement clarifying or justifying the action. From our point of view these documents have, although doubtless unintentionally, embodied exaggerations, misrepresentations, or slants that render them of questionable accuracy.

As an example, one such statement under the title "...Issues Currently Under Question" spoke of "carelessly" reflecting against Mennonite Heritage, and "recklessly" seeking alternatives and reflecting against "overall" Mennonite tradition. To use such descriptive terms when referring to issues presently under question seems like a rather reckless insinuation of Bro. Stephen's position as well as the position of any of the rest of us.

The above referred to document has been revised and at my insistence the title has been changed to "Bishop Statement for Unifying and Strengthening our Position."...

As pressure grew for an explanation for the action against Stephen's ministry, the bishops wrote a statement which attempted to identify where the different positions were stemming from doctrinally. On July 19, 1990, a four-point statement was distributed to the bishops, but there was no author identified on the statement.

1. We believe that Christ and His church are inseparable. We further recognize that Christ's call to the believer will result in loyalty and commitment for the church which is his body. To emphasize loyalty to Christ without a corresponding call to loyalty and commitment to the church will result in a scriptural imbalance.

2. We believe that spiritual gifts are given to the church corporately. Therefore, we conclude that a spiritual group's judgments on issues and interpretations of the Scriptures are more valid than the individual's. Even though we recognize the individual's contribution, the individual is still responsible to group consensus as long as the overall emphasis of the group is in harmony with the Scriptures and should rather be suspicious of his own opinions in favor of the group's position.

3. We believe that the traditional Mennonite understanding and application of Bible principle are valid and in harmony with the N.T. teaching and practice. We believe that a respect and an adherence to the time-tested "Mennonite way" will

bless us with spiritual advancement and growth. Even though there may be other God-approved alternatives, for us to reflect against this heritage or to wrecklessly [sic] seek alternatives robs us of our stability and opens us for apostasy [sic].

4. We believe that the church has a mandate to provide direction beyond the mere letter of Scripture. We are to discern attitudes and patterns of conduct that condition in a direction contrary to Scriptures and to discern that which brings the church in harmony with Scriptures. To confine church voice to a mere letter observance is to open her to the influence of the new gods that arise.

In response to these four points, Aaron wrote to the Bishop Board.

Dear Brethren,

Greetings in the Name of the One whom we believe continues to multiply His grace, mercy, and peace unto us His unworthy creatures.

Reflections on our church life over the recent past are quite humbling to say the least and, of course, embody some heart-rending and disappointing aspects.

References to our problems at our Ministers Conferring Meeting and the inferences of the legitimacy or need for church division given at such a time as this indicate that a significant state of unrest still exists on the part of some in our fellowship. The echo of the emphasis on division in our meeting has sounded across our continent and even across our national borders.

An ordained brother outside our district recently diagnosed our church as being divided into three factions over the action of the bishops in relation to the temporary silencing of one of our number.

Group one feels that the action was unjust, unfair, and far too drastic for the offense caused.

Group two feels that the action was just and has accomplished its purpose and that the book should now be closed on the issue.

Group three feels that the action was just but that it has not produced the desired results and that more drastic action is needed to bring the church to rest.

Group three seems to be the most vocal of these groups. According to the action taken at the time of the silencing, the church will need to be brought to a satisfactory rest by January 1 for things to become normal again. On the surface the present situation does not look very hopeful because of the dissatisfaction of faction three and in light of the public references to division at our last Conferring Meeting.

Those of us who have been most closely and most seriously affected by the action continue to have apprehensions and unanswered questions about the original actions taken as well as about some of the continued efforts made toward stabilizing conditions. Our failure to have a clear-cut and understandable statement of the basis for the action before the action was taken and our failure in repeated efforts to draw up a statement to identify or clarify the issues seems only to add to our perplexity and also perhaps to our confusion. The current seven point statement under consideration seems to be no exception.

As an example point number three on the statement is virtually saying that presently the person or persons under question are "carelessly" reflecting against past Mennonite practice and are "recklessly" seeking alternatives to, and are reflecting against "overall" Mennonite traditions.

The descriptive terms "carelessly", "recklessly," and "overall" seem to us to be grossly exaggerated terms related to the issues. If the writers of this statement and others on the board really believe that these descriptive terms represent accuracy and honesty we can certainly appreciate the patience and forbearance you have exercised in the situation.

Maybe we should just let the statement rest and let God be the judge as to whether this represents the truth but permit us, at least once more, to plead your mercies and compassionate consideration in any finalizing of further statements or actions. To some of us the assumptions of the statement cannot be considered solid truth by any stretch of our imagination. We also feel that there are a number of other distorted assumptions and inferences in the statement. Any statement adopted by this board becomes a part of the historical record of the Eastern Pennsylvania Mennonite Church and historical records are worse than worthless if there are inaccuracies involved.

The above concern illustrates what appears to some to be a continuing effort to justify a drastic action that was taken by unduly slanting things a certain direction and by magnifying or misrepresenting reasons for the action taken.

We stated in our very first letter of concern (March 1990) regarding the proposed action that "we believe there are due causes for concern but that these can and should be addressed through brotherly procedures."

From among our bishop group, in discussion on the situation it has been stated several times that the concern Brother Stephen meant to address in the censured sermon was not an invalid concern. For the problems that were embodied in that message he has acknowledged error and made suitable confession and sought forgiveness.

It is our sincere desire that our church fellowship comes to rest. We are not interested in continuing to agitate the situation or challenge what the Bishop Board decides. However, come January 1 and if faction three continues to agitate unrest and promote division to the point that the bishops feel that more drastic action must be imposed— unless some new flagrant inconsistencies come to the surface and unless the E.P.M.C. Discipline formula for dealing with ordained brethren is consistently and conscientiously employed we do not at this juncture see how we can honor any further or more drastic action.

May I suggest that we give serious consideration to the possibility of our present church condition being similar to the Ephesus crisis (Revelation 2:1-5). The church at Ephesus was perhaps second to none in their church labors, in their practice of sound doctrine, in their ability to detect and avoid error and erroneous teachers and in their untiring perseverance in the faith. But they were failing in the one greatest of all virtues—the virtue on which the whole design of redemption is based. In spite of all the commendable aspects of their church life our Lord Jesus diagnosed them as a fallen church in need of repentance in order to keep from becoming extinct as a part of the church of Jesus Christ. In their efforts to keep soundness of faith they were actually destroying the faith.

Would it be too arrogant or egotistical to say that in our day, at least for our local area and out-reach, our church has been second to none in some of the same qualities that were true and commendable at Ephesus? And would it be too suggestive to say that we may also be guilty of having left the same qualities for which Ephesus was censured by our Lord?

If this inference to our problem being similar to the Ephesus crisis problem is a wrong inference please be gracious and forgive me for this inferred error. The indications seem pretty clear that we are guilty. Might we not do well indeed to acknowledge our condition and blow the trumpet and issue a church-wide call to repentance in order to keep our candlestick from being removed.

I do not hesitate to identify myself as one of those in need of a greater measure of divine love shed abroad in my heart.

Whatever the need, may God be gracious to us and supply that need for our rest and for His glory.

In brotherly love and hope,

Aaron M. Shank

Silence was the only response to Aaron's letter.

In addition to Aaron's personal response, the Lebanon District bishops felt there was a tone to the four points statement that needed a clarifying response. They soon called for a meeting with their district ministry to formulate their position. On August 23, 1990, with prayer and fasting, the Lebanon District Ministry adopted the following response. The statement which follows was shared with the Bishop Board. By this time, blame for the church-wide stress was shifting from Stephen Ebersole to the Lebanon District.

1. We believe that while Christ and His Church will be inseparable in eternity, no church group can claim infallibility here on earth. 2 Cor. 11:2-4; Gal. 4:11; Rev. 2:5; 3:20. Any individual or group may among other snares fall into spiritual fornication (worldliness Jas. 4:4), or into self love (traditionalism Col. 2:19-23), and thus forfeit their betrothal to the Lamb of God. We recognize that a believer's commitment to Christ will cause him to be loyal to fellow-believers as members in the body which is Christ's Church. Eph. 4:15,16; 2 Tim. 2:22 We believe the primary emphasis of preaching will be one of personal obedience to the Lordship of Jesus Christ (2 Cor. 4:5; Col. 2:6-10), which will result in growth (Eph. 2:20-22) and visible expressions of unity as believers "walk by the same rule" (Phil. 3:16). To overemphasize loyalty and commitment to a leader or a church group may result in: 1. straying into false doctrine (2 Peter 2:13-15), 2. schisms and divisions (1 Cor. 4:6), 3. a de-emphasis on the place of the Word and the Holy Spirit in the life of the believer (2 Tim. 3:15; John 16:13; 1 John 2:20).

2. We believe the Scriptures to teach obedience to church traditions (2 Thess. 2:15), subjection to church leaders (Heb. 13:7,17), and submission to each other (Eph. 5:21). Therefore, we conclude a believer is to harmonize himself with the applications of a Scriptural group (Phil. 3:16). However, since only the Scriptures are infallible (2 Peter 1:19), and since each individual must give account of himself to God (Rom. 14:12), and since the criteria of judgment is the Gospel alone (Romans 2:16), we conclude the church is organized to bring believers to submission to the Word of God, and to herself but not ultimately to herself. Every believer is encouraged to diligently study the Bible, and thus develop convictions to guide his life's choices (2 Tim. 3:16,17). No church group is so spiritual that they are above a Biblical challenge, nor so Scriptural that they may decide a given Scripture does not mean what it says (Gal. 1:8). Special blessing was pronounced upon those in Sardis who dared to stand true to their convictions, in spite of the consensus decline (Rev. 3:4).

3. We respect the traditions and practices of the Mennonite Church that are expressions of the precepts and principles of the New Testament. We recognize however, that it is possible for traditions to creep in that actually prohibit spiritual advancement and growth (Mark 7:4,8). The only true standard whereby one may discern the validity of traditions is the Word of God. To blindly adhere to traditions of the past that have no Biblical basis, or to recklessly abandon traditions that have well expressed Biblical principles will rob us of spirituality and guarantee apostasy.

4. We believe the church has a mandate to make applications to the teachings of the Eternal Word of God (Matt. 16:18,19; Acts 15). The church should continue to examine new practices, inventions and innovations, and weigh these by the principles of the Word of God to determine their value, or their detrimental influence. That which is basically good will still need direction. Where no Biblical principles are violated or jeopardized, the church may

safely conclude the issue is within the realm of Christian liberty (Romans 14; 1 Cor. 8).

The rest of the Eastern bishops did not agree with the above statement. In an effort to answer the above statement, in an effort to resolve the difficulties, and in an effort to bring unity to the Eastern Church, the bishops formulated a statement of their own which they issued to the church-wide ministry on January 9, 1991. They titled it "Issues Currently Under Question," but at Aaron's insistence renamed it "Bishop Statement for Unifying and Strengthening Our Position." The title implies that the Lebanon District Bishops shared the position, when in reality they had formulated their own position to which the following is an answer.

1. We believe that Christ and His body, the Church that is loyal to Him and to His Word, are one. We recognize that Christ's call to the believer will result in loyalty and commitment to the Church. To emphasize that loyalty to the Church is inferior to loyalty to Christ or to emphasize loyalty to Christ in a way that reflects against loyalty to the Church results in undermining the New Testament place of the Church. While it is understood that Christ is infallible and that the Church on earth is ever imperfect and prone to apostasy, loyalty to a faithful Church is part of loyalty to Christ. To emphasize loyalty to Christ without a definite call to loyalty and commitment to the Church is an imbalanced emphasis. A basic proof that the individual is loyal to Christ is his loyalty and faithfulness to a Scriptural Church. John 17:21-23; Acts 2:41; Eph. 1:22,23; Col. 1:18; 2 Thess. 2:15; 3:6; Rev. 1:20.

2. We believe that spiritual gifts are given to the Church. The body is made up of many members. No one member has all the gifts given by Christ. Therefore, we conclude that a spiritual group's judgment on issues and interpretations of the Scriptures are safer than the individual's. Even though we recognize the individual's contribution and that the individual may be more right than the group in some instances, the individual still has a responsibility to the body so long as the overall position of the group is in harmony with the Scripture, and should first of all question his own opinion in favor of the group's. Matt. 18:17; Acts 2; Rom. 12; 1 Cor. 12; Eph. 4:8-16; Phil. 2:1,2; 3:16; Heb. 13:7,17; Rev. 2:7,11,17,29; 3:6,13,22.

3. We believe the traditional Mennonite understanding and application of Bible principles are valid and in harmony with New Testament teaching and practice. We believe that respect for and adherence to this time-tested "Mennonite way" will enhance stability and spiritual growth. Even though there may be other God-approved alternatives, for us to reflect against this heritage or to freely seek alternatives robs us of our stability and opens us to

apostasy. Even though there have been some unwholesome aspects to the past, these inconsistencies should not be used to reflect against the value of the overall Mennonite tradition. We believe that to be overly suspicious of tradition leads to undue experimentation. 1 Thess. 5:14,21; 2 Thess. 2:15.

4. We believe that the Church is responsible to provide direction beyond the letter of Scripture and the Church Discipline. The Church has this obligation in the face of ever-changing world practices and in light of the fact that the standards of Scripture are given mainly in principle form. In addition, our church Discipline is a minimum standard and does not address all expressions of worldliness. We are to discern the "new gods" and the attitudes and patterns of conduct that condition in a direction contrary to Scripture and the Discipline, and to discern that which brings the Church in harmony. If administration is limited to the letter only for giving a voice or taking disciplinary action, spirits and attitudes will remain and develop that are destructive to spiritual life and will even be undermining to the keeping of the letter. We believe that an openness and a commitment to the Church consensus helps us keep a balance in working this out practically. Deut. 32:16,17; 1 Cor. 12:10; 14:29; 1 Thess. 5:21; 1 John 2:15-17; 4:1.

5. We believe that a strong teaching ministry coupled with fair and consistent discipline is the Scriptural approach. The teaching ministry is finally understood by what is allowed or not allowed by church administration. Personal conviction develops as the Biblical basis for a position is taught and as sound administration admonishes and insists on compliance in patience and love. To imply that carefulness to detail in regard to Bible application is being legal and is spiritually destructive, and that more tolerance fosters spirituality, is to militate against the Biblical emphasis relating to indoctrination and sound administration. True spirituality is measured by one's carefulness and concern for Biblical obedience. Matt. 7:21; Luke 6:46; Matt. 18:15-18; 1 Tim. 5:20; Phil. 2:12; 1 Peter 1:13-15; 2 Tim. 4:1,2; 2 Peter 1:5.

6. We believe that churches that are sponsored in outlying areas or in other cultures should hold a standard that is comparable to that of the sending churches. This is vital to maintaining a conferring relationship and for safeguarding the mission church from independent thinking. It is also necessary for protecting the mission from the influence of the surrounding religious thought and for providing the new church with a sense of stability and roots. To have the difference between the sponsoring and the sponsored churches too broad results in the undermining of the conviction of the home church and in stifling of the spiritual growth of the developing church. Acts 16:4,5; 1 Cor. 1:2; 4:17; 7:17; 1 Thess. 2:14.

7. We believe that one of the dangers facing the Church is a distaste for Mennonite practice and the separated life. The present questioning of long-standing practices and subtle reflections against standards and church authority reveal this malady.

When expressions of concern about legalism and traditionalism result in a weakening of standards and reflect against careful Church administration, the ground is being laid for further drift and apostasy.

Aaron wrote later in a letter to a friend in April of 1991:

I suppose the truth of the matter is that if we were as ready to separate as the other side is to have us separated it would have happened long ago....

At the fall 1990 Conferring Meeting Bro. Isaac [Sensenig] preached on the legitimacy of church divisions. The purpose of such emphasis at such a time seems quite obvious. (Maybe that's a false assumption.)

Several times at our bishop meetings one of the bishops has suggested how we should go about having a division if it comes to that. At our recent church-wide Ministers' Meeting at Denver, [spring 1991] it was pretty evident to those of us who are closest to the church operations that there was an element bent on shoving us out....

Why haven't we separated? Because we love the church and deplore the reproach of divisions. I have told a number of the bishops that I'm afraid we might not make it successfully without the help and influence of the larger body of the church. But I have also recently told a few of them that if this perpetually critical element of the church is allowed to continue their agitations, I do not see how we can make it with that either. Perhaps it would be less of a reproach on the cause to separate than to try to live on and work with that particular perpetually critical element in the church. That element was pretty clearly identifiable at the Wednesday afternoon meeting.

Dear brother, what would you do?

Perhaps we have reacted too much to what we believe to be unfair criticism and undue drastic actions taken against us. We have much room for improvement to come up to the standard pattern of our Lord Jesus Christ. We still live in that biggest room in the world—the room for improvement....

The Bishop Board Minutes on November 30, 1990 state:

We shared for a while on some of the issues that are causing unrest among our people and we tried to discover ways to bring unity...

We continued discussing the needs that face us and how we can work through our difficulties. We talked about some discipline variations and how we can best help and lead our people to victory and we be at peace among ourselves.

On November 30, 1990, the Bishop Board received a letter of concern relating to Stephen Ebersole's restoration to public ministry. It was signed by three deacons from the Denver District. Among other concerns, the letter stated, "We all desire to avoid a division among us...However, in essence a division of doctrine and practice already exists." The letter proceeded to list six alleged doctrinal issues involved in the disunity and stress.

To Aaron, blaming the problems of the Eastern Church on the Lebanon District was nothing new. Since the middle 1970's, the Lebanon District was receiving blame from the neighboring Richland District for being too tolerant of problems they were facing.

On January 9, 1991, there was a special church-wide ministerial meeting held at Blue Rock. This was to reinstate Stephen's bishop responsibility. The Bishop Board Minutes state:

> This is to inform the churches that regarding Bro. Stephen Ebersole's bishop responsibilities; As of January 9, 1991 he is again free to function and a review of the situation will be made around July 1, 1991.

It seemed obvious to some onlookers that the Eastern Church had made it very convenient for the Lebanon District to split off and form their own group in reaction to Stephen Ebersole's silencing. The responsibility for the division of course would be upon those leaving. In fact, one bishop made the statement, "We have a new situation not faced before; the church will not divide."

Church groupings

On February 12, 1991, the Ministerial board of the Lebanon District met to discuss concerns within the district as it related to church-wide relationships. At that meeting, they decided to hold two district-wide members' meetings, one at Rehrersburg and one at Dohners, at the end of February to present the following.

> 1. An exhibit which analyzes various church goals and crystalizes where we want to be. This will also clarify which direction we want to travel as a church....
>
> 2. To report on our request to the Bishop Board the following items:
>
> a. From a minute we quote, "We request the Bishop Board for the appointment of a committee of bishops from outside (not connected in any way to) our church fellowship to help analyze and give recommendations regarding our present church stress in the capacity of non-binding arbitration. The committee should be made of three bishops, one chosen by our district bishops, one chosen by the rest of the

Bishop Board, and the third chosen by these two bishops. If the Bishop Board cannot grant this request, we then sense a need to correspond with bishops outside our church fellowship for further counsel."

b. "We request the Bishop Board to consider placing a moratorium on the next discipline review for two years."

At the meetings an analysis of various church goals was presented. The analysis as it was offered follows.

We believe it is important that any group of people who are going to work together as a group, understand what their united goals are. This is especially important for those who are endeavoring to be the people of God. If the goals are clear and understood, the group will more likely find it is pulling in one direction. Whenever new issues arise, it will be able to ascertain when it is making progress and be able to give the rising generation a vision worth living and dying for.

The following analysis is being presented as a brief sketch of what different church groups have as their goals. It is not intended that any one particular church group be pinpointed and reflected against. Furthermore, we sense a danger in using a comparison like this to judge and label others for usually we cannot as accurately assess other's reasons and motives as we think. Let us heed the direction given us by the Apostle Paul, "For we dare not make ourselves of the number, or compare ourselves with some that commend themselves: but they measuring themselves by themselves and comparing themselves among themselves are not wise" (2 Cor. 10:12).

Rather this analysis is being shared for us to challenge ourselves as to whether or not we are really accomplishing what God has placed us here on earth for.

As a district leadership we want to identify ourselves as having "Group C" goals. It is our intention to maintain characteristics that clearly identify ourselves as being in that group.

Group A

1. Goal: To maintain traditional Mennonite practices.

2. Identifying characteristics:

a. A rigid adherence to customs and practices of the past, even preserving practices that conflict with the Word of God.

b. Salvation based on outward conformity to group practices, with no teaching or belief in assurance of salvation.

c. Strong emphasis on group loyalty, so much so that if one leaves the group his salvation is questioned, even if he continues to live in Biblical discipleship.

d. Conviction for certain practices is built by strong rejection for anyone who dares to suggest or to practice anything different.

e. The Holy Spirit exists only as a theological point. Practically no place is given for His work in the life of individuals.

f. Mission efforts and personal evangelism are practically nonexistent.

Group B

1. Goals:

Primary: To maintain traditional Mennonite practices.

Secondary: To keep the mentality spiritual.

2. Identifying characteristics:

a. Effort is put forth to follow the Scriptures but if there is some conflict between the Word and the traditional Mennonite way, the traditional way will supercede.

b. Assurance of salvation is taught, but is reserved for those who come out with the same thinking and practices of the group.

c. Group loyalty is emphasized, and if one challenges the status quo whether it be from the Bible or not, he may face severe rejection. Uniformity is stressed and those who would differ from an unwritten norm are regarded as rebellious.

d. Conviction is built by appeal to the group consensus and Scripture verses are added to give the teachings extra support.

e. The Holy Spirit speaks through group voice. There can be no individual prophetism, for all revelation is given through the group.

f. Mission work and personal evangelism are engaged in with the intention of reproducing as nearly as possible the identical applications of the group.

Group C

1. Goals:

Primary: To build a Biblical Spiritual church

Secondary: To make application to the Scriptures with respect to our Mennonite heritage.

2. Identifying characteristics:

a. Effort is made to exalt the Word of God and apply it in the traditional manner of the Mennonite Church, but if in any way there is found conflict between the two, the Scriptures are followed. Furthermore, the Bible is studied and sought to be applied even in areas not formerly noticed or given emphasis to.

b. Assurance of salvation is taught and believed but is reserved for those who maintain a relationship with Jesus, pursue Biblical discipleship, and bring themselves under the authority of a Biblical church.

c. Loyalty for the Lord Jesus and His Word are the foremost emphasis of the teaching, and a submission one to another is promoted as decisions and applications need to be made. Loyal opposition is welcomed if it is not given in a spirit of contention, but in an effort to honor the Word. Other church groups are recognized if they are sound in doctrine and practice even though some applications are different.

d. Conviction is built by appealing to the Word of God, expressing strong personal example and practicing Biblical discipline. Areas where no Biblical principles are at stake are left to Christian liberty.

e. The Holy Spirit speaks through the Word, and will never contradict its authority. He also works in the believer's life through: authorities, (including the church), circumstances, and a still small voice within; but never contrary to the Word.

f. Mission work and personal evangelism are encouraged, and converts are expected to subscribe to the doctrines of the Word as understood by the church doing the mission work. In other cultural settings some applications may vary if they better illustrate the teachings of the New Testament in that setting.

Group D

1. Goals: To be a Biblical spiritual church

2. Identifying characteristics:

a. Effort is made to apply the Word of God but no preference is given to any particular historical Christian heritage. All Christian heritages are considered viable and worthwhile.

b. Assurance of salvation is guaranteed to those who believe in Jesus and practice discipleship regardless of whether or not they bring themselves under the authority of a church fellowship.

c. Teaching that would build loyalty to one particular heritage is reflected against.

d. Conviction is built by teaching the Word of God, and strong personal example.

Most of life's daily choices are left to individual decision.

e. The Holy Spirit will not override the Word, but will rule and guide the believer in such a powerful way so as to make church standards or discipline largely unnecessary.

f. Mission work and personal evangelism are enthusiastically engaged in with effort to bring new disciples into obedience to the Word.

Group E

1. Goals: To celebrate Christian liberties.

2. Identifying characteristics:

a. Effort is made to teach the Bible, but few direct applications are made.

b. Assurance of salvation is guaranteed to all who believe in Jesus.

c. No effort is made to preserve or appreciate practices from the past.

d. Convictions are left up to the individual and are largely considered unnecessary.

e. The Holy Spirit continues to give revelations as authoritative as the Scriptures and may permit certain Bible teachings to be regarded as obsolete.

f. Missions and personal work are emphasized but no visible expression of discipleship is expected.

We recognize the above given analysis is not comprehensive or exhaustive, but is only a brief sketch of the goals of a church.

Another dimension to consider is that within a fellowship there also exists the spirituality factor. When the spiritual temperature is hot, the goals will become purified and God-honoring. The converse is also true. When spiritual interests wane and apathy or carnality set in, the goals become more obscure and unlikely to be achieved.

We as the leadership of the district want to do better in setting the example by growing in our own spiritual interests and in the exercise of Biblical discipline. Furthermore, we encourage the brotherhood to more fervent prayer, diligent Bible study, earnest evangelistic efforts, and continuing growth in holiness of life. We believe God will be pleased to bless us only when we sincerely love and exalt Him with all our heart, soul, mind, and strength. But when His blessing is poured out then no foe or obstacle on earth can prevent Him from accomplishing great things for His Kingdom.

Sincerely in Christ,

The Lebanon District Ministry

The non-Lebanon bishops would not consent to arbitration by an outside committee of bishops. Nor would they accept the "groupings" method of evaluating churches. The minutes state a motion carried, "That we do not apply the 'groupings' to our church as a way of evaluating. Nor are we approving the Lebanon District's using the method [constructive dialogue and charitable discussion] as they requested. We do not believe that any of the 'groups' adequately represent our church but we support the idea of following the Bible in all of the applications as understood by the 18 Articles of Faith and the Church Discipline."

The "groupings" letter distributed

On March 25, 1991, the final proverbial "straw that broke the camel's back" happened when a minister sent the unabridged version of the "groupings" letter to all the ordained of the EPMC. The "groupings" letter that was shared with the Lebanon District members was a condensed version of a larger letter shared with the bishop board. It endeavored to highlight why the numerous conflicts in the earlier years between the Lebanon District and the rest of the EPMC had come to pass.

The brother who sent it to all the EPMC ministry gave two explanations on a cover letter:

> 1. To present material that gives clarity to the thought pattern of those responsible for the enclosed exhibit. We need to understand our brethren's concept in order to effect a solid reconciliation, so we can build together with strength and purpose. This exhibit will also hopefully reduce misunderstandings, insinuations, surmising, and thus more loss of unity.

> 2. To stimulate constructive dialogue and charitable discussion; possibly even at a conferring type meeting where the strengths and dangers of any desired course of travel could be mutually shared for united progress of a safe and holy way. John 17:21b.

As this letter went to each minister in the entire group, it stimulated a serious backlash that the bishops found impossible to squash.

During the summer, the relationships continued to grow more tense.

On June 28, 1991, David Wadel, Jesse Neuenschwander, Lynn Martin, and Alvin Snyder presented a paper to the Bishop Board entitled "An Effort to Understand Our Present Need."

The Lebanon bishops feel that the problem is basically that some do not appreciate their district and are reflecting unfairly against them with sinister motives. They view the situation as basically a "love" problem. They feel that certain individuals control the group and that the group tilts more and more toward a legalistic position.

In contrast the rest of us feel that a force is trying to change the church from what she has been. We sense that the concepts and ideas expressed parallel too closely the thought patterns of thirty or forty years ago when a similar force subtly moved the church into apostasy. We feel that we are now deciding whether we will be a plain church or not 20 years from now and to compromise to the new ideas afloat is to fail the Lord and our God-given trust. We recognize that the differences among us are deeply rooted and relate to what it takes to maintain and perpetuate a plain conservative church.

The document went on to include a possible solution, such as Stephen changing his thinking on seven points. Also, it had a section on other alternative suggestions, including Stephen's personally withdrawing himself from the ministry, a disengagement for two years, or a division.

In a letter dated July 1, 1991, Stephen Ebersole presented a five-page response to the June 28 paper. The same day, three motions carried in a bishop meeting. The first related to a planned meeting. The second stated, "That Bro. Stephen should withdraw the influence of the February 12 letter [the groupings]...." The third stated, "That we appoint a committee of bishops to direct the administrative functions of the district. They would be held responsible for what happens in the district. They would not do all the administrative work but would be in touch and in communication and would answer to the bishop board. They would review wedding plans, transfers, activities, etc."

Two days later, in another bishop meeting, Stephen Ebersole "expressed himself as not being able to withdraw the influence of the February 12, 1991 letter." Stephen reported that the Lebanon District Ministry voted 5 in favor and 15 not in favor of the third motion carried in the July 1 bishop meeting. In the same meeting the bishops took action:

That the bishops hereafter will meet without Bro. Stephen and will give him time to think through the implication of not submitting to the bishops and recall the influence of the Feb. 12 letter.

We will be open to negotiate the things included in the July 2, 1991 letter to the bishops from the Lebanon District Ministry as soon as he is ready to give a favorable response.

Furthermore, on July 26, 1991, the Lebanon bishops presented a letter to the Bishop Board suggesting three possible ways to resolve the difficulties.

1. The first option is that if there is strong enough feeling that "group C" goals are a false foundation to build upon, then the powers that be will need to dismiss us for having these foundational goals. The board should be reminded that such action would be out of keeping with the board's commitment to "follow the Bible in all of the applications as understood by the 18 Articles of Faith and the Church discipline. Ref Min 91B4 #8C, and is not in harmony with the historic practices of the Old Mennonite Church or the principles of Christianity.

2. One legitimate solution for those who want to honor the Discipline in their response to this situation and yet feel us unfit for any continued fellowship, would be for them to withdraw and form a fellowship upon whatever foundation and according to whatever rules they decide. Historically it has already happened that some ordained have just stopped coming to conference meetings and organized to form their own fellowship.

3. The only other solution that we can think of if there is not sufficient grace and charity to make it work together, is to have a truly amicable separation. We realize that the common ground between us is very great. We represent this idea reluctantly but do so because apparently there are some who feel strongly that we cannot continue within the same lines of fellowship. In a separation like this, there would be a decision for each of the groups to completely recognize and honor the other, much like Eastern currently does with the groups such as Washington Co., York and Adams Co. churches, or the various other conservative churches on the North American continent. We feel that a separation or realignment like this could more nearly fulfill the Scriptures, "...that there be no division in the body..." If the separation could not be completely amicable then we are not interested in a separation at all, because such a relationship would constitute a breach in the body of Christ.

On August 26, 1991, Alvin Snyder gave a report to the bishops of a committee meeting with Stephen Ebersole on August 13. The committee communicated with Stephen that he needed to retract three things:

A. That the February 12 letter undermines the agreement of the Jan. 9, 1991 meeting at Blue Rock.

B. The letter indicts the church in a way that is unfair, presenting the view that the church moves in some cases on the basis of tradition instead of the Scriptures and has a continuing tendency to do so. He should recall this influence as much as possible.

C. The essence of the letter encourages dissenting thinkers to be more vocal.

The August 26 meeting recorded reasons as to why Stephen Ebersole was made inactive the second time and why he was no longer meeting with the bishops.

A. Some of his beliefs and ideology are not right and consequently this affects how he looks at his work and responsibility.

B. His refusal to put forth an effort to recall what has been damaging in the Feb. 12 letter and not following the bishops' direction to recall it.

C. His claiming to be in support of the Eastern Church and yet he has not worked in harmony with the rest of the bishops and considers them as being too traditional.

At the same meeting Aaron and Sidney were excused for two and a half hours while the rest deliberated as to what should be done. In that time, they reached a decision.

Recognizing that we as a group are now at a crossroad and the church is in unrest due to this conflict, a working unity seems impossible. And so we are suggesting the following. In order to preserve the faith of the Gospel and fulfill our duty before God we will continue to uphold the principles of the Eastern Church.

A. Motion carried: That we send a letter to every ordained brother in the Lebanon District as an answer to a report from the July 2 district meeting.

B. Motion carried: That we work out a separation in which the Brethren Aaron, Sidney, and Stephen would provide leadership to those ordained men who support them and that provision be made for any ordained brethren or members in the Lebanon District (southern part) who desire to remain with the Eastern Church. Individual members or ministry of any district could relate to the new group through proper negotiations without letter until March 1, 1992. The bishops are ready to support those members and ministry who desire to remain with the Eastern Church.

C. Motion carried: That if the Brethren Aaron, Sidney, and Stephen are not ready to accept the responsibility of a new group, then we would consider the following recourse.

For our working relation to continue together we would consider Bro. Stephen inactive and the bishop administration for the district would be by bishop board appointment.

Bro. Aaron and Sidney would fit into that program and their role would be determined by the bishop board.

D. Motion carried: That we will set a review date for Sept. 1, 1992 to see if we can mend our differences and decide to be reunited if we follow part B.

A letter dated September 3, 1991 from the Lebanon District bishops answered this action.

This letter is being written in response to the action of the Bishop Board taken on August 26, 1991 (in which we brethren Aaron Shank, Sidney Gingrich, and Stephen Ebersole were not allowed to participate)....

INASMUCH as repeated efforts on our part to clarify our loyalty to the Eastern Pennsylvania Mennonite Church and our intentions to consistently administrate the church on the basis of the E.P.M.C. discipline seems to be disbelieved or unacceptable to the Bishop Board; and,

INASMUCH as the repeated requests from the Lebanon District bishops and ministry to call in an unrelated committee of bishops outside our E.P.M.C. fellowship to assist in resolving our problems has been given some consideration but continually rejected; and,

Steve and Sandra Ebersole, 1992.

INASMUCH as in our judgment the discipline's outlined procedures have on occasions been ignored or laid aside in relation to the present church situation (A list of these violations will be given to you at your request); and,

INASMUCH as it has been stated numbers of times on our Board that we are not that far apart in our thinking and yet our repeated appeals to the Bishop Board that we renew our love and appreciation for each other and get on with the business of building church again have been rejected; and,

INASMUCH as a separation is being talked about and promoted in certain sections of our church and has been alluded to numbers of times in documents and discussions on the Bishop Board as well as in the spring 1991 conferring meeting message; and,

INASMUCH as the only recourse offered is not in harmony with Scriptures such as 1 Cor. 12:18-22, has an element in it that has formerly not been acceptable to the district ministry involved, and in the recourse as a whole would likely place our district and perhaps the whole E.P.M.C. in a still greater state of confusion, consequently we believe it is not a legitimate recourse; therefore,

WE HEREWITH agree (reluctantly) to submit to and accept the Bishop Board action (minute 91 B13) "to work out a separation" and will endeavor by God's grace and divine enablement to organize a separate fellowship. We suggest January 1, 1992 as the official date for the new fellowship's inception.

WE HEREWITH wish to express our regrets that conditions are such that you feel that a separation must be worked out.

WE ALSO HEREWITH express our sincere appreciation for the spiritual benefits which we have re-

Steve Ebersole family, 1992.

ceived from our E.P.M.C. fellowship over the years. We hope that the worthy causes we have championed together will continue to benefit both us and you until our Lord Jesus returns for His own.

Furthermore, we wish to thank you for the patience you have manifested toward us over the years of our working together. If the statements, letters, and announcements shared from time to time are believed to be the unbiased truth you have been very gracious and patient with us.

We will wait for the Judge of all the earth to determine the rightness and the fairness of the assumptions and actions that have been taken. Meanwhile we pray that our gracious Lord will find sufficient sincerity on the part of both you and us to grant unto us His eternal mercies in that day.....

Pushed Out

At a bishop meeting at White Oak Mennonite Church on September 11, 1991, again in the absence of Aaron, Sidney, and Stephen, a paper entitled "Procedure for Relating to the Brethren Aaron Shank, Sidney Gingrich, and Stephen Ebersole" was adopted.

At the same meeting, plans were formulated for a meeting to be held at

White Oak for those of the Lebanon District who rejected Aaron, Sidney, and Stephen's leadership. The Eastern Bishop Board would be in charge of the meeting.

The minutes of the meeting state, "As we discussed the situation where we are now it is noted that the new group which is forming is not because Bro. Stephen has refused being made inactive."

At the next Bishop Board meeting held at the same place, on September 23, 1991, again in the absence of Aaron, Sidney, and Stephen, a paper entitled "Procedures for Relating .... the New Group" was adopted. The minutes for the meeting record the following action.

> This suggests that the 3 bishops in question take the responsibility to work out a separation. Inasmuch as the Brethren Aaron Shank, Sidney Gingrich, and Stephen Ebersole have a group supporting them and they have formulated a working standard and since they are not interested in accepting the recourse.
>
> We at this point recognize that the Brethren Aaron Shank, Sidney Gingrich, and Stephen Ebersole have not taken action to withdraw from the Eastern PA Mennonite Church and yet, we are at a place where it does not seem like this continued conflict can be resolved. The following motion was made and supported.
>
> Motion carried: That the Brethren Aaron Shank, Sidney Gingrich, and Stephen Ebersole are no longer a part of the Bishop Board of the Eastern PA Mennonite Church and we recognize them and those who follow them as a separate group.
>
> We recommend that we be charitable toward them and do what we can to avoid the hard feelings that are associated with this type of circumstance.
>
> We come to the above conclusions due to the following reasons:
>
> A. There are those who identify with the charges and spirit of the February 12, 1991 letter sent by the Lebanon District Ministry.
>
> B. And there are those who rejected the Bishops' recommendations regarding administration in the Lebanon District.
>
> C. And there are those who are identifying with this new interest in formulating a new discipline and plans for a new group and are no doubt the ones who will be giving support to those three bishops.

After the above was formulated, Aaron, Sidney, and Stephen entered the meeting at 10:30 A.M. They received the action of the other bishops. These three suggested that the action take effect on January 1, 1992. This would give the three bishops and their supporting ministry some time to organize and prepare for leading a separate group.

At 1:00 P.M. a group of ordained men, composed mostly of those who chose not to remain with Aaron, Sidney, and Stephen, met with the Eastern Bishop Board. They discussed:

A. the practical matters of separation.

B. the issues wherein Stephen Ebersole does not think with the rest.

C. the idea and responsibility of a separate group.

D. the forms of church government and how disciplinary action is viewed.

E. the "Procedures for Relating to the New Group."

F. practices and how to relate to the standards.

On September 27, 1991, the Lebanon District bishops issued a letter to their membership. The first sheet contained general information concerning what was happening. The second sheet contained the Lebanon District response to the Bishop Board request, shown above. The third sheet is the announcement made to the Eastern Church as a whole concerning the division.

You are probably aware of some of the new developments within the Lebanon District as a result of the decision of the Bishop Board of the Eastern Pennsylvania Mennonite Church. This decision requested the Lebanon District bishops Bre. Aaron Shank, Sidney Gingrich, and Stephen Ebersole to give leadership to a "new group."

A number of the ministry of the Lebanon District have shared together for several days over the past weeks in order to formulate this "new group," and to give a sense of direction for its future.

The ministerial group decided that the name of the new group shall be "Pilgrim Mennonite Conference."

The major work of this ministerial body was the formulation of the Pilgrim Mennonite Conference discipline which is titled "Decrees for to Keep." This booklet of Decrees is herewith being sent to you for your study and consideration....

We are aware that this situation has caused a great deal of confusion in the minds of many, and that for some it will be difficult to make a decision on this matter. We have felt that the best way we know to give an impartial view of the situation and to dispel some of the rumors that are a part of an occasion like this is to share correspondence that documents the progression of this stress to the point where we are today. We are not adding our analysis to these documents, realizing that as you study them, you will want to reach your own conclusions....

The Eastern Bishop Board formulated a statement to be shared with the congregations of the Eastern Pennsylvania Mennonite Church. Concerning it, the Pilgrim Bishops state, "While we feel that the charges contained in this statement are not accurate, we share this document with you for your consideration and evaluation." Interestingly, the momentous division experience merited only a single paragraph of 38 words in the November issue of *The Eastern Mennonite Testimony*.

Following is the statement presented to the congregations of the Eastern Pennsylvania Mennonite Church.

> It is with a deep burden and with sadness that we share the following information with you.
>
> You are no doubt aware of the stressful condition that has surrounded our church due to a situation that has developed among the bishops and leadership.
>
> It does come clear that the principles that have influenced and directed the Eastern PA Mennonite Church since its beginning have been challenged to the point where we feel that for us to continue in these goals some definite action is needed.
>
> We sincerely regret that we need to work out a separation among us at this time. But in light of the present circumstances we present the following to help you understand the situation between the Eastern Pennsylvania Mennonite Church and the "New Group" which is being formed under the leadership of the three bishops, Aaron Shank, Sidney Gingrich, and Stephen Ebersole.
>
> The future relationship between the E.P.M.C. and the New Group will be dependent on the course the New Group takes. The New Group's performance in relation to standards and in regard to respecting the E.P.M.C. work will have a direct bearing on future relationships. Naturally, we have deep reservations toward the new movement and hold a wait-and-see attitude. While we wish to exercise charity toward the New Group and to any other group who may relate to them, we cannot endorse the new movement under the present circumstances.

While the official statement indicated sadness at what developed, on a private level there was rejoicing "that the church is purged." This rejoicing even carried over into public meetings.

Whereas Milford watched his father conduct a "war" in defense of truth as the Lancaster Conference departed from it, Milford watched his father suffer "grief" in the second ordeal. Aaron had poured his heart and soul into the revival of conviction which developed into the Eastern Pennsylvania Mennonite Church. Now the church he had helped to father refused to operate according to the principles he had always stood for. In the end, it pushed him out and broke his heart. It would not even offer an amiable release. Aaron would repeatedly lament, "There should have been a better way..."

In 1997, after both men had read an early draft of this biography, Aaron wrote to Isaac Sensenig:

> I am enjoying my present church life with its challenges and opportunities, but the pain of being dismissed from the church I had a vital part in bringing into existence, for holy reasons and justifiable causes, in a holy and honorable way, lingers with me. I love the EPMC and am praying that the worthy causes for which she was organized will not be unduly reproached or die.

But work remained to be done.

Organizing Pilgrim Mennonite Conference

In accordance with Aaron's stated concerns, a working discipline was formulated in September 1991 by the leadership of the new Pilgrim Conference. It was characteristically titled *Decrees for to Keep*.

A preliminary statement introducing the *Decrees* stated,

> You may notice some different features about these Decrees which we would like to explain.

> We understand the place of a discipline not as replacing the Scriptures, but as giving a consistent uniform practice to the principles of the Scripture. Many of these Scriptures are printed out so it is easier to understand the relationship of the Bible principle to the Pilgrim practice.

> As we formulated these Decrees we tried to keep in mind that along with our own people we should consider an audience that may not be familiar with the various Mennonite beliefs and practices. Consequently, we have included more explanations than is normally found in a discipline.

> We also have striven for a more detailed explanation for the benefit of our own people, realizing that there exists the possibility that some would maintain practices without really understanding the reasons behind these practices....

Milford kept a close eye on his father through the years.

Dad is more relaxed today than he used to be. For years and years you could see strain on his face. Dealing with the drift in Lancaster Conference was an ongoing war for him.

Dad was more mellow about the Pilgrim division than the first one. He didn't say much; Mother would tell me about it. He wasn't in a fighting mood. When he did talk, he was very subdued. He couldn't understand it. When I made comments about the situation, he would say, 'The Lord knows all things.'

While the Lancaster Conference situation was warfare for him, the Pilgrim situation was like a shock or a death. First he couldn't believe it was happening, then he accepted it, and finally he grieved.

The following reply to a letter from a former Lebanon District member reveals Aaron's heart.

Thank you, Bro. Dale [Heisey] for your surprise correspondence of July 22, 1991. I did not think I would wait so long to answer but with all the abnormal goings on around here the past couple of years, some things have been pushed aside or neglected altogether. It causes us to be deeply humbled to be caught up in a church tangle that hinders so seriously the work of the kingdom of Christ. We hope the Lord will take up the tangled strands and somehow make them show forth His praise....

Another more lengthy letter (end of 1991) to one of his friends reveals even more.

Dear _____— My esteemed and beloved brother in Christ.

Greetings in the name of our condescending Savior, our interceding Elder Brother, and our hopefully soon coming Lord Jesus.

Recently someone shared with me that you had written a letter to _____ in which you shared some of your insights related to his and my involvements in the present E.P.M.C. struggles and crisis.

After "a bird of the air" carried this noise and "that which hath wings" told me of the matter, I contacted _____ and inquired about the truth of that which the birdie that had wings had reported to me.

You may be very right in your judgment about the Lord sending leanness of soul into my aged life. Your evaluation calls me to a renewed examination of myself and my present experiences. I confess I am a very weak and inefficient bishop and that I am really not meet to be called a bishop. Looking at some of the abilities of my brethren, I feel they can walk circles around me while I am running at top speed. I have always felt that my responsibilities have been far beyond my abilities. The reason I have served the church in the capacity of a bishop for 34 years is because the Lord called me to this office and work. The call was crystal clear and while I have never doubted the call, I have often wondered why.

However, if you will grant me a little clemency, dear brother, I will try to share with you some facts that may put a different slant on the things whereof you speak.

First, let me clear the record with you that Brother Stephen was not my vote for bishop at the time of his ordination. He was my man for the place after what I believed was the leading of the Holy Ghost in making him an overseer of the church of God. I don't usually tell people how I voted but since you say "The Lord gave Brother Aaron his choice", I will tell you that my vote went to _____. However, when Brother Stephen was named to share the lot, I was very well satisfied from my firsthand experience with him, that he was qualified and would make a valuable contribution to the bishop leadership of the church.

I simply do not know of any faulty procedures followed during the process of the ordination. Along with other concerns, I was very sensitive to the problem of taking a good leader away from one of our small outlying congregations, when they are so badly needed for the ongoing witness in their community. Because of this concern we had, previous to the voting, told those congregations that if any of their ministry were nominated they would have the right to appeal that their minister be excused from sharing the lot. There was no such appeal forthcoming. Incidentally, shortly before the nominations were given, _____ stated clearly that he would have no problem if either _____ or Stephen Ebersole were nominated. Through the influence of his local ministers, he has since become a militant opposer of Brother Stephen.

When the nominations were announced and some concerns were registered about Brother Stephen's involvement, I offered to cancel out the plans and consider Brother Alvin Snyder for the bishop oversight of the district. Brother Alvin meekly stated his reluctance for such a consideration and the offer was pursued no further. Previous to the nominations I asked the bishops for the consideration of Brother Lester Martin. It was Bishop Board action that Brother Lester was not to be eligible for this place. It was my embarrassing responsibility to announce this to the congregations.

Perhaps I should tell you, too, that I listened today to the taped meeting held at White Oak on October 21 which was held to give encouragement to the Lebanon District folks who may desire to remain with the E.P.M.C. On the tape Brother David Wadel states that when some concerns came about Brother Stephen that the bishops "felt no real justifiable reason to exclude him and proceeded with the ordination."

The thing that finally settled the decision to go ahead with the ordination with all three men sharing the lot was that the other two brethren voluntarily stated that they were not interested in proceeding with the ordination if Brother Stephen must withdraw or be excused from the lot.

Incidentally, it seemed that the concerns against Brother Stephen came basically from one geographical area of the church.

We were told recently by one of the bishops that when it was decided to go ahead with the ordination that some of the bishops said if it falls to Brother Stephen they will believe the Lord is telling us that it is time for a division in the church. The fact is, and I think you know it too, that division has been in the air for 15 years or more -- coming basically from one general area of the church. That area has finally "called the shots" and brought the division to fulfillment. I well remember you coming to one of our ministerial meetings years ago, after visiting in _____ and saying to the effect "What is all this talk about a big split coming in the E.P.M.C.?" In 1976 the bishops got a letter from one of the districts blaming the Lebanon District for their problems and implying that a separation may be necessary. The Lebanon District has been perpetually blamed for the ills of the E.P.M.C. A conservative minded brother from another part of the church observed recently that this is not a Stephen Ebersole problem but that the problem existed before Stephen was a baby on his mother's lap.

_____ do you know Brother Stephen personally? Do you know first-hand what his real doctrinal position is? Do you know what his position is on church traditions? Do you know anything about his performance, especially as it relates to upholding the E.P.M.C. discipline and his exercise of the discipline where there has been violation? Do you know anything about his personal life and conduct? Have you come to your conclusion that he is "a young and ambitious and inexperienced bishop --- insubordinate to his elders and drawing away disciples after him" on the basis of your personal knowledge of him or on the basis of hear-say and assumptions?

I think he has done just about everything he could do to keep from "drawing away disciples after him". If he had not done so he could conceivably have thousands of people following him today.

Early in this struggle the bishops got a letter from a comparatively young minister denouncing the bishops for not taking immediate action against Brother Stephen. He had a number of heavy charges laid against Brother Stephen. When he was spoken to about his accusations, he admitted that he based his charges on what he heard rather than what he actually knows. "He that justifieth the wicked, and he that condemneth the just, even they both are abomination to the Lord."

May I suggest that since it was the determinate counsel of some brethren before the ordination that if Brother Stephen is ordained there should be a division effected, that it was the natural thing for those brethren to see evidences that may not have existed to justify their predetermined concepts. At one of the last bishop meetings we attended, one bishop said Brother Stephen thinks that if you put enough steam back of evangelism that will take care of everything. Brother Stephen doesn't believe that any more than the bishop who said it does. At another time he told a group that Brother Stephen hates tradition more than he loves the Bible. In spite of all our Lebanon District weaknesses, the special meeting at White Oak on the evening of October 21, according to my evaluation, was full of false slants, distortions, and misrepresentations. May God have mercy.

At one of our recent bishop meetings shortly before the decree was made that a separation be worked out, it was stated that the turmoil in the church is the judgment of God on us for ordaining a man we all know should not have been ordained. Maybe such is a possibility but just suppose he was made overseer by the Holy Ghost and we imply it is the work of the devil—then what?

You have at times given your testimony of appreciation for the conservative position of the church. You did it again at Blue Rock on January 9. I believe you 100%. But I also believe your conservatism and Brother Stephen's conservatism may be more compatible than your conservatism and some of the other bishops. You helped me to see the consistency and modesty of the draped cape for the maternity dress. Some of the bishops wanted to expel me from their coasts for taking a position in favor of this more modest dress. When you became a member of the E.P.M.C., I was told to ask you to wear a frock coat suit. I told the bishops that for various reasons I would have a problem requiring dear _____ to get a frock coat suit. Whereupon Bishop _____ said, "I'll talk to _____ about that. I can easily talk to _____." I never found out that he talked to you about it. Maybe by now you have a frock coat. If not and you want to bring yourself up a notch with some bishops and add some fulness to your aged life, get a frock coat.

I said at the beginning of the censuring of Brother Stephen that if he has done anything worthy of death, we will not refuse to have him die, but if nothing worthy of death can be laid upon him and he must die, some of us feel we will need to die with him. A goodly number of brethren across the church are in serious doubt about the actions taken. About 20 of us feel there was nothing worthy of death found in him and therefore feel we need to die with him. We see him as a man of like passion in need of help and encouragement along the way but in no way deserving of drastic actions taken against him.

"Smite the shepherd, and the sheep shall be scattered." I do not believe that it was God who smote His dear Son at Calvary and scattered the sheep. It must have been Satan who said "I will smite the shepherd, and the sheep shall be scattered." We want to leave it to the righteous Judge to determine who is smiting the three bishop shepherds and scattering the sheep. There does seem to be a scattering of sheep all over the E.P.M.C. today. Do you think it could at all be possible that the Lord is sending leanness of soul on the E.P.M.C. because of their ruthless and austere way of handling one or several of their fallible brethren -- some of their anointed fellow-laborers whom the Holy Ghost has made co-overseers of the church?

We want to remain open to any evidence that the Lord is smiting us and be ready to repent. At present it seems the Lord is leading us to chart a course similar to what we have been removed from. You have called upon _____ to repent of his "doings and lead in the way of conservatism." We believe _____ is continuing to lead in the way of conservatism and that he is a gift from God to the Pilgrim Mennonite Conference to help us walk in the highway of holy conservatism.

No doubt you are tired reading this letter. I confess I am tired writing. Perhaps this information will not change your personal thinking or position but I hope it will at least help you understand in a small measure why some of us are where we are.

I do hope I can remain in your good graces and still be included in your "best friends" list. I will be happy to meet you anytime, greet you with a greeting of love, and share any further clarification that may be desirable. We share very little of this information with others outside of the brethren who are knit together in this church problem, unless we are asked or we hear of false rumors floating around.

May the gracious Lord direct our hearts into the love of God and into the patient waiting of Christ. The grace of our Lord Jesus Christ be with you.

Love and best wishes for the days that lie ahead and the eternity that is not far away.

Your brother and companion in the Lord,

Aaron M. Shank

The letter was fruitful in that it cleared misunderstandings and renewed the closeness of long-standing friendship.

In the fall of 1992, the newly founded Pilgrim Mennonite Conference sensed the need for additional bishop help. While several congregations that had formerly been a part of the Lebanon District remained with Eastern, several other congregations with different backgrounds soon sought membership with the new group. Brother Ivan Martin Jr. was chosen by lot on November 23, 1993, to take up this work. Within the space of one year, the Pilgrim Conference sensed a need to divide the expanding circle of churches between the younger two bishops. As a result of this, Ivan Jr. received oversight of the Swatara congregation where Aaron and Marjorie were members. Aaron and Ivan also formed a close friendship and worked closely together until Aaron's death. Incidentally, when the new districts received names, Ivan's district most closely resembled the former Lebanon District and received that name.

Marjorie's decline

On their 50th wedding anniversary, May 29, 1990, the Shank children with Aaron and Marjorie's knowledge held a drop-in open house at the old homestead, where Louise and her husband Ira Mast lived. Those for whom Aaron served as bishop were invited. Many, many people honored Aaron and Marjorie by their presence that day.

At the anniversary, Marjorie was able to function without needing a wheelchair. She had suffered from Lou Gehrig's Disease for several years. After the anniversary, she continued to steadily regress. She gradually lost control of her muscles while her mind was as active as ever. Increasingly she became a prisoner in her own body. She required more and more care.

Finally, Aaron told his co-laborers in church work, "I need to keep a promise I made over fifty years ago. I must provide and care for Marjorie in her sickness. You will need to excuse me from a regular active role in church work."

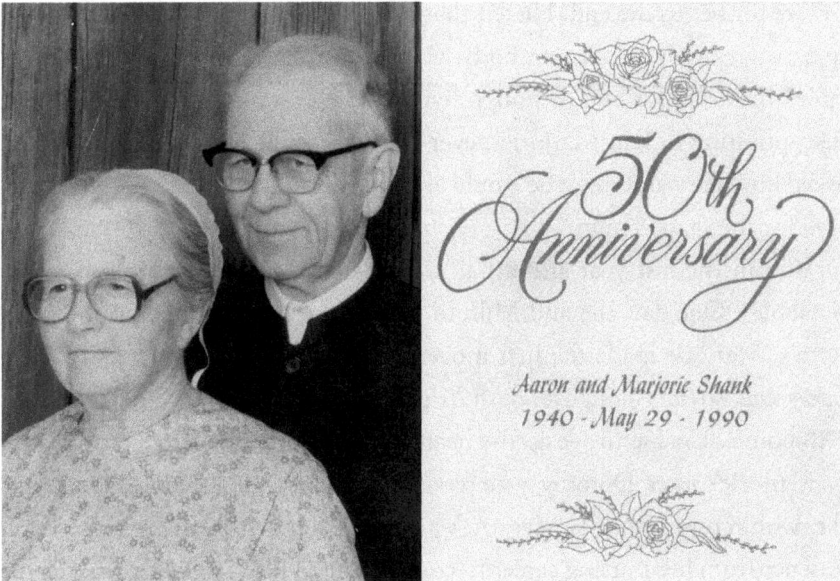

Left: Aaron and Marjorie at the time of their fiftieth anniversary. Right: A thank-you card from the Shanks for the fiftieth anniversary event.

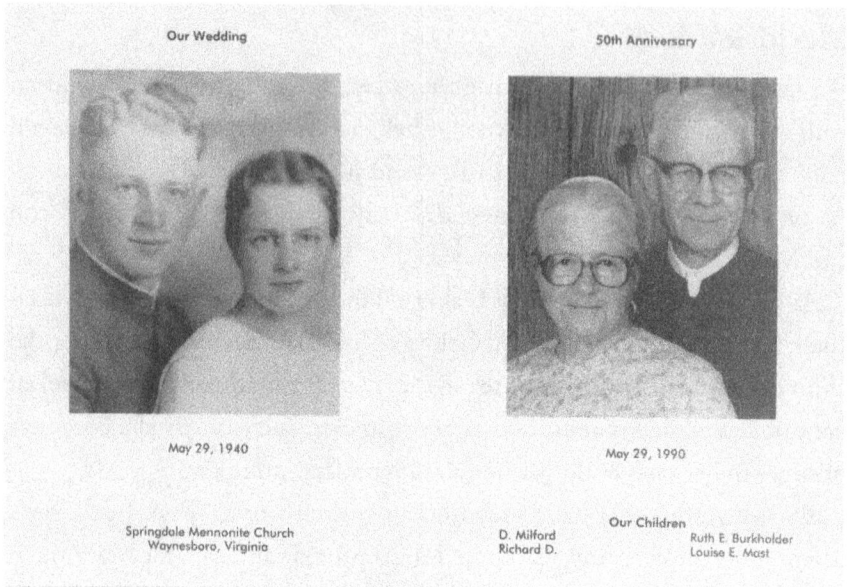

Inside of the fiftieth anniversary thank-you card.

Marjorie's health continued to worsen. In his devoted care of his wife, Aaron was able by the help of God and the kindness of family and friends to care for her to the end. He felt that Marjorie's emotional strains of living in a progressively weakening body were greater than the stresses he experienced in caring for her. Although living as a handicapped person was very disappointing to her, Marjorie never complained of her condition. When asked how she was doing, she would always cheerfully reply, "I'm doing quite well for the shape I'm in."

Within the last year and a half of her life, Marjorie was still playing Scrabble®. One day, she and Milford began a game by each choosing nine letters. Marjorie made the first move by laying out all nine letters to spell *hexagrams*, stretched out over both "triple word" and "double word" to garner 188 points. Unable to speak, she beamed at Milford.

Marjorie's sister, Dorothy, who served as her caregiver, had an accident one day within one month of Marjorie's passing. Daughter Ruth took a leave of absence from her nursing career to come home to help with Marjorie's care. Thus Ruth, Louise, Milford, and Aaron surrounded her bed as she passed into eternity. Aaron began to sing,

O come angel band,
Come and around her stand,
O bear her away on your snowy wings
To her immortal home.
O bear her away on your snowy wings
To her immortal home!

The love that Marjorie had poured out on others for a lifetime was returned to her in song as she was ushered into eternity.

On June 23, 1995, at the age of 78 years, she went to be at rest with the Lord. She passed away within the walls she had made home with Aaron for the last twenty years. They had enjoyed a little over fifty-five years of the Lord's leading and blessing together. She was buried at the Swatara Mennonite Cemetery, land which originally she and Aaron had jointly owned.

Marjorie Remembered

One day in the late 1980s, Marjorie had shocked Steve Ebersole by announcing that she wanted him to preach her funeral sermon, and that she wanted no eulogy, but rather an evangelistic message. Thus, at her funeral, one speaker noted that Marjorie was a very capable woman, possessing a sharp mind, a keen wit, and native intelligence. Marjorie expressed who she was by choosing the following songs for her funeral: "Only Remembered by What We Have Done," "Come Ye Disconsolate," "If on a Quiet Sea," "While the Years of Eternity Roll," "There Waits for Me a Glad Tomorrow," and "We Shall Be Like Him." Steve preached the funeral on Philippians 3:21, her chosen text. Furthermore, she chose 1 Corinthians 15:51-58 as the devotional meditation, emphasizing abounding in the work of the Lord. Ivan Martin, Jr. noted that she abounded in serving the Lord for 67 years, beginning her commitment at age twelve. She abounded as a married woman for 55 years, as a mother for 54 years and the same amount of time as a minister's wife. She abounded 38 years as a bishop's wife, pouring her heart out into many journals. She abounded as a school teacher for 19 consecutive years, agreeing at the last minute to teach because no one else could be found. She influenced over 300 students during that time and finally chose six former students to be pallbearers at her funeral.

Sidney Gingrich, who moderated Marjorie's funeral, reminded the attendees of Marjorie's sanctified sense of humor. Then he proceeded to recount his memory of a time when he accompanied Aaron and Marjorie on a trip to visit the southern churches. When he and Aaron had returned to the motel from an errand, Marjorie met them with face aglow to report, "I just finished reading through the Bible again." Sometimes she would read through the entire Bible three times in one year and sometimes six times. The marathon of Bible reading was motivated by the single passion of learning and doing the will of her Master. Aaron and Marjorie shared one heart!

At the age of eighty, without his companion of fifty-five years, Aaron Shank grieved.

CHAPTER 10

Aching Eighties

FOUR MONTHS BEYOND his eightieth birthday, Aaron was a widower. While he did not worship her, his life had been bound up with Marjorie. Once she was gone, he needed to handle life and its duties alone. While he grieved, he refused to sink into depression and self-pity.

About six months after Marjorie died, Aaron wrote a letter to "Brothers, Sisters, Sons, Daughters, Nieces, Nephews, Grandchildren, and Friends," most of whom were still in the Conference Mennonite churches.

> It has now been six months since the angels took Marjorie out of our temporary care of her, into their exclusive care of her, in the wee hours of the morning of June 23, 1995. While we were expecting her to be taken from us, the changes that it brought seemed so sudden and so final. It is not the easiest thing to adjust to a separated life of singlehood after 55 years of togetherness. But the Bible says, 'He giveth more grace.' It does not say how much He gives—just more. So when people ask me how I am doing I generally say—like Marjorie used to say when she could talk, 'Just fine for me.'

> ...For those of you who may not know, Marjorie died of Lou Gehrigs disease (Amyostophic Lateral Sclerosis—ALS). ALS is a slow creeping type of paralysis. It destroys the muscle tissue of the body, gradually immobilizing its victims to final and complete helplessness and death. There is no known cause or cure for the disease.

> When the doctor first diagnosed Marjorie's problem, he said that her feet were good and her head was good but that the telephone wires were down in between. He told us later that we could expect a gradual weakening until there is complete loss or lack of control of her muscular system.

> From all evidences her mind continued clear until very close to the time of her passing, but she could not actively communicate because even the whispering muscles, and the bat of the eyes or the squeeze of the hand wouldn't work. For

someone who had always had an unusually active mind and a keen interest in almost everything, it must have been extreme mental torture and anguish to have her active mind penned up in such a weak helpless body.

It seems most significant that many years before she had any idea that she might become afflicted with such a debilitating disease, when she was still strong and going fast, she had chosen as her main funeral text Philippians 3:21 with a special emphasis on the phrase '...who shall change our vile body....' Those of you who were at the funeral may remember that in his message Bro. Stephen Ebersole explained that the word 'vile' as used in the text means 'humiliation' or 'to be brought low.' For Marjorie to see folks come and go, talk and laugh, work and rest, sing and pray, etc., etc., and not be able to share or even to respond in any possible manner must have been humiliation in the ultimate. She often cried in those closing moments of her life but she could not tell us why she was crying.

What a glorious moment it must have been to suddenly be removed from her mortal prison-house body into the ultimate of freedom in Christ and into the comfort of the 'God of all comfort.' We praise God for the rest of the verse of Philippians 3:21 with its promise of our vile body being finally 'fashioned like unto His glorious body.' Looking back from the eternal 'excellent glory' I am sure that what seemed to her, and to us, as long, wearisome days, months, and years of her suffering and humiliation here, must now seem like a mere light affliction which was but for a moment. To move so suddenly from the ultimate of humiliation into the ultimate of comfort and glorification is certainly beyond our comprehension, and as the song writer says, 'will surely be worth it all.'

...But Marjorie had another text also with another concern in view. That text was 1 Corinthians 15:58. Bro. Ivan Martin used this text in the devotional meditation. Part of that verse reads '...be ye stedfast, unmoveable, always abounding in the work of the Lord...' In choosing that text she was not thinking only of herself but also of all our immediate families and kinfolk, and the many changes that have taken place church-wise, and the biblical practices that have been moved away from in our life time.

Marjorie and I had or have for a long time felt we should give some kind of testimony to our families as it relates to the need for stability and steadfastness of faith in Christ and the essential accompanying practical expressions of that faith. The same Bible that says, 'Believe on the Lord Jesus Christ and thou shalt be saved' also declares that 'He is the author of eternal salvation to all those that obey Him.'

For nearly 18 centuries practically every professing Christian denomination understood and respected the command of 1 Corinthians 11:1-16 that Christian women should wear a special sign covering of sufficient size to carry with it a spiritual significance. In the past 200 years, or so, most of these denominations have moved away from the Scriptural covering of 1 Cor. 11—and in just the past 50 years or less most of the larger bodies of Mennonites have also moved away from the commandment. Along with wearing a covering with spiritual significance, Christian women did not even think of having their hair shorn (using a shears on it) or being shaven (cut close). It was considered Scripturally disgraceful to do so. The influence of Christian women made it also socially disgraceful. In one of Reiman Reminisce's recent publications a woman reminisces on her first haircut. She says, 'When Dad saw my short bobbed hair, he was so shocked he couldn't talk! If a bombshell had dropped at his feet he could not have looked more stricken.' Of course, her reminiscing was not one of concern over what she had done or how it affected her father but rather of a sacrilegious nature. It says how far society has moved since professing Christianity has moved.

I well remember when some of you who once wore a consistent covering over uncut hair believed in and defended its use both in oral argument and in document form. What has happened? Has the message of the Bible changed? Is the covering no longer a divinely ordered praiseworthy ordinance (1 Cor. 11:2)? Has the Holy Spirit removed the once delivered 'shame to be shorn' and the 'let her be covered' from the Holy Oracles? Or have we done the moving away from the 'forever-settled' commandment.

Next—I would like to call attention to a movement away from what has been understood as a Biblical and traditional practice of the church on the wedding ring. [Here Aaron quotes from the tract 'Marriage and the Wedding Ring' which he had written. He included a copy of it with the letter.]

It seems rather strange that on one hand that which the Mennonite Church has from its inception understood the Bible to teach (the covering) has been moved away from while at the same time that which the church has from its inception understood the Bible to teach against (the wedding ring) has been moved into. Is this what the Bible means when it says we are to be 'unmoveable!?' God says that we are not to keep the ordinances of the world but that '...ye...shall keep mine ordinances, to walk therein.' (Lev. 18:2,3; See also 2 Thess. 2:15)

On the doctrine and practice of nonconformity in personal appearance many of us have moved far away from what we and our parents practiced. In the Preface of his book on *Christianity and Dress*, John C. Wenger declares, '... The Battle against worldliness [in dress] will not have been won until each believer has decided for himself to live the non-conformed life.' According to this statement it would seem, without doubt, that the battle against worldly dress has been lost and moved away from. The god or goddess of fashion has had its appeal and fastened itself on us until there is no distinct separation any longer in evidence. Has the world gotten so much better that it is now biblical and right to follow the appearances of the world or have we moved away from that which was once a proper Biblical expression of a principle that runs through the Bible? When a principle does not find a proper expression it is a lost principle.

[Here Aaron gives the story of the black lady's testimony at the Atmore post office; see page 81.]

From the divinely inspired writings of the late Apostle Paul we are told that Christian women are to dress in 'modest apparel' (garments that adequately cover the body including the lower limbs)—the kind of apparel that 'becometh women professing godliness.' Dress that manifests godliness must be different from that of an ungodly world.

From the divinely inspired writings of the late Apostle Peter we are told 'not... the wearing of gold, or the putting on of apparel.' 'Not the putting on of apparel' cannot mean that we are to be unclothed but rather that the superfluous, unnecessary items designed and suggested by the world are not to be worn. The laces, frills, ruffles, ties, etc., etc. would doubtless come in this category.

Both the Old Testament and the New Testament teach us that the practice of nonconformity in our bodily appearance is essential to our understanding and maintaining the total structure of divine truth. (Numbers 15:37-41; Rom. 12:1,2). In Numbers 15 God required a distinct mark of identification in their dress as a reminder to keep all His commandments. In Rom. 12:2 we are told to be non-conformed as a help in knowing or understanding what is that 'good, and acceptable, and perfect will of God.'

We do not in any way mean that these Bible principles are more important than other Bible teachings but rather that they are also a part of the divine injunctions enjoined upon us which should be trembled at and practiced, rather than ignored or rejected.

Of course, we all have our weaknesses along the way but personal weaknesses are vastly different from intentional ignorance or willful rejection or disobedience. Unintentional weaknesses of sincere Christians are doubtless covered by the blood which cleanseth from all sin (1 John 1:7).

Please grant me your patience for one more concern. This relates to the free exchange of hugs and kisses between the sexes when we meet and separate. This kind of exchange between blood brothers and sisters, when done with reserve might not be objectionable. But when it is practiced between in-laws, it is hardly in keeping with Biblical purity and discretion. It is rather the way of the sensual world which is becoming more morally corrupt as this age draws to a close. I personally have steered clear from such meeting-greetings and while Marjorie did not resist it she never appreciated it.

May the gracious Holy Spirit grant us the correction, the guidance, and the grace that is needed to bring us all into His holy, glorious, and eternal presence.

Best wishes to one and all for now and forever.

Devotedly yours, with love and prayers,

Aaron and (Marjorie—Retrospectively)

As Marjorie had slipped into her handicapped state, it seemed natural that Dorothy would help in her older sister's care. Dorothy had started helping tend to Marjorie's needs over the weekends, when the regular caregiver would have time off. But who was Dorothy? Up until that time Dorothy had experienced a life of her own.

Dorothy Showalter Newswanger

As a teenager, Dorothy wished to attend the Eastern Mennonite School at Harrisonburg, Virginia, not far north of where she lived. But she had a problem—not enough dresses. She and her next sister shared dresses, and washed, dried, and prepared them so each could wear a different one each day.

As a single person, Dorothy involved herself in various kinds of work. She worked at the publishing house at Scottdale for a while, at a hatchery in Harrisonburg, Virginia, and in the osteopathic office of her brother-in-law, Dr. Paul Herr. She later served under the Lancaster Conference for more than eleven years in mission work in Honduras.

Dorothy (Showalter) Newswanger as Numdia Bible School secretary.

At age forty-four, Dorothy married the widowed Walter Newswanger. Five years later, Walter died, leaving Dorothy a widow. Sometime after Walter died, Dorothy served as secretary at the Numidia Mennonite Bible School for eleven years.

Several months after Marjorie's death, Aaron was ready for companionship again. He had little desire to become acquainted with someone entirely new. Marjorie's younger sister, Dorothy, was just the person.

Foreign

Testimony of Outgoing Worker
Dorothy Showalter

News Notes . . .

FOREIGN

A farewell service was held for Dorothy Showalter, Quarryville, Pa., short-term missionary appointee under the Eastern Board to Honduras, at the Rawlinsville Mennonite Church on Sunday evening, December 22. Bro. Aaron Shank was the speaker. Sister Showalter left for Honduras December 28 to serve as living companion and helper to the nurse at Tocoa. She arrived on the field the same day.

"The Lord is my light and my salvation; whom shall I fear? the Lord is the strength of my life; of whom shall I be afraid?" I praise God for His great salvation, for His love, mercy, and forgiveness in my life, and for His keeping power.

When I think of all the Lord has done for me and of the great need in the world, I want to serve Him and my fellow men as best I can. I am happy for the privilege of serving Christ in Honduras and feel there will be many rich experiences and blessings ahead in this field of service. There will likely be some problems, disappointments, or times of discouragement, too; but we do have the promise that God will be with us.

"And the Lord, he it is that doth go before thee; he will be with thee, he will not fail thee, neither forsake thee; fear not, neither be dismayed." Also, "My grace is sufficient for thee."

There will need to be a constant abiding in Christ. "Abide in me, and I in you. As the branch cannot bear fruit of itself, except it abide in the vine; no more can ye, except ye abide in me."

Pray that Christ will be seen in my life as I assist the workers in Honduras.

Missionary
Messenger
Vol. XXXIV   February, 1958   No. 10

In Honduras
Eager Listeners
Hear the Gospel

The February 1958 *Missionary Messenger* covered Dorothy Showalter's departure for Honduras under the Eastern Board of Missions and Charities.

After Dorothy's death, the president of Eastern Mennonite Missions wrote to her family:

At Eastern Mennonite Missions, we hold a deep appreciation for the years of service that Dorothy gave to the kingdom of God. Back in 1961, when Dorothy concluded her first term of service through EMM, Paul Kraybill wrote this to her:

"I would like to express to you our deep and sincere appreciation for the way in which you gave of yourself so generously and so efficiently to assist in the program of our mission in Honduras. You may be sure that it was much appreciated and that your service made a very effective and meaningful contribution."

Norman Hockman, who served with Dorothy in Honduras, said this about her when she completed her last term:

"Dorothy was appreciated by everyone. She selflessly gave of herself to the work, not only in the office, but to a host of additional requests that came her way. She will be hard to replace here."

I'm sure you feel the same way…We give thanks to God for Dorothy's life and ministry.

After Sidney Gingrich's wife had died, Sidney married his wife's sister two years later. Considering this example, Aaron contemplated doing the same.

Aaron would "stop in" to see Dorothy while she continued living on Walter's farm. He would bring an ice chest full of produce from his garden. Initially, she considered these gestures as acts of consideration from her brother-in-law. But in December of 1995, Aaron approached Dorothy about the possibility of a deeper relationship. Dorothy remained uncertain. The adjustments needed in another marriage, the change in church life,[1] and a variety of other reasons prevented her from giving Aaron a commitment at that point. The issue was left open. In the spring of 1996, Aaron traveled to Dublin, Georgia, to assist in the church work there. While he was gone, Dorothy received "one or two" letters from Aaron. When Aaron returned north, he again approached Dorothy for consideration of a courting relationship. Dorothy

---

1 She was a member of the EPMC.

again asked him for time to consider his proposition. After due consideration and some unusual developments, she finally consented.

The couple had their first "date" in July at the Shirksville congregation's fellowship meal. Aaron told the group that night that he had received "A rumor from the Lord!" He went on to explain how Dorothy had received her confirmation that this friendship might be acceptable. In some way the rumor got out that Dorothy and Aaron were courting. When Dorothy went to church at Danville, a number of people came to congratulate her for her social change. When she realized how her people saw this development, it dispelled her doubts and she consented to his special friendship.

Aaron and Dorothy attended a number of church activities, weddings, and social events together. Dorothy was sensitive to the thoughts of others and sought affirmation that this was the Lord's will. Having received encouragement from her family, brothers and sisters in her church, and those who were considered "friends of the couple," Dorothy concluded that she was within God's plan for her life.

Dorothy Pearl Showalter Newswanger became Mrs. Aaron Shank on Sunday evening, November 3, 1996. The wedding service was held at Swatara Mennonite Church, with Stephen Ebersole preaching the wedding sermon and Sidney Gingrich performing the marriage ceremony.

Week-long revival services which had been scheduled for the Swatara congregation were canceled for the first Sunday evening. That Sunday evening, open to anyone desiring to attend, Aaron and Dorothy were married. The couple attended each of the subsequent meetings during the week. The following Sunday's planned fellowship meal included a special table set for Aaron and Dorothy with their attendants. After the meal Aaron, in a short speech, said publicly in his characteristic way, "I have married Dorothy twice—first when she married Walter Newswanger and second when I married her."

Sometime later Aaron took Dorothy on a trip to her Springdale church home in Virginia. While Springdale retained little of its Mennonite distinctives, Aaron graciously credited the sermon for the good it contained.

1 Corinthians 13 marriage

Aaron had high aspirations for marriage. In a card written to Dorothy sometime later, he paraphrased 1 Corinthians 13:4-8. He wrote, "Aaron and Dorothy suffer long and are kind; Aaron and Dorothy are not envious; Aaron and Dorothy do not vaunt themselves and are not puffed up; Aaron and Dorothy do not behave themselves unseemingly; they do not seek their own; Aaron and Dorothy are not easily provoked; they do not think evil of people; Aaron and Dorothy do not rejoice in others' iniquity; but they rejoice together in the truth. Aaron and Dorothy bear all things, believe all things (good), hope for all things, and endure all things. Aaron and Dorothy never fail." He concluded, "This idealism may not always be attainable but may we diligently strive for this kind of perfection." He signed the card, "Affectionately yours, Hubby Aaron."

Big Picture Sermon Summaries

Aaron preached countless messages in his lifetime, each dedicated to the needs of the hour as he saw them. But Aaron also preached several key messages, each of which offers a unique window into Aaron's heart as a responsible church leader. In each of these Aaron united "the big picture" with the details which created "the big picture." Aaron understood that the far-seeing eye of a church leader must be able to comprehend "the big picture" so that the details remain in perspective. He knew better than to major on minors, to focus on details. Aaron's broad experience, including both time and geography, qualified him to speak authoritatively about the particular issues he addressed. Summaries of three such messages follow; recordings for the same are available.

In 1988, Aaron preached a sermon entitled "Why is There an Eastern Pennsylvania Mennonite Church?" In that sermon he pointed out several callings of the EPMC. If God can raise up a group, God can keep a group adhering to His principles. There is no reason why we cannot be successful.

1. To witness to the importance and value of a consistent observance of the Christian ordinances.

2. To maintain the principle of modest apparel.

Aaron Shank's second wedding day. Aaron and Dorothy with their attendants, Ira and Louise (Shank) Mast.

3. To maintain a Scriptural approach to brotherhood assistance.

4. To maintain a Scriptural approach to divorce and remarriage issues.

5. To maintain a Scriptural position on peace and nonresistance.

6. To maintain a proper attitude toward payment of taxes.

7. To maintain a Biblical concept between faith and works, grace and faith, and conditional salvation.

8. To maintain inner and outer holiness of life.

9. To be strong promoters and exalters of Jesus Christ.

Then he mentioned some threats and dangers facing the EPMC.

1. The Ephesus Church syndrome. This is the greatest danger that faces any orthodox group. Orthodox people are strong-minded people and thus they have special problems appreciating each other if they differ in viewpoint.

2. Respect for church leadership and authority. Some present trends and attitudes will threaten the existence of the EPMC.

3. Considering the Church infallible. One Lancaster Conference bishop

said, "Do you think that this Board which works and prays together and tries to find a right solution together, can make a mistake?" Consensus can go wrong.

We are responsible to be obedient to the Church until the church requires something of us that would violate a Bible principle. At that point the Church loses its authority because it exercises delegated authority.

We must guard against the dual errors of disrespect for church authority and church infallibility.

4. Religious pride. Church people tend to look around and compare their group's best with other groups' worst. It is right to be loyal, but not by putting other people down. "We look over and see other churches' problems and we say their problems result from the wrong kind of organization. Then we say our problems are because we are keeping the faith. If we are going to continue as the EPMC, we will need to be very humble, very, very humble."

5. Laziness in administration. The Church will naturally decay under lazy administrators.

In October 1991, Aaron preached a sermon at Shirksville entitled "50 Years in the Ministry" at the request of Pastor Raymond High. He hesitated to preach the message lest he be preaching himself, not Jesus Christ. With his usual modesty he acknowledged that he could have done better. His actual frequent failures were embarrassing to him. What has happened has happened.

He contrasted his fifty years of feeble and frail efforts to Christ's three and one half short years. "My ministry is an awesome embarrassment to me as I compare it with Jesus Christ's work and ministry. It fades away into insignificance and nothingness."

"Jesus never talked about his accomplishments and neither did Apostle Paul."

"I have no count of the number of sermons I preached, the home visits made, how many revival meetings I've held, at how many Bible Conferences I've spoken, nor the number of converts in revival meetings, nor the number of baptisms I've performed. I have no account of the amount of money I've given to the church, the number of bishop meetings I've attended, the number of mission board meetings I've attended, the number of committee meetings I attended when I served on the LMS board, and the Publishing House Board. I don't know how many council meetings I've conducted, nor the number of communion services, nor the number of marriages I officiated."

"I get comfort from Jesus' words of commendation for 'very little.' The rewards are out of proportion for the service rendered or the suffering experienced."

"I aimed at dedication to Christ above everything else all my life. God favored me by placing me in the ministry when I didn't deserve being called at all. I endeavored to be faithful. I think I have fought a good fight. I believe I have kept the faith. But faithfulness has been a fallible faithfulness. No one knows any better about my own fallibility than I do."

"My deep burden and concern has been for sound doctrine."

Aaron listed areas of growth he had seen in the Lebanon District over the years.

1. Use and production of tobacco challenged in Lancaster Conference.
2. Increased loyalty to the Church.
3. Regular services are held in all the buildings of the District.
4. Christian literature distribution program.
5. Young People's Institute.
6. Christian Day Schools.
7. Prison ministry.
8. Shepherd's Fold.[2]

Then he listed some changes that he made during his administration as bishop in the Lebanon District. Some of these he remembered his father being concerned about.

1. Sunday School was eliminated on Communion Sundays.
2. Years earlier the feet washing service had been optional. After communion, the service was dismissed. Those present could remain after communion for feet washing or they could go home.
3. The ministers used to only wash feet among themselves. Basins in

---

2 Shepherd's Fold is a ministry dedicated to helping men gain personal victory over sinful strongholds in their lives.

the pulpit served the ordained men, thus they did not mingle with the congregation.

4. Every council service employed the Matthew 18 text. Aaron discontinued the tradition.

5. Every preparatory service employed Matthew 6, 7. Aaron discontinued this tradition as well.

6. Leavened bread and fermented wine changed to unleavened bread and grape juice.

7. There had been no annual business meetings. There were no nominations. Meetings to place people into church offices were termed *reelections*, and the terminology was correct.

8. When ordained men went to the pulpit, they always sat in the order of their ordination. All of the ordained men gave testimony after a sermon. Both of these traditions were discontinued.

9. The ordained men did not participate in the Sunday School discussion. They spent the time in a counsel room. Aaron discontinued the practice.

10. Only one vote was required to place a man in the lot as a candidate for ordination. Aaron required more.

11. Ministers' meetings did not exist. Aaron valued ministers' meetings.

Looking beyond 1991, Aaron asked some questions about the future.

1. Will the Church continue a strong spiritual emphasis?

2. Will Christ have the preeminence in the Church?

3. Will the Church remain separate from the world? "The Bible teaches and history proves that we cannot maintain the full structure of Biblical truth without maintaining a consistent position on nonconformity in attire."

4. Will brotherhood assistance remain functional?

5. Will there be increased respect for Church authority and Church leadership?

6. Will true nonresistance be maintained?

7. Will the Church maintain an enthusiastic and energetic evangelistic outreach?

8. Will a strong emphasis on moral purity continue?

Pilgrim youth on an evangelistic trip to New York City in 1999 pose with a Jewish tour guide.

More than twenty-five years later, we marvel at the prophetic insight expressed that day!

In April of 1996, Aaron preached another significant sermon at Swatara Mennonite Church. It was entitled "Things to Remember After My Decease." By this time, he had regained his former vigor and dynamic in preaching following Marjorie's illness and death. He made several observations.

He maintained that being "what we are" is proof that "we have learned some things from history." In spite of the fact that "no church group has ever been permanently successful," the conservative Mennonite church still survived. "I claim to belong to the same religious body, doctrinally, principly [*sic*], Biblically, that I joined nearly seventy years ago. The name of my church organization has changed a few times but the basic principles have remained unchanged. I am still a part of the group that continues the practices, principles, and standards that I joined nearly seventy years ago."

"When I was ordained to the ministry, one of the things which was indelibly impressed upon me was Apostle Paul's charge to Titus to speak sound doctrine and sound speech which cannot be condemned. I have majored on these in my ministry."

"I admired and learned a lot from J. Paul Graybill, a strong conservative in the Lancaster Conference. He taught the principles which were embraced and maintained by a large block of people who came into the Eastern Pennsylvania Mennonite Church. These people maintained these principles because their leader had built these principles into their system. Even though Conference drifted away, these people remained a part of the system of principle from previous years."

1. "The principles of practical holiness in experiential salvation are permanently fixed. I hope our brotherhood will never try to invalidate or change the Bible standard. No individual, no ministerial board, no congregational counsel has any right to invalidate or change any Scriptural principle."

Aaron Shank enjoys a day of fishing with grandson Darvin.

"The Roman Catholic Church has deceived its millions by claiming infallibility in its headship. If we ever get to the place where we claim infallibility, we're claiming something not given us from heaven. Such a claim puts no difference between the Church and Jesus Christ. The Church is not infallible, Jesus Christ is; the Church can go wrong, Jesus Christ can't. Until the Church is in heaven with Christ without spot or wrinkle, it cannot claim to be equal with Jesus Christ."

"When we bind and loose in making proper applications to the Word of God, I solemnly believe that God holds us responsible to honor and respect the Church. When Church standards turn us toward the truth, God in heaven recognizes them."

2. "The truth, to be preserved, must be repeated and reemphasized. Repeated truths become the truths most surely known to a people. To be silent in one generation on a Bible doctrine means that it will be lost to the

next generation. It doesn't even take that long. People can depart quickly from the truth."

3. "We have a personal responsibility concerning our election to salvation. We need some help here. Some say, 'There is nothing we can do to experience salvation. We only do good works as a result of salvation.' One of our conservative papers recently made the statement, 'Good works are not even a consideration in the first step of salvation.' I have heard numbers of times, 'There is nothing we can do to be saved; all our works are as filthy rags.' The provisional works by God for salvation are supernatural; the conditional works of response to God's offer by mankind are good works." Aaron was referring to the human responses of repentance for personal rebellion against God and personal faith in the Lord Jesus Christ.

Aaron and Dorothy, c. 1997.

4. "We must keep emphasizing the soon return of our Lord Jesus Christ. I hope as long as I live and after my decease that we'll keep remembering these eternal unchangeables and keep our hope alive in the imminent coming of Christ. We must have our churches ready to be caught up to see Him like He is. I hope we provide the kind of leadership which keeps us constantly expecting, constantly looking up."

Racing home

In the early summer of 2001, Aaron was increasingly aware of the limitations of his mortal body. Twice that year he was hospitalized for respiratory difficulties. But he preached as he was able, warning the one requesting the sermon that he "might not be able" to fulfill the request.

On April 23, 2002, Aaron preached his last church-wide sermon at the funeral of a close friend. Young John Earl Hollinger had married, had a son, and was a member at Swatara when he was diagnosed with cancer. As his sickness progressed, he and Aaron formed a close friendship. One day Aaron told young John Earl, "You and I are in a race to see who gets home first." When John Earl won that race, it was his request that Aaron preach the funeral sermon.

The closing months of 2002 saw Aaron continue to decline, especially with respiratory problems. On prior occasions, Aaron had expressed his desire to be alive at the rapture of the Church. Now he stated that to experience physical death would be interesting.

Although Aaron was racing Home, his legacy continued. In 2003, Pilgrim Mennonite Conference counted seventeen congregations and 1,078 members. The Eastern Pennsylvania Mennonite Church had sixty-three congregations and 4,284 members. Yet the legacy which Aaron and his fellow-laborers contributed to the church was larger. In 2003, there were two other church groups which traced their roots to the "honorable release" of 1968. Hope Mennonite Fellowship had five congregations and 372 members, and the Mid-Atlantic Mennonite Fellowship had eighteen congregations and 1,402 members.

Aaron's last home sermon (Swatara) was shared with deacon Henry Klassen on the Sunday when Henry was bidding farewell to the congregation for a short term at the Children's home in Honduras. He preached his very last sermon on earth (July 14, 2002) at Bethany Mennonite Church in Virginia. Characteristically, he preached on "The Lord Shall Roar out of Zion."

Aaron labored to the end, even in his last years when his active public preaching was over. He titled a treatise on the subject of Faith and Works, "Your Most Holy Faith."[3] Aaron believed that Faith was necessary for Salvation, but he could not see any difference between the faith and faith. In other words, he believed that a person needed to commit himself to the entire body of New Testament truth in order to experience salvation.

On September 10, 2002, Aaron wrote a letter to Dorothy inside of a birthday card. He noted that the letter was being written nineteen days in advance, "just in case I am not here in 19 days."

3 This work is still in print under the title *Faith and Works in Salvation*, from Rod & Staff Publishers.

My Dearest Dorothy Pearl,

Wishing you a very happy birthday in the wonderful name and love of our heavenly Father and the Lord Jesus Christ, our precious Lord and Savior. You are my pearl of great value. When Jesus used the term "pearl of great price," He was referring to the church, His bride-to-be which He found in a field (the world) and purchased it at a very great price. Your name suggests what you are to me—a pearl of great value to me—now and until either one of us may move into the world where "they neither marry nor are given in marriage." Then all the saints, including those who had marriage partners here will become the eternal glorified Bride of Christ. But you came into my "wife-life" as a pearl of great value free of charge, without any great cost to me. And you have been most efficient and more than sufficient as a "helpmeet" for me. Your ready adaptation to a new marriage union, to a new home and family life, new community life, along with your untiring physical energy, and your spiritual devotion, and your captivating smile, etc., etc. has been satisfying and comforting—physically and spiritually. I thank you and thank God for your saying "yes" about seven years ago. May God continue to bless you richly and reward you greatly. Wishing you His best for the remaining time here and for eternity there.

Aaron then drew an arrow to the printed text of the card. *Thank you for the miracle of you... You are, and always will be the love of my life.* He signed the card, *Yours lovingly, Husband Aaron*

CHAPTER 11

Death, Sod, God

JANUARY 2003 INCLUDED a hospital stay of three days. The summer months brought increased shortness of breath and difficulty with breathing. On September 28, Aaron participated in his last communion service with the Elm Street congregation. It was apparent to everyone that Aaron's life would now be measured by days rather than years.

Thursday, December 11, Aaron suffered intense pain. Aaron asked Ira Mast, his son-in-law, to "please pray that God would deliver me from this pain in one way or another." Aaron did not wish to return to the hospital.

At the very end, Aaron somehow realized that he was confused. He referred to the story Marjorie had enjoyed telling about the man who finally admitted, "I A T K."

Someone who heard the man say this wondered, "What does that stand for?"

He replied, "I am terribly confused."

"Well," came the retort, "Confused is spelled with a 'C' not a 'K.'"

"Oh, well, that just shows how confused I am," came the answer.

When Dorothy tried to clear up the confusion, Aaron replied, "I A T K."

Aaron received his call home on Monday evening, December 15, 2003. Aaron had anticipated these moments while he was healthy and strong. "Won't that be something. To be absent from the body is to be present with the Lord. When I close my eyes to this earth, I will open them in the presence of Jesus!

"Oh, the joy of the privilege of seeing my Lord and Savior face to face!"

"And then, according to what the apostle Jude wrote, He will take me to the Holy Father who is sitting on the throne. He will take me by the hand and present me faultless to the Eternal God....

"Imagine, one with as many faults as I have ... presented faultless to a thrice Holy God and be able to praise Him with all the saints of all the ages. My mind just collapses with the thought!"

Funeral services were held on December 20, 2003 at the Swatara Mennonite Church. His memorial read:

In Loving Memory,

On Monday evening, December 15, 2003, about 9:00, Bro. Aaron Shank was called home to be with the Lord. He had moved into the Lebanon District with his family in the fall of 1919, from Virginia, when he was 2 ½ years old. At the age of twenty-six, Aaron was ordained minister at Meckville on October 12, 1941. Later on July 4, 1957, he was ordained bishop of the Lebanon District. In all Brother Aaron served as an ordained brother for sixty-two years, out of which forty-six were served in the bishop responsibility. Bro. Aaron will be remembered for his thorough and sound doctrinal understanding of the Scriptures, his fervency in preaching, and his fairness in administration. His burden for the conservative Mennonite Church was that she not move away from her Scriptural foundation, but ever walk more closely with the Lord.

Viewings were held on Thursday evening from 6-8 at the Fairview Reception Center on Friday afternoon 2-4 and 6-8 at Swatara Mennonite Church. The funeral was held on Saturday at Swatara at 10:00. His body is laid to rest beside his first wife, Marjorie, who passed on June 23, 1995.

We extend our sympathies to Sister Dorothy, (his faithful companion since November 3, 1996, and caregiver for these last months), to his daughter Louise, wife of Ira Mast, and to the rest of the family. To those of us who remain of the next generations the challenge is to live and teach the doctrines and practices of the Word, that we too may leave a legacy for succeeding generations to follow as Brother Aaron has done.

Characteristically, Aaron had written about death and desired that the following be read or referred to at his funeral service.

In Hebrews 2:15 we are told that outside of Christ death is a lifetime fear. While the child of God anticipates with joy what comes after death, the experience of death, nevertheless, has many distasteful, uncomfortable, and undesirable aspects, -- it is in reality an enemy. But as children of God we can actually look forward to this last enemy attack upon us with a degree of anticipation because it is in the experience of death, that for us death is destroyed.

The Pilgrim Conference Bishop Board in a photo taken only three months before Aaron's death. L to R, back row: Earl Ray Hursh, Ivan Martin Jr., Steve Ebersole, Simon R. Yoder; front row: Sidney Gingerich, Aaron Shank, Harry Neuenschwander.

Death is a very cruel enemy. We sing sometimes, "Death comes down with reckless footsteps to the hall and hut." And it comes to the costliest mansions, too.

It comes at any time in life—from infancy to old age, expected or unexpected. It takes sweet little babes from their mothers' loving arms. It tears husbands and wives away from each other's companionship, from the beginning of wedded life and anytime thereafter. (As a child I have vivid memories of my parents lamenting the tragic death of a dedicated young groom married to a dedicated young bride, only a few days after their marriage.) It sometimes takes a young father or mother away from a family of young children leaving a widow or widower to raise the family alone. It snatches fathers and mothers, grandfathers and grandmothers away from children and grandchildren.

Death will at times take its victims at the most inconvenient places – in the shop, in the field, on the highway, in the hospital, in the church pew or pulpit. (I was personally acquainted with a Mennonite minister in Virginia who, while delivering a Sunday morning sermon, was stricken by death and fell lifeless from his pulpit).

Death strikes in many cruel and varied ways. It may strike through lingering disabilities or painful diseases, through sudden accident or prolonged illnesses. Many of God's children have, by the hands of wicked, ruthless tyrants, died cruel deaths by devouring flames, by stonings, by drownings, by mutilation of their bodies. It tears to pieces or murders in other cruel ways, by the millions, the tiny bodies of aborted babies. It is sometimes inflicted by storming elements, enemy germs, and demon-inspired enemy human agents.

The enemy of death never returns its victims. It takes bodies and gives them over to decadence and corruption. Sometimes it gives bodies to be devoured by worms and scavengers of the earth and sea (see Job 19:26)....

How was this destruction of death made possible? God sent His Son into the world, "made in the likeness of sinful flesh." He was born in the flesh so he could die in the flesh. In due time He gave Himself over to the enemy of death. It was the most shameful, disgraceful, humiliating death known to man—"even the death of the cross." Although He was all powerful and the enemy authorities and the enemy of death could have "had no power at all over Him," in that hour of the cross He humbly rendered Himself a helpless victim of death and a helpless subject of the grave. But that hour of helplessness was brief. Death could not keep Him as a victim long and the grave could not hold Him long. He awoke from His momentary sleep of death, tore the poisonous sting out of death, and broke loose from the short hold the grave had on Him. And "up from the grave He arose, with a mighty triumph o'er His foes"—His human foes, His demonic foes, and His foe of death.

In that moment of matchless and humanly inconceivable power over death and the grave, there was a graphic demonstration of what He had accomplished for His followers. As He arose from the grave, many graves of past centuries exploded and Old Testament saints followed Jesus triumphantly out of the cold hold the grave had on them....

The message for us is clear, comforting, and conclusive. As children of God we can in the face of the enemy of death shout triumphantly, "O [enemy of] death, where is thy sting? O [holding] grave, where is thy victory?" We can cry out in jubilation, "Thanks be unto God which giveth us the victory [over sin, over the enemy of death, over the hold of the grave, over the tormenting flames of hell, over the lake of fire, and over the second death] through our Lord Jesus Christ" 1 Corinthians 15:55-57....

Praise the holy, precious, powerful, and worthy name of Jesus—the uniquely exclusive One who alone brought destruction to the enemy of death for the children of God. The One who gives eternal life in the place of eternal death.

Aaron's funeral planning was simple because Aaron had the funeral plans written out beforehand. He and Sidney had conferred together on the subject previously and both had agreed that the survivor would take part in the other's funeral. At the funeral, Sidney testified that Aaron was an able leader, of noble character, one who had run his race well. He noted the God-given wisdom evident in his work, his consistent life and testimony, his depth of understanding (he was chosen to deal publicly with hard subjects), and his ability to be a wise challenger. "I felt like a little boy by Aaron's side."

Aaron's choice of the following funeral songs testifies to his commanding presence, even in death: "God Himself Is Present," "The Time for Toil," "Not I but Christ Be Honored," and "Go Labor On." Ivan Martin, Jr., moderated the funeral, with Anthony Good leading the songs, Sidney Gingrich having the devotional thoughts, and Steve Ebersole preaching the funeral sermon. Aaron had requested that Harry Neuenschwander and Sim Yoder share a testimony following the message. At the cemetery, Clair Burkholder conducted the graveside service. Harry noted in his testimony, "Aaron did not try to do the work of twelve men; he tried to put twelve men to work." This snippet eloquently and concisely states the attitude and mentality out of which Aaron functioned.

As brothers and sisters grieved beside his lifeless body, Aaron M. Shank stood before the glorious presence of his God, awaiting the full resurrection and the complete triumph of life over death.

Dorothy

Dorothy played "second fiddle" to two different men, each widowers. At age forty-four she returned to the States from Honduras to marry Walter Newswanger and step into his home to become a step-mother to his four children (two of his children were married before Walter and Dorothy were married), his wife as a dairyman, and his confidante as a church leader. Five and a half years later, she was abruptly widowed, but continued to live on Walter's farm to care for the needs of the family.

At age sixty-eight, after caring for her sister Marjorie until shortly before she died, she became Aaron Shank's second wife, outliving him by more than fourteen years. By this marriage she became step-mother to Aaron's four children, although none of them lived at home any longer. In one lifetime she had become step-mother to two different sets of children, not a common achievement. By the time of her death, she was step-grandmother to 40 step-grandchildren (28 Newswanger step-grandchildren and 12 Shank step-grandchildren). Although Dorothy never had any children of her own, she earned a good name by seeking to be a servant everywhere she went. No complaining, no self-pity, always conscious of bothering others, she was universally known for her quiet smile. No one knows how many "Little Jewel Books" she distributed to the children of the families she loved. When she needed care near the end of her life, she was a joy to care for; she never wanted to "be a bother." It took some time to convince her to ring her call bell when she wanted something.

Ten days before she died, she told some visiting ladies, "I love Him, I praise Him, you need to serve Him." On the day before she died, she raised her hands from her bed and said semi-consciously in the hearing of those nearby, "Celebrate! Celebrate!" (not her normal choice of words). What was she witnessing in those final earthly days?

As the widow of two different men, where should her body rest until the resurrection? Her earthly body was placed on the opposite side of Marjorie. Thus Aaron's body awaits the resurrection between his two beloved wives.

Aaron and Marjorie Shank's tombstone. As of this publication, Dorothy's tombstone has not been placed.

CHAPTER 12

Postlude

ELIE WIESEL, JEWISH holocaust survivor, might have been speaking for Aaron on April 12, 1999, when he spoke on "The Perils of Indifference" at a public gathering.

"Indifference considers the lives of others of no consequence. Indifference is tragic, a denial of the purpose for our creation, the ultimate unbelief, an unconscious death, more dangerous than anger or hatred, the friend of the enemy, a betrayal of one's own humanity by being indifferent to the plight of others. Where I came from society was composed of three kinds of people, the killers, the victims, and the bystanders."

At another time and place, treading the blazed but rugged path of both his great-great uncle John M. Brenneman and the Shank family friend, George R. Brunk I, Aaron M. Shank demonstrated fearless loyalty to Christ and His Church, untiring, energetic leadership in His service, dedication to sound Bible doctrine in both preaching and writing, an entire lifetime devoid of indifference. Indifference could do no credit to the cause of Christ.

Since the ascension of Jesus Christ, God has used men filled with the Holy Ghost to lead the true church. The variation seen in the effectiveness of church leaders is no reflection on the provisions of God; rather, success or failure in church leadership, as well as any other venture in life, depends predominately upon submission to the direction of God through His Word and Spirit. Aaron Shank was a man gifted with many natural talents. He had a keen understanding and comprehension of human character. He had the ability to instill a desire to "do right" in the hearts of those who fell through their own human weakness. His dynamic preaching style, quick humor, and homespun sermon illustrations all combined to make him effective in his pulpit ministry. But perhaps the greatest single asset Aaron Shank possessed in his years of service to the church was a steadfast commitment to follow the Spirit of Christ as revealed in the Word of God. This "asset" formed a core around which his ministry could be built. It provided him with stability and direction when others foundered in leadership.

While he was exceptionally gifted, Aaron experienced and fully comprehended failure. Years after his separation from the Eastern Pennsylvania Mennonite Church and the formation of the Pilgrim Mennonite Conference, he lamented with tears "there had to be a better way." He felt a great burden for the apostasy within his own family, and yet felt powerless to alter the direction of their lives. In church life, he sadly witnessed many of his flock depart into liberalism and worldliness. Yet, the commitment to hold fast the Spirit of Christ as revealed by the Word of God kept Aaron effective as a leader at home and in the churches he served.

It has been said that a man can be measured by the size of the shadow he casts. This method has only one shortcoming in that it is required to have knowledge of where the man is standing in relationship to the source of light illuminating him. The largest shadow is created when the man stands fully upright, directly before the light. As Aaron Shank stood before the illuminating power of God, his shadow fell on generations of family, friends, and church members. To many, the shadow seemed to intimate that Aaron Shank was a huge man. Aaron would have seen himself more accurately. He would have informed us that the size of the shadow cast by this small man was no reflection of his stature, simply the result of his standing directly before the Light of the Lord and Savior, Jesus Christ.

Aaron Shank's farm as it appeared in 2019. Swatara Mennonite Church dominates the center of the photo. Aaron's house is in the left center. The graveyard where Aaron and his wives are buried is visible behind the Swatara meetinghouse. On the right is Steve Ebersole's home and business.

A chart Aaron made for study of the Tabernacle—Version 1 (1959).

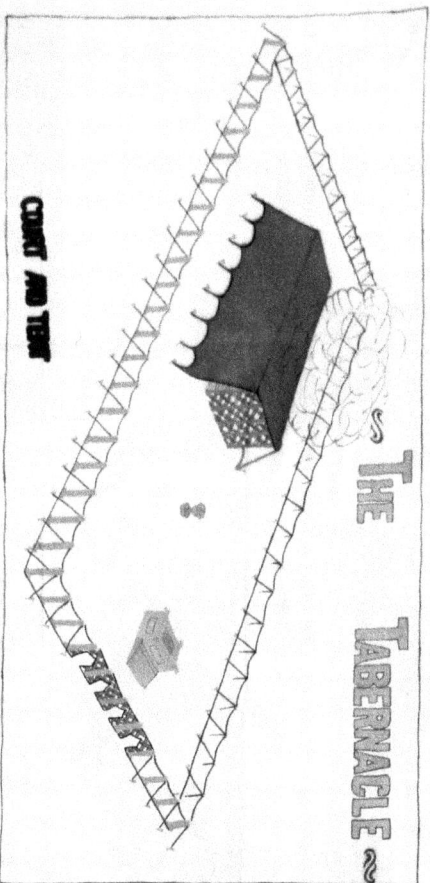

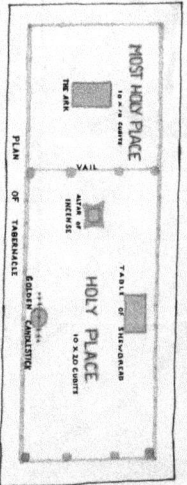

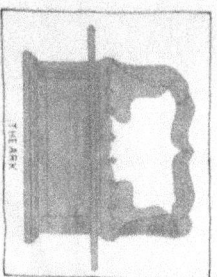

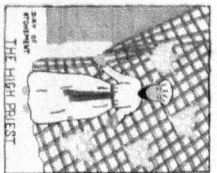

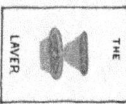

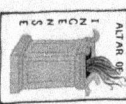

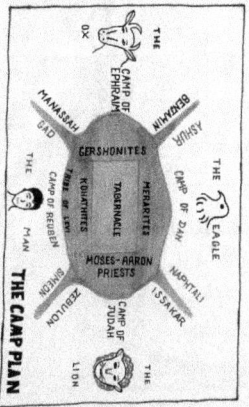

A second version of Aaron's Tabernacle chart.

THE ARK

COURT AND TENT

THE TABERNACLE 2

THE HIGH PRIEST

FIVE OF TRUMPETS

LEVITE PRIEST

IN ROBES OF GLORY AND BEAUTY

THE HIGH PRIEST

THE ALTAR

THE LAVER

CANDLESTICK

TABLE OF SHEW-BREAD

ALTAR OF INCENSE

PLAN OF TABERNACLE

MOST HOLY PLACE
18 x 1/2 CUBITS

THE ARK

VAIL

ALTAR OF INCENSE

TABLE OF SHEWBREAD

HOLY PLACE
10 X 20 CUBITS

GOLDEN CANDLESTICK

TABERNACLE FRAMEWORK

THE CAMP PLAN

CAMP OF EPHRAIM

THE OX

MANASSEH

GAD

BENJAMIN

ASHUR

GERSHONITES

MERARITES

TABERNACLE

KOHATHITES

CAMP OF REUBEN

TRIBE OF LEVI

THE MAN

MOSES-AARON PRIESTS

REUBEN

ZEBULON

CAMP OF JUDAH

ISSAKAR

NAPHTALI

CAMP OF DAN

THE EAGLE

THE LION

PROPERTY OF AARON H. SMOCK

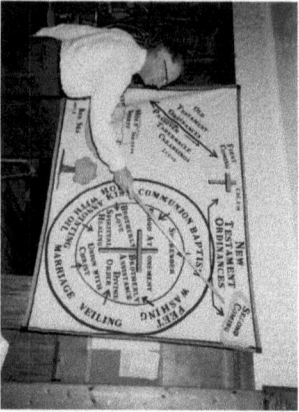

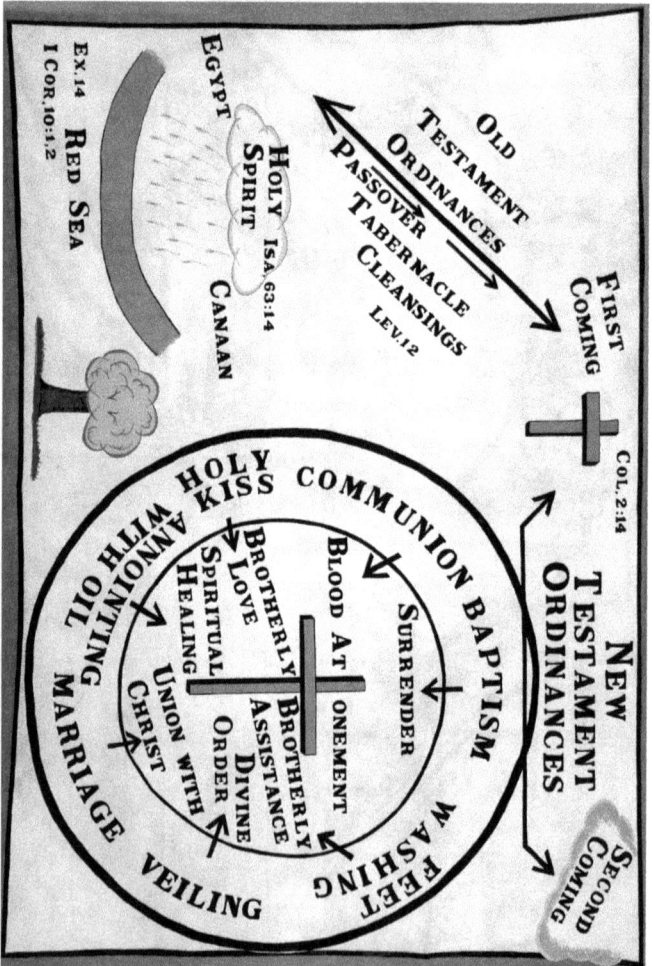

The chart that Aaron designed regarding ordinances is packed with meaning. Beginning on the bottom left, the way God led the Children of Israel to Canaan with ordinances becomes a pattern for the New Testament Church ordinances. Old Testament ordinances were Passover, the Tabernacle, the Cleansings, and Circumcision. While they brought Israel out of Egypt to Canaan, they also pointed forward to the cross of Christ. The tree in the bottom center represents spiritual life. While the life is hidden beneath the bark (what is seen on the outside) the life is what is inside. The large ring on the right with an inner ring represents a cross section of that living tree. The ordinances which the church practices on the outside represent the spiritual life within. The ordinances are intended to help us journey from the cross to the second coming of our Lord Jesus.

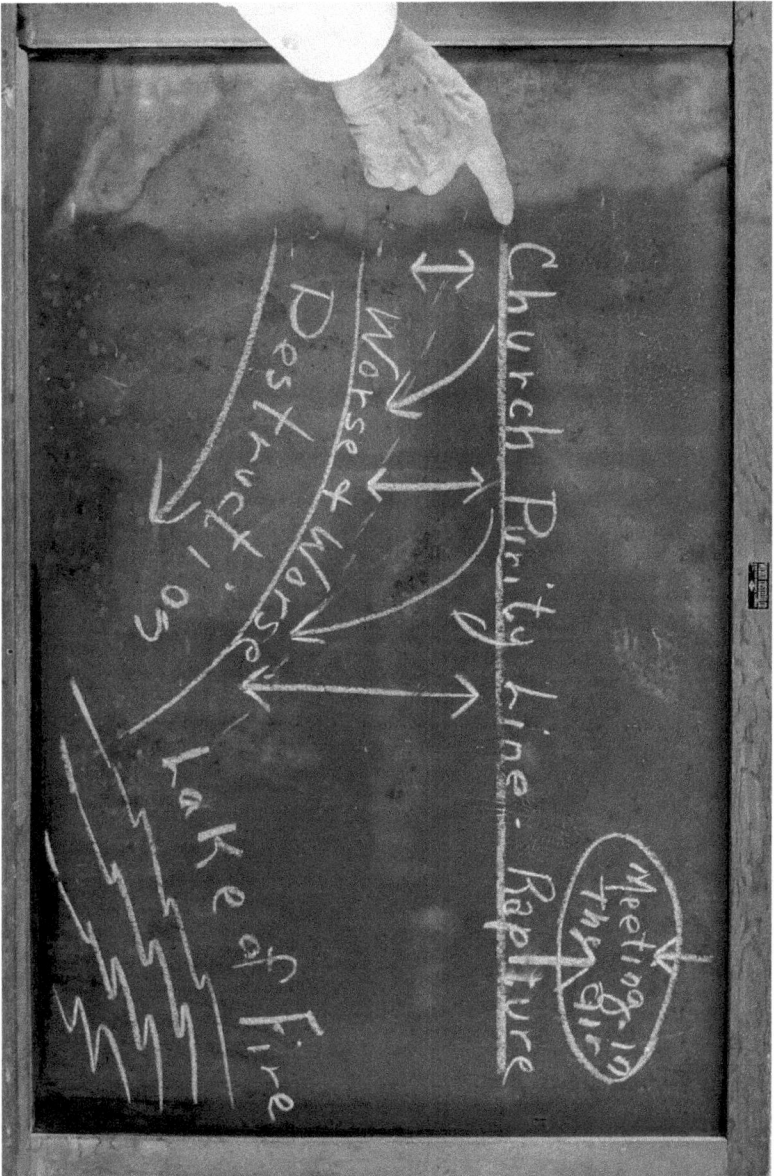

Aaron was a teacher to the end. After his death, this chalkboard drawing depicting the progressively increasing distance between the corrupt world and the pure church was found in his basement.

APPENDICES

Frank Observations
by Close Co-Workers

DAVID THOMAS WORKED closely with Aaron in the Lancaster
Conference. As Conference Moderator when the Eastern Pennsylvania
Mennonite Church formed, David is credited for lending his influence to-
ward an amiable release from Conference. David said:

> Aaron was an evangelist and prophet. He will go down in history as a staunch
> conservative. He took very seriously his call and accountability as bishop and was
> conscientious to do what was right. He worked absolutely honestly, never deceit-
> fully or by maneuvering. When he had a burden, he communicated it by writing.
>
> He was often used as an evangelist, not so much on Christian Life Conferences.
>
> His weakness was related to his gifts. He was not a warm personal counsellor which
> is natural for a prophet. Nor did he have the gift of mercy. Crisis situations were
> part of Aaron's prophetic gift.
>
> When he served on the Lancaster Mennonite School Board, he did not feel the
> same kind of responsibility there that he did on the Bishop Board. On the School
> Board, the responsibility did not stop with him like it did with his bishop work.
>
> In those days he served without remuneration for his services. He spent all day once
> a month with the Bishop Board. He spent three days twice a year for Conference
> work. In addition, he served on the personnel committee for the Eastern Board of
> Missions and Charities and spent time interviewing prospective missionaries and
> visiting the field. He really threw himself into Regional Bible School Board work.
>
> I give my full blessing on Aaron Shank.

David Thomas
former Moderator of Lancaster Conference

As a member of the Weaverland Conference, Isaac Sensenig attended revival meetings at Ephrata Mennonite Church when Aaron had meetings there March 20-April 3, 1949. The meetings were Isaac's first encounter with Aaron.

> I developed nonconformity convictions during that time. I used to wear a bow tie. I told my wife when we got home after hearing Aaron at Ephrata, "My bow tie is going off to stay. I'll never wear one again."

Aaron had said characteristically, "The necktie is superfluous whether it sticks out crosswise or hangs down lengthwise. It makes no difference." Isaac had not had much teaching on the issue.

> I knew the church didn't approve of it. The young men all wore ties; those who wanted to be more faithful wore bow ties because long ties were looked on with disfavor.

Aaron's Lebanon District had no neck ties.

Isaac was also impressed with Aaron's logic on the need for black hosiery. "If dresses came to the floor, we wouldn't talk about hosiery. Since they don't, we have black hosiery to cover the lower legs."

> I accepted what he gave as Bible. The way he gave it was convicting.

> I appreciated Aaron's personality; he was forthright and dynamic in his preaching. People who liked what Aaron stood for in terms of issues liked his personality; those who did not, minded his personality.

> He took a more tolerant administrative approach in church life. This approach was not by default but resulted from his convictions on how to administrate. We had honest differences here. I hold nothing against Aaron for all the differences we had.

> Aaron's ability lay in being able to explain doctrinal issues. He could explain the doctrinal reasons for the various conservative applications.

> He took the leadership in presenting the case for an honorable separation from Conference to the Bishop Board. I respected him for that.

> He did have a problem taking criticism personally and could easily remember the hurts of the past.

> I consider Aaron to be a man of integrity in every way. I miss his contribution to

the Eastern Church today.

Isaac Sensenig
fellow bishop in the Eastern Pennsylvania Mennonite Church

Aaron ordained Alvin Snyder to assist with the bishop work in the northern part of the Lebanon District. Aaron's long-range plans were to eventually form another district there after working with Alvin in administrative work for a period of time. Alvin says:

> I first met Aaron Shank at the Mennonite Messianic Mission meetings. I developed a relationship with him at the Elm Street Church in Lebanon. I was looking for a church which knew why they did what they did and Aaron provided that better than any other person I have ever met. I did not have much Bible knowledge at all when I came to the church. Much of what I believe today I attribute to Bro. Aaron.
>
> He very capably helped me understand the principles of nonconformity and separation from the world. He very ably substantiated practical separation from the world with Biblical principle. His inspirational preaching effectively moved me to desire to practice applications which crossed the flesh. His strong Bible base, his logic, his sound doctrine, and his thoroughness when he dealt with a subject was very convincing to me. He could approach a subject in such a positive way that the negatives he had to share seemed so much more palatable. His preaching and conversation, along with his sense of humor, presented such a wealth of knowledge that I desired to tap into it.
>
> Aaron was an effective spiritual leader with the ability to inspire people to love God and the Scriptures. He was also an inspiration in church administration. I thought he had such a nice way with people in that he was fair and honest. When he dealt with dissatisfied people, he would say, 'The church door swings both ways.' He encouraged dissatisfied people to look elsewhere when it became obvious that the Lebanon District could not meet their needs.
>
> I always felt I could go to Aaron and talk whenever I had questions. He corrected me when I pronounced 'shew' as 'shoe' and when I said that sin was black, he pointed out that sin was darkness, not black. When he made corrections like these, I did not feel intimidated. And he was quite ready to give me public commendation when he felt that it was in order.
>
> When under challenge he was not easily moved from what he believed. One brother commented to me, "You can be sure when all the smoke is cleared, Aaron will be standing at the same place he always stood." He was not harsh with people who differed from him on eschatology. Even though he retained his logic during a discussion or disagreement, you still had to like him after the discussion was concluded.

When dealing with opposing sides which were obviously both at fault in a situation, Aaron would say, "It's no use the one donkey calls the other donkey 'Long Ears.'"

Aaron made several unique contributions to the conservative Mennonite Church. He took a strong, consistent stand against tobacco production and use. He, along with his father, made a significant contribution to a sound doctrinal position on nonresistance. The two understood firmly that nonresistance was a unique teaching of the New Testament and that God in His basic nature was not nonresistant.

Furthermore, other leaders depended upon his logic in formulating church positions. He did the logical thinking during the formation of the Eastern Church.

When the Eastern Church formed, he brought a large number of his District into the Eastern Church. This accomplishment was due to his effective preaching and superior method of church administration.

I looked on with interest when Wilmer Shenk moved to Georgia against the counsel of the church and yet Aaron helped him establish the church at Dublin.

There was no difficulty between Aaron and Sidney in their working relationship as bishop teammates.

J. Alvin Snyder
junior bishop in the Lebanon District of the Eastern Pennsylvania
Mennonite Church

Aaron ordained Sidney Gingrich in 1970 to assist him as bishop in the Lebanon District. Aaron had always appreciated the team approach to ministry which he had shared with Simon Bucher. Two years after Sidney was ordained, Simon departed this life. Sidney worked shoulder to shoulder with Aaron in the bishop office for several decades. He says:

> If Aaron had thought something through, it was pretty hard to change his mind. This quality aggravated some people and blessed others. When he would defend his firm position, he would become rather emphatic. In this he was misunderstood as being aggravated, but I don't think it was that. He was just being deeply earnest.
>
> For example, when we [the Gingrichs] came into the District in 1941, he was a strong contender against tobacco production and use. He influenced many people against tobacco even though much was grown in Lebanon County.
>
> His preaching was dynamic, captivating, and easy to follow. He had a way of making his points easy to grasp.

Some people criticized his manner in the pulpit. He probably overdid his emphasis by becoming red in the face, especially when he was younger. Even though he overdid his emphasis, the content still remained. As he looks back, I think he himself would think his preaching was a little too explosive at times.

Some people interpreted his arched back, his braced feet, his spread out arms, and flung back head as pride. I don't think so. He still does that.

Sidney Gingrich
bishop assistant in the Lebanon District

Steve Ebersole says:

"I'll tell you like Simon Bucher told me years ago. We're in this work as a team. At first, I'll walk ahead and you will walk behind. Then, as you have more experience, we will walk side by side. Then if the Lord tarries, you will walk ahead, and I will follow behind. Then someday I will slip away with my course finished on earth..."

It was a beautiful spring day, and we were walking the property Aaron was arranging for us to have for our future house and workshop. The clouds were billowy in a deep blue sky, but the deeper peace was in working with a man I trusted completely.

And that is how it was. At the time, I don't know how I could have had a more trusting relationship with any man. It seemed I had known Brother Aaron all my life, and my parents had stories about his life even before I was born. That I would one day serve with him as bishop of the Lebanon district had never entered my mind.

(My father had chosen to cast his lot with the Lebanon District of the Lancaster Conference when he and my mother married. They had moved to the Philhaven Hospital Farm, and joined Gingrich's Mennonite Church. Simon Bucher and Aaron Shank were the ministerial team. After about three years of married life, Gingrich's had an ordination, and my father was ordained as minister with the understanding that they would go serve in a church planting effort somewhere. My earliest memory of Brother Aaron was when he and Brother Simon Bucher ordained a bishop for the south, Bro. Paul Dagan.)

In the beginning of my bishop service, we went almost everywhere together. I also took trips with Bro. Sidney, and both of them honored my questions with personal stories and anecdotes. I heard stories from childhood, ministry, family, business, and church life. I feel very indebted for the time both of them took with me, in giving me encouragement and also criticisms.

One of Bro. Aaron's criticisms for me was that I should raise questions when I was bringing a correction, rather than to make accusations. I still think of that today when I find myself working with a sensitive issue.

Another aspect for which I shall be forever grateful was having had the privilege of going to Bro. Aaron with all my questions. Having received my education in the public school system of Florida, I had much exposure to other Protestant and Catholic ideas. This gave me many questions about why the Mennonite church had the practices they did.

I would go to Bro. Aaron and he would take my questions seriously. I asked him things like:

1. Why do we have communion twice a year? His answer was that there is no Bible mandate, but the Old Testament example was a spring and fall Feast of the Lord that honored Israel's redemption. In the Spring there was Passover. In the Fall there was the Day of Atonement. In Aaron's opinion our practice had Bible support.

2. Why don't we baptize right away upon conversion? Aaron admitted this was one of his and his father's most serious questions about Mennonite tradition. He then shared that since we don't tie baptism with regeneration (and he had us remove the statement used after baptism about rising to walk in newness of life, since a person was already walking in newness of life), and since we connect baptism with church membership, which involves a good deal of trust, then he could support waiting until after instruction, but that instruction should not be too long.

There were many other items we discussed, like faith and works, speaking in tongues, the three-office ministry, and mode of baptism.

Aaron's strong interest in sound doctrine surfaced in *Instructions for Christian Living and Church Membership*. After much deliberation, Aaron prepared a chart that outlined the importance of keeping the ordinances in order to maintain a relationship with God. This diagram illustrated the Old Testament ordinances, the transition into the New Testament because of the work of Christ, and the New Testament ordinances and the place they fill in the life of the Church and the individual believer.

After developing this chart, Aaron set his thoughts in order in a series of articles for the *Eastern Mennonite Testimony*. Later this series was incorporated into the booklet that is still published by the Eastern Pennsylvania Publication Board and is used to instruct new believers in preparation for baptism.

When Lester Shirk withdrew from the Shirksville congregation, Aaron took up pastoral oversight there. Then when Raymond High was ordained pastor, he continued to serve as lead pastor. Consequent to the Ebersoles moving into the area, Aaron and Sidney recommended that the Ebersoles make Shirksville their church home in order to help with the ministerial team there. Aaron asked Steve to take over the instruction classes.

One evening after I had taught the lesson, Aaron had some rebuke for me.

"If you keep veering so far off the lesson, you will discourage the students from studying their lessons," he admonished. "What you had to say might have been important, but it wasn't staying close to what the text covers. You need to teach what is in the lesson and make sure you go over the questions at the end. That will greatly enhance the students' willingness to study."

I appreciated the counsel, and quickly adjusted my teaching approach.

One of the things shared in those lessons that many of the students will remember was Aaron's emphasis on song memorization. He shared his own intense temptations as a youth to think on things that would have destroyed his spiritual life. This caused him to grow concerned that he would be ready before a siege of temptation would come. He felt he should have a plan in place so he could escape the temptation. For this reason he committed many songs to memory. He could sing all the verses to scores of songs, especially those related to Christian victory.

I often thank God for having had the privilege of working with Brother Aaron. I have met other leaders who I felt would shame me for raising questions, but I never felt that from Brother Aaron. In fact, he wanted to know all my questions because he wanted me to have a good foundation under my life and ministry.

Steve Ebersole
ordained as the "next generation bishop to serve the Lebanon District"

Son Milford Shank says:

Thank you, Dad for –

Living and demonstrating a steadfast faith that "would not shrink tho' pressed by many a foe,"

The long days of hard labor to provide for family and to give to the church and to those with less,

A lifetime of expressing and showing affection toward Mother,

The countless petitions to God on behalf of each of us children,

The near lifetime of endless giving of time to various programs of the church,

Taking time to hit a softball (for me to catch) and taking the family to local ponds for a couple of hours of fishing and then stopping for ice cream sandwiches on the way home,

--and for much, much more.

Thank you, Mom for the giving of yourself –

In many church related activities,

In your total support of Dad in his responsibilities and ministry,

In your abundant love and concern for each of your children,

In the incredible amount of physical labor in the home, on the farm, and in the schoolroom,

In the abundant kindness and affection you conveyed to my "special" friends,

In your utter commitment to study and learning while teaching and guiding hundreds of students,

--and for much, much more.

I miss you very, very much.

The following tribute written April 2, 1987, by Karla Jean (Boll) Strite puts into words the unspoken sentiments of many under the spiritual care of Aaron Shank.

Last night after my personal devotions I was thinking about our service Wednesday evening and how I felt the sermon was just what I needed!!

I appreciate so much what you both have done for me – in sermons and in many ways of your Christian walk of life and setting a GOOD example. Also, your interest in the young people really impresses me. And Aaron, it always touches my heart – your deep concern for our spiritual well-being and it gives me a renewed zeal to keep striving on and do better. I feel I have a lot of room to grow in and sometimes wonder if I'll ever succeed but with the Lord's help, I know it's possible. Like you often said, "The biggest room in the world is the room for improvement!"

If there is ever anything you would like to see me change or have a concern in my life, I want to know! I hope I don't ever put you in that spot – I do want to do what's right but like you said Wednesday evening in your message, 'We are soooo---prone to forget and cool off a bit. I want you to know your reminders have been a great help to me!

Keep praying for me....I realize your position in the church puts a great responsibility on you! Thanks so much and may the Lord richly bless you for it!

Teach me to do thy will, for thou art my God: thy Spirit is good: lead me into the land of uprightness. Psalm 143:10 is my prayer!

An anonymous person wrote:

Aaron was a sharp, keen-edged thinker. His sharpness greatly disturbed some people, fuzzy-edged people. The clarity he carried in himself tended to sharpen those who worked around him. He applied his sharpness to sorting through business issues, home issues, church issues, doctrinal issues, all the issues he faced, insisting upon consistency and uprightness. This sharpness greatly contributed to his successful business and church life; people trusted him because of it.

But this same sharpness tended to create enemies where something other than the truth was at stake. Then Aaron could not be met on his own terms; smokescreens needed to be employed. But Aaron's perceptive heart and mind penetrated the smokescreens to observe what was actually going on. Hypocrisy cannot be helped and so he committed the matter to God. He was a leader in every sense of the word.

Record of Meetings

Record of the series of places and times of revival meetings and other extended meetings held during Aaron's lifetime of service. Blanks may exist in the record.

1944 Gingrichs—Lebanon County, PA; two weeks in autumn

1945 Rawlinsville—Lancaster County, PA; two weeks in summer
　　　　　Rissers—Lancaster County, PA; December 2-16

1946　　Marion—Franklin County, PA; April 3-14
　　　　　Mummasburg—York County, PA; May 26-June 2
　　　　　Garbers—York County, PA; July 14-21
　　　　　Salunga—Lancaster County, PA; October 13-27
　　　　　Gantz—Lancaster County, PA; November 17-Dec. 1
　　　　　Willow Street—Lancaster County, PA; December 8-22
　　　　　Millwood Bible School—Lancaster County, PA;
　　　　　　　　　　December 30, 1946-January 10, 1947
　　　　　　　　　　Five subjects, with four courses daily.

1947　　Knoxville, TN—April 30-May 11
　　　　　Hildebrand—VA (southern district); May 14-25
　　　　　Pond Bank—Franklin County, PA; June 22-July 2
　　　　　Masonville—Lancaster County, PA; November 16-30

Millwood Bible School—Lancaster County, PA;
December 29, 1947-January 9, 1948
Five subjects, with four courses daily.

1948   Red Hill Church—Harrisonburg, VA; February 29-March 11
Newport News (Huntington Ave.)—VA; March 17-31
Coatesville—Lancaster County, PA; April 11-18
Rossmere—Lancaster City, PA; May 9-16
Manheim—Lancaster County, PA; October 23-31
Reading (12th Street Mission)—Reading, PA;
November 25-December 5
Millwood Bible School—Lancaster County, PA;
December 27, 1948-January 9?, 1949
Five subjects, with four courses daily.

1949   Ephrata—Lancaster County, PA; March 20-April 3
Vincent—Franconia Conference, PA; June 5-12
Perkasie—Franconia Conference, PA; July 14-24
Homeville—Lancaster County, PA; August 21-28

1950   Millwood Bible School—Lancaster County, PA; January 2-13
Cedar Hill—Lancaster County, PA;
August 27-September 3
Stauffers—Dauphin County, PA; November 5-19

1951   Millwood Bible School—Lancaster County, PA; January 1-12
Bairs Codorus—York County, PA; April 15-22
Salem—Franconia Conference, PA; November 4-11
East Petersburg—Lancaster County, PA;
November 18-December 2
Millwood Bible School—Lancaster County, PA;
December 31-January 11

1952   Rock Hill—Franconia Conference, PA; March 18-23
          Buffalo—Juniata County, PA; March 30-April 6
          North Lebanon, PA (Tent Meetings); June 3-13
          Reading, PA (Tent Meetings); August 12-24
          Bridgeport—Franconia Conference, PA;
                        September 28-October 5
          Bertlets—Franconia Conference, PA; November 9-16
          Gingrichs—Lebanon County, PA;
                        November 23-December 7
          Millwood Bible School—Lancaster County, PA;
                        December 29-January 9

1953   Osaka—Alabama; February 22-March 1
          Freemansville—Alabama; March 4-15
          North Lebanon, PA (Tent Meetings); June 28-July 12
          Harrisburg, PA; August 30 – September 10
          Bosslers—Lancaster County, PA; November 1-15
          Millwood Bible School—Lancaster County, PA;
                        December 28-January 8

1954   Lancaster Mennonite School—Special Bible Term; January 11-February 19
          Three courses.
          Blainsport—Lancaster County, PA; April 7-18
          Pensacola, FL (Tent Meetings); September 19-29
          Skippack—Franconia Conference; October 10-17
          Millwood Bible School—Lancaster County, PA;
                        December 27-January 7

1955   Lancaster Mennonite School—Special Bible Term; January 10-February 18
          Three courses.
          Erbs—Lancaster County, PA; February 27-March 13
          Rock—Franconia Conference, PA; April 10-15

Brushy Run—West Virginia; September 7-18

Williamson—Franklin County, PA;

September 26-October 9

Pinecraft Tourist Church—Sarasota, FL; December 15-25

1956 Lancaster Mennonite School—Special Bible Term;

January 9-February 17

Millwood—Lancaster County, PA; February 3-11

Dohner—Lebanon County, PA; March 30-April 8

Fort Seyhert—West Virginia; October 9-21

Oak Shade—Lancaster County, PA; November 11-22

Hanover—York County, PA.; December 2-16

Millwood Bible School—Lancaster County, PA;

December 31-January 11, 1957

1957   Fourpoint, OH; March 21-31

Ordained Bishop July 4, 1957. With his added responsibility Aaron discontinued teaching at Millwood Bible School as well as the Special Bible Term at Lancaster Mennonite School.

Cottage City, MD; September 15-29

Osaka, Alabama; November 3-9

Straight Mountain—Springville, Alabama;

November 10-17

Poarch (Indian Mission)—Atmore, Alabama;

November 20-27

Mechanics Grove—Lancaster County, PA; December 8-15

1958   Deep Creek, Virginia; March 9-16

Freemansville, Alabama; March 30-April 6

Following the Freemansville revivals, he preached a week at Osaka, Florida, and a week at Poarch (Indian Mission), Alabama. No service was held on Monday evenings.

Red Run (Tent Meetings)—Lancaster County, PA;

August 27-September 3

Fox Street, New York; September 2-9

Conestoga—Morgantown, PA; September 7-14

1959   Turkey Run—Logan, Ohio, Ohio Conference; August 23-30

Maple Grove, Maryland; September 20-29

Dillers—Cumberland County, PA; Tabernacle Study—

October 18-29

1960   Dillers—Cumberland County, PA; Revivals

September 24-October 2

1961   Riverside, West Virginia; August 13-20

Wayside—Tower City, PA; October 22-29

Pike—Elida, Ohio; November 8-16

Palm Grove—Sarasota, Florida; November 26-30

1962   Records are lost.

1963   Pinecraft—Sarasota, Florida; February 17-24

Cambridge (Tent Meetings)—Lancaster County, PA;

July14-21

Bank—Virginia Conference; October 23-November 3

Myerstown—Lebanon County, PA; November 14-24

1964 Gilford Road, Maryland; March 1-11

North Lebanon—Lebanon, PA; April 8-19

Milford, Nebraska; September 20-30

Springdale, Virginia (Marjorie's home church);

November 4-5

Mountville—Lancaster County, PA;

November 26-December 6

1965 North Fork, West Virginia; August 15-22

Providence—Franconia Conference, PA; October 24-31

Hammer Creek—Lancaster County, PA;
November 24-December 5

1966   Goods—Lancaster County, PA; March 24-April 3
Bernville—Berks County, PA; September 18-25

1967   Rawleigh Springs, Virginia; August 9-20
Wilmington, Delaware (Voluntary Service Unit);
December 18-22

1968   Records are lost.

1969   Gospel Light, Ohio; October 12-19
New Hamburg, Ontario; November 22-30

1970   Bridgeport—Montgomery County, PA; October 4-11

1971   Numidia Mennonite Bible School—Columbia County, PA;
January 20-27

1972   No record of any series of meetings.

1973   Elm Street—Lebanon, PA; August 19-26

1974   No record of any series of meetings.

1975   Carbon Hill, Ohio; March 1-9
Dublin, Georgia; July 6-13
Danskin, British Columbia; July 20-27
Sharon, Elida, Ohio; December 7-14

1976   Miners Village—Lebanon County, PA; March 7-14

1977   Hopewell, Oregon; February 27-March 6

1978   Hopewell, Maryland; May 14-21

1979   Carbon Hill Bible School, Ohio; January 7-14
            Kenton, Delaware; March 18-25
            Dublin, Georgia (Tent Meetings); August 31-September 9
            Danville, PA; December 2-9

1980   Numidia Mennonite Bible School—Columbia County, PA;
February 15-22
            Simmontown—Lancaster County, PA; March 22-30
            Kenton, Delaware (Tent Meetings); July 20-27
            Bethel—Lancaster County, PA; November 16-23

1981   Rheems—Lancaster County, PA; April 13-19

1982   No record of any series of meetings.

1983   Pensacola, Florida; December 11-18

1984   Richland—Lebanon County, PA; March 18-25

1985   Carbon Hill, Ohio; January 13-15
            Numidia Mennonite Bible School—
                    Columbia County, PA; January 25-February 1
            Hartleton—Union County, PA; April 14-21
            Brookside, Ontario; July 22-28
            Blue Rock—Lancaster County, PA; November 10-17

1986   No record of any series of meetings.

1987   Bridgeport—Montgomery County, PA; October 11-18

1988   Danskin, British Columbia; March 20-27

1989 – 1995 Aaron did not accept lengthy assignments, believing that it was his primary duty to care for his ailing wife. The only exception during these years was the first annual tent meeting held at the Lebanon Fair Grounds, August 16-25, 1991.

1996   Mt. Joy—Columbiana, Ohio; September 30-October 6

1997   Newville Bible School—Newville, PA; February 14-21
        Leola—Lancaster County, PA; April 20-27
        Grandview, TX; May 26-June 1

Note: It seems quite obvious that both the format and course content instituted at Numidia Mennonite Bible School flows out of Aaron's previous Bible School experiences, including Eastern Mennonite School, Millwood Bible School, and the Special Bible Term at Lancaster Mennonite School.

Committees
on which Aaron Shank Served

Lancaster Mennonite School Board

Lancaster Conference Bible School Board

Lancaster Conference Nonconformity Committee

Lancaster Conference Representatives on [Scottdale] Mennonite Publication Board

Lancaster Conference Bishop Board

Lancaster Conference Joint Bishop and Mission Board

Lancaster Conference Bishops Foreign Missions Counsel (Included several visits to Lancaster Conference missions in Honduras)

Mennonite Messianic Mission Board

Eastern Pennsylvania Mennonite Church Bishop Board

Chair of interviews for Eastern Pennsylvania Mennonite Church Voluntary Service Units at Wilmington, DE, and Danville, PA

Led initial trip (accompanied by Elvin Graybill) to Guatemala to investigate possible mission work and location for EPMC foreign mission work

Led initial trip (accompanied by David Wadel) to Paraguay to investigate helping the Stephen Stoltzfus group (formerly part of Nationwide Fellowship)

Assorted Quotes
Gleaned from Aaron Shank

Sound Doctrine

Sound doctrine will produce sound living; sound doctrine and sound living will prepare us for an eternity with Christ.

Eagerly sit at the feet of those who teach sound doctrine; right teaching will produce right living.

Sound doctrine will guide through both the changing experiences of life and the crisis experiences of life, providing both anchor and direction. Sound doctrine preserves people in changing times.

Show me one reference in the New Testament of an invisible church. Every church mentioned in the New Testament was a visible church composed of visible people just like you and me.

For truth to be preserved it needs to be repeated and reemphasized. Truth has a cumulative effect; what people don't remember, understand, or believe in one sitting is eventually comprehended by repetition.

We must go from where we are; we cannot go from where we aren't.

The Bible is a "know" book, it is not a "guess" book.

The abuse of a good thing never makes that good thing bad. (When the Israelites abused the sacrifice system, and Isaiah needed to call their righteousness "filthy rags," he was not saying the sacrificial system instituted by God was filthy rags, he was just saying their abuse of it was.)

On Christian Experience

Elijah was a man with his ups and downs, but his ups were upper than his downs were down, and one day he went up to stay up, and didn't come down again.

Let us sing "I'll Live for Him who Died for Me" only this time let us sing, "I'll die for Him who lives for me, how happy then my death shall be"...

God searched all through heaven to give us His very best. Let us all give our very best to Him.

Let us never become satisfied with ourselves. When we become satisfied with ourselves, we come to a standstill and are in danger of a downfall.

When I became a man, I put away childish things. When do I become a man? The Bible also says a man shall leave father and mother...When a man is old enough to seek a wife, he is old enough to stop playing.

As soon as a man stops growing in grace he comes to a standstill and is in danger of a downfall.

The biggest room in all the world is the room for improvement.

The Bible says "He giveth more grace..." It doesn't say how much grace he will give, it just says more grace.

Jesus came to make a big difference for us in this life, and is coming again to make an even bigger difference in the world to come! (At John Earl Hollinger's funeral)

On Authority

Leadership is of Divine Origin—God Himself is the moderator of eternity, the chairman of eternity. He designed archangels over angels, leaders over Israel and the concept of establishing leaders in the New Testament church.

All authority finds its source in a higher authority. Whenever an authority steps out from under the authority of God, it ceases to be an authority.

It is hard to do an ugly thing in a nice way.

On Church Life

If we are not a help to you in your new church relationship, then we are not fair with you. But likewise, if you are not a help to us, then you are not fair to us either.

Since Christ is the most wonderful person who ever lived, if He is living in us, then we are among the most wonderful people who ever lived, so let's enjoy each other!

The product of a birth is a new baby. The product of the new birth is a baby as well. These new Christians are baby Christians. We all know that we don't put babies in the refrigerator. Rather we endeavor to help them grow by giving them attention, keeping them warm, and giving them plenty of spiritual nourishment.

A need constitutes a call. If there is a house on fire, you don't wait until someone calls you. The need calls you.

In an ordination one receives a special charge, but all of us should receive a recharge.

We are here to make a preacher. Paul says a number of times, "Made a preacher." Jesus told his disciples, "I have chosen you." Whenever there were self-appointed men, they were troublemakers as is evidenced in Acts 15.

While division is always proof that something has gone wrong, it is not true that division always wrecks the cause.

God generally is against division, except when division is necessary to save the cause. God had to cause division when Satan rebelled or else heaven would have become a devilish place.

I appreciate being a part of a church that wants to help us safely get through a world that is on its way to hell.

A thing overdone, is a thing undone. We do not help the cause when we overdo it.

On Obedience

We must have an application to a principle or else the principle is dead or dying.

There are three reasons for doing something:

　　1. Personal conviction.

　　2. To avoid causing offence.

　　3. For the sake of submission.

If we always had to have a conviction for everything before we would do it, there would be no need for Bible teaching on submission. Submission is not submission when we understand everything before we do it.

A thing is basically good or it is basically bad. If it is bad, it should be rejected. If it is good, it still needs to be protected and done in moderation.

About His Courtship with Dorothy

All the desirable availables are either unknown or are non-existent.

We have heard a rumor from the Lord (Obadiah 1:1) about the rumor that went around to Dorothy that she was saying yes to Aaron's pursuits when she really was saying no.

I have married Dorothy twice—first when she married Walter Newswanger and second when I married her.

On the Aging Process

God heals us over and over again until one day our bodies are too old and worn out to heal anymore. Then he gives us an eternal body that will never need healing again. Hallelujah!

I am a 1915 model with a few squeaks and rust spots. The squeaks are in my joints, and the rust spots are in my eyes, ears and in my memory.

When you have the eighties excuses you can be excused from almost anything.

James says our life is like a vapor, and at its longest life is only a vaporizing life. We have been brought into an existence from which we can never enter into a non-existence. My vaporizing life is almost all steamed out. (August 20, 2001).

On the Trinity

He, Jesus is the Word of God. He, in being the Alpha and the Omega is the whole alphabet of God. All of God's message to the human family is written through Jesus Christ.

The Holy Spirit is the behind-the-scenes operator of the Church.

Put your name in the place of Charity in 1 Cor 13... how does it sound? But you know, when you put the worthy name of Jesus in, it fits all the way.

On Prophecy

Prophecy is simply history in advance, and time is only a parenthesis in eternity.

You may think I am too literal when it comes to Bible prophecy. I would rather get to heaven and have God tell me, "Aaron, you took me too literal on those passages of Scripture" than to get to heaven and have him tell me, "Couldn't you read plain English?"

Selections from Aaron Shank's Writings

A Letter on Church Government and Conference Structure

After the Discipline Review process was completed, Aaron wrote a letter to his fellow bishops at the beginning of 1988. This writing offers a window into how Aaron viewed the responsibility of church leadership.

Church government represents a major difference between the two major groupings of Swiss Brethren descendants, the Amish and regular Mennonites. While the Mennonites have adopted the conference model for church government and regard it as almost essential for inter-generational continuity, the Amish consider the conference model as anathema. They understand that leaders handing conference decisions down to members without the members wrestling with the issues themselves to be a violation of the New Testament body concept. To be valid, the church, led by servant leaders, needs to speak as a united voice to the issues at hand. Consensus, not a vote, is the proper way for the church to move forward. In doing so, consideration is also given to how other similarly-minded congregations deal with similar issues. Ministers' Meetings are held for ministers to hear each other speak to issues, but no binding vote by the ministers should be taken.

As Mennonites relocated to Pennsylvania from Europe and soon spread to distant places, the situation seemed to invite the Conference model. The Amish, on the other hand, staunchly held to their congregational government model. However, the two experienced switching the distinctive group ideals. Today, many Old Order Amish still insist upon congregational government while using a strong leadership method to carrying out church discipline, a Conference-like method for governing. The Swiss Brethren non-Amish Mennonites formed district conferences which eventually combined into Mennonite General Conference.

Aaron Shank grew up in the lap of Conference, first Virginia and then Lancaster. He had no other practical church experience. Thus his story grows out of his experiences with conference. Readers from non-conference backgrounds are invited to graciously respect Aaron for his staunch loyalty to the conference model. Furthermore, the people Aaron led were trained to function under the conference model and appreciated the stability of that model. They desired their leaders to provide leadership accordingly.

The Eastern Pennsylvania Mennonite Church, in response to some of the negative aspects of their experience in Lancaster Conference, attempted to hybridize the traditional Conference structure with the "fellowship" structure which the Nationwide churches had developed, which was similar to Amish-Mennonite structure. Aaron felt that this hybridization, which was referred to as a "conferring fellowship," had serious weaknesses, and explained his viewpoint in this letter.

A number of times over the years I have indicated my apprehension related to the Scripturalness or the wisdom of our procedure in our periodic discipline review work. Since I have been asked a few times to give my reasons, I have decided to share my observations in writing....These observations are shared out of a concern for the spiritual health, spiritual rest, and spiritual growth of the Church.

1. I have difficulty finding any Scriptural concept, precept, or precedent for a procedure such as we follow. In the Old Testament Moses and Aaron along with the Levitical priesthood were given the Law and were responsible to administer it to Israel; elders were also chosen to an administrative role. The people were responsible to respect faithful leaders and suffered severe consequences when they did not do so.

In the New Testament "the decrees for to keep" were ordained of the apostles and elders at Jerusalem and then delivered to the Churches by the appointed officials as a finished and finalized package. The result—"and so were the churches established and increased in numbers daily."

To say that the decision-making in Acts 15 was by the whole church membership—leaders and laity alike—may be reading something into the text that really is not there. The thing that pleased "the apostles and elders with the whole church" was the decision to send a delegation to Antioch with the good news of the good changes of the New Testament era. "The decrees for to keep" that were delivered to the churches were reported to have been established by the apostles and elders at Jerusalem. (Acts 16:4)

The New Testament repeatedly emphasizes the place and responsibility of leadership, and that faithful leaders are to be respected, submitted to, and followed. In giving our people a share of the leadership in establishing standards for the Church, we may be educating them in the direction of laity rule....

2. The membership who are to comprise 50% of the vote necessarily includes a large number of immature youth whose vote may be influenced by their peers or other influential persons rather than being based on personal conviction. When young members need to be told how to vote, it would seem they are too immature to vote.

3. In some of the issues presented for decision there are always members--and sometimes their number could be very large--who are unaffected personally or disinterested in the item under consideration and will, therefore, take a passive attitude and vote one way or the other simply because it is all right with them either way.

4. It is well-nigh impossible for committee members whose concerns are adopted for voting, as well as for the ministry who may favor adopting the items, to keep from using their efforts to influence the vote. In our recent review recommendations, between the time that the ministry approved the items and the time of our local congregational voting, there were a number of visitors who had been invited to serve in our pulpits who took the opportunity, apparently, to influence the vote.

In a previous review one family testified that in their setting practically everyone was going to vote negatively on an item, but that in its presentation they were made to feel that they would be rebelling against the leadership of the Church if they do not approve the recommended item. Because of this, in order not to be guilty of rebellion, they voted affirmatively from pressure rather than from personal conviction.

I think we all believe that generally it is altogether right for the ministry to seek to influence our people in what we believe to be principles of righteousness, but when we ask for their counsel or their vote on matters of opinion and application, and then tell them how to vote or make them feel guilty if they do not vote a certain way, we may be inviting a rapid deterioration in wholesome relationships between the leadership and the membership of the Church. When members are made to feel guilty or disloyal if they vote a certain way, then it seems, without doubt, that this is one way we do manipulate the vote. If it is indeed a sin to vote "No" on any given item, then we should never give our people the opportunity to do so. We do believe it would be a sin to vote negatively on such things as the veiling and cut hair for women. In such cases the leadership would sin in presenting it for a vote. Perhaps this rule could be applied to any recommendations. If it is a sin to vote negatively, and we give our members that privilege then we most surely sin by granting them the privilege to sin. (If members must vote a certain way out of respect for leadership, then we would far better call for that respect without asking for their opinion in the matter.)

5. The Review Committee usually spends much time in many meetings involving months and sometimes years sharing concerns before arriving at a decision. The ministry are then given a half day, or more time if needed, to share in and reshape the recommendations. Our members are then asked to make their decision on comparatively short notice, and without the benefit of the discussions that went into the decision-making in the first place. In the meeting where the ballots are first shared with the members, and in the voting meeting, the membership is given the privilege of asking questions and sharing concerns or making suggestions. However, the concerns and contributions shared in these meetings can never benefit the Review Committee or affect the recommendations before they are presented to the membership for a vote.

If the membership is to have equal percentage of the vote with the ministry, it would seem only fair for them to have at least some opportunity, if not equal opportunity, to present their concerns to the Committee before the recommendations are finalized for voting. A number of lay brethren across the Church wondered whether their concerns would get back to the responsible persons for consideration....

6. There is always a grave possibility or danger of members who have been growing in their love and appreciation for the Church—some of them babes from non-Mennonite background—becoming discouraged through the added unrest over the discipline review....

Perhaps Acts 15 is not a fair parallel to our present method of establishing or adding rules and standards for the Church. The problem that disturbed the Church then was not a problem of the setting up of standards for the Church, but one of understanding and relating properly to the transition from the Old Testament era to the New Testament era. Their basic problem seems to have been a problem of over-regulation, and how best to deregulate the things of the Old Testament that were not necessary.

Or maybe we do have a similar problem of understanding how to relate properly and when to apply Old Testament principles to New Testament church life. For example—with the exception of the occasions when the Early Church assembled on the first day of the week for fellowship, the New Testament is completely silent on the sacred observance of the Lord's day. We go to the Old Testament for our convictions on keeping the Lord's day holy. We do the same for the principle of spanking or for the using of the rod in child-training, for dress distinction of the sexes, for specific identification dress for God's children, for our use of the lot (which practice was never even alluded to after the birth of the Church), etc.

Just when is it right to profit by and base our practice on Old Testament principles and when is it right to make authentic change where the New Testament does not require such a change? Maybe we should have a "Jerusalem Conference" on this problem sometime.

You brethren may not be in agreement with the convictions or ideas herein presented. You need not give any consideration to them, if you do not care to do so. However, I would like to have these concerns on the record, either to be proven wrong or to be validated in time to come should our gracious Lord delay His coming.

Devotedly yours,
Aaron M. Shank

Why I Feel Comfortable with My Hair Shorn and my Face Shaven

In 1988, an ordination was conducted at Hartleton, one of the churches in the northern part of the Lebanon District. One of the men named as qualified for the office of minister wore a beard. One of the bishops said, "We don't have any bearded preachers and we don't want to start."

The bearded nominee was asked whether he would shave off his beard if he was ordained to fill the office. Since he was unwilling to shave his beard, he was dismissed from the class of nominees who would share the lot.

Since Aaron was the senior bishop there, he was asked to explain the situation at the ordination. He did not relish the task. Nevertheless, it appeared that since he made the announcement, he was opposed to beard-wearing. The report went out that Aaron considered the victory over the beard in question as a personal victory. In reality, Aaron was neutral on the beard issue. Today, Pilgrim Conference has beard-wearing preachers. Aaron wrote the following to explain his position on the beard.

I have never worn a beard on my face. I have always had the hair on the top of my head shorn.

Physically, I think I am more comfortable being shorn and shaven than if I were to just let the hair on my head, face, and neck grown naturally.

Spiritually, I am more comfortable being shorn because the New Testament declares it is a shame for a man to let his hair take its natural course of growth (1Cor. 11:14). Likewise, for reasons that follow, I feel spiritually comfortable without a beard. I can also believe that many religious professors who wear beards could testify to feeling spiritually comfortable doing so.

It is not the intention of this testimony to seek to make anyone feel uncomfortable for wearing a beard, unless as some have confessed after wearing the beard for awhile that they were motivated by pride, individualism, or some other ill motivation. It is hoped, however, to help those who do not wear beards to feel comfortable in not doing so.

Although I do not see any Scriptural basis for its use, I respect those religious groups whose general practice has been to promote or require the wearing of the beard. Neither do I condemn anyone else who from proper motivation wears a consistent beard. I do think it is quite obvious, however, that there are times when we do not understand our own motives. In using the term "consistent beard" it seems to me that a long uncut beard would be a violation of the Bible teaching in 1Cor. 11:14.

I feel comfortable without a beard because it is not commanded for general use anywhere in the Bible. In the New Testament there is no reference whatsoever to the beard. There is not even an indication that any man wore a beard.

In the Old Testament reference is frequently made to men wearing beards. The proper care of the beard is referred to in Lev. 19:27 which indicates its general use among men. That the beard was worn is implied, but it is never specifically commanded for general use.

The beard and all the other hair growth on the head, face, and neck was, however, specifically required for any one taking the Nazarite vow. The Nazarite perhaps symbolized the greatest degree of humility, self denial, and separation in a system that was to wax old and vanish away (Heb. 8:13).

The Nazarite was to have "no razor come upon his head." He was to "let the locks of his hair grow." He was not to eat grapes or raisins or drink grape juice of any kind. He could not touch a dead body without losing his Nazarite position (Num. 6:1-8).

But the Nazarite requirement was not a part of the law for general practice. Jesus fulfilled the law and since He is never identified as, or declared to be a Nazarite, the Nazarite requirement was an exception to the law and was not for general practice.

The New Testament completely nullifies the Old Testament Nazarite method of separation. Jesus used grape juice and instituted its use in one of the holiest, most significant, perpetual memorial services of the New Testament era. Through the inspired pen of the Apostle Paul, it is now a shame to practice the Nazarite type of separation (1Cor. 11:14).

In Lev. 19:27, Israelite men were commanded to "not mar the corners of thy beard." This was not a command to wear the beard, but instructions for those who wore beards. In Deut. 21:15-17, instruction is also given for men who had more than one wife, but this was not a command for men to practice polygamy nor do we ever use it as an argument for men to have multiple wives today.

In 2Chron. 29:25, during the religious reform of good king Hezekiah, it is stated that "he set the Levites in the house of the Lord with cymbals, with psalteries, and with harps…for so was the commandment of God by the prophets." Again in 1Chron. 16:42, Israel thanked and praised the Lord "with musical instruments of God." From these and many other Scriptures it is clear that musical instruments, properly used, had an approved and vital place in the worship of God in Old Testament times. (Amos 8:5 represents a sensual usage of musical instruments rejected by God.)

Today we reject the use of musical instruments in church worship because we do not find them used or commanded for use in New Testament church worship. Since I firmly believe we should leave the musical instruments for church worship in the Old Testament where they were used by the "commandment of the Lord by the prophets," I feel very comfortable to leave the implied usage of the beard there also.

I feel comfortable today with both my hair shorn and my face shaven because in the New Covenant—the Covenant that remaineth (2Cor. 3:11) which is far more glorious than that which waxed old and vanished away, of which the Nazarite may well have been a type—we are told that it is a shame for a man to let his hair take its normal course of growth.

I feel comfortable being shaven and shorn because the New Testament declares it to be a shame for a woman to be "shorn or shaven" (1Cor. 11:6), and in the same context it is declared that there is to be a difference between men and women, implying that men are to be the opposite of women in this respect.

I feel comfortable to reject the argument that the beard should be worn because God put it there and that it represents the "image of God." "Made in the image of God" (Gen. 1:27) represents man in his original unfallen state. Could it be that whiskers and a bushy head on a man are a natural part of man's head and face for the same reason that thorns and thistles are natural on the face of the earth? For those who contend that the beard represents the image of God I feel comfortable to believe that it might just as well, or maybe rather, represent man only after his fallen state.

It hardly seems possible that letting hair grow naturally, which God now says creates a shameful appearance on man, should have been a part of the original creation of man—the creation that God declared was "very good" (Gen. 1:31). Must we believe there was a part of original man, made in the image and likeness of God, that God would later forbid and declare to be shameful to Him?

I feel very comfortable without a beard when I think of the possibility of taking the Gospel to certain tribes and people of the earth who do not naturally grow beards. To take the Gospel to the American Indians, many of whom have no natural beard growth, presenting myself with a beard, as one of the ideal marks of manhood and separation would doubtless render my witness useless and ineffective. Might not the American Indian just as well have the right to believe that his smooth face is the proper representation of the image of God?

I feel comfortable without a beard because if Jesus wore a beard when He was here on earth it was not important enough to have any reference made to it in the New Testament record of His life. It is generally accepted that He did wear a beard, however, based primarily on Isa. 50:6. The context of this verse indicates that the prophet's experience recorded in Isa. 50 was a type of Messianic experience when Christ was here on this earth. The New Testament does say that God sent His Son "in the likeness of sinful flesh" and since men of Jewish race do normally have beard growth and since Jesus was a part of that race, He would have had natural beard growth.

Joseph, who was perhaps one of the most striking person-types of Christ in the Old Testament was doubtless a type of Christ's resurrection when he came hastily out of the dungeon in Egypt at which time he "shaved himself and changed his raiment" (Gen. 41:14).

I feel comfortable not wearing a beard as a sign of masculinity or maleness, especially since a percentage of the world's men do not have natural beard growth. I am sure that their masculinity is readily identifiable. With my shaven face I know of no time when I was mistaken for a woman. Even when I was a child with curly hair and some of my dear old aunts would sometimes say, "Isn't it a pity he isn't a girl?" I was not mistaken for a female.

I feel comfortable not wearing a beard as a special mark of separation from the world because many times in many places in the world and for many men of the world the beard has been and is presently used as a special mark of worldliness. The Encyclopedia International states that "from time immemorial it [the beard] has served as an ornament, a mark of social distinction, and a symbol of manhood." We see evidence of this on every side in today's worldly society. The beard therefore can hardly be said to be a distinct mark of separation from the world.

Finally, I can feel comfortable with my face shaven because Jesus said, "If ye love me keep my commandments" (John 14:15), and I believe I can love Him and keep all His commands without needing to wear a beard.

This testimony, "Why I Feel Comfortable With My Face Shaven and My Hair Shorn" may sound a bit judgmental of beard wearers. It is not intended to be that. Stating a preference for anything and giving reasons for the same can hardly be done without reflecting on that which one may not prefer. I do confess, however, that this testimony is intended to help those who may come under undue pressure or influence to wear the beard to feel Scripturally comfortable to continue the practice of being both shorn and shaven.

Since some men naturally have beard growth and some men naturally do not have beard growth, and since the Bible does not directly teach for or against the wearing of a consistent beard, it would seem logical to believe that the matter is optional with God. The rightness or the wrongness of what I do on amoral issues may well be determined by my motive in doing it. And it is often true that others may understand my motives better than I do.

When one is motivated by a holier than thou attitude, by pride, individualism, worldliness, a desire for distinction, rebellion, or a negative attitude toward the church, etc., etc., what he does on an amoral issue may well constitute an abomination unto the Lord. Since others may understand our motives at times better than we do, there may be times when the church will need to look at motives and give direction accordingly.

"Whether therefore ye eat, or drink, or whatsoever ye do, do all to the glory of God" (1Cor. 10:31).

Respectfully,

Aaron M. Shank

Ideals Necessary for Healthy Congregational Life

Aaron Shank's range of spiritual care stretched from doctrinal position statements, to proper administrative protocol, to practical spiritual advice (such as the following), to passionate preaching to those he served, to private counsel, and to all matters related to the spiritual well-being of those under his care. And, best of all, Aaron stretched for excellence in his own personal life as a pattern for those observing him. May God give us more leaders like Aaron!

Some time ago while visiting at one of our churches, I heard a brother say, "I'm enjoying my church fellowship more than I ever did in my lifetime." I replied, "And what are we going to do to keep it that way?"

We always have a tendency to degenerate. Think of Israel's glorious beginning and how they degenerated. Look at the beautiful beginning of the early church, yet it was not long until some were turning the grace of God into lasciviousness, denying the only Lord God that bought them. We have on record the beautiful start of the Reformation and the Anabaptist movement in the sixteenth century. Then we read of the apostasy in Holland and

Germany where church life almost became extinct. It will always take work to keep our fellowship healthy.

An ideal is a standard in its highest state of perfection and excellence. Thus we could say we are looking for ideals that comprise the perfect church. Do we ever attain to a perfect church? No, there is no perfection in this world. What then? Shall we give up and not strive for perfection? The Scripture indicates that any standard less than perfection is too low a standard for the child of God or for the church of God. In Colossians 1:28-29 the Apostle Paul says that the purpose of his preaching and teaching was to make "every man perfect in Christ Jesus." Then he adds, "For which I also labour, striving according to His working, which worketh in me mightily." He had not yet reached perfection himself, but was striving toward the same goal. According to Ephesians 5:27, the church will be without spot or wrinkle when Christ presents it unto Himself. Until that time we will need to work on the spots, and keep ironing out the wrinkles. The best spot remover is the blood of Jesus Christ and the best wrinkle removers are the Spirit of God and the Word of God.

The Church at Thessalonica was a model of healthy congregational life. In I Thessalonians 1, Paul commended their work of faith, their labor of love, and patience of hope in Jesus (v. 3). In verse 8 he commends them for their community and country wide witness. Yet in I Thessalonians 4:1,10 he encourages them to "abound more and more." One of the surest ways of decline is to become satisfied with ourselves. When we become satisfied with our spiritual attainments we come to a standstill and are in danger of a down fall.

The foundation of healthy church life is the preeminence of the IDEAL PERSON, Jesus Christ. He must be the focal point of our worship, the pivot around whom our love, our devotion, and our loyalties revolve. In Sunday morning services, in prayer meetings, in Bible conferences, and in revival meetings we study Jesus Christ. And there is so much more to learn about Him. He is all in all. In all things He must have the preeminence.

Another foundational ideal is the provision of Christ's cleansing blood. In our physical bodies, as our blood carries nourishment to all parts of the body, it also picks up the impurities found throughout the body and brings those impurities to places where they are expelled from the body. In the body of believers, Christ's blood carries our sins away as far as the east is from the west, cleansing us from sin and making us healthy.

A third ideal is to have leadership who seek to guide every member toward perfection (Eph 4:11-12). The purpose of Christ giving leadership gifts to the church is that the body would grow "to the measure of the stature of the fulness of Christ" (v.13).

For healthy congregational life we also need the ideal of constant prayer. "Praying always with all prayer and supplication in the Spirit and watching thereunto with all perseverance and supplication for all saints" (Eph 6:18). Are we praying for each other as we ought to be? Romans 12 says that we are to be instant in prayer. When we hear something about someone that is unfavorable, what is the first thing we do? The first thing we should do is talk to the Lord about it, instead of talking to the first person we see. A good prayer plan at times is to use the alphabet to think about people we could pray for. Start with those whose names begin with A, and think of something you can pray for about that person.

As we relate to each other in the congregation, we need the practical ideal of love. Read I Corinthians 13 and say your name in place of the place of the word charity, then strive to live up to it. It is possible for us, like the church at Ephesus (Rev 2:1 5), to possess and defend what we believe to be the full Gospel, including our practice of separation from the world and nonresistance to evil, and be a sick, fallen church because we lack the greatest of all ingredient of a healthy church, brotherly love. In our church gatherings, it is ideal to have a special meeting place and a special meeting time. If the service starts at 9:00 AM, the ideal is to be there several minutes before 9:00 and calm ourselves before the Lord. The Bible says, "Be still and know that I am God." While every family experiences emergencies that may make them late occasionally, tardiness should be the exception rather than the rule. If we have any business that makes us habitually late to church, it is time to change businesses or revise our schedules.

Some other ideals include having as nearly perfect attendance as possible to our local congregation, and every member participating in our services in some way. A warm handshake, a kiss of love, a cheery "God bless you", and a smile also contribute greatly to the health and fullness of joy in church fellowship. We come together to see Jesus Christ in our services, and we want to see Him in each other.

We can contribute to the health of our congregation when we all sense our responsibility to come with a contribution. Bring a prepared lesson, a testimony, an open ear, and bring an offering. All that we have is from God, and our tithes and offerings are a recognition of His divine ownership. If a renter refuses to pay his rental fee, we would say he is robbing his landlord and he ought to make it right. If we are robbing God, do you think it might be a good idea to make it right with Him and pay up?

There are also a few things we should leave at home when we come to church. We do not need to bring along our businesses or the meal we plan to serve to our guests when we get back home. And we certainly do not need any chewing gum. It does not contribute to our spiritual health.

Ideally, for the highest level of spiritual health, we need to come hungering and thirsting for the things of the Lord. The manna from heaven is what nourishes our souls. The children of Israel never got indigestion from manna. They became sick when they grew tired of manna and desired other things. If we come to church with a desire to be fed, we can be filled and anxious to come back for another filling of manna from heaven.

As we come into the holy sanctuary of God, we are experiencing the ultimate in Christian fellowship. Apostle Paul referred to this fellowship as sitting "together in heavenly places in Christ Jesus." Let us come together appreciating the greatest gatherings that can be held on this side of eternity, until the day when Jesus Christ presents the church unto Himself without spot or wrinkle.

The Tongues Movement

Originally published in the Pilgrim Witness.

In the Gospel of Saint Mark we have the first mention in the New Testament of speaking in new tongues. It is given in our Lord's last commission to His disciples (Mark 16:15-18). According to <u>Strong's Greek Concordance</u>, the word "tongues" as used in this text is translated from the Greek word glossa and means "a language." Glossa is used in the New Testament fifty times. Once it is used for "cloven tongues of fire." Sixteen times it is used in speaking of the physical tongue, and thirty-three times it refers to genuine, existing, intelligible languages. In all of the Scriptures referring to tongues-speaking, this word glossa (language) is used. Throughout the Bible, "tongues" stands for languages or speech. The "cloven" (split, divided) tongues with their split flames shooting from a base might well symbolize the fiery tongues that God would use to spread the word of the Gospel to every nation and people and tongue.

In Acts 1, as Jesus was with His disciples for His closing moments on this earth, He assured them that something new and unexpected was about to happen. It would not be what they were expecting, but they would be involved. They were to stay at Jerusalem and wait for the empowering of the Holy Spirit which would come upon them, enabling them for the new task on which they were to embark. He assured them they would not need to wait very many days.

In keeping with His promise, after only ten days of waiting, "suddenly" they were all filled in a new way, with the newly-promised Holy Ghost power, and began to speak in a new way with other tongues (languages) as the Holy Spirit gave them utterance. The word "utterance" is from a Greek word meaning "to enunciate plainly — to declare" (Strong).

In this very first experience of speaking in new tongues (languages), the multitude of people who were gathered together at Jerusalem "out of every nation under heaven" heard in his own tongue wherein he was born "the wonderful works of God." This new, first-ever-heard-of, miraculous manifestation of tongues-speaking both amazed and confounded the hearers (Acts 2:511). This confounding, astounding miracle of speaking and hearing, along with "the wonderful works of God" message which was conveyed through the new tongues, brought to them conviction, surrender, repentance, faith in Christ, and salvation. The New Testament Church was born.

In this initial new-tongues phenomenon at Pentecost, there is nothing to indicate that the converts spoke in new tongues. Rather, the very opposite is indicated. It is specifically stated in the context that "many wonders and signs were done by the apostles" (Acts 2:43). Acts 2:14 also implies that the apostles were exclusively in charge of this uniquely phenomenal gathering. It may be worthy of note that, other than on the day of Pentecost, we have no record of the apostles ever speaking in new tongues again.

In Acts 10 it was the new Gentile converts who spake in new tongues. The record says nothing about the possibility of Peter and his Jewish companions speaking in tongues on that occasion. The reason for this change is clearly indicated in the fact that the Jewish brethren who accompanied Peter to the house of Cornelius "were astonished…that on the Gentiles also was poured out the gift of the Holy Ghost." Just as on the day of Pentecost, where the converts needed confirmation that the apostles were God's approved agents, so now the Jewish leaders needed the same confirmation that God was accepting the Gentiles on the same basic conditions. When Peter was "called on the carpet" for going in unto the unclean Gentiles, he had all the evidence and all the witnesses he needed to prove that he had moved under the direction of the same Holy Spirit that had led on the day of Pentecost. When the shocked and apprehensive critics heard the testimony of Peter and his accompanying brethren, they "glorified God, saying, Then hath God also to the Gentiles granted repentance unto life" (Acts 11:18). This was God's way of getting the Jewish leaders and Jewish converts to see that in this new New Testament Church era God "put no difference between us [favored Jews] and them [despised Gentiles]" (Acts 15:9).

In Acts 19:1-7 we have the last of the three recorded new tongues speaking experiences which took place in the beginning of the new church era. Here Paul found a group of sincere believers who were totally ignorant of the new outpouring of and baptism of the Holy Ghost. They responded to Paul's teaching and were baptized. As Paul laid hands on them, "the Holy Ghost came on them; and they spake with tongues, and prophesied."

Each of these phenomenal new tongues experiences was in connection with new circumstances and new revelations related to the birth and forma-tion of the new body of Christ. On the day of Pentecost the multitudes of Old Testament "dyed-in-the-wool" Jews and proselytes needed special con-firmation that the apostles were God's true representatives for the occasion.

At the house of Cornelius the Jewish leaders, in this never-before-heard-of relationship with Gentiles, needed miraculous evidence that God was now putting no difference between the "select Jews" and the "Gentile dogs" (Acts 15:7-18). The middle wall of partition was now broken down (Eph 2:11-22).

The Ephesus group doubtless needed miraculous confirmation that Christ and the Holy Ghost baptism which Paul presented was in reality that which John the Baptist had prophesied should come (Matt 3:11).

The glorious unforeseen changes of religious life from the Old Testament's cumbersome types-and-shadows religious practices to the new Testament's "more glorious" era of fulfilled types and shadows, along with other significant experiential changes, was so different and drastic that God saw fit to graciously confirm His representatives of the change by "bearing them witness, both with signs and wonders, and with divers miracles, and gifts of the Holy Ghost, according to his own will. (Heb 2:4). Perhaps the last great confirming miracle of the transitional era was the giving of our Lord's last Will and Testament to man by divine inspiration. Today we need no other sign. We still have that great miraculous sign with us. Borrowing the phrase of Abraham to the rich man in hell, when the latter pled for a miraculous witness from the dead to be sent to his living brethren to keep them out of hell (Luke 16:27-31), we can say with equal or even more emphasis than Abraham. "If we hear not the Gospels and the Epistles, neither will we be persuaded, though one rose from the dead." Those early authorized agents of the transitional period did not have the miracle of the New Testament Scriptures to carry with them. God's confirming "signs and wonders" were conferred upon them in a unique way. God confirming Scripture writers with miracle signs was not new. Moses and the prophets were also confirmed in this way as they penned the words of Holy Writ.

Following the Holy Spirit-directed new tongues-speaking associated with the birth and early formation of the new New Testament Church fellowship, the only other New Testament reference we have to active tongues-speaking is in 1 Corinthians 14, where the Apostle Paul seeks to correct the confusion and heresy of tongues-speaking as it was being practiced in their church life. As we look at this corrective treatise on tongues, we are impressed with how different Corinthian tongues-speaking was from the original Holy Spirit-directed tongues on the three occasions in Acts. And on the other hand, in how many ways it was similar to twentieth century tongues practices.

It should be noted that the term "unknown," as used in 1 Corinthians 14:2,4,14,19,27, is in italics, which means it is not in the Greek text from which our King James Bible is translated. "Tongues" stands for languages and constitutes intelligible words or utterances. At Pentecost the "other tongues" conveyed a message of "the wonderful works of God." At the house of Cornelius their speaking in tongues was understood to "magnify God." At Ephesus they spake with tongues and "prophesied." Prophesy is to speak "unto men to edification, and exhortation, and comfort" (1Cor 14:3). With the exception of verse 21, every time the word "tongue" or "tongues" is used in this chapter, it is translated from the Greek word glossa, meaning an intelligible, already-existing language. Biblical tongues (languages) always conveyed a message that could be directly understood or was to be understood by interpretation.

Paul's concern for the church at Corinth was that all who hear utterances in the church gatherings — whether believer or unbeliever — would be able to understand and be edified. He indicated that the tongues speakers were benefitting no one who heard them (verse 8), with the possible exception of some personal edification (verse 4). Since the word "tongues" (glossa) has reference to an existing language, that person must have been speaking in his own language which he himself understood but no one else did. How else could he have been edified if he himself did not know what he was saying?

The Corinthians' tongues-speaking gave the church no sense of direction (verses 7-9). It was as useless as speaking into the air (verse 9). It was heathenish (verse 11). It was very inferior to plain, simple, understandable speech (verse 19). It was disorderly, confusing, and took on the form of insanity (verses 23-27). It made them feel like an exclusively superior group (verse 36).

To add weight to Paul's concern, he reminded them that although he could speak in tongues (not unknown tongues) more than any of them (verse 18), it would be of no value for him to speak to them except his speaking reveal some truth, impart some knowledge, edify someone, or teach some doctrinal truths (verse 6).

We believe that if properly understood and properly interpreted, the Bible gives no place for a "peeping and muttering" (Isa 8:19), indistinct, inarticulate, unknown tongues speaking for any purpose. Again, the meaning of "tongues" in the Bible when referring to speech always means an intelligible, meaningful, existing language. We might ask the question here: Did God, or His Holy Son, or His Holy Spirit, or His holy angels, or His holy prophets, or His holy apostles, ever deliver a message or speak to the world in a tongue that could not be understood or interpreted by His children? Another question: Did God ever promise that His children would ever speak in unknown tongues? Did "new tongues" (Mark 16:17), "other tongues" (Acts 2:4), "divers kinds of tongues" (1 Cor 12:10), "diversities of tongues" (1 Cor 12:28), ever mean unknown, nonexisting tongues? If we can trust our Greek theologians who tell us that in all these references "tongues" means intelligible, understandable languages, the answer is "No!"

Paul's ability to speak in many tongues (1 Cor 14:18), existing languages, may well account for the fact that he seems to have had no problem communicating to people everywhere as he went from country to country and to different nationalities with the Gospel.

In my younger days as a mission pastor, we were blessed with a community convert who could converse intelligibly in about a half dozen different foreign languages. As he became known across the church, he was frequently called upon to come and communicate the Gospel to foreigners with whom the local folks had difficult language problems. He seemed to always be able to understand and communicate with such folks. He spake in tongues more than we all. He used his gift of tongues for edification.

A few times in my lifetime, all unplanned for, and, in fact, not previously known to me, I found myself in the presence of unknown tongues speaking. One of these occasions was in community visitation during a series of revival meetings. We visited a woman who had been a member of the church, had backslidden, and had apparently given herself over to demonic influence. As we introduced our interest and started to share the love and claims of Christ to her, she burst into vulgar and blasphemous speech such as I had never heard before. Suddenly she changed her talk into meaningless, unknown, tongue-twisting syllable speech with fire flashing, as it were, out of her eyes and spit flying out of her mouth. There was no question as to the source of both her known and her unknown tongue. We were relieved to get away from that kind of open-sepulcher-throat stench and asp-poisoned, tongue-polluted talk (Rom 3:13).

The other occasion was vastly different. We were visiting our churches in the South and were invited to attend a Pentecostal revival service. Following an orderly church service, the pastor invited interested folks to come forward and join in a prayer period. About a dozen and a half went forward. After a brief period with a number of folks praying in the English tongue, the pastor began supposedly praying in another tongue. Soon it sounded like the whole group was engaged in what seemed to us strangers as some confusing babbling into the air which nobody could understand. While this speaking in tongues was different from the other, it was not patterned after tongues in Acts and fell short under the tests and corrections of 1 Corinthians 14.

The "unknown tongues movement," as it is generally practiced today, could be discontinued completely without disobeying or doing violence to any Scriptural teaching whatsoever. In fact, we believe it would be spiritually honorable to replace that kind of unknown, strange speaking "into the air" with tongues that would be understandable and would convey a convicting or upbuilding and edifying message to the hearers. It would be God glorifying! In 1 Corinthians 14:12, Paul admonishes, "Seek that ye may excel to the edifying of the church." This he indicated they could not do, speaking in unknown tongues.

The proper and safe understanding and use of tongues, as promised by Christ, is seen in the way new tongues were used or witnessed by the foundational New Testament "apostles and prophets" in the birth and formation of the New Testament Church (Eph 2.20; Heb 2:3,4). These tongues experiences are found in Acts, chapters 2, 10, and 19. If speaking in unknown tongues as it is practiced today were God-ordained and Holy Ghost directed, the practice would be patterned over these examples and would stand up to every test of 1 Corinthians 14. Sadly, the very opposite seems to be true.

It has been claimed by unknown-tongues speakers today that their experience in tongues was supernatural. While they were "seeking the power or baptism of the Spirit," some mysterious power took control of their tongue and made them speak or pray in an unknown tongue. Sometimes these claims are made by those who have known and practiced the simple, easy-to-understand commandments of the New Testament but have disliked them and have turned "from the holy commandment delivered unto them" (2Pet 2:21).

They may use their "supernatural" experience as an excuse, or justification, or a refuge for not loving some of the truths they had learned and had previously practiced (2Thess 2:10-15). Commands like, "Greet one another with an holy kiss" (five times commanded in the Holy Word), or the unshorn hair and veiled-head command for Christian women, or, "Wash one another's feet," or the command to be separate from the world related to worldly dress and fashions, or perhaps the command to "obey them that have the rule over you," etc., etc. These are plainly stated holy commandments of our Lord. Whereas speaking in unknown tongues is never once commanded in the Bible.

God sometimes lets people actually believe they are right when they are actually wrong because "they received not the love of the truth" (2Thess 2:10,11).

The Bible is replete with warnings and examples of deception. Jesus warned that "many shall come in my name, saying, "I am Christ: and shall deceive many" (Matt 24:5). One of the subtlest forms of deception is to exalt the name of Christ and to minimize or wrest the commands of Christ.

Paul informs us that there are false apostles who transform themselves into fake apostles of Christ, a Satan who transforms himself into a fake angel of light, and ministers of Satan who are transformed into fake ministers of righteousness (2Cor 11:13-15). He prophesied also, that the end times would be characterized by many "signs and lying wonders" (2Thess 2:9), and that "evil men and seducers shall wax worse and worse, deceiving, and being deceived" (2Tim 3:13).

Peter warns that "there shall be false teachers among you ... and many shall follow their pernicious [destructive] ways" (2Pet 2:1,2).

John warns us to, "Try the spirits whether they are of God: because many false prophets are gone out into the world" (1John 4:1).

Jude warns in verse 4 that men creep in "unawares" who turn "the grace of our God into lasciviousness" (a license to loose living).

Jeremiah 23 speaks of the reality of false prophets and how they work. They cause God's people to err (verse 13); they speak a vision out of their own heart (verse 16); they are very energetic — they run even though God has not sent them (verse 21). They prophesy lies on the basis of their dreams, which God declares is nothing but "chaff" compared to the "wheat" of His word (verses 25-28). They deceive their own hearts (verse 26); they steal God's words, thus adding power to their chaffy dreams (verse 30); they claim to have a burden from the Lord (verse 34). They are prophets who could have led — would have had the ability to lead — God's people aright if they had stood in God's counsels (verse 22). They were prophets (religious leaders) whom God was against (verse 30).

It seems Scripturally clear that at the beginning of the New Testament era and through the transitional period from the Old Testament on until the New Testament Scriptures were finalized, God confirmed His initially-authorized agents for that period with special miracle-working manifestations. On the day of Pentecost it was specifically stated that "many wonders and signs were done by the apostles" (Acts 2:43).

It was the apostles Peter and John who healed the forty-year-old cripple in Acts 3. Again in Acts 5:12, after the schemed deception of Ananias and Sapphira and their sudden judgment of death pronouncement by the Apostle Peter, it is stated that "by the hands of the apostles were many signs and wonders wrought among the people." In verses 14-16 we are further told that as multitudes of believers were added to the Lord, they brought forth the sick to Peter for healing. At the same time "there came also a multitude out of the cities round about unto Jerusalem," (where the apostles were giving themselves continually to prayer and to the ministry of the word - Acts 6:4) "bringing sick folks, and them which were vexed with unclean spirits: and they were healed every one" — no failures whatsoever.

In Acts 8:5-7, Philip, one of the initially authorized agents of the new era, "went down to the city of Samaria, and preached Christ unto them. And the people with one accord gave heed unto those things which Philip spoke, hearing and seeing the miracles which he did. For unclean spirits, crying with loud voices, came out of many ... and many taken with palsies, and that were lame, were healed."

In Acts 9:32-35, it is again Peter who, coming to the saints at Lydda, found Aeneas, who had been bedridden for eight years, sick of the palsy, to whom he spoke the word, and he was instantly well and strong. The result: all that dwelt in Lydda and Saron turned to the Lord. In the following verses of this chapter, Peter performs an only-once-recorded type of miracle by the apostles in the raising of Dorcas to life. The result: "And it was known throughout all Joppa; and many believed in the Lord "

In Acts 19, through the Apostle Paul's two-year stay at Ephesus, "all they ... in Asia heard the word of the Lord Jesus." Here it is said that "God wrought special miracles by the hands of Paul" (verses 10,11). Paul was one of the special, initially authorized agents of the new era, to spread the Gospel in all the world.

In 2 Corinthians 12:11,12, Paul, who had earlier referred to himself as an apostle who saw the Lord, "as of one born out of due time," (1Cor 15:8), humbly testifies, "For in nothing am I behind the very chiefest apostles, though I be nothing. Truly the signs of an apostle were wrought among you in all patience, in signs, and wonders, and mighty deeds."

As the apostolic era, the transitional era, and the confirming-by-signs era drew to a close, and the New Testament Scriptures were given and finalized, there was no longer a need for the confirming physical, miracle signs. Paul, who had healed people of all kinds of sickness many times during his ministry, stated near the close of his life, "Trophimus have I left at Miletum sick" (2Tim 4:20), and recommended something other than divine healing to Timothy for his "often infirmities" (1Tim 5:23).

The era of the birth and early formation of the church was uniquely different from any other era in that it was made up basically of people who lived in two drastically different dispensations. Inasmuch as the "New" fulfilled and therefore concluded the "Old," believers needed to move out of the one into the other in order to be saved (Gal 5:1-4) and receive the baptism of the Holy Ghost (Acts 1:4,5). The apostles who previously had their names "written in heaven," (Luke 10:20) needed to wait till Pentecost for their experience of Holy Spirit baptism. It could have been no other way for them. The three thousand repenting converts were promised (Acts 2:38) and received, the same day, the Holy Spirit. (Acts 2:39). They immediately became part of the newly born church (Acts 2:41).

Ever since the formation of the Church, "by one Spirit" (1Cor. 12:31), we are all baptized into "one body" when we become part of that body. We cannot therefore find a basic or complete pattern of experience for the entire church era in the experiences of the apostles or in the birth, early formation, and activities of the church. There will not be any other church born and there will never be another Bible written.

An infallible commentary of the exclusiveness and uniqueness of a select group of authorized agents for the transitional era, and who those agents were, is given to us in Hebrews 2:3,4. "How shall we escape, if we neglect so great salvation; <u>which at the first began to be spoken by the Lord, and was confirmed unto us by them that heard him</u>; God also bearing <u>them</u> witness, both with signs and wonders, and with divers miracles, and gifts of the Holy Ghost, according to his own will?"

In the finalized New Testament Scriptures we have given unto us all things that pertain unto life and godliness (2Pet 1:3) and all we need to throughly furnish us and finish us out in Christian sojourn (2Tim 3:1517). We do not need to depend on physical miracles. Neither do we prove what is right or wrong by such evident miracles. Moses performed a great miracle in an act of flagrant disobedience to God.

No miraculous manifestation, nor a messenger from another world, could make the goodness of God more lovable, sin and hell more terrible, Christ more divine, Calvary more cleansing, salvation more wonderful, decision more urgent, or lift death, and eternity more solemn, than do the Scriptures we hold in our hands. An angel from heaven (Gal 1:8) or one risen from the dead (Rev 13:3; 17:8) might lie — the Holy Scriptures cannot.

In the Gospels we have recorded for us the miraculous birth, beautiful life, gracious words, wonderful works, and divine sacrifice of Jesus in providing salvation for the world. The church is only once mentioned and is seen only in its embryonic stage (Matt 16:15-19). In Acts the church is seen in its miraculous birth, its early formation, and its initial rapid growth — all associated with Holy Ghost miraculously confirmed activity.

With the exception of the called-together council at Jerusalem (Acts 15) and Paul's message to the elders at Miletus (Acts 20), all the messages recorded in Acts are directed to

those who were not yet Christian, and needed to be saved. It remained therefore for the Epistles to set forth for us the inner character, the solemn responsibilities, the holy walk and talk, the faith, hope, and love, and the heavenly fellowship that is called for and characterizes the true church. In these Holy Ghost inspired Epistles, in which we have the most demand-ing and heavenly aspects required of the church, the speaking in unknown tongues and the performing of physical miracles is not once promised or set forth as a requirement or even as an evidence of

the blessing and power of God on the church or any individual in the church. The truest blessings and the richest experiences are promised to those who live a life of faith and holiness in loving obedience to the gracious and eternal commands of our loving Lord Jesus Christ.

Now that the New Testament doctrine is fully given — "Take heed unto thyself and unto the doctrine; continue in them: for in doing this thou shalt both save thyself and them that hear thee" (1Tim 4:16). And "seeing ye know these things before, beware lest ye also, being led away with the error of the wicked, fall from your own stedfastness" (2Pet 3:17).

In response to the above article printed in the Pilgrim Witness, *a charismatic pastor from Canada wrote a very critical letter to editor Luke Bennetch. When Luke showed the letter to Aaron, he asked Dorothy for a pencil and paper and produced the following response in very short order.*

July 7, 2000

Dear Pastor _____

Thank you for your correspondence of 3/13/2000 addressed to Pastor Luke Bennetch, Editor of our monthly publication, The Pilgrim Witness, in response to my article on "The Tongues Movement" in the February issue. Your letter was forwarded to me for my reflection and possible response. It is good for us at times to have our doctrinal beliefs challenged by other Bible scholars - either for correction where we may be in error or to help to strengthen our convictions in what we believe to be Biblically sound. I experienced both of these benefits from your letter. I do not propose my article to have been an infallible treatise on the subject.

In order to give a little system to my answer I have numbered your paragraphs (¶). Your apology for not knowing what title to give me in re-ferring to the article was not at all necessary. The dictionary defines the "Mr" title, which you used throughout your letter when referring to me as "a conventional title of respect for men." That's good enough for me. The ordained ministers of the church group I am a part of never have accepted the title "Reverend," neither do we address any other ordained ministers as "Reverend" for the simple reason that "holy and reverend is his name" (Psa 111:9). I have been an ordained minister since 1941, and an ordained bishop since 1957. We do accept such titles as Deacon, Minister, Pastor or Bishop.

¶'s 9-16. I do appreciate your pointing out my failure to include Peter's Holy Spirit empowered message as that which brought the people to repentance and salvation. That was an unintentional oversight on my part. I do firmly believe, have always believed, that Peter's sermon was the climactic influence the Holy Ghost used to bring the people to salvation on the day of Pentecost. However, I do also believe that "the wonderful works of God" made known to the people through the miraculous hearing of "every man in our own tongue, wherein we were born" was a contributing factor in getting them ready to hear and respond to the message of Peter.

The magnitude of the almost unbelievable and important changes that were so suddenly taking place in the ushering in of the new church age (which only 10 days earlier was not even understood by the Apostles, and possibly much less understood by the devout Jews that were there) needed those "wonderful works of God" manifestations as a confirmation (Heb 2:3,4) that this wonderfully unique newness was without doubt God-designed and heaven-sent.

The "Wonderful works of God" they were hearing about might well have included discussion and explanation on the drastic changes embodied in the unexpected new church age. Whatever it was, it gave the multitude assembled an openness and it gave Peter, one of those Ephesians 2:20 foundational apostles, a ready opportunity to use the keys given to him by the Lord to open the door of the church kingdom for the 3000 souls ready to enter on that same day, as well as the continuing flow of additions in subsequent days.

I note with interest that in your criticism of the foregoing statement you state that my point "is without Biblical support and is his opinion only" (¶ 16). Also, in response to my statement that in Acts 10, "The record says nothing about Peter and his Jewish companions speaking in tongues on that occasion," you state that "Mr. Shank is trying to make a point on what the

Bible DOESN'T say instead of what it does say" (¶19). In this connection it is also interesting to note that again and again throughout your letter, both your conclusions and your quotes from others are based on your assumptions - on what the Bible DOESN'T say rather than what the record actually does say. I will not in any way fault you for this. Sincere Bible students and teachers always have, always will, seek to interpret or explain Bible principles as they understand them for practical use.

In ¶ 4, your criticism seems unfounded and unnecessary. The new tongues the disciples were using could well have been and doubtless were "naturally unacquired" (Strongs) languages. This does not prove whether they were or were not already existing languages. Whatever the language used it was understood by 16 different nationalities in their own native language which was already in use when they were born.

¶'s 5-7. I did not purposely (as you imply in your correspondence) evade commenting on "Though I speak with the tongues of men and of angels" (1 Cor. 13:1). Along with many other Bible scholars I do not believe that Paul was here referring to any type of strange, mystical, unknown tongues speaking. A much more simple and consistent understanding would seem to be that with all the gifts, and all the abilities, and all the revelations, and all the authority, and all the understanding, and all the faith possessed by the Apostle Paul he was acknowledging that even if he were to speak in the most beautiful and powerful oratory of any language or even of all languages, or if he were to speak with all the perfection, and with all the eloquence, and with all the persuasiveness of angelic beings (Galatians 1:8), without the practical expressions of divine love, it would be as worthless as "a tinkling cymbal" noise or as vain and meaningless as merely speaking "into the air" (1 Cor. 13:1-8; 14:9; Jas. 3:15,16; 1 Jn 3:18) The practical expressions of divine love comprise "a more excellent way" than any other of the best and greatest gifts man can possess. Dr. M. D. Treece whom you quote on this verse seems to be basing his conclusions on his personal assumptions rather than on what the Bible says.

In ¶18 you comment on Acts 2:16 thus: "'But this is that,' 'This' meaning the people speaking in other tongues and appearing to be drunk is what Peter is referring to as a fulfillment of Joel 2:28-29. In Joel 2:28-29, God promises to pour out His Spirit on daughters and handmaidens!... So this shows that there were women on the day of Pentecost speaking in other tongues and appearing to be drunk!" My response — In the first place, the record does not say that when they were speaking in other tongues they appeared to be drunk. These critics were mockers who didn't believe and didn't want others to believe, so in mockery they said that "these men (not women) are full of new wine." Days later the same kind of critics had Peter and John imprisoned as criminals. Were they acting like criminals? Earlier in the life of Jesus the same kind of critics said He was possessed with a devil when He was actually acting like the very Son of God. Does that prove that in acting like the Son of God He was also acting like He was demon possessed? Saint Paul in seeking to correct the disorderly Corinthians on the tongues issue, by divine inspiration ordered, "Let all things be done decently and in order." We have no reason to believe that the Holy Spirit was leading in any other way at Pentecost. When you say that the women, or any others, were speaking in tongues and appearing to be drunk you are saying something that the Bible DOESN'T say.

Secondly: In the interpretation of the prophetic Word, there is such a thing as a near, distant and final or complete fulfillment. Peter did not actually say that the "wonderful works of God" they were seeing and hearing about was an actual fulfillment of Joel's prophecy. Among the things Joel said are to come to pass are "signs in the heavens above... the sun turned into darkness and the moon into blood." The final fulfillment is to be "before the great and notable day of the Lord come." So another possible and more plausible meaning of Peter's explanation could be, "This is that Spirit which was spoken of by the Prophet Joel." A little later on in his sermon Peter assured the repentant multitude that they, their children and many that are afar off, could receive "that" same Holy Spirit gift who was directing the disciples in this phenomenal meeting.

Thirdly: Acts 2:4 does not say that they all spake in other tongues. It does say "they were all filled with the Holy Ghost, and began to speak in other tongues as the Spirit gave them utterance." (Utterance — "to enunciate plainly - to declare" Strongs 669) The terms "began to speak," and " as the spirit gave them utterance," would at least imply that only those whom the Spirit gave a message were speaking. In 1 Corinthians 14:26, Paul by inspiration of the same Spirit that was directing at Pentecost ordered the Corinthians to do all things decently and in order. Also, when there were several who wanted to speak, they were to speak by course, doubtless meaning one after the other (v.27).

It seems unthinkable that all 120 disciples would speak in other tongues all at one time with thousands of people understanding clearly what they were saying. And although it might have been possible for all 120 to each take a turn, it is quite unlikely that such was the case. And if indeed the women present were at this time given prophecies to utter, according to the Holy Spirit New Testament directives, it would have needed to be done in meekness and sobriety (1 Timothy 2:9,10) and not in an appearance of drunkenness as you so confidently affirm in your letter. In giving direction to the disorderly Corinthians, Paul, by divine inspiration ordered their women to keep silence altogether. The fact that the critics mockingly said "these men are full of new wine" might well suggest that the women were not among those prophesying in other tongues at that time.

¶'s 22-28. In your rebuttal to my suggestion that Paul's ability to speak in many tongues (languages) enabled him to preach the gospel to any of the possible different tongues he may have encountered in his missionary journeys, you argue that because Greek was the common international language of the time there would have been no need for Paul to use any other language than Greek. It is an historical fact, however, that there were other languages in general use at the time. Hebrew, Syriac, Latin and perhaps others. Pennsylvania has been known as Dutch country and Berks Co. where I live, as predominantly Dutch but I still need an interpreter to know what a Dutch tongue is saying. It is hardly conceivable that Greek was readily understood in every area to which Paul took the Gospel. At Pentecost there were many different tongues represented. You state "I am certain that Paul being a well-educated man could speak several languages." If Greek was the only language used at that time and well understood why was it necessary for Paul to be educated in several different languages?

¶'s 29-34 Coming to 1 Corinthians 14, Paul's paramount concern is that the use of tongues should be edifying and fruitful to both hearers and speakers. His contention is that unless one understands the tongue or language being used he cannot be edified, whether in speaking or in praying. Since there is no edification without understanding, the man in v.4 who alone is edified by the tongue he is using must be understanding the tongue he is being edified by. Paul's argument is that a language understood only by the speaker would be of no value in their public gatherings. Again, by the same reasoning, in vv.14-16 praying in a language no one else understands is altogether unfruitful to those who should be inspired and edified by what is being prayed and therefore they cannot say amen. Paul follows in v.15 that when he prays it is "with the spirit and the understanding."

If we take the italicized word *unknown* out of 1 Corinthians 14, and if we follow the divinely inspired directives of the Apostle Paul in 1 Corinthians 14, do we have any basic foundational Scripture to build on for the present day unknown tongues practices? If I may use your terms in your critique of my article on "The Tongues Movement" it would seem to me that you are building your doctrine and practice of unknown tongues speaking on what the Bible DOESN'T say rather than what it does say.

¶ 35. You state rather emphatically "Mr. Shank's assertion that the apostles were the authorized special agents during a time of transition is wrong." Who do you think the subjects of Hebrews 2:3-4 were to whom God bore witness, both with signs and wonders, and with divers miracles, and gifts of the Holy Ghost, if they were not a select group from among those who heard Jesus speak? Who do you think the foundational agents of Ephesians 2:20 were if they were not the apostles and prophets of the apostolic transitional era?

Leaders of subsequent eras like Martin Luther, Ulrich Zwingli, Menno Simons, John Wesley, Edward Irving, the organizers of Bethel College at Topeka, Kansas, etc, may have been foundational in starting certain segments of professing Christendom, but no one (other than those of the apostle's era) however great, can be said to be the initiators under whose direction the church was born and formed. They did not have the foundational New Testament Manual to guide them hence God bore them witness with "special miracles", "divers miracles," etc.

¶'s 35-42. In your belief that the same miraculous manifestations of the apostolic era should be continued in the church today may I ask you if you are practicing what you preach? Are you demonstrating the same kind of miracles as are recorded for us in the Acts of the Apostles?

- Are you having new tongues speaking sessions wherein every man in your audience hears in his own native language " the wonderful works of God?" (2:8)
- Are your leaders being confirmed by doing "many wonders and signs" bringing fear upon every soul? (2:43)
- Do you "in the name of Jesus Christ" bring immediate healing to 40 year old lifetime cripples? (3:7-9)
- Have any of you been imprisoned for preaching Jesus, only to have the locked prison doors miraculously swing open? (5:19; 12:7; 16:26)
- Are you having multitudes bringing sick and evil-spirited people to your churches and healing "every one" — no exceptions? (5:14-16)
- Do you without any information or indication whatsoever detect and confront hypocrisy with a pronouncement of judgment and see the guilty persons fall over dead? (6:8, 15)
- Do you have any remarkable Stephens full of faith and power doing great wonders among the people dying a martyr's death with a face looking like the face of an angel? (6:8, 15)
- Do you have any Philips going into new areas being confirmed before the multitudes by casting out unclean spirits and healing the incurables and the disabled? (8:5-8)
- Do you have traveling evangelists directed by angels to traveling strangers, leading them to Christ, and then suddenly, miraculously being caught up and transported by the Spirit of God about 35 miles? (From Gaza to Azotus) to continue their evangelism in other areas? (8:26-40)
- Have you found any 8 year incurable, bedridden Aeneas' getting up at your word and carrying away his own bed? (9:33-34)
- Have you raised any well-loved, dead Dorcas' to life by the word of one of your leading leaders? (9:40)
- Have you ever had an angel appear to a seeking soul of a new nationality and naming one of your leaders to send to for help? (10:1-6)

- Have any of your evangelists ever encountered one who opposed the truth and been confirmed by sentencing blindness on the one who opposed? (13:10-11)
- Have you ever had one of your missionaries stoned and drug [*sic*] away from his preaching area for dead and have him get up and continue his mission work as though nothing happened? (14:19-21)
- Have you ever had a Eutychus fall from a third floor taken back up as dead and immediately restored to life? (20:9-10)
- Have you ever had an evangelist stranded in a foreign area spending his time healing many people of their diseases? (28:8-9)
- Have any of your people been bitten by what is known as a poisonous viper and without any medical aid whatsoever receive no harm? (28:3-5)

In our day of multiplied infirmities, incurable diseases, lifetime disabilities, along with the increased social, and moral corruptions, religious confusions, etc. it would seem that the need for, and opportunities of a Pentecostal, Apostolic type of church would be limitless and greater than ever — If that were God's way of making Himself known in the world today.

Another question, in your unknown tongues speaking do you follow the divinely inspired guidelines of 1 Corinthians 14?

Do you:

- Emphasize that speaking in a known tongue is much more useful and beneficial than speaking in an unknown tongue?
- Stress that the person is greater who prophesieth (speaking to edification, exhortation and comfort) (v.4), than the person who speaks in an unknown tongue?(5)
- Teach that without the use of an interpreter speaking or praying in an unknown tongue is nonedifying (5, 17) and unfruitful (14) to the hearers, and that if there be no interpreter unknown tongues speakers are to "keep silence in the church?" (v.28)
- Believe that unless the message of a tongue is understood it is as worthless to the hearer as merely speaking into the air? (9)
- Understand that if the significance of a voice is not understood it is

like one barbarian (one who did not understand Greek) speaking to another barbarian, each telling the other something but neither one understanding the other one? (11)

- Teach that those who are zealous of spiritual gifts should seek to excel to the edifying (using words that build up) of the church? (12)

- Agree that Paul, as an example, prayed and sang with the spirit and with the understanding, and that he deemed a five-word testimony given in an understandable language preferable to 10,000 words given in an unknown tongue? (19)

- Believe that speaking in tongues is not a sign to them that believe, but for them that believe not (22) as to the thousands at Pentecost (Acts 2) or as to the unbelieving Jewish skeptics in relation to the acceptance of Gentiles into the church? (Acts 10,11)

- Maintain that all things are to be done decently and orderly?(40) Tongues speaking is to be limited to two or three each in turn-one after the other, restricted only to those who can have their tongues interpreted. No interpreter? No speaking. (27-28)

- Teach that women are to "keep silence in the churches; for it is not permitted unto them to speak?" (37)

- Accept that the things which the Apostle Paul wrote are the commandments of the Lord? (37)

We as a church group are not among those people who do not believe in miracles. We are completely ready to accept any miracles God wants to perform among us or through us "according to His own will." Since we have the miracle and finality of the New Testament Scriptures, which the initial foundational agents of the church did not have to build with, this is all the proof or confirmation we need for experiencing so great salvation (Romans 1:16), for assurance of being baptized by one Spirit into the body of Christ (1 Corinthians 12:13), for knowing and doing the will of God and for knowing how to serve Him faithfully, "...and [we] forbid not to speak in tongues" if it meets the criteria of Holy Spirit orderliness (26-32,40), spiritual saneness (22-25), conveys a message that can be readily interpreted by someone present (28), keeps women in silence (34) and presents truths that are understandable and edifying to both speaker and hearer (12,26).

Respectfully in Christian love,

Aaron M. Shank, Bishop

Pilgrim Mennonite Conference

Letter to Stephen Scott

In 1996, Good Books published An Introduction to Old Order and Conservative Mennonite Groups. *While its treatment of the Pilgrim Conference was basically accurate, Aaron was concerned about one sentence which inaccurately described the formation of the Pilgrim Conference.*

The sentence in question stated, "They [the founders of the Pilgrim Mennonite Conference] believed the EPMC had become too legalistic in its church discipline requirements, and they wished for more activities for the young people."

Bishop Ivan Martin Jr. wrote the following letter to the book's author.

As an EPMC teenage member 25 years ago, I remember the various play activities that we as young people across the church (not only in the Lebanon District) engaged in. I was involved in more play (which was not as much as some other young people) in the first four years of EPMC than my teenage son is involved in with PMC today. The truth is that EPMC has sought to eliminate youth activities while PMC is permitting activities with some direction as you reflected on p. 222. However, this was not an issue with which we were not working with the church at large.

If I gave you the impression that the preceding two items represent the reasons for the development of the PMC, I assume the responsibility for not making myself more clear. I and my fellow ministry of the PMC feel misrepresented by this evaluation....

While the EPMC had its origin with a concern for the liberal drift in the Lancaster Conference, the growth of the EPMC in other areas of the church included a large number of people who were dissatisfied with the lack of spirituality of other more traditional Old Order and Conservative Mennonite groups. A number of congregations increased in significant size because of primary interest from these people. Wherever people go, they tend to take their background with them. This was the case in Eastern and helped to present the problems that needed to be addressed. During the latter 1980's there was a growing voice heard concerning maintaining some (Old Order) traditions of the past. A number of times it was declared at church-wide meetings that Old Orderism is the preferred way to go. Hence, the place of traditions became more of an issue. This became apparent as the black hat and bonnet were required to be worn regularly in some settings. Alterations of the cape dress for maternity needs was not allowed (again in some areas of the church). The frock coat for the ordained was expected in some districts. This growing difference was interpreted by some as a difference of conservatism and liberalism. While the increasingly stronger voice of the EPMC was to conserve the traditions of the past, the voice of the Lebanon district was for adhering to those practices that help us conserve the principles of the Scriptures. The document (referred to as the Feb. 12 letter) that classifies churches as "A,B,C,D, or E" churches was an effort to identify the differing goals of traditional vs Biblical vs liberal churches. This document was not appreciated by the strong tradition supporters of the EPMC. While some of the leading leaders of the EPMC admitted they could identify with "Group C", they opposed the document's method of comparison.

Another factor that brought on the division was a conflict in administration. Throughout the history of the EPMC, there were some who did not appreciate the administration of Aaron Shank. Some of this may reflect a difference of personalities, and some may have been due to the methods of dealing with problems. While the Lebanon District was probably the most conservative of the districts and churches that left the Lancaster Conference, it was painted as the liberals of Eastern. It is my evaluation that the Lebanon District was the most stable area in Pennsylvania in the last 50 years. The position under Lancaster Conference and the position under EPMC did not vary as much as some churches who were very liberal under Lancaster Conference and became ultra-conservative under Eastern. The bishop ordination of Stephen Ebersole was viewed by some as ordaining a bishop that was too much like Aaron in thought and administration. This produced more stress that some felt could only be resolved with a division.

It should be of interest that the three original bishops of the PMC did not desire to leave but were told to leave the EPMC. Many of us who left had desired that the growing problems and stress in the church would be resolved without a division. Our ministry had in written form requested that bishops from other conservative groups would be asked to give their evaluation of our problems. The Eastern Bishop Board would not consent to such a committee. The growing pressure to make something happen was illustrated on January 24, 1990, when a vocal element of the EPMC ministry boycotted a meeting, requiring the bishop board to take more positive steps in dealing with the Lebanon District. Later that year, Stephen Ebersole was silenced for a period of five months. This action failed to produce the division some had desired. Since there was no reason for him not to be reinstated, he resumed his office, much to the displeasure of some of the church. Had there been sufficient evidence to permanently silence Stephen, there would have been no reluctance to do what some felt must be done. The bishop board was eventually "forced" to do something. This resulted in the decision that either bishops Aaron Shank, Sidney Gingrich, and Stephen Ebersole leave Eastern and start another group or else the bishop board would render their offices to a more or less degree inactive and appoint a bishop committee over the Lebanon District. The three bishops accepted the bishop recommendation that they leave. Thus was the beginning of another church. Thus was also the beginning of a group that many have wondered why it came into existence. To my knowledge, the bishop board never put in writing why they called for a division. It was an unexplained action that was simply to be accepted. Of significance is the fact that from a certain geographical area of the EPMC soon after its inception, overtones of division were being heard until the division became a reality....

It appears to me that you received information about us from those who desire to question the integrity of the PMC. Even though those who do not appreciate the PMC may use your opinion to discredit the scriptural integrity of the PMC by referring to us as a group who does not like rules and we defend all sorts of youth activities, I am satisfied to allow God to be the final judge of the history of our church. It is my prayer that the PMC may be among other conservative groups who go down in the pages of history as those who were not ashamed to live the Bible principles and traditions in their day....

Sincerely yours,

Ivan Martin, Jr.

List of Selected Sermon Titles

Sermons by Aaron Shank available at www.pilgrimministry.org.

Atonement – 07/07/1997
Beyond Death's Door – 08/17/1992
Bible Brotherhood Assistance – 10/12/1997
Biblical Basis for the Unified Church – 04/21/1993
Choosing and Charging Leaders from Among Leaders – 03/05/1995
Christ Hath Once Suffered – 10/18/1992
Christian Assurance – 06/17/2000
Christian Growth and Development – 04/22/2001
Christ's Intercessory Work in Heaven – 10/06/1996
Church Issues Facing Us Today – 07/07/1977
Come and Reason – 12/02/1951
Developing Respect for Authority – 06/06/1965
Discerning the Lord's Body – 10/02/1994
Doctrine of the Deacons – 07/09/1996
Does God Still Wink at Sin? – 06/13/1999
End Time Delusions – 12/19/1966
Every Member - Good for Something – 03/22/1998
Facing a Church Crisis Realistically – 08/27/1968
Faith and Works – 03/11/2001
Fortification against Deceptive Voices – 03/01/2000
From Egypt's Heavy Bondage into Canaan's Blissful Rest – 04/22/1999
Fullness of Joy in Christian Fellowship – 12/05/1993

Genuine Evidences of the Holy Spirit – 03/29/1997

Giving Thanks Always – 12/17/1995

Go in this thy Might – 03/26/1993

Goals for our Sons and Daughters – 08/14/1983

God is for us to Help us to Get to Heaven – 10/20/1996

God is Working for Us – 10/18/1996

God's Answer for Cynicism – 05/16/1999

God's Heavenly Dress Standard for New Believers – 04/23/2000

God's Regulations on Dress – 07/13/1997

God's Spiritual and Natural Laws – 10/05/1996

Heaven – 08/13/1995

How Big and How Great is our God? – 01/02/2000

Ideals Necessary for Healthy Congregational Life – 02/19/1995

Jesus Exalted Among Us – 12/11/1994

Joseph - A Type of Christ – 02/09/1997

Judas the Unkept Disciple – 08/22/1991

Keeping and Sharing our Faith - Member's Meeting – 07/27/1994

Looking Forward to and Earnestly Desiring Immortality – 04/18/1999

Making Our Calling and Election Sure – 08/09/1998

Me First – 05/31/1992

Messages from the Realms of Hades – 08/24/1991

Millennium in Prospect – 07/25/1999

Modern Jewish History and Fulfilled Prophecy – 07/07/1977

Moving Forward with God in Faith – 05/14/1993

New Testament Forgiveness and Reconciliation – 09/24/1995

Nomination service for a Minister – 11/24/1985

Old Testament Sabbath and New Testament Lord's Day – 07/23/2000

Our Lord's Amazement – 09/12/1999

Our Meeting House - A Gift from God for God – 03/26/1995

Our Response and Responsibilities to Faithful Leadership – 12/06/1992

Overcoming Conflict in the Church – 01/11/1997

Please Get in Touch with Jesus – 03/25/1998

Principles of Prophetic Perceptions – 07/07/1977

Progressive Sanctification – 01/01/1959

Prophecy – 07/07/1977

Rapture – 10/13/1996

Respectful Fathers and Mothers and Honoring Sons and Daughters
– 05/08/1994

Salvation - Before, After and What We Will Be – 08/08/1999

Salvation by Faith, Works or Both – 02/08/1995

Sealed Unto the Day of Redemption – 06/23/1996

Servants and Services of Eternity (Rev 21:24-22:5) – 06/06/1993

Tests for our Christian Standing – 03/11/1999

The Age of the Ceaseless Ages – 12/14/1997

The Amazement & Heaviness of Jesus on the Dark Side of the
Cross– 09/08/1996

The Anabaptist Church – 11/15/1952

The Ascension of Jesus Christ – 05/19/1996

The Bible For Us, For Now and Forever – 01/12/1997

The Christian's Anticipated Change from this Life to the Next Life
– 12/04/1992

The Christian's Call and Commitment to Suffering in the World – 11/17/1985

The Christian's Call to Evangelism – 04/09/1995

The Danger of being in a Neutral Position – 05/14/1968

The Doctrine of the Resurrections – 01/05/1995

The Eternal Destinies of Man – 06/05/1983

The Exclusiveness of the Cross of Jesus – 10/07/1993

The Fulfilment of Old Testament Prophecies – 07/07/1977

The Fullness of God For the Fullness of Man in the Fullness of Time for
the Fullness of Eternity 12/12/1997

The Glories of Heaven – 03/16/1997

The Grace of God – 02/01/1998

The History of Non-Conformity – 06/05/1980

The Holy Kiss – 02/11/2001

The Holy Spirit – 03/26/1998

The Judgment – 01/11/1998

The Lord Shall Be King Over All the Earth – 03/23/1997

The Lord shall Roar Out of Zion – 07/14/2002

The Love of God – 10/04/1998

The Manna of God's Word – 03/07/1999

The Ordinance of Divine Authority – 01/10/1993

The Ordinance of Divine Order of Authority – 11/07/1993

The Place, Placement, Replacement, & Misplacement of Leadership in the
Church – 06/08/1997

The Recharging of a Minister for the Work of a Bishop – 11/27/1992

The Return of the Days of Noah – 01/31/1999

The Sacredness of Human Life – 04/27/1997

The Second Coming of Jesus – 07/19/1993

The Significance of Almighty God – 08/17/1991

The Significance of Tears – 06/20/1999

The Spirit of the Living God – 08/14/1994

The Sufferings of this Present Time – 09/10/1995

The Value of a Soul – 08/18/1991

The Voice of Jesus will Wake up the Dead Now – 03/23/1998

The Wars of the Devil – 10/02/1996

Transitional Activities in the Book of Acts – 08/16/1993

Unashamed Students on God's Honor Roll – 03/21/1993

Voices from the Dead – 11/13/1952

We are Made for Something Better – 10/01/1995

"What Shall we Have Therefore?" Matt 19:27 – 11/28/1992

When you read the Bible Through – 04/16/1997

Where is the Place of My Rest – 02/06/1994

Who Is the Lord that I Should Obey Him?– 01/03/1992

Why there is an Eastern PA Mennonite Church – 05/23/1982

Worthy is the Lamb – 08/01/1993

Shank Genealogy

Aaron's Genealogy

Aaron M. Shank, Feb. 5, 1915-Dec. 15, 2003
m.(1) Marjorie Catherine Showalter, Aug. 3, 1916-Jan. 23, 1995
m.(2) Dorothy P. Showalter, Sept. 29, 1927-Apr. 10, 2018 (widow of Walter
   R. Newswanger)

John M. Shank, Oct. 12, 1880-Nov. 10, 1945
m. Mary Mae Miller, May 30, 1881-Sept. 17, 1975

Martin B. Shank, Sept. 7, 1854-Mar. 6, 1930
m.(1) Catherine "Katie" Shenk, Oct. 31, 1852-Aug. 12, 1921
m.(2) Elizabeth Vincent, July 9, 1858-June 2, 1935 (widow of Fayette S.
   Furman)

Samuel J. Shank, Nov. 7, 1830-Oct. 7, 1872
m. Sarah Catherine Rhoades, Sept. 5, 1835-Nov. 1, 1862

Henry Shank, Feb. 16, 1787-Dec. 7, 1839
m. Elizabeth Heatwole, Sept. 3, 1795-Jan. 3, 1836

Henry Shank, Nov. 25, 1758-Oct. 10, 1836; ordained as minister in 1784
   in Rockingham Co., Va. and as bishop 1810
m. 1782, Anna Magdalena Reiff, Oct. 30, 1762-Mar. 30, 1819

Michael Shank, ca. 1718-1775
m. Magdalena

Michael Shank, ca. 1695-1759
m. Mary

Christian Schenk, b. June 15, 1662, Eggiwil, Switzerland; d. 1724, Lancaster
    Co., Pa. (then part of Chester Co.); immigrated Aug. 24, 1717

Michael Schenk, b. Sept. 21, 1639, Switzerland; d. Ibersheim, Germany
m. Sept. 21, 1660, Anna Stauffer

Michael Schenk, b. June 22, 1590, Eggiwil; Anabaptist exiled from
    Switzerland in 1671; d. 1672, Ibersheim, Germany
m. Dec. 16, 1616, Barbli [Barbara] Risser

Ulrich Schenk, b. ca. 1568
m. Annali [Anna] Rytz

Ulli [Ulrich] Schenk, b. ca. 1546, Rothenbach
m. Anneli [Anna] Neuenschwander

Hans Schenk, b. ca. 1522, Rothenbach
m.(1) unknown; m.(2)May 25, 1584, Elsbeth Neueschwander at Rothenbach;
    m.(3) Feb. 7, 1594, Margareth Wenger

Hans Schenk, b. ca. 1500

Hans Schenk, b. ca. 1470; lived at Rothenbach in 1494

Marjorie and Dorothy's Genealogy

Through their mother (as traced here), Marjorie and Dorothy were third cousins to Aaron and shared his Shank ancestors. Bold font in both lists indicates the common ancestor.

(1) Marjorie Catherine Showalter, Aug. 3, 1916-Jan. 23, 1995

(2) Dorothy P. Showalter, Sept. 29, 1927-Apr. 10, 2018 (widow of Walter R. Newswanger)

m. Aaron M. Shank, Feb. 5, 1915-Dec. 15, 2003

Ira Showalter, October 3, 1893-Aril 24, 1953 (see family photo, p. 36)

m. Edna Mae Shank, November 20, 1893-January 9, 1975

Erasmus Coffman Shank, January 2, 1861-July 18, 1943

m. Ida Rhodes, February 24, 1862-May 6 1931 (see family photo, p. 38).

Jacob Shank Jr., May 14, 1819-August 13, 1889

m. Barbara Beery

Jacob Shank Sr., 1793-1871

m. Francis Miller

Ira and Edna Showalter's wedding photo.

Henry Shank, Nov. 25, 1758-Oct. 10, 1836; or-
dained as minister in 1784 in Rockingham Co., Va. and as bishop 1810

m. 1782, Anna Magdalena Reiff, Oct. 30, 1762-Mar. 30, 1819

Anthony and Elizabeth (Landes) Showalter, Marjorie's paternal grandparents.

Additional Showalter Family Photos

Ira and Edna Showalter

Ira and Edna Showalter's tombstone.

Marjorie as a toddler.

The Showalter siblings, L to R: Milton, Dorothy, Marjorie, Leonard, Lois, Winfred.

Ira and Edna, later in life.

Springdale, the Showalter family's home church, where Aaron and Marjorie were married.

Walter Newswanger and Dorothy Showalter's wedding day, January 1, 1972. Ed and Shirley Kerr are attendants.

A Final Word
from Steve Ebersole

BROTHER AARON SHANK'S story needs to be told. We have rising waves of generations who need the vision and pursuit of Bible doctrine that follows the example of Brother Aaron's faith and vision in his generation.

Mentor, confidant, friend, advisor? What title shall I give Bro. Aaron? Words fail me as memories come back from across the years. How I miss him! I don't think anyone (besides my wife) knew my faults and gave me as much love and trust as Brother Aaron. So patient with me in my immaturity! So ready to give me the resources I needed for my responsibilities. So forgiving in my failures and in the times when I hurt him. So trusting with his own struggles and failures. Truly I could not have wanted a better spiritual father as I endeavored to fill his shoes and wear his mantle.

Next to my earthly father, I consider Aaron Shank to have been my spiritual father and guide. Best of all, I knew that I could take any question to him, and he would give the question honest consideration and most often, a Bible answer. He never belittled me for asking. I know it hurt him deeply when we faced the EPMC/PMC division, because he loved the EPMC and he did not want to face another division in his lifetime. But he also knew the vision of holding the Bible before anything else was the vision of his own heart.

I found Aaron to have a profound respect for Mennonite tradition that exemplified and demonstrated Bible principle. I also found him willing to counter long-honored traditions when they contradicted or did not express Bible principle. In our long hours of traveling together he would recount numerous lessons he had learned from his walk with Christ in the changing tests of time. These gave me a secure sense in knowing the Bible is a safe guide in the issues of life.

And in his advancing years, Bro. Aaron did not lose his keen vision of his responsibility here nor of his hope of eternity. He shared that he understood that Bro. George R. Brunk I was busy working on another article when God called him home and that he wished to pass on doing the same. He would write out his articles and ask me to type them for him, and he had a half-finished document in the works when God called him home.

His clear vision of eternity led him to tell me one day, "A lot of folks would like the Lord to come back while they are alive. If that is God's will, then I want that too. But my preference would be to experience all that God has for saints. I'd like to experience what there is in death, and then open my eyes to see Christ's presence without my mortal body. I'd like to share in with the multitude of the saints, and then share the excitement of coming back with Jesus to receive my glorified body and the rest of the saints! Why that would be the very best anyone could hope for! The only drawback is the inconvenience it would put you folks through in having to bury my dead body!"

As Bro. Aaron drew closer to his day of death, he told me one day, "I can't wait until the Lord calls me home! Why I believe when I close my eyes here, I'll open them and see the face of my Lord Jesus! And then He'll take me by the hand and say, Aaron, I want to present you to the Father. And this is the part I find it hard to imagine. He'll say, 'Father, this is my son Aaron. He is faultless because of his trust in my finished work at Calvary. Why that's almost impossible to believe! Me with all my faults! Presented faultless to the One who inhabits eternity! Oh I thrill to anticipate the glory of that hour!"

Aaron knew doctrine and theology of the Bible better than anyone else I knew, but the wonderful part was how he thrilled in that doctrine. He didn't just know the truth, he embraced it and it filled him with wonder, awe and hope. Not only did Aaron rejoice in the truth of Scripture, he also rejoiced in the Person of Jesus Christ Himself!

Those of us who knew Bro. Aaron have a responsibility to the generation we mentor. No, not to glorify Aaron, but to glorify our Lord Jesus. He needs to be precious to us and we should live in such a way that the next generation wants to serve Him too.

BIBLIOGRAPHY

Interviews

Gladys Baer

Cletus Doutrich

Sidney Gingrich

Mary Louise Martin

Jesse Neuenschwander

Steve Olesh

Isaac Sensenig

Dorothy (Showalter) Newswanger Shank

Milford Shank

Alvin Snyder

David Thomas

David Wadel

I have worked closely with Ira and Louise (Shank) Mast as well as with
Steve Ebersole to collect information, pictures, and textual documents. I
worked most closely with Aaron M. Shank himself, who most graciously
spent hours on this project, in the interest of gaining the facts and

chronology of this story. Others have volunteered information outside of formal interviews.

Other sources

Lancaster Conference Bishop Board Minutes

Eastern Pennsylvania Mennonite Church Bishop Board Minutes

Allen, David C. and Lucille Shank. 2002. *The Genealogy of Erasmus Coffman Shank 1861-1942*. Self-published.

Auker, Kenneth. 2013. *Keeping the Trust*. Eastern Mennonite Publications.

Graber, Robert B. "An Amiable Mennonite Schism: The Origin of the Eastern Pennsylvania Mennonite Church." *Pennsylvania Mennonite Heritage* 7(4) (October 1984).

Runion-Slear, Ruth. 2005. *Gingrichs Mennonite Church and Cemetery*. Self-published.

Shank, Aaron M. Personal correspondence and papers.

Shank, Aaron M. 2011. *Faith and Works in Salvation*. Rod & Staff Publishers.

Shank, Aaron M. *Marriage and the Wedding Ring*. 1966, Lancaster Mennonite Conference; reprinted with modifications by Rod & Staff.

[Shank, Aaron M.] 1984. *Instructions for Christian Living and Church Membership*. Eastern Mennonite Publications.

Shank, John M. First printed 1945. *A Time to Kill and a Time to Heal*.

Stambaugh, Sara. 1984. *I Hear the Reaper's Song*. Good Books.

For Further Study

For readers wishing to know more about Aaron Shank, the website www.sounddoctrinearchives.org has a collection of Aaron's writings and sermons, as well as documents (letters, meeting minutes, etc.) relating to his life.

PHOTO CREDITS

p. 97—LMS Board of Trustees and Religious Welfare Committee. *Laurel Wreath*, 1960, p. 48. Public domain.

p. 99—Amos Weaver. *Laurel Wreath*, 1960, p. 49. Public domain.

p. 100—LMS officials. *Laurel Wreath*, 1959, p. 50. Public domain.

pp. 104-105—LMS students. *Laurel Wreath*, 1960. Public domain.

pp. 111—Ben and Anna Eshbach. Courtesy of Kendall Eshbach.

p. 115—Daniel Wert family. Courtesy of Daniel Stover.

p. 117—David Thomas. Laurel Wreath. Public domain.

p. 120—Roxbury Holiness Campground. Courtesy of Ethan Weaver.

p. 122—Homer and Naomi Bomberger. Courtesy of Joann Weaver.

p. 127—David Thomas. *Laurel Wreath*. Public domain.

p. 146—H. Raymond Charles. *Laurel Wreath*. Public domain.

p. 154—Rehrersburg, c. 1976. Rehrersburg 1977 church calendar.

p. 162—Numidia Bible School teachers. Courtesy of *The Reflector*.

p. 163—J. Paul Graybill. Courtesy of the Lancaster Mennonite Historical Society.

p. 166—Ann(a) (Olesh) Showalter. Courtesy of Lily A. Weaver.

p. 174—Eschatology chart. By Justin Ebersole, based closely on an original by Aaron Shank.

pp. 182-183—Numidia Bible School teachers and cooks. Courtesy of *The Reflector*.

p. 192—Myerstown school. Courtesy of Lorene Mast.

p. 193—Myerstown school teachers. Courtesy of Lorene Mast.

p. 200—George R. Brunk tent revival. Courtesy of the Lancaster Mennonite Historical Society.

p. 205—Darlene Herman. Courtesy of Ervin and Darlene Martin.

p. 211—Sidney and Mabel Gingerich. Courtesy of Galen Martin.

p. 213—Steve Ebersole family. Courtesy of Steve Ebersole.

p. 216—Maternity dress. Courtesy Pilgrim Mennonite Conference.

p. 254—Steve and Sandra Ebersole. Courtesy Steve Ebersole.

p. 255—Steve Ebersole family. Courtesy Steve Ebersole.

p. 273—Dorothy Newswanger. Courtesy of *The Reflector*.

p. 274—*Missionary Messenger*. Public domain.

p. 282—New York 4 Jesus. Courtesy of Steve Ebersole.

ABOUT THE AUTHOR

CHESTER WEAVER IS a son of the Lancaster Conference Mennonite Church (baptized 1965) and also a son of the Eastern Pennsylvania Mennonite Church, becoming a member in 1972. He transitioned to the Amish-Mennonite expression of Anabaptism in 1994 and has continued in that tradition to the present.

He has taught full time in Christian Day schools for 36 years, twelve years in Pennsylvania at the Allen Christian Day School and at the Rheems Mennonite School, sixteen years at Grandview/Osceola, Texas, and eight years at the Hebron Christian School in Lagrange County, Indiana. He has also taught more than twenty years in youth Bible Schools such as Calvary Bible School, (Calico Rock, Arkansas), and in the Area Wide Bible Schools.

He serves as Administrative Dean of The Shepherds' Institute, a traveling, week-long pastor training effort. He has regularly spoken at the annual Anabaptist Identity Conference. He serves on the board responsible for Anabaptist Perspectives. Recently he has become a consultant to Sattler College in Boston, Massachusetts, serving as liaison between the Anabaptist community and Sattler College.

He married Barbara Sauder in 1974. Their union is blessed with eight children, three in California, two in Texas, two in Virginia, and one in Ireland. Presently they have forty-one grandchildren.

Chester was ordained in 1997 and maintains an active interest in Anabaptist history and theology, always hoping to stimulate further interest in the subject of his passion. Chester and his wife are members of the Cedar Creek Mennonite Church near the Dallas/Ft. Worth Metroplex in Texas. They presently reside in the village of Itasca.

For additional titles, contact:

SERMON ON THE **MOUNT**
P U B L I S H I N G
P.O. Box 246
Manchester, MI 48158
(734) 428-0488
the-witness@sbcglobal.net
www.kingdomreading.com